746.14 £25.00

R18878 A 23

This book is due for return on or before the last date shown below.

17 JUL 2003
- 5 JAN 2009

The Color of Henna Die Farbe Henna

ARNOLDSCHE
Art Publishers

The Color of Henna

Painted Textiles from Southern Morocco

Annette Korolnik-Andersch
Marcel Korolnik

Die Farbe Henna

Bemalte Textilien aus Süd-Marokko

With contributions by/Mit Beiträgen von

Edward Badeen
Mourad Kusserow

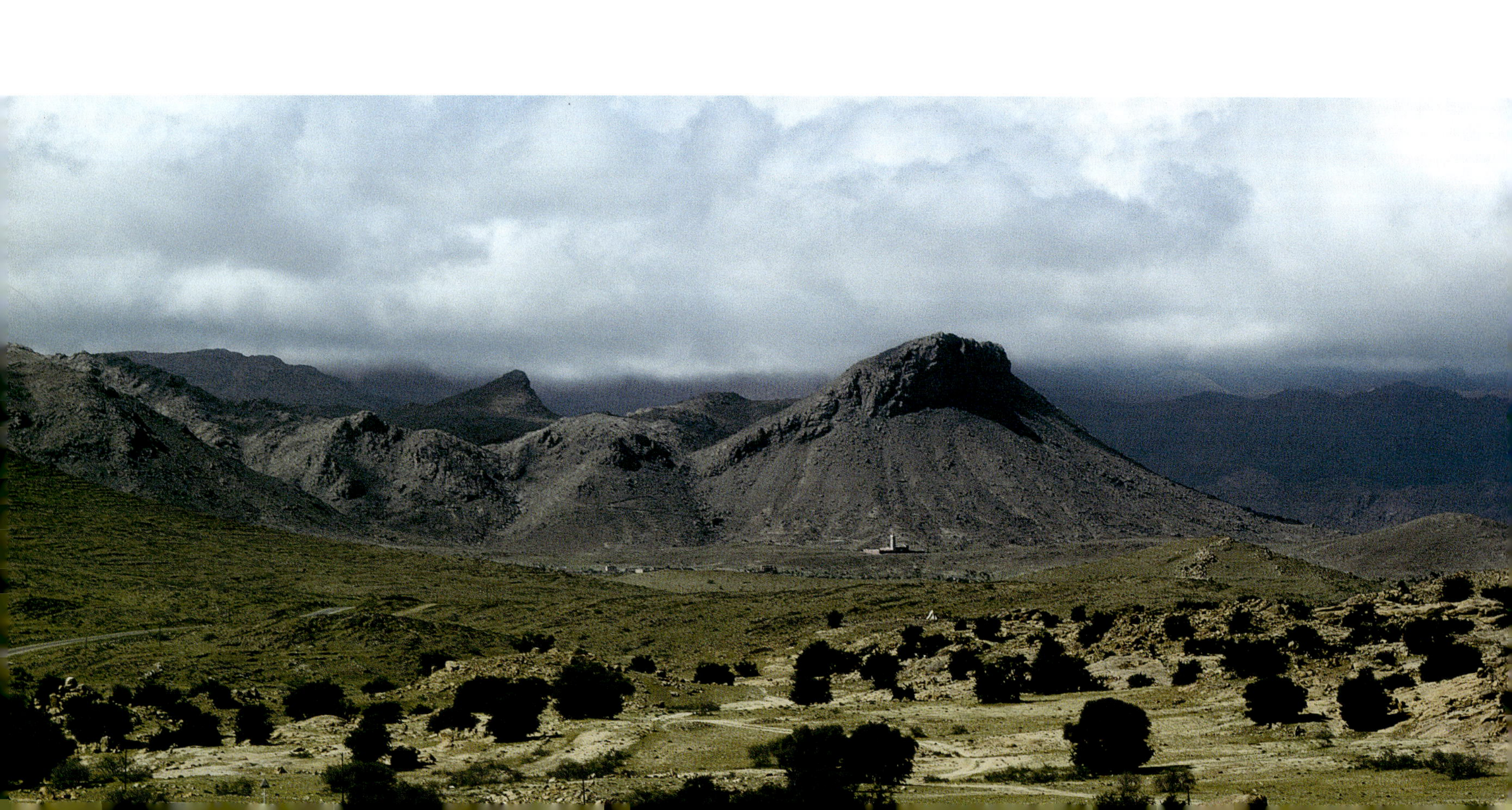

Contents

Foreword 7
Introduction 8

The Anti-Atlas as Lebensraum 12
The Sahara as a cultural landscape 18

Mourad Kusserow
The Imazighen and their Tifinagh 22

The people of the Anti-Atlas 28
The Feija 32
The Feija and Islam 38

Edward Badeen
Traditional popular medicine and the fqîh 45

Wool and weaving among the Feija 48

Markus Ritter
Henna 54

The henna-painted textiles of the Feija 62

Textiles from the Feija territory 68
- Aït Manesour 70
- Tisfrioudine and Tisnassemine 74
- Iligh and Afouzar 80
- Erkoune 92
- Imi n'Tatelt 106
  - Chorfa textiles in Imi n'Tatelt 111
  - Textiles from the shrines at Imi n'Tatelt 118
  - The haik of the fqîh 128
  - *Edward Badeen*
    The Symbols on the haik of the fqîh 131

Appendix
- Map of tribal territories 136
- Technical Analyses 138
- Bibliography 140
- Abbreviations 141
- Glossary 142
- Authors 143

Inhalt

Vorwort 7
Einleitung 8

Lebensraum Anti-Atlas 12
Kulturraum Sahara 18

Mourad Kusserow
Die Imazighen und ihr Tifinagh 22

Die Menschen im Anti-Atlas 28
Die Feija 32
Die Feija und der Islam 38

Edward Badeen
Die traditionelle Volksmedizin und der Fqîh 45

Wolle und Weben bei den Feija 48

Markus Ritter
Henna 54

Die hennabmemalten Textilien der Feija 62

Textilien aus dem Gebiet der Feija 68
- Aït Manesour 70
- Tisfrioudine und Tisnassemine 74
- Iligh und Afouzar 80
- Erkoune 92
- Imi n'Tatelt 106
  - Textilien der Chorfa in Imi n'Tatelt 111
  - Textilien aus den Heiligtümern von Imi n'Tatelt 118
  - Der Haik des Fqîh 128
  - *Edward Badeen*
    Die Symbole des Haik des Fqîh 131

Anhang
- Karte der Stammesgebiete 136
- Strukturanalysen 138
- Bibliographie 140
- Abkürzungen 141
- Glossar 142
- Autoren 143

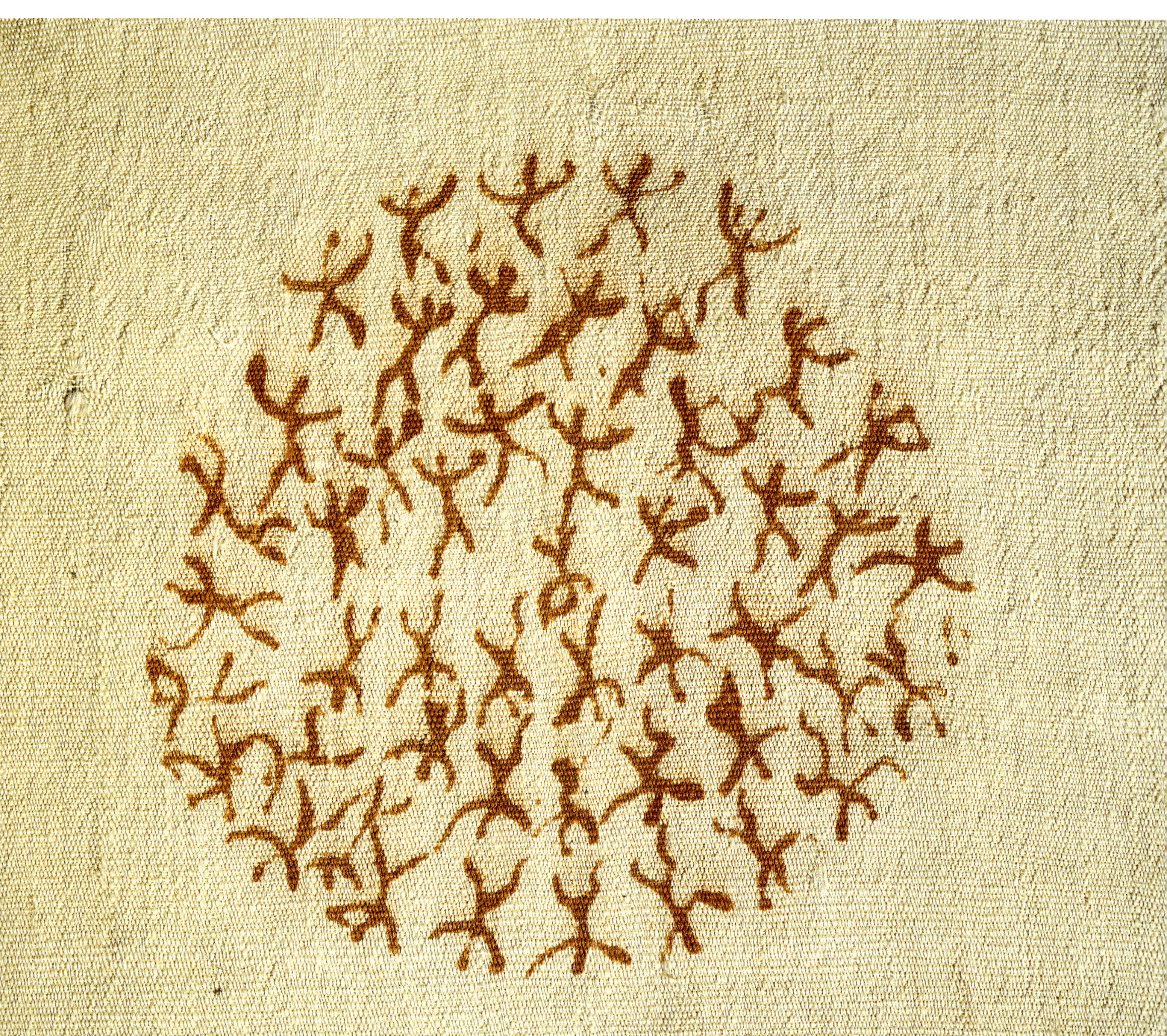

Foreword

On their extensive travels through the mountains of the Anti-Atlas, Annette Korolnik-Andersch and Marcel Korolnik have encountered a form of textile design which has hitherto been virtually overlooked: weavings painted with a natural dyestuff made from the henna plant. Unlike the textiles usually woven from dyed wool yarn in southern Morocco, the weavings from a handful of villages inhabited by members of the Feija tribe boast architectural motifs, good-luck symbols as well as apotropaic symbols to ward off evil or even enigmatic signs in Arab and Berber script. All these symbols and signs are painted directly on the cloth. The representations unfolding across the large, undyed surfaces of these Feija weavings are, in the modern observer's eyes, of breathtaking simplicity and, at the same time, startling expressiveness.

Many of these textiles - some are over four meters long - were wrappers or headscarves that were worn as part of traditional women's dress. By the mid-20th century, however, knowledge of the technique of painting textiles with henna had been virtually lost. The last use to which this form of design was put was for the occasional decoration of wedding blankets.

Annette and Marcel Korolnik-Andersch have amassed a remarkable body of henna-painted weavings while conducting field studies over a period of many years. Their scholarly research on these textiles has made it possible to present this art for the first time to an international public. For their contribution to scholarship and their unswerving commitment to their chosen field we owe a great debt of gratitude indeed to the collectors.

The present book and exhibitions in Zurich, Mönchengladbach, Locarno and Santa Fe - as well as other museums worldwide - show a selection of the finest and most exemplary pieces and are highly informative on the influences and background which have brought forth the designs and repertoire of patterns distinguishing this unique textile tradition.

Roger Fayet
Museum Bellerive, Zurich

Vorwort

Bei ihren Reisen in das Anti-Atlasgebirge sind Annette Korolnik-Andersch und Marcel Korolnik auf eine bislang kaum wahrgenommene Form der Textilgestaltung gestoßen: Gewebe, die mit dem pflanzlichen Farbstoff Henna bemalt sind. Im Unterschied zu den im südlichen Marokko sonst üblichen Wirkereien aus gefärbten Wollfäden, zeigen die Textilien einiger weniger Dörfer des Feija-Stammes architektonische Motive, Glücks- und Schutzsymbole oder auch geheimnisvolle arabische und berberische Schriftzeichen, die direkt auf das Gewebe gemalt sind. Die Darstellungen, die sich auf den großen, ungefärbten Gewebeflächen ausbreiten, sind für das Auge des modernen Betrachters von atemberaubender Schlichtheit und Expressivität zugleich.

Viele der Textilien – manche sind über vier Meter lang – gehörten als Wickel- oder Kopftücher zur traditionellen Ausstattung der Frauenkostüme. Gegen Mitte des 20. Jahrhunderts ging das Wissen um die Technik der textilen Henna-Malerei jedoch weitgehend verloren. Zuletzt wurde diese Form der Gestaltung nur noch vereinzelt bei Hochzeitsdecken angewandt.

Über viele Jahre hinweg hat das Sammler- und Forscher-Ehepaar einen bemerkenswerten Corpus von hennabemalten Geweben zusammengetragen und wissenschaftlich aufgearbeitet, so daß heute erstmals die Möglichkeit besteht, diese Kunst einer internationalen Öffentlichkeit zu präsentieren. Hierfür und für ihr unermüdliches Engagement danken wir den beiden Sammlern herzlich.

Die vorliegende Publikation und die Ausstellungen in Zürich, Mönchengladbach, Locarno, Santa Fe – und in weiteren internationalen Museen – zeigen eine Auswahl der schönsten und repräsentativsten Stücke und informieren über die Einflüsse und Hintergründe, welche die Gestaltung und den Musterschatz dieser einzigartigen Textiltradition hervorgebracht haben.

Roger Fayet
Museum Bellerive, Zürich

Introduction

And not of me is the tale,
but of my mother [...].

Euripides, frg. 488 ed. Nauck

Since the early 1990s we have been studying tribal carpets and textiles from Morocco. For us this is more than a field for collecting, for here we have really been able to trace the origins of a traditional textile art - in the families who made them, on their own territory.

In the following we shall present the results of a second study we conducted in the field. Whereas the first took us to the area around Marrakesh several years ago, to the descendants of Beduins, this time we went to the Feija, a tribe of the Chleuh Berbers, into their territory on the southern slopes of the central Anti-Atlas.

We first traveled through the region in 1997 for the purpose of obtaining reliable information on textiles and carpets which had recently appeared on the market at Marrakesh. They came allegedly from the above mentioned area in the southern Anti-Atlas and their provenance was noted as "Beni Yâacoub". On arriving in the area, however, we soon ascertained that there was no tradition of knotted carpet weaving there. Instead we were shown textiles of a type unknown to us: their decoration consisted mainly in henna paintings. What was so extraordinary was that henna-painted textiles were used for a variety of purposes. And the most valuable result of all: we found the pieces directly in the families where they had been made, received first-hand information on them and could even acquire some of these textiles ourselves.

Einleitung

Und nicht von mir ist der Mythos,
sondern von meiner Mutter [...].

Euripides, frg. 488 ed. Nauck

Seit Beginn der 1990er Jahre beschäftigen wir uns mit Stammesteppichen und Textilien aus Marokko. Für uns ist das mehr als ein Sammelgebiet, denn hier konnten wir wirklich den Ursprüngen einer traditionellen Textilkunst nachgehen – bei den Herstellerfamilien, in ihrem Lebensraum.

Wir legen hier die Ergebnisse einer zweiten von uns durchgeführten Feldstudie vor. Während uns die erste einige Jahre früher in die Umgebung von Marrakech führte, zu den Nachfahren früherer Beduinen, sind es hier die Feija, ein Stamm der Chleuh-Berber in ihrem Gebiet an der Südflanke des zentralen Anti-Atlas.

Die Gegend bereisten wir erstmals 1997 mit dem Ziel, verlässliche Informationen über neu im Handel von Marrakech aufgetauchte Gewebe und Teppiche zu erhalten. Diese sollten angeblich aus dem besagten Gebiet im südlichen Anti-Atlas stammen und die Herkunftsbezeichnung lautete "Beni Yâacoub". Als wir in das Gebiet kamen, stellte sich bald heraus, dass es dort keine Knüpftradition gibt. Stattdessen bekamen wir Textilien einer Art zu Gesicht, die uns unbekannt war: ihre Dekorationen bestanden hauptsächlich aus Hennabemalungen. Außergewöhnlich war, dass sich hennabemalte Gewebe für verschiedene Verwendungszwecke fanden. Und das Wertvollste dabei: Wir fanden die Stücke direkt bei den Herstellerfamilien, erhielten die Informationen dazu aus erster Hand und konnten einige der Textilien anschließend sogar erwerben.

Kenner der Materie erwarten im Anti-Atlas sorgfältig gewobene Textilien, mit vielfarbigen Mustern dekoriert, ausgeführt in verschiedenen, komplizierten Web- und Wirktechniken. Noch nie zuvor hatten wir jedoch von nur einem Stamm sowohl Wickel- wie Kopftücher und auch noch weitere Textilien gesehen, die anstelle farbiger Muster fast ausschließlich Hennabemalungen trugen. Noch nie hatten wir Bemalungen gesehen, die uns wie Schriftzeichen erschienen und Motive, die offensichtlich magische, amulettartige Bedeutung hatten. Und kaum je sahen wir in Marokko Textilien, von denen eine ähnlich starke Ausstrahlung ausging.

What those knowledgeable in this field expect to find in the Anti-Atlas are meticulously woven textiles, decorated with multicolored patterns and executed in various different sophisticated weaving and tapestry weaving techniques. Never before, however, had we seen from a single tribe both woman's wrappers as well as headscarves and other textiles which bore henna paintings to the exclusion of almost anything else instead of colored patterns. We had never until then seen paintings which looked to us like characters used in writing and motifs which evidently had magical, talismanic significance. And we had hardly ever seen textiles in Morocco which were as strikingly powerful as these.

We were soon aware that we had discovered something special, possibly unique. And, because this was the case, we decided to go into the phenomenon in depth. Every step of exploring virgin territory is an adventure: neither scholarly studies on these textiles nor significant quantities of material for comparison were available to back us up.

Not until 2001 did we find out that the Musée de l'Homme in Paris had six Feija textiles in its magazines; these pieces had been collected during a field study on Berber jewelry and taken to the museum in 1970 along with a some scanty bits of information which, however, entirely agreed with ours. Splendid confirmation for both the museum and for us. More material for comparison is only available in the form of individual pieces in private collections; there is, however, virtually no information on them.

The tradition of painting textiles with henna became extinct among the Feija in about 1950. This may be one of the reasons why only a few isolated pieces could be found. Some of the women who owned them have died and their daughters, too, are by now elderly. Consequently we felt it was urgent to conduct our research as intensively as possible so as to be able to finish it.

Bald wurde uns bewusst, dass wir etwas Besonderes, möglicherweise Einmaliges entdeckt hatten. Und weil dies so war, beschlossen wir, den Phänomenen auf den Grund zu gehen. Das Betreten von Neuland ist Schritt für Schritt ein Abenteuer: Wir konnten uns weder auf wissenschaftliche Arbeiten zu diesen Textilien noch auf Vergleichsmaterial in nennenswerter Quantität abstützen.

Erst 2001 stellten wir fest, dass das Musée de l'Homme in Paris sechs Textilien der Feija im Depot hat; diese Stücke wurden anlässlich einer Feldstudie über Berberschmuck gesammelt und kamen 1970 ins Museum, begleitet von wenigen Informationen, die jedoch völlig mit unseren übereinstimmten. Eine für das Museum wie für uns schöne Bestätigung. Weiteres Vergleichsmaterial existiert nur vereinzelt in privaten Sammlungen; Informationen dazu fehlen weitgehend.

Die Tradition, Textilien mit Henna zu bemalen, ist bei den Feija um 1950 erloschen. Dies mag mit ein Grund dafür sein, warum nur wenige Einzelstücke aufzufinden waren. Die Besitzerinnen sind zum Teil schon verstorben, und auch deren Töchter haben inzwischen ein hohes Alter erreicht. Wir fühlten uns daher veranlasst, die Forschung mit größtmöglicher Intensität voranzutreiben und abzuschließen.

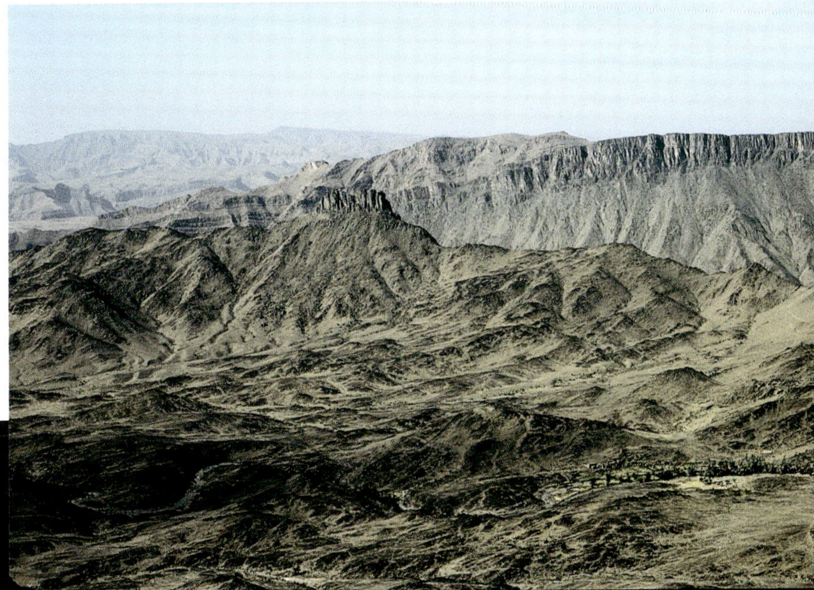

A small oasis in the crater of the extinct Tagragra volcano, 2000

Kleinoase im erloschenen Krater von Tagragra, 2000

The present publication is an attempt to answer the questions raised when Feija fabrics are looked at, questions which must be answered if these textiles are to be understood. A selection of the questions arising in this connection follows:

- Did lack of resources in the remote area inhabited by the Feija or the absence of dyers and dyes cause them to use henna for painting their textiles?
- Did the Feija seek to distinguish themselves from the other groups of Chleuh in the region by developing designs and ideas of their own?
- How did it come about that influences from the Tuareg, the Berbers relatives of the Feija in the Sahara, became evident in the repertoire of motifs used in Feija textiles?
- What effect did the presence of the Beni Yâacoub shrine complex in the Feija territory have on their textiles?
- Did the spontaneous manner of painting with henna lead to the development of a multifaceted range of design types which - compared with the decorations executed by neighboring population groups in rigidly adhered to weaving techniques - are so utterly astonishing?

The concept for the present book grew out of these questions. We obtained the necessary scholarly publications and studied the sources in the La Source Library in Rabat. Although we found unequivocal, clear answers to some questions, we had to be content with merely approaching others, especially with anything touching on the esoteric. We have eschewed conjecture and have supported the inferences drawn as far as possible with information received from the locals (in so far as such information could be checked by multiple statements) and from specialist publications. Answers emerged as we worked through the material and many a connection was clarified.

Die vorliegende Publikation versucht, Antworten auf die Fragen zu geben, welche die Feija-Gewebe beim Betrachten und Verstehenwollen stellen. Hier eine Auswahl:

- Führten die fehlenden Ressourcen im abgelegenen Gebiet der Feija, bzw. die Abwesenheit von Färbern und Farben zur Verwendung von Henna zum Bemalen der Textilien?
- War es das Bestreben der Feija, sich mit einer eigenständigen Gestaltung und eigenen Ideen von den anderen Chleuh-Bevölkerungsgruppen in der Region zu unterscheiden?
- Wie kommt es, dass Einflüsse der Tuareg, den berberischen Verwandten der Feija in der Sahara, im Motivrepertoire ihrer Textilien sichtbar werden?
- Wie wirkt sich die Präsenz des Beni Yâacoub-Heiligtums im Gebiet der Feija auf die Textilien aus?
- Führte die spontane Art der Hennabemalung zur Entwicklung der facettenreichen Palette an Gestaltungsarten, die – im Vergleich zu den in rigiden Webtechniken ausgeführten Dekorationen der benachbarten Bevölkerungsgruppen – voller Überraschungen steckt?

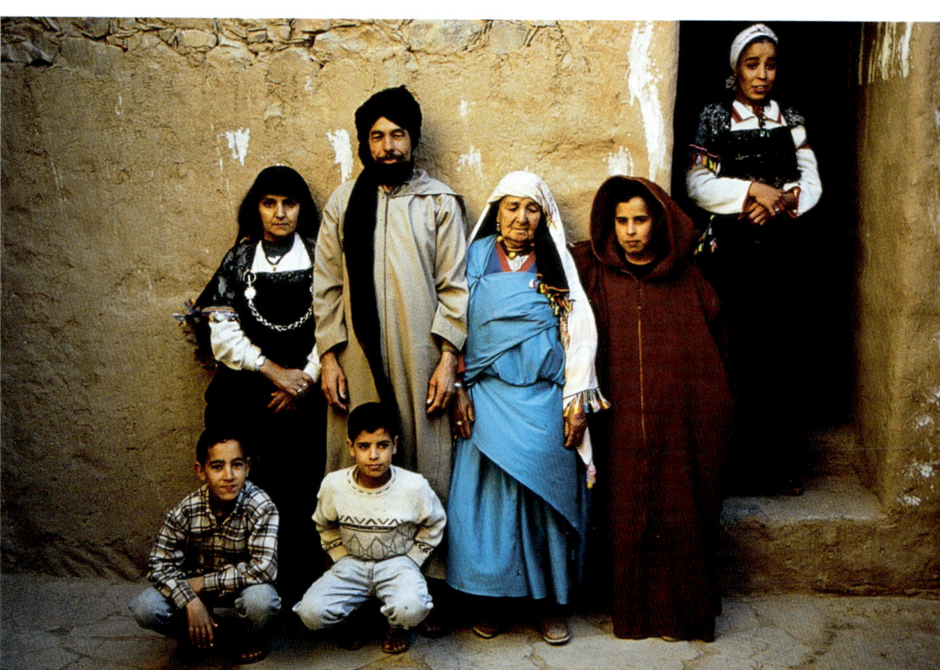

Aisha (left), Lahcen, Hadja, Brahim, Fatimah - the Feija family whom we cannot thank enough for their hospitality and patience, for the information they have given us on textiles and for letting us watch them weave and paint with henna, 2001

Aischa (links), Lahcen, Hadja, Brahim, Fatimah – die Feija-Familie, der wir nicht genug danken können für ihre Gastfreundschaft und Geduld, für ihre Informationen über Textilien und dafür, dass sie uns beim Weben und beim Malen mit Henna zusehen ließ, 2001

The Feija created textiles which are unique in their kind and in what they express so that they are utterly distinctive. We are fortunate indeed to have made contact with interested museums and a publishing house which have supported us in our efforts to make this extremely interesting material available to the public.

Anhand dieser Fragen entstand das Konzept für die vorliegende Publikation. Wir beschafften die notwendige wissenschaftliche Literatur und studierten die Quellen in der Bibliothek La Source in Rabat. Auf manche Fragen fanden wir eindeutige und klare Antworten, bei anderen mussten wir uns mit Annäherungen zufrieden geben; insbesondere da, wo der esoterische Bereich berührt wird. Wir vermieden Spekulationen und stützten eigene Schlüsse möglichst auf Informationen der lokalen Bevölkerung (soweit diese durch Mehrfachaussagen überprüfbar waren) sowie auf wissenschaftliche Literatur. Mit der Aufarbeitung des Materials kamen Antworten und mancher Zusammenhang wurde klar.

In Art und Ausdruck haben die Feija Textilien geschaffen, die einzigartig sind und eine ganz eigene Identität verkörpern. Wir sind glücklich, mit interessierten Museen und einem Verlag in Kontakt gekommen zu sein, die uns dabei unterstützen, das überaus interessante Material der Öffentlichkeit zugänglich zu machen.

On the present publication

Since Morocco is a francophone country, names and terms in Arabic or Berber dialect are written as they are in French, in accordance with standard practice in the country itself. Place-names or tribal names are, therefore, spelt as they are on maps and in standard works of reference (or in a form which is recognizably similar). Only in the article by Edward Badeen has the phonetic transcription of the Arabic used by the author himself been retained. Arabic or Berber terms in *italics* are explained in the glossary (p. 142).

In French - and, therefore, in Morocco as well - terms such as "tribe" *(tribu)* are still used as a matter of course; this also holds for the majority of the publications used and quoted in the following, some of them of fairly early date. The authors would like to take this opportunity to emphasize that they are fully cognizant of the problems related to this terminology and have chosen to use these terms solely for the sake of easier comprehension - no disrespect to the people or groups thus designated is meant. To facilitate understanding, therefore, and because the term is so widely known, the designation "Berber" is used throughout (except for the article by Mourad Kusserow) although the authors realize that this name is not particularly appreciated by the people to whom it is generally applied. However, the preferred designation - "Imazighen" - has not yet become widely known.

Descriptions of customs and observances refer to the Feija discussed here, a Chleuh Berber tribe living on the southern slopes of the central Anti-Atlas. They can only be applied to other groups, even neighboring ones, with reservations. When no specialist publications are mentioned in the text, results presented are those of our own studies. Wherever statements made by the inhabitants of the region are referred to, they are quoted as such.

Zu dieser Publikation

Da Marokko ein frankophones Land ist, sind Namen und Ausdrücke in arabischer oder berberischer Sprache in der landesüblichen, französischen Schreibweise wiedergegeben. Somit finden sich zum Beispiel Ortsnamen oder Stammesbezeichnungen in Karten- und Nachschlagewerken gleich (oder wiedererkennbar ähnlich) geschrieben wieder. Nur im Artikel von Edward Badeen wurde die vom Autor verwendete Umschreibung der arabischen Sprache beibehalten. Die *kursiv* gesetzten arabischen oder berberischen Begriffe sind im Glossar (S. 142) erklärt.

Im Französischen – und damit auch in Marokko – werden Begriffe wie etwa "Stamm" *(tribu)* nach wie vor ganz selbstverständlich verwendet; dies trifft auch auf einen Großteil der hier verwendeten und zitierten, teilweise älteren Literatur zu. Es sei an dieser Stelle ausdrücklich betont, dass die Autoren dieser Publikation sich der Problematik dieser Terminologie bewusst sind und diese Begriffe nur der einfacheren Verständlichkeit halber benutzen – mit allem Respekt gegenüber den so bezeichneten Menschen oder Gruppen. Der Einfachheit und allgemeinen Bekanntheit halber wird auch (außer im Beitrag von Mourad Kusserow) zumeist die Bezeichnung "Berber" benützt, im Bewusstsein, dass dieser Name von den Betroffenen nicht sehr geschätzt wird. Die bevorzugte Bezeichnung "Imazighen" ist jedoch bislang noch wenig bekannt.

Beschreibungen von Sitten und Gebräuchen gelten für die hier behandelten Feija, einem Stamm der Chleuh-Berber an der Südseite des zentralen Anti-Atlas. Übertragungen auf andere Gruppen, auch in der Nachbarschaft, sind nur mit Vorbehalt möglich. Wenn im Text keine Literatur angegeben ist, handelt es sich um Ergebnisse unserer eigenen Nachforschungen. Wo es sich um Aussagen der lokalen Bevölkerung handelt, sind diese als solche bezeichnet.

The Anti-Atlas as Lebensraum

The tribal territory of the Feija is in the central Anti-Atlas in southern Morocco. This area is often called the pre-Sahara. It marks a boundary as far as climate, plate tectonics and vegetation as well as population are concerned. There are many drawings carved into the rocks along the southern slopes of the Anti-Atlas and in the adjacent regions and they indicate early settlement of the region.

Lebensraum Anti-Atlas

Das Stammesgebiet der Feija liegt im zentralen Anti-Atlas im Süden Marokkos. Dieses Gebiet wird häufig als Vorsahara bezeichnet – es bildet eine Grenze, sowohl was Klima, Tektonik und Vegetation als auch was die Bevölkerung angeht. Entlang der Südflanke des Anti-Atlas und in den angrenzenden Gebieten befinden sich viele Felsritzungen, die auf eine frühe Besiedlung des Gebiets verweisen.

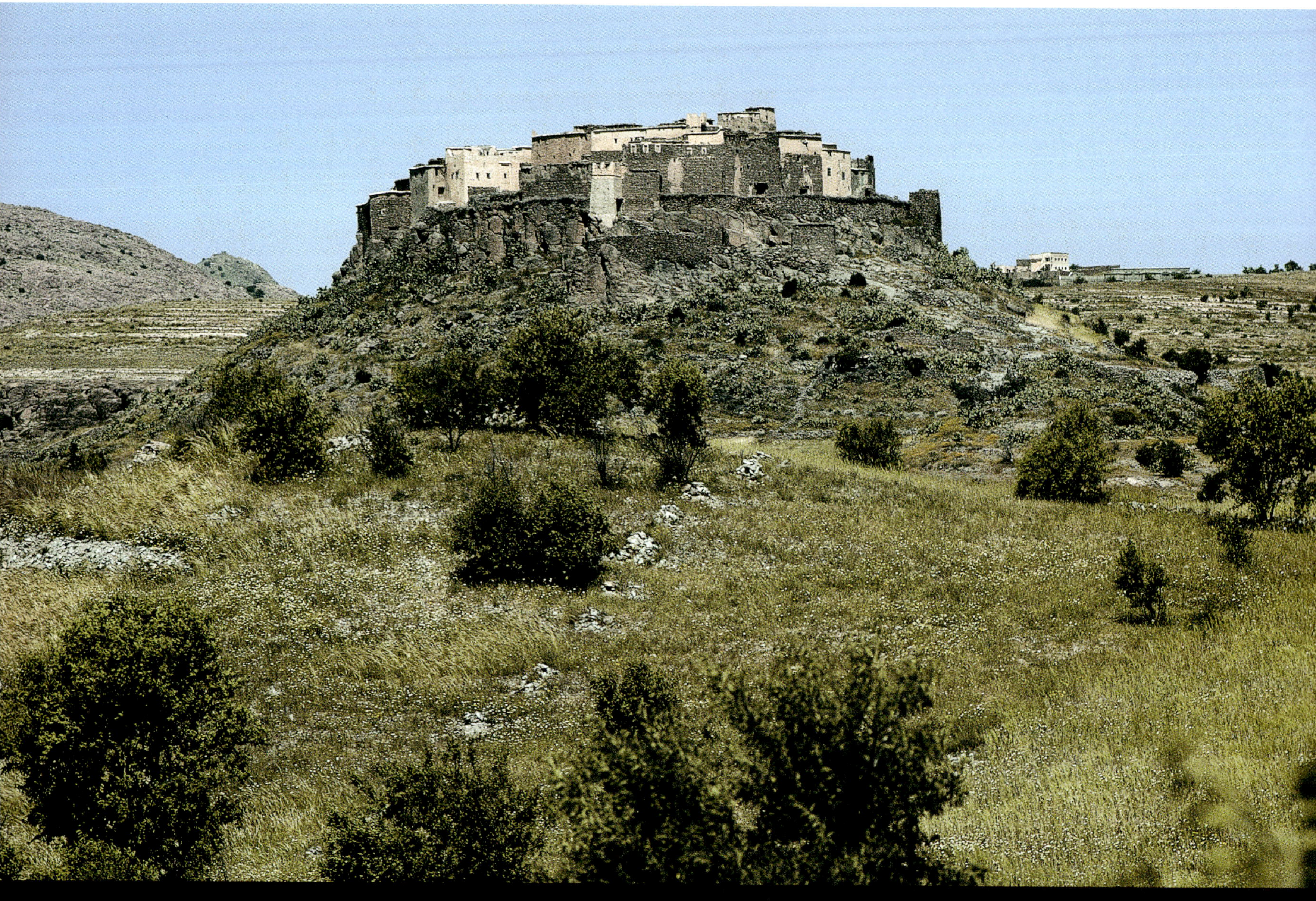

Fortified village in the Ammeln Valley near Tafraoute, 1996

Wehrdorf im Tal der Ammeln bei Tafraoute, 1996

The Anti-Atlas

The Anti-Atlas (see map p. 136) is part of the African plate. Geologically speaking, Europe begins north of it. The area extends for more than 660 kilometers from the Atlantic Ocean in the south-west to the Hamada du Guir in the north-east. The mountain range lies at a latitude between 29° and 32° north and, with the Amalou-n-Mansour in the Jebel Sarhro, rises to an elevation of 2712 meters. The area is on average not more than 100 kilometers wide.

Der Anti-Atlas

Der Anti-Atlas (siehe Karte S. 136) ist Teil der afrikanischen Kontinental-Platte. Nördlich davon beginnt geologisch Europa. Das Gebiet erstreckt sich über 660 Kilometer vom Atlantischen Ozean im Südwesten bis zur Hamada du Guir im Nordosten. Die Gebirgskette befindet sich zwischen 29° und 32° nördlicher Breite und erhebt sich mit dem Amalou-n-Mansour im Jebel Sarhro bis auf 2.712 Meter. Das Gebiet ist durchschnittlich nicht mehr als 100 Kilometer breit.

Klimatische Abstufungen sind von Westen nach Osten sowie von Norden nach Süden zu beobachten: Die Einflüsse des Atlantischen Ozeans werden nach Osten hin, ungefähr vom Ort Ifrane an, von trockenerem, kontinentalem Klima abgelöst; die der Sahara zugewandte Südflanke des Massivs hat Wüstenklima. Die Regenmenge nimmt von Westen nach Osten und von Norden nach Süden rasch ab – in gleicher Richtung steigen die Durchschnittstemperaturen ebenso rasch an: Die Sommermaxima erreichen z.B. in Zagora 52 °C. Die Berggebiete der Sarhro-Nordflanke erhalten noch 20 bis 40 Regentage pro Jahr.

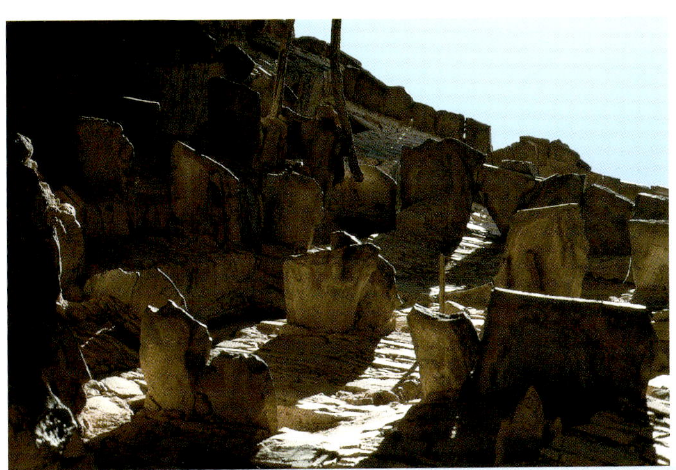

Stone slabs make steps to the storerooms in the *agadir* in Tasguent, 1996

Steinplatten dienen als Stufen zu den Vorratsräumen im *agadir* in Tasguent, 1996

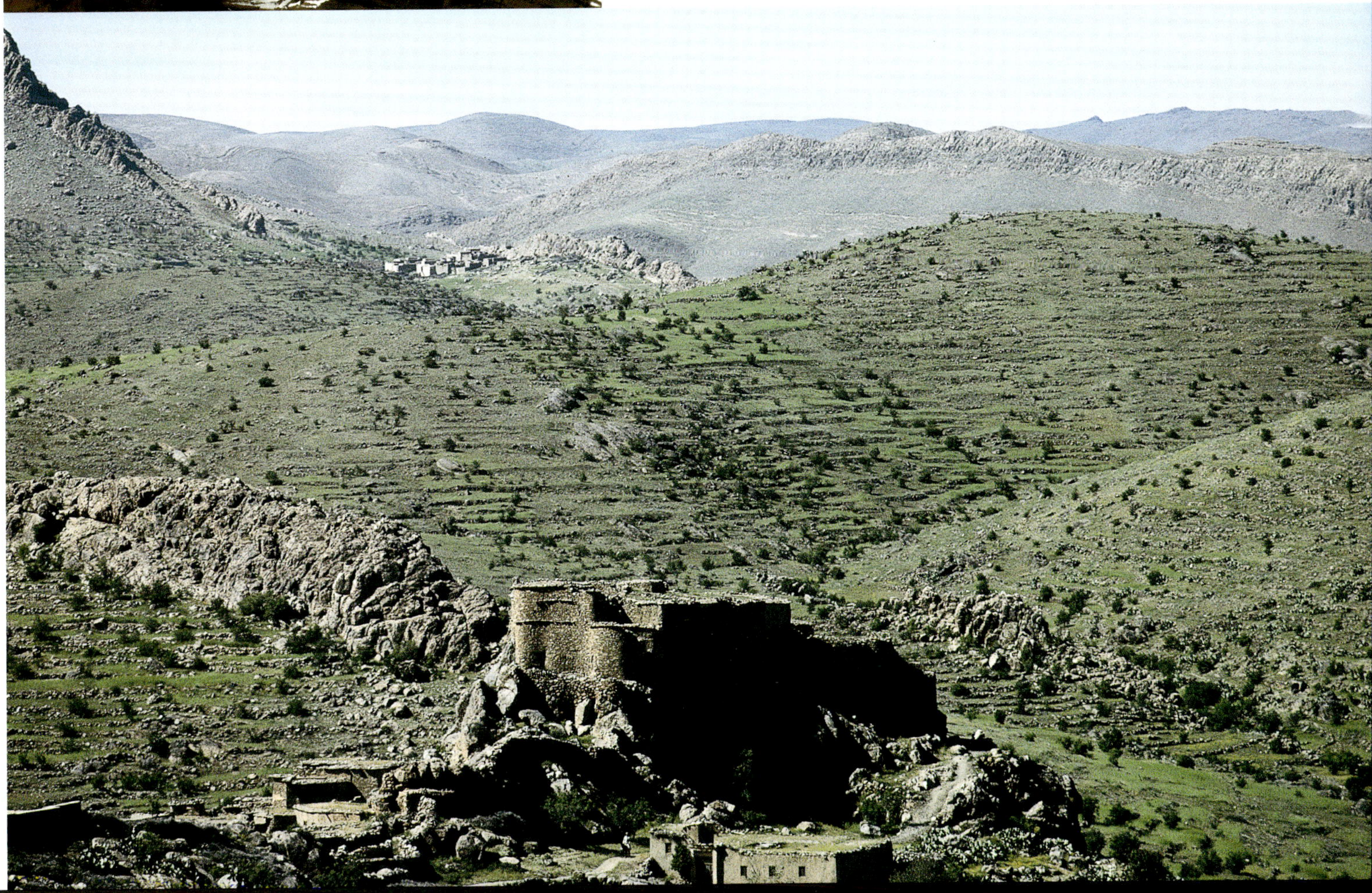

Communal fortified granary *(agadir)* in Tasguent, 1996

Gemeinschaftsspeicher *(agadir)* in Tasguent, 1996

There are noticeable differences in climate from west to east as well as from north to south: the moderating influence of the Atlantic Ocean yields towards the east, approximately from the town of Ifrane, to a more arid, continental climate; the southern slopes of the range, which face the Sahara, have a desert climate. Mean annual rainfall diminishes sharply from west to east and from north to south - in the same directions the rise in mean annual temperature is just as steep: the summer maximum temperature can reach 52° C in Zagora, for instance. The mountainous regions of the Sarhro north slopes still have from 20 to 40 days of rainfall a year.

The Anti-Atlas subdivides into three zones: the western, the central and the eastern section. The climate and vegetation of the western part are moderated for a stretch of about 30 kilometers by the Atlantic and its morning mists. This is hilly and largely verdant country. To the east the terrain rises steeply. At Tafraoute the Jebel Lekst rises to an elevation of 2359 meters. The region is semi-arid, yet thuya, juniper, argan trees, nut trees, palms and euphorbia thrive here.

Der Anti-Atlas kann in drei Zonen unterteilt werden: in den westlichen, den zentralen und den östlichen Teil. Klima und Vegetation des westlichen Teils werden auf einer Breite von ungefähr 30 Kilometern vom Atlantik mit seinen Morgennebeln bestimmt. Die Landschaft ist hügelig und überwiegend grün. Weiter östlich steigt das Gelände rasch an. Bei Tafraoute erreicht der Jebel Lekst bereits 2359 Meter. Die Gegend ist semiarid, doch gedeihen Thuja, Wacholder, Arganien, Nussbäume, Palmen und Euphorbien.

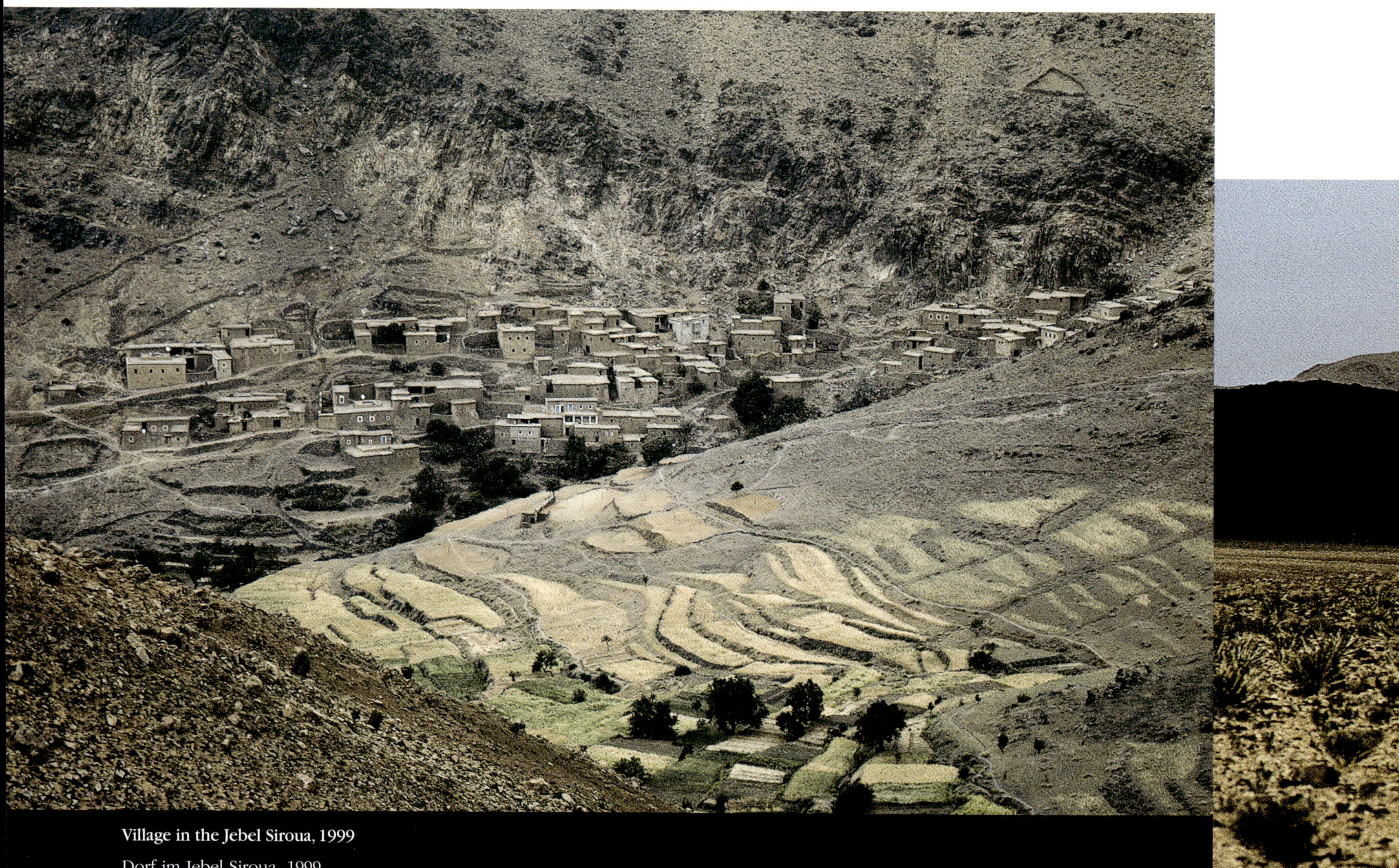

Village in the Jebel Siroua, 1999

Dorf im Jebel Siroua, 1999

The boundaries of the central Anti-Atlas can be sketched briefly as follows: not far from the well known city of Taroudannt, which is set in the fertile Sous plain, one of the few north-south roads in the region runs through the Anti-Atlas to Tata. This road forms roughly the western boundary. The Drâa Valley can be viewed as the eastern boundary. Except for small oases tended by the inhabitants, the central Anti-Atlas terrain ranges from steppe to stony desert.

The territory of the Feija lies on the southern slopes of the central Anti-Atlas. Until 2001 it could only be reached by a track *(piste)*. From the north it turns south in the region of Taliouine. The same track runs from the south into the area at Akka Irhèn.

The Jebel Siroua massif is made up of extinct volcanoes and is a northern outlier of the long Anti-Atlas range. The Jebel Siroua is bounded on the east by the Sous Valley. Lichens, mosses and primitive vegetation are still found growing at higher altitudes in the Siroua.

The elongated massif of the Jebel Sarhro, the eastern section of the Anti-Atlas, stretches from the upper Drâa Valley to the east, ending at the Tafilalt Valley. Its southern slopes are a landscape fissured with bizarre canyons; their walls are faced with basalt or almost black desert varnish. In the north-east the massif terminates in a chain of hills. Mines are operated here: silver is mined at Imiter, cobalt at Bou Azzer, copper as well as nickel and lead at Tiouit and Tizi Moudou.

Das Gebiet des zentralen Anti-Atlas wird etwa wie folgt begrenzt: Unweit der bekannten, in der fruchtbaren Sous-Ebene gelegenen Stadt Taroudannt führt eine der wenigen Nord-Süd-Straßenverbindungen durch den Anti-Atlas nach Tata. Diese Straße bildet ungefähr die Westgrenze. Als Ostgrenze kann das Drâa-Tal angesehen werden. Der zentrale Anti-Atlas ist mit Ausnahme kleiner, von Menschen gepflegter Oasen steppen- bis steinwüstenartig.

An der Südflanke des zentralen Anti-Atlas liegt das Gebiet der Feija. Es konnte bis 2001 nur über eine Piste erreicht werden. Von Norden her geht sie in der Gegend von Taliouine nach Süden ab. Von Süden her führt die gleiche Piste bei Akka Irhèn in das Gebiet.

Das Massiv des Jebel Siroua besteht aus erloschenen Vulkanen und ist ein nördlicher Trabant der langen Anti-Atlas-Kette. Der Jebel Siroua schließt das Sous-Tal nach Osten ab. In den höheren Lagen des Siroua gibt es noch Flechten, Moose und niedrige Vegetation.

Das ausgedehnte Massiv des Jebel Sarhro, der Ostteil des Anti-Atlas, erstreckt sich vom oberen Drâa-Tal ostwärts und endet mit dem Tafilalt-Tal. An seiner Südflanke gibt es bizarre, canyonartige Landschaftsformen, die Felsen sind aus Basalt oder von fast schwarzem Wüstenlack überzogen. Im Nordosten läuft das Massiv in einer Hügelkette aus. In Minen wird hier Bergbau betrieben: Man fördert Silber in Imiter, Kobalt in Bou Azzer, Kupfer in Tiouit und Tizi Moudou sowie Nickel und Blei.

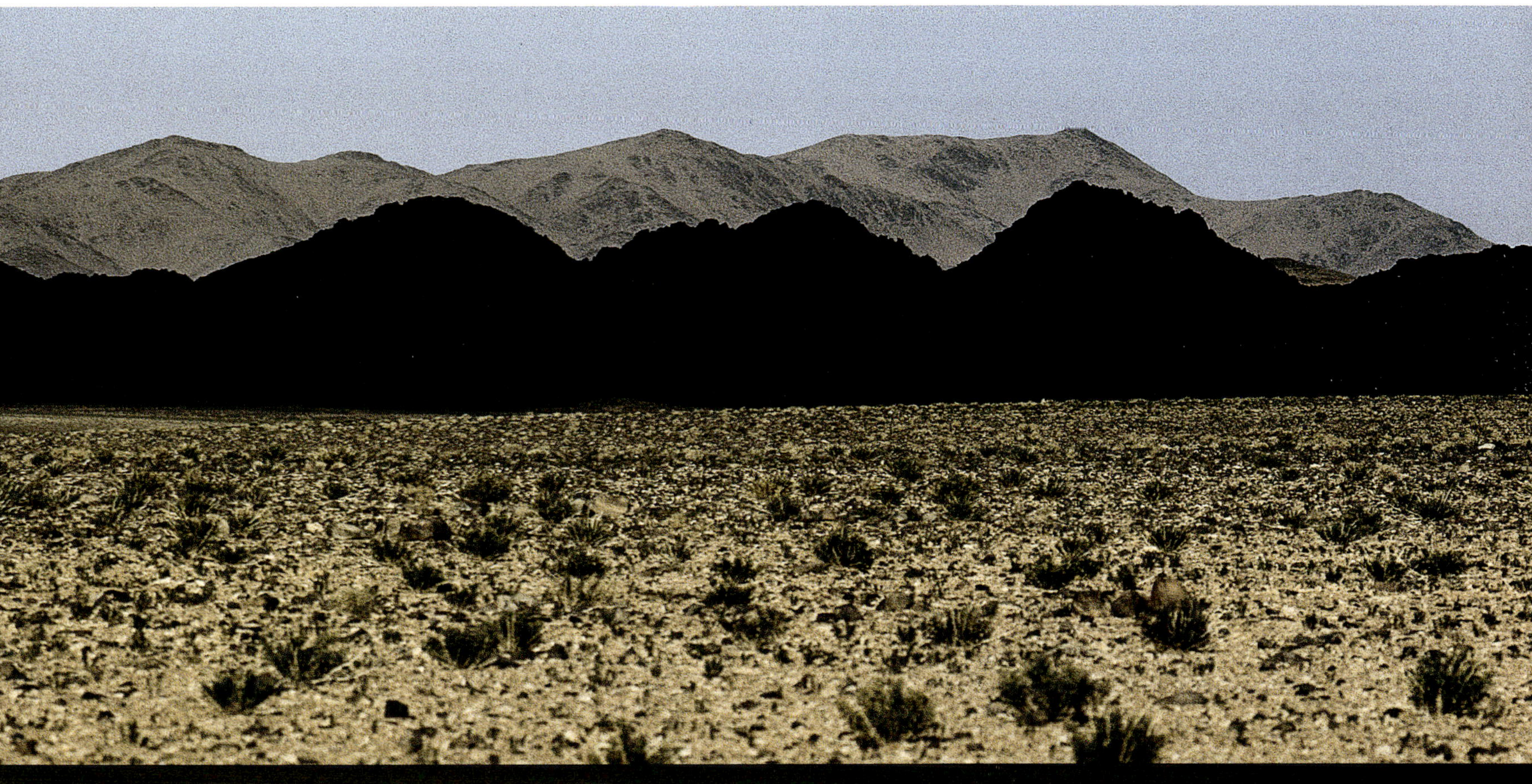

The Jebel Sarhro near Boumalne-du-Dades, 1999

Der Jebel Sarhro bei Boumalne-du-Dades, 1999

Early traces of man

The age of the rock pictures in the Maghreb has been discussed for a long time and at great length. They used to be attributed to the Capsian (13 500 - ca. 8 000 BC) because the earliest figurative representations on ostrich eggshells are known from that period. Now the majority view is that rock pictures set in with the Early Neolithic. The earliest Stone Age finds in the Saharan Atlas - where most rock picture stations in the Maghreb are found - date from the 6th millennium BC (Ain Naga, Djelfa region: 5 550 BC). Even if the early date may seem questionable, we can at least assume that the Maghreb tradition of making pictures on rocks originated in the early 5th millennium.

Frühe menschliche Spuren

Über das Alter der Felsbilder, die sich im Maghreb finden, wurde lange und ausgiebig diskutiert. Früher wurden sie häufig dem Capsien (13 500 - ca. 8 000 v. Chr.) zugeschrieben, denn aus jener Zeit waren die ersten bildhaften Darstellungen auf Straußeneischalen bekannt. Heute neigt man überwiegend zur Annahme, dass die Felsbildkunst mit dem frühen Neolithikum einsetzte. Die ältesten Steinzeitfunde im Sahara-Atlas – dort liegen die meisten Felsbildstationen des Maghreb – stammen aus dem sechsten vorchristlichen Jahrtausend (Ain Naga, Region Djelfa: 5550 v. Chr.). Wenn nicht schon zu diesem Zeitpunkt, so dürfen wir doch zumindest davon ausgehen, dass die Felsbildtradition des Maghreb am Anfang des fünften Jahrtausends ihren Ursprung hat.

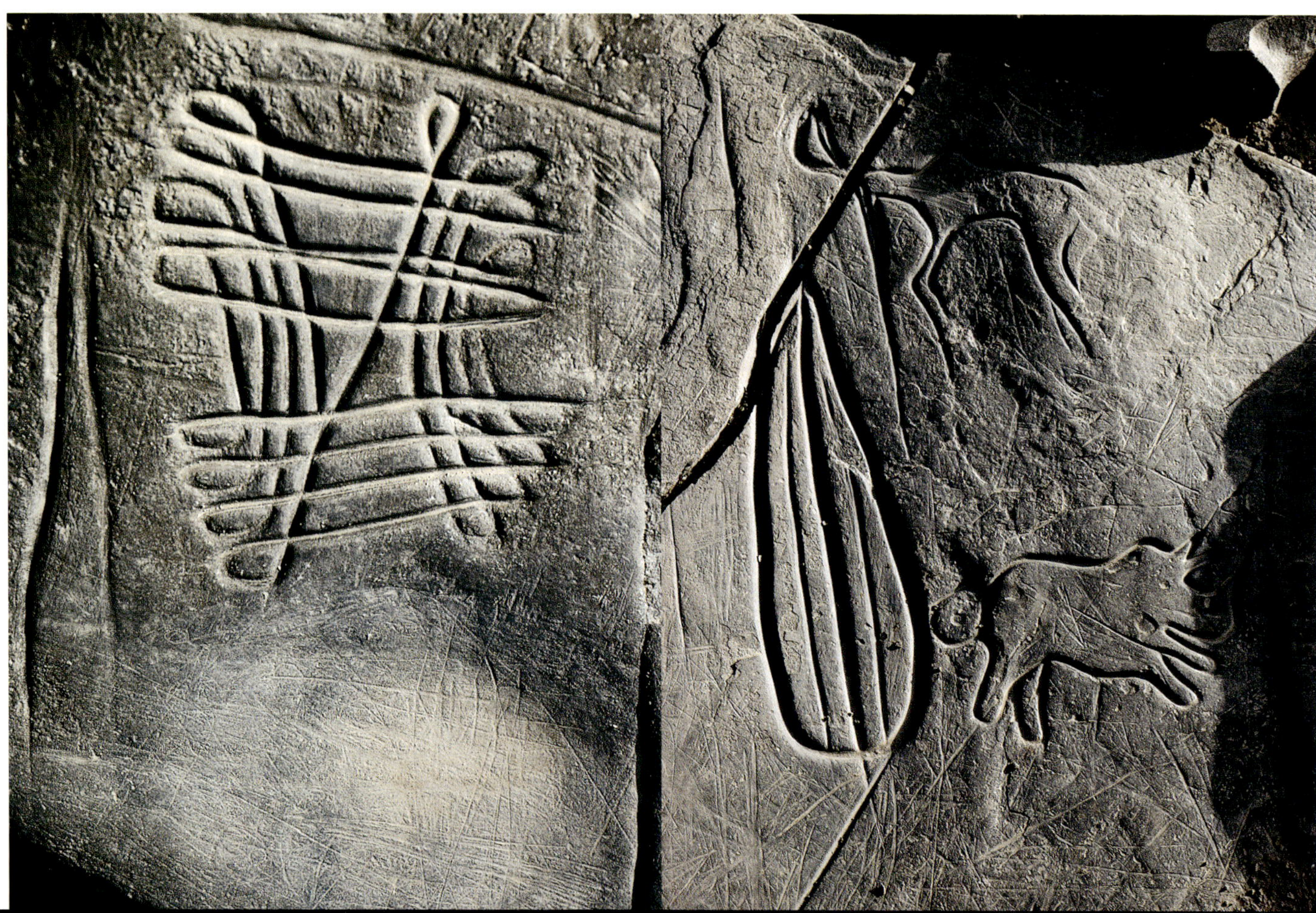

Polished rock pictures, Early Neolithic, ca. 5 000 BC or more recent, Aït Ouazigh, upper Drâa Valley, 2001
Probably a representation of snaring (similar to that in the Hoggar mountains). Left and top: The grooves are assumed to have been cut by arrowheads and similar implements. Below the snare symbol a depression for grinding grain is visible.

Polierte Felsbilder, frühes Neolithikum, ca. 5000 v. Chr. oder jünger, Aït Ouazigh, oberes Drâa-Tal, 2001
Wahrscheinlich eine Fallendarstellung (ähnlich auch im Hoggar-Gebirge). Links und oben: Man nimmt an, dass die Rillen vom Schleifen von Pfeilspitzen und dergleichen herrühren. Unterhalb des Schlingensymbols ist eine Mahlvertiefung erkennbar.

Polished rock pictures, Early Neolithic, ca. 5 000 BC, Aït Ouazigh, upper Drâa Valley, 2001
Representation of African wild animals which are no longer found in Morocco: a rhinoceros and a gazelle; to the left probably a net for capturing game.

Polierte Felsbilder, frühes Neolithikum, ca. 5000 v. Chr, Aït Ouazigh, oberes Drâa-Tal, 2001
Darstellung afrikanischer Wildtiere, die heute in Marokko nicht mehr vorkommen: ein Rhinozeros und eine Gazelle; links daneben wahrscheinlich ein Fangnetz.

A fundamental distinction should be drawn between polished and hewn rock pictures. The polished rock pictures probably date from the Early Neolithic whereas the carved pictures, known as „Libyco-Berber", also reveal the earliest *tifinagh* characters (cf. on this „The Imazighen and their Tifinagh", p.22), are dated to about the 1st millennium BC.

References: Nehr 1992, Riser 1984, Striedter 1984

We are indebted to: Dr. Peter Jablonka, Tübingen University

Es ist grundsätzlich zu unterscheiden zwischen polierten und geschlagenen Felsbildern. Die polierten Felsbilder dürften im frühen Neolithikum entstanden sein, während die geschlagenen, „libyco-berber" genannten Bilder auch erste *tifinagh*-Schriftzeichen (vgl. z.B. „Die Imazighen und ihr Tifinagh", S. 22) aufweisen und etwa um das erste Jahrtausend v.Chr. entstanden sind.

Literatur: Nehr 1992, Riser 1984, Striedter 1984

Dank an: Dr. Peter Jablonka, Universität Tübingen

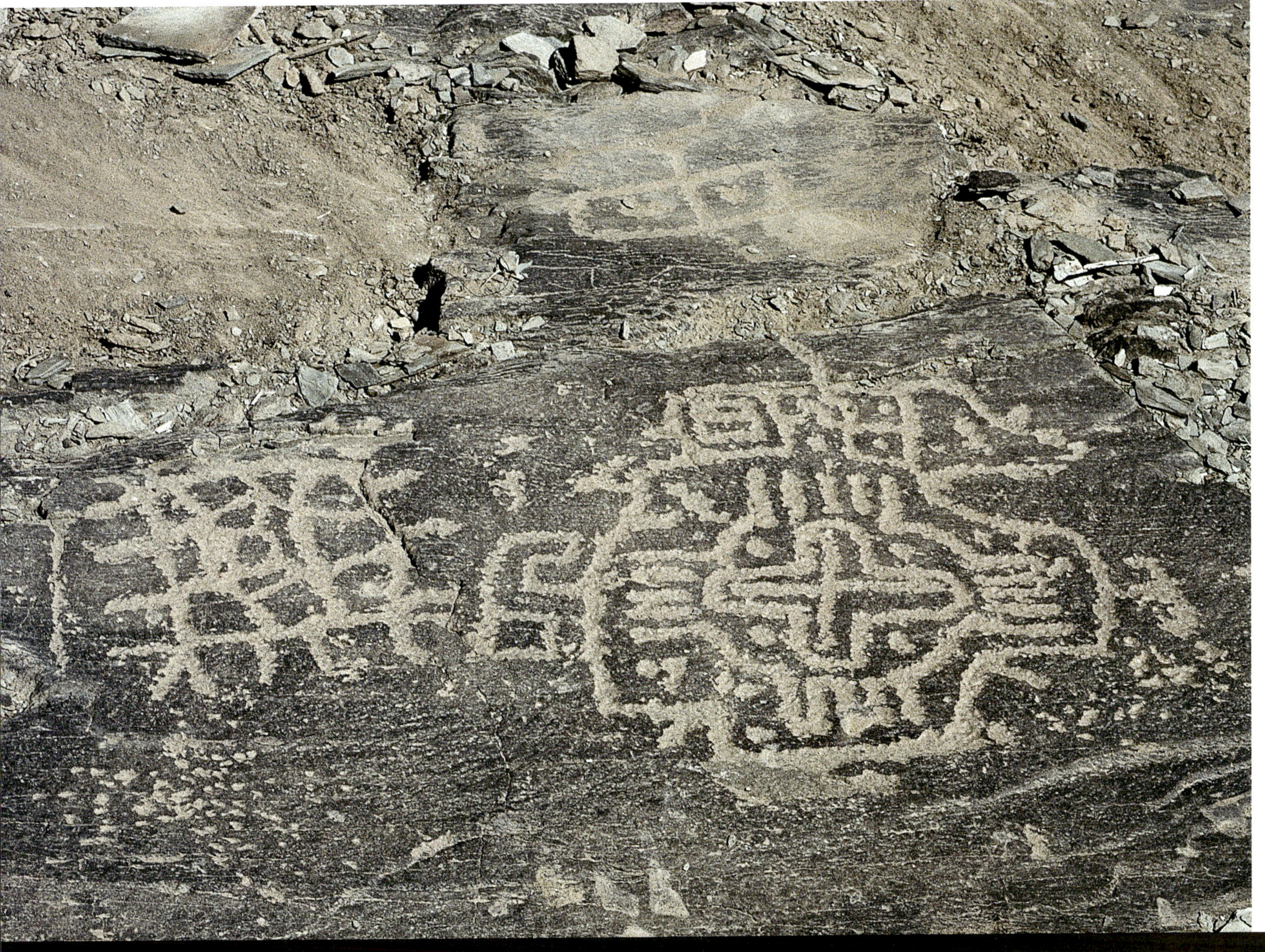

Pictures carved in the rock near Tagragra, ca. 1000 BC

The Sahara as a cultural landscape

The tribal territory of the Feija, with whose textiles we are concerned here, is situated on the southern slopes of the Anti-Atlas facing the Sahara. A lively cultural and economic exchange took place between the inhabitants of the Sahara and the peoples who live on its fringes. Contact with the Tuareg is of paramount importance for the Feija and also influenced the motifs on Feija weavings.

Kulturraum Sahara

Das Stammesgebiet der Feija, um deren Textilien es hier geht, liegt an der Anti-Atlas-Südseite, der Sahara zugewandt. Zwischen den Bewohnern der Sahara und denen der Wüstenränder gab es einen regen kulturellen und wirtschaftlichen Austausch. Von besonderer Bedeutung für die Feija sind die Kontakte mit den Tuareg, was auch die Motive auf den Feija-Geweben beeinflusste.

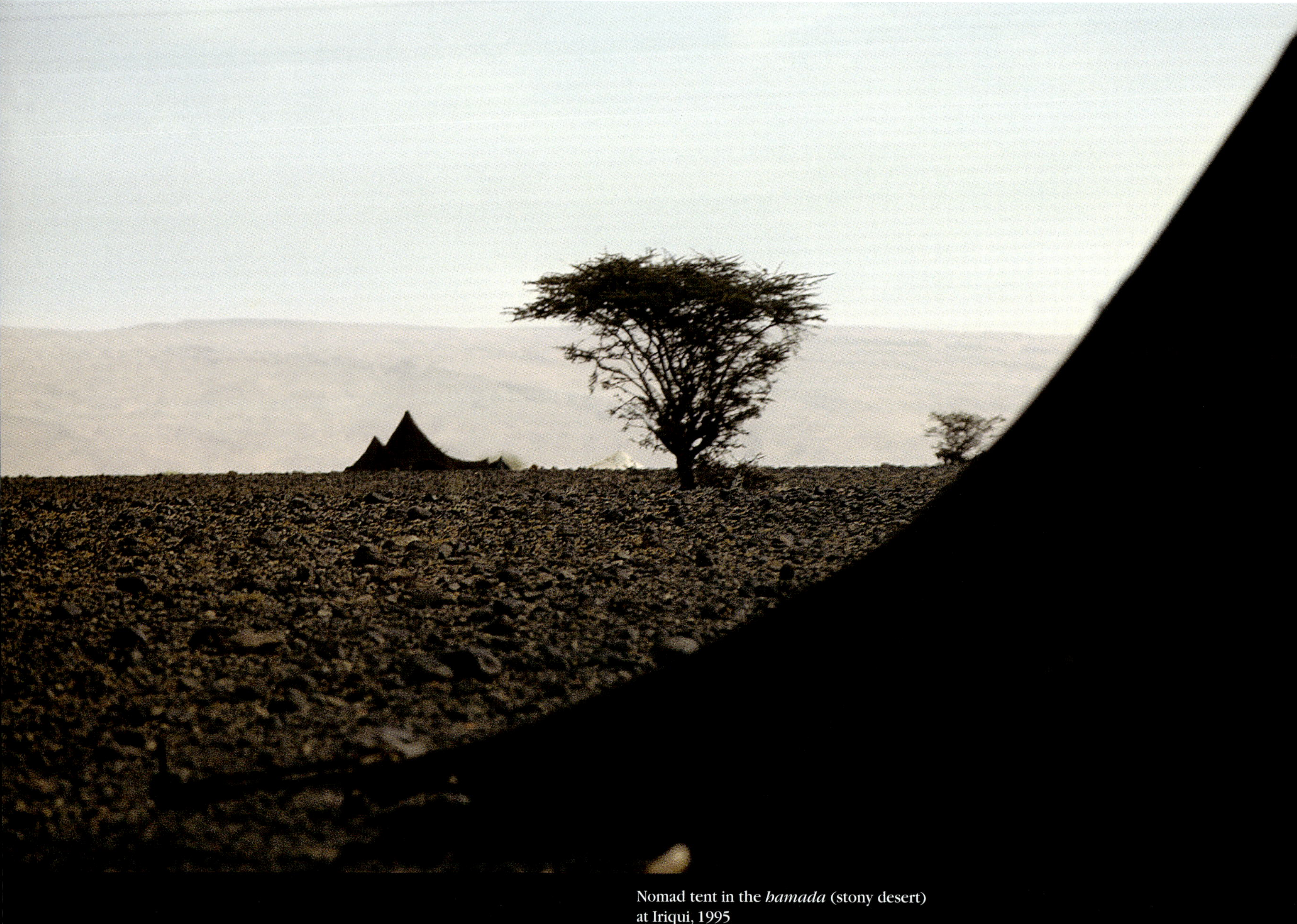

Nomad tent in the *hamada* (stony desert) at Iriqui, 1995

Nomadenzelt in der *hamada* (Steinwüste) bei Iriqui, 1995

Caravans, salt and sugar

The Sahara, its inhabitants and the trans-Saharan trade routes they used have played a major role in the lifestyle and thinking of the Feija since time immemorial. Intensive long-term study of the Feija as well as the inhabitants of the southern Drâa Valley has led us to conclude that the Sahara should be viewed as a single cultural landscape - much as the Mediterranean littoral so often is.

The far-flung trans-Saharan caravan routes have yet to be exhaustively studied. However, it is known that a network of well-established caravan routes criss-crossed the Sahara from the earliest times. Such trans-Saharan routes enabled the neighboring peoples to engage in uninterrupted economic and cultural exchange. Historically of particular importance for the region discussed here was what was known as the "Salt War" which was waged from 1539 until 1591 between Morocco and the old kingdom of Sudan. The real significance of this war rests in the circumstance that Morocco had regular secure access to the gold of the old kingdom of Sudan from then on via the ancient caravan routes. Between 1590 and 1750 nineteen of the pashas in Timbuktu were, in fact, aristocrats from the Drâa Valley. Moreover, from the latter half of the 16th century this development led to the routes used by the salt trade also running through the Anti-Atlas region - through Imi n'Tatelt and the Drâa Valley.

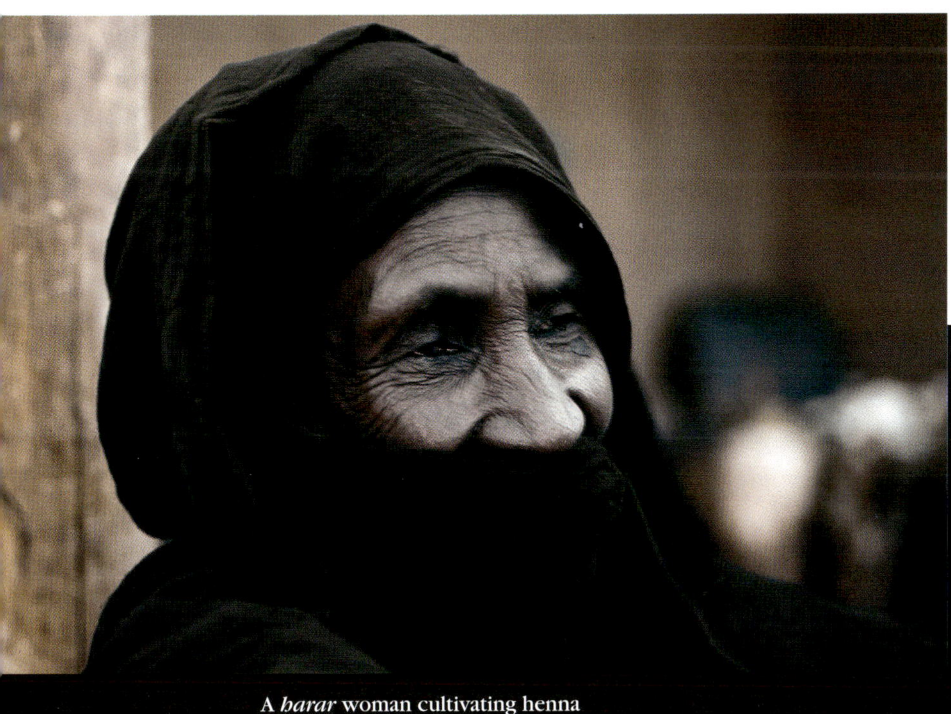

A *harar* woman cultivating henna in the lower Drâa Valley, 2001

Hennabäuerin – eine *harar* – im unteren Drâa-Tal, 2001

Karawanen, Salz und Zucker

Die Sahara, ihre Bewohner und deren Handelswege spielen seit jeher eine wichtige Rolle im Leben und Denken der Feija. Die intensive und lange andauernde Beschäftigung mit den Feija sowie mit den Bewohnern des südlichen Drâa-Tales führte uns zu dem Schluss, dass die Sahara als zusammenhängender Kulturraum angesehen werden sollte – fast genauso, wie dies für den Mittelmeerraum selbstverständlich ist.

Die Wege der Saharakarawanen sind nach wie vor nicht erschöpfend erforscht. Man weiß jedoch, dass die Sahara seit frühen Zeiten von einem Netz bekannter Karawanenwege durchzogen wird. Sie ermöglichten einen kontinuierlichen wirtschaftlichen und kulturellen Austausch unter den Anrainern. Besonders wichtig für das hier besprochene Gebiet war der sogenannte "Salzkrieg", der von 1539 bis 1591 zwischen Marokko und dem alten Sudan (heute Mali und Niger) ausgetragen wurde. Die wahre Bedeutung dieses Krieges liegt darin, dass Marokko von nun an auf den alten Karawanenwegen regelmäßigen und gesicherten Zugang zum Gold des alten Sudan hatte. Zwischen 1590 und 1750 waren sogar 19 der Paschas in Tombouctou Vornehme aus dem Drâa-Tal. Von der zweiten Hälfte des 16. Jahrhunderts an führten aufgrund dieser Entwicklung auch die Wege des Salzhandels durch das Gebiet des Anti-Atlas – durch Imi n'Tatelt und durch das Drâa-Tal.

Die vielen sogenannten *agadir romanni* (frei übersetzt: Speicherburg der Römer/Fremden), welche entlang der alten Karawanenrouten der Sahara (z.B. in Touat[1]) bis in den Anti-Atlas hinein errichtet worden waren, und die auch heute noch als dichte Kette auf den Bergspitzen thronen, sind Zeugen dafür, dass wichtige Wege durch das Gebiet der Feija führten (siehe Abb. S. 93). Das Alter dieser Festungen lässt sich kaum bestimmen: Einmal beschädigt, können sie in kurzer Zeit zu Steinhaufen verfallen.[2]

1 Vgl. z.B. Oliel 1994, S. 38.

2 Für Archäologen sind diese Festungen wenig ergiebig, da die lokale Bevölkerung auf der Suche nach sagenhaften Schätzen auch Scherben, Holz oder Metallfundstücke mitgenommen hat. Viele Märchen und Sagen erzählen vom "Judengold", vom "Christenschatz" und sehr wertvollen Dingen, die an bestimmten und bezeichneten Stellen in der Landschaft und in den *agadir romanni* vergraben sein sollen. Dieser Schatzglaube entbehrt zwar einer wissenschaftlichen Grundlage, ist jedoch tief im Bewusstsein der Bevölkerung verankert und hat vielen Tälern, Hochweiden und Orten ihre Namen gegeben. Der Ursprung der *agadir romanni* wird irrtümlich oft nur auf die Portugiesen zurückgeführt.

The numerous *agadir romanni* (free translation: granary of the Romans/foreigners), as they are called, which were set up along the old caravan routes (for instance, in Touat[1]) criss-crossing the Sahara and extending into the Anti-Atlas, still crown the mountain peaks to form a close-knit chain (see fig. p. 93). They attest that important routes led through the Feija territory. The age of these fortifications cannot be determined; once damaged, they tend to collapse within a short time into heaps of rubble.[2]

An *agadir romanni* differs from a village communal granary in that it corresponds in layout to a small barracks or a caravanserai. Caravans passing through found safe lodgings for man, beast and wares at an *agadir*. Small cells as well as quite a large communal kitchen are grouped about an inner court. Such structures are generally round and adapted to the terrain. At least one other *agadir romanni* is always within sight of each. Smoke signals or beacons conveyed messages from *agadir* to *agadir*. It could not be ascertained whether the *agadir romanni* were used by the Feija as a refuge in times of emergency.

Just as vital as the links between the Anti-Atlas and the Sahara were those that extended from the Anti-Atlas into the Sous, the valley bordering it immediately to the north, which was mainly inhabited by peoples of Arab descent. The Beni Yâacoub shrine in Imi n'Tatelt possesses vast domains in the Sous (see "The Feija and Islam", p. 38).

The Tuareg and their Tifinagh alphabet

The caravan trade between Timbuktu in the south and the Sous in the north was controlled by the "knights of the desert", the Tuareg. Gold, salt and slaves were some of the most important "trade goods". According to our informants, intermarriage between the Feija and the Tuareg must have been

1 Cf. for instance Oliel 1994, S. 38.

2 These fortified structures are not of much use to archaeologists since the locals, always on the lookout for fabulous treasure, have also appropriated sherds, wood and metal finds. Numerous fairy tales and legends tell of "Jewish gold" or "Christian hoards" and valuables which are supposed to have been buried at specified, designated places throughout the countryside and in the *agadir romanni*. Scholarship does not bear out this myth of buried treasure yet it is deeply rooted in the consciousness of the local population and many valleys, high summer pas-

Ein *agadir romanni* unterscheidet sich von einer dörflichen Speicherburg: Seine Anlage entspricht eher einer kleinen Kaserne oder einer Karawanserei. Durchziehende Karawanen fanden mit Tieren und Waren sichere Unterkunft. Kleine Zellen sowie eine größere Gemeinschaftsküche gruppieren sich um einen Innenhof. Die Anlage ist in der Regel rund, der Topographie angepasst, und es besteht Sichtkontakt zu mindestens einem weiteren *agadir romanni*. Von *agadir* zu *agadir* wurden mit Rauch oder Feuer Botschaften übermittelt. Ob die *agadir romanni* in Zeiten der Bedrängnis von den Feija je als Fluchtburgen gebraucht wurden, war nicht zu erfahren.

Ebenso bedeutend wie die Verbindungen zum Sahararaum waren vom Anti-Atlas aus auch jene in den Sous, dem unmittelbar nördlich benachbarten Tal, mit seiner mehrheitlich arabischstämmigen Bevölkerung. Im Sous besitzt das Heiligtum von Beni Yâacoub in Imi n'Tatelt große Ländereien (siehe "Die Feija und der Islam", S. 38).

Die Tuareg und ihr Tifinagh-Alphabet

Beherrscht wurde der Karawanenhandel zwischen Tombouctou im Süden und dem Sous im Norden von den "Rittern der Wüste", den Tuareg. Gold, Salz und Sklaven gehörten zu den wichtigsten "Gütern". Eheliche Verbindungen zwischen den Feija und den Tuareg müssen gemäß unseren Informanten recht häufig gewesen sein. Für die vielfältigen Beziehungen der Feija zu den Tuareg finden sich sowohl im Musterschatz der Gewebe als auch in der Literatur Belege.

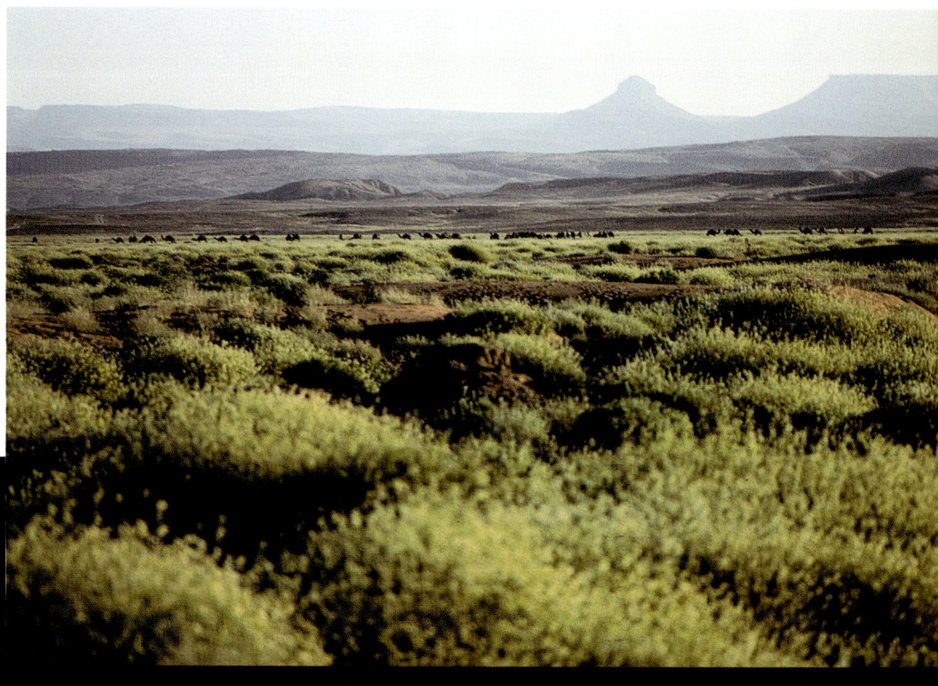

A view of the Anti-Atlas and the Jebel Bani from the blooming desert at Chegagate, 1995

quite frequent. There is evidence for diverse links between the Feija and the Tuareg both in the repertoire of patterns found on textiles and in literature. The catalog section of the present publication shows what can be seen of this on the fabrics. Here the Tuareg alphabet, called *tifinagh*, is especially important. *Tifinagh* characters were used by the Feija and evidently by the "white magicians" of this region as a sort of secret code. The signs were probably used for this purpose because they were recognizable in the area yet could only be read by a handful of people. More efficacious powers and positive energies are ascribed to whatever is written in *tifinagh* characters.

Points of conformity between the Tuareg and Feija or Chleuh Berber cultures also appear in other areas. Since there is not enough space in the present book to describe these in detail, let it suffice here to point out keywords related to the magic and symbolism of materials (silver, wood) as well as the medicine and therapeutic uses to which medicinal herbs - and henna in particular - were put.

References:
Brett/Fentress 1996, Oliel 1994, Soldini et al. 1983, Spillmann 1931

Der Katalogteil dieser Publikation zeigt, was davon auf den Textilien sichtbar wird. Insbesondere ist hier das Alphabet der Tuareg, *tifinagh* genannt, von Bedeutung. *Tifinagh*-Zeichen wurden bei den Feija und offenbar bei den "weißen Magiern" dieses Gebietes als eine Art Geheimschrift verwendet. Man bediente sich der Zeichen wohl deshalb, weil sie in der Gegend bekannt waren, jedoch nur von ganz wenigen Menschen gelesen werden konnten. Was mit den *tifinagh*-Zeichen geschrieben ist, dem wird mehr Kraft und positive Energie zugesprochen.

Übereinstimmungen zwischen den Kulturen der Tuareg und den Feija, bzw. den Chleuh-Berbern zeigen sich auch in weiteren Bereichen. Es würde den Rahmen dieser Publikation sprengen, diese ausführlich darzustellen, daher sei hier nur stichwortartig auf die Bereiche Magie und Symbolik von Materialien (Silber, Holz) sowie Heilkunde und Verwendung von Heilpflanzen – insbesondere von Henna – verwiesen.

Literatur:
Brett/Fentress 1996, Oliel 1994, Soldini et al. 1983, Spillmann 1931

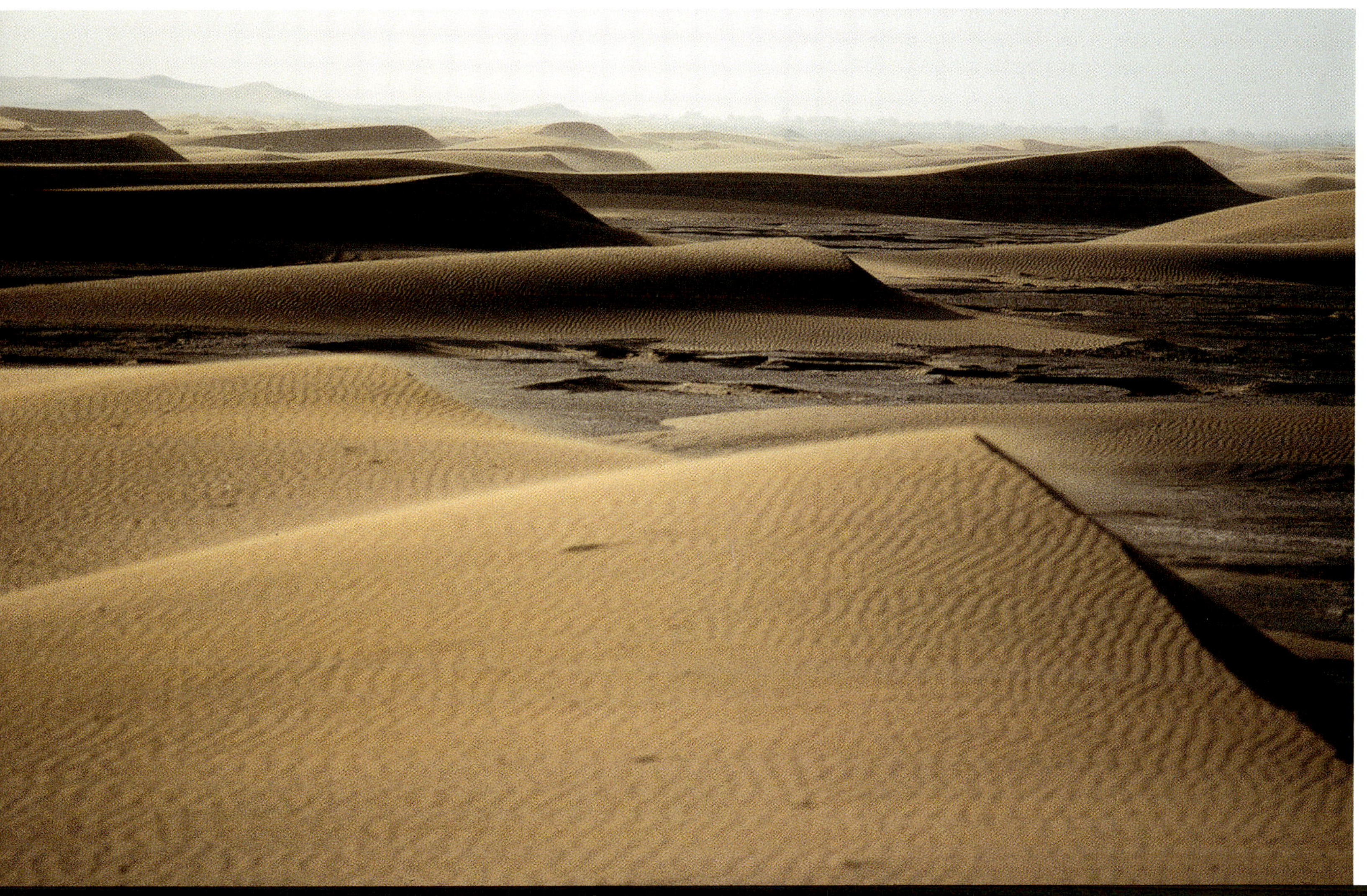

The sand dunes at Lac Iriqui, 1994

Die Sanddünen am Lac Iriqui, 1994

The Imazighen and their Tifinagh

Mourad Kusserow

Only the Tuareg had an alphabet in the form of the *tifinagh*; the Imazighen literary tradition is otherwise an oral one. The Imazighen of Morocco, however, have a *tifinagh* of their own, developed from the original Tuareg alphabet. These are the *tifinagh* characters which are so important in connection with Feija textiles.

Die Imazighen und ihr Tifinagh

Mourad Kusserow

Nur die Tuareg hatten mit dem *tifinagh* ein Alphabet, ansonsten war die literarische Tradition der Imazighen eine mündliche. Die Imazighen Marokkos haben jedoch ein eigenes, aus dem ursprünglichen Tuareg-Alphabeth entwickeltes *tifinagh*. Diese *tifinagh*-Schriftzeichen spielen in den Textilien der Feija eine wichtige Rolle.

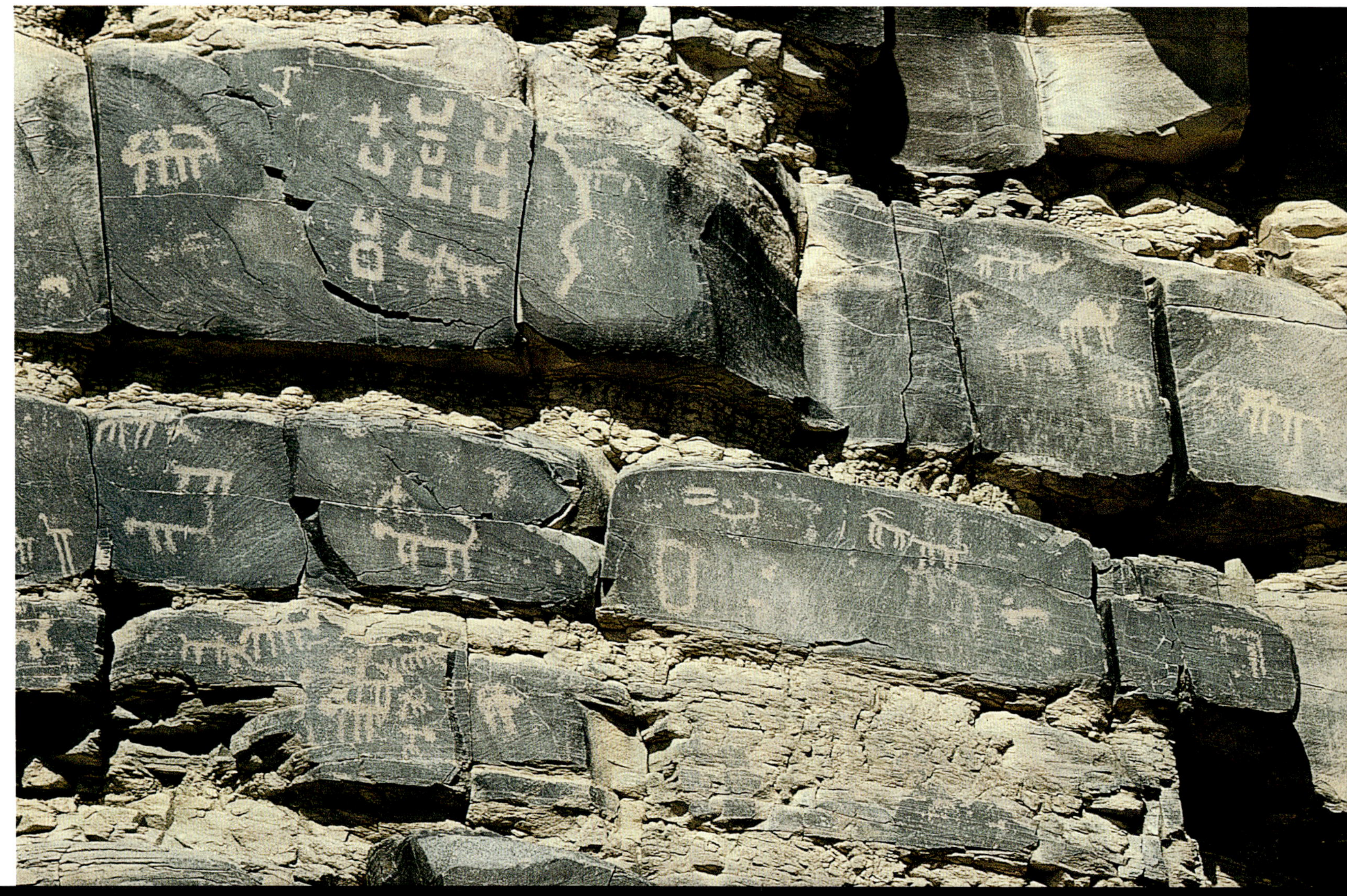

Pictures carved in the rock near Tinzouline, ca 1000 BC (central Drâa Valley): *tifinagh* characters, domestic animals such as horses and dromedaries, 1992

Geschlagene Felsbilder bei Tinzouline, ca. 1000 v. Chr. (mittleres Drâa-Tal): *tifinagh*-Schriftzeichen, Haustiere wie Pferde und Dromedare, 1992

If we wish to study Imazighen culture - language, script, poetry and narrative literature, weaving, ceramics, decoration and domestic architecture - we must first clarify several aspects of cultural history. First of all, let us begin with the term "Berber", derived from the Greek "bárbaros", an expression which, even though it has been used in the present book to facilitate comprehension, basically should be quickly forgotten since those so designated call themselves "Imazighen" (pronounced "imasieren"), which means "free people". Because of its all too obviously negative connotations - uncivilized, barbaric, uneducated, savage, etc. - the term "Berber" is rejected.

The origins of the Imazighen, the indigenous population of Morocco and large parts of North Africa, are obscure. All that is known about this is that they had links with the great powers of antiquity - the Egyptians, Greeks and Romans. In the course of their turbulent history, the Imazighen experienced the incursions of many different peoples: the Phoenicians, Hebrews, Romans, Vandals, Byzantines and Arabs - and thus the arrival of Islam in the 7th century - as well as European colonialism, in 1830 in Algeria, 1881 in Tunesia and 1912 in Morocco. Nowadays the geographic spread of the Imazighen is limited to a fairly extensive territory bounded in the north by the Mediterranean, in the east by Egypt (the Siwa Oasis), in the west by the Atlantic and in the south by Niger and Mali. There are smaller Imazighen oases in Mauretania and in northern Senegal.

The language of all Imazighen groups is *tamazight*, a collective term for various main dialects assigned to one of the five branches of the Semito-Hamitic - Afro-Asiatic - language family.

Beschäftigen wir uns mit der Kultur der Imazighen – Sprache, Schrift, Dicht- und Erzählkunst, Webkunst, Keramik, Dekor sowie Wohnkultur – so müssen wir uns zunächst über einige kulturhistorische Aspekte Klarheit verschaffen. Das beginnt bereits mit dem aus dem Griechischen stammenden Ausdruck "Berber", den wir, auch wenn er in dieser Publikation der Einfachheit halber verwendet wird, im Grunde schnell vergessen sollten, denn die Betroffenen nennen sich selbst "Imazighen" (sprich: "imasieren"), das heißt "freie Menschen". Der Begriff "Berber" wird wegen seines pejorativen Inhalts – unzivilisiert, barbarisch, ungebildet, wild etc. – abgelehnt.

Die Herkunft der Imazighen, der Urbevölkerung Marokkos und weiter Teile Nordafrikas, liegt im Dunkeln. Fest steht lediglich, dass sie mit den antiken Großmächten – Ägyptern, Griechen und Römer – in Verbindung standen. Im Verlaufe ihrer wechselvollen Geschichte erlebten die Imazighen die Ankunft unterschiedlicher Völker: Phönizier, Hebräer, Römer, Vandalen, Byzantiner, Araber – und damit des Islam – im 7. Jahrhundert – und des europäischen Kolonialismus – 1830 in Algerien, 1881 in Tunesien und 1912 in Marokko. Heute beschränkt sich die geographische Verbreitung der Imazighen auf mehr oder weniger große Lebensräume, die im Norden vom Mittelmeer, im Osten von Ägypten (Oase Siwa), im Westen vom Atlantik und im Süden von Niger und Mali begrenzt werden. Kleinere Imazighen-Oasen gibt es in Mauretanien und im Norden des Senegal.

Allen Imazighen-Volksgruppen gemeinsam ist die Sprache *tamazight*, ein Sammelname für verschiedene Hauptdialekte, die einen der fünf Zweige der semito-hamitischen – afro-asiatischen – Sprachfamilie zugerechnet werden.

TRANSCRIPT. LATINE	TIFINAGH MAROCAIN	BOUDRIS BELAÏD	SALEM CHAKER	AGRAW IMAZIGHEN	LIBYQUE HORIZONTAL	LIBYQUE VERTICAL	SAHARIEN ANCIEN	TIFINAGH TOUAREG	TRANSCRIPT. ARABE
a	• •	•	•	•	• •—	•	•—	•	ـَـ
aïn	ⵄ	A	—	ⵄ					ع
b	Φ	Φ	Θ	Φ	⊙ ⊡	⊙ ⊡	⊡ Φ ⊟ Θ	⊡ Φ ⊟ Θ	ب
c (ch)	C	G	C	C	} { ⊏ C	ʍ {		⊃ ⊃ ⊐ ⊂	ش
d	Λ	Λ	Λ	Λ	Π U	⊐ ⊏	Π Λ U V	Π Λ U V	د
ḏ	V								ڎ
ḍ̣	E								ظ
ḍ	Ɑ	E	E	E	≻—	m		Ǝ E ш	ض
e (é)	÷ ÷	%							ـِـ
f (ph)	⊐	⊐	ⵊ	ⵊ	ⵅ ∝ U	ⵅ ⵅ ⵅ		ⵊ ⵅ	ف
g	ⵅ	ⵅ	ⵅ	ⵅ					ڭ
ḡ	Ⴟ	Ⴟ	ⵖ	ⵅ		V Λ	ⵖ ⊥	ⵖ ⊥ ⊢	ڭي
ġ (gh)	Y	Y	!	Y	≡ ÷	ⵉⵉⵉ +	≡	⁝	غ
h	Φ	Φ	≡	O	≡	ⵉⵉⵉ	≡	⁝ ::	ه
ḥ	ⵃ	ⵃ	•••	ⵃ	⊢	⊥ T		::	ح
i	Σ Ɛ	Σ	ϟ	Σ	Z N ʕ ʔ ~	N Z	ʔ ʕ ʔ }	{ } ʔ ʕ	ـِـ
j (ž)	I	I	I	I	H	H I		I H ⵅ X X	ج
dj	ⴵ								دج
k	K	K	ⵍ	K				∵ ⁖ ⁖ ∵	ک
ǩ	ⴿ	K							کش
ḵ (kh)	ⵅ								خ
l	ǁ	ǁ	ǁ	ǁ	ǁ	=	ǁ	ǁ	ل
m	⊏	[	⊏	⊏	⊐ ⊃	⊔ ∪	⊐ ⊃	⊐ ⊏	م
n	I	I	I	I	I	I	I	I	ن
ñ			≠						
q	ⵇ	ⵇ	≡	ⵇ		≡		•••	ق
r	O	O	O	O	O ⊡	O ⊡	O ⊡	O ⊡	ر
s	● ⊙	⊙	⋈	⊙	ⵅ	ⵅ 8 ∞	⊙ ⊡	⊙ ⊡	س
ṣ	ⵚ	ⵚ	⊢	O	[C G	Π			ص
t	+	+	X	+	+ X	+	+	+	ت
ṯ (th)	X	X			Ǝ Ǝ	⊔	[⊐ ⊏	Ǝ	ث
ṭ	ⵟ	ⵟ	E	E	≻— ≻—	m	→ ≻—	Ǝ E ш Ǝ	ط
ts	ⵜ				X		X		تس
tch	ⴵ								تش
u (ou)	⁝ ⁝	:	:	:	=	ǁ	—	: .:	ـُـ
v (b)	◺ ◿								پ
w	ⵡ	U	=	:					و
x		X	::	X					خ
y	Π	∩	Ɛ	Σ	Z N ʕ ʔ ~		ʔ ʕ ʔ }	ʔ ʕ ʔ }	ي
z	ⵣ	ⵣ	ⵣ	ⵣ	— H	—	H	ⵣ ⵣ ⵣ	ز
ẓ	ⵥ	ⵥ	ⵥ	ⵥ	∩ m	ш	m ш ⵣ	ⵥ ⵣ ⵥ	صز

"Tableau comparatif des alphabets libyco-berbères", from *Tifinagh* 9, 1996

"Tableau comparatif des alphabets libyco-berbères", aus *Tifinagh* 9, 1996

From the 11th to the 13th centuries three Imazighen dynasties - the Almoravids, the Almohads and the Merinids - held sway in Morocco, ruling vast areas of North Africa. This led to centuries of intermingling between Arabs and Imazighen although, when it occurred, it was limited to the flat country and urban centres near the coasts, especially the Atlantic coastal plain. Remote mountainous regions, on the other hand, have remained purely "Imazighen" down to the present day. In other words, the Arabs introduced Islam and the Arabic language but culturally they otherwise merged totally with the Imazighen. As a result, quite large groups of Imazighen became "Arabised". The Moroccan colloquial vernacular *darija* consists in quite a considerable number of loanwords from Arabic yet is really an Arabised Imazighen idiom. Many of those who were once Imazighen have lost all knowledge of their origins - they have become genuine Moroccans. The rural depopulation of recent years as well as rapid adoption of electricity - and linked with the latter the invasion of remote regions by the electronic media as well as continuing advances in literacy - have forced the Imazighen to be multilingual - speaking Arabic, French and Spanish. Attempts at establishing classroom teaching in indigenous Imazighen languages, which are only spoken but not written, have been unsuccessful. The Sahara Imazighen, the Tuareg (*at-tawarik* = the "trackless" ones), are the only group to use an alphabet, the *tifinagh*; they have a tradition of written literature, especially poetry.

Against this background, what interests us is the question of the origins of the *tifinagh*. The ancestors of the Imazighen spoke "Libyan" and were called "Libyans" in Pharaonic Egypt.[1]

Vom 11. bis 13. Jahrhundert gelangten drei Imazighen-Dynastien – die Almoraviden, die Almohaden und die Meriniden – in Marokko an die Macht und beherrschten weite Teile Nordafrikas. Damit setzte eine jahrhundertelange Vermischung zwischen Arabern und Imazighen ein, die sich jedoch nur auf das flache Land und urbane Zentren in Nähe der Küsten, vor allem des Atlantik, beschränkte. Unwegsame Bergregionen sind bis heute rein "imazighisch" geblieben. Mit anderen Worten: die Araber brachten den Islam und die arabische Sprache, aber als Volk gingen sie weitestgehend in den Imazighen auf. Das führte dazu, dass größere Imazighen-Gruppen sich "arabisierten". Die marokkanische Umgangssprache *darija* besteht aus einer nicht unerheblichen Zahl von arabischen Lehnwörtern, ist aber in Wirklichkeit ein arabisiertes Imazighen-Idiom. Im Bewusstsein vieler ehemaliger Imazighen ging das Wissen um die Abstammung verloren – sie wurden zu echten Marokkanern. Die in den letzten Jahren sich verschärfende Landflucht, aber auch die rasche Elektrifizierung – und damit verbunden das Eindringen elektronischer Medien in abgelegene Regionen sowie die fortschreitende Alphabetisierung – sorgen dafür, dass die Imazighen zur Mehrsprachigkeit – Arabisch, Französisch und Spanisch – gezwungen werden, wodurch die Versuche, Unterricht in imazighischen Muttersprachen, die nur gesprochen werden, einzurichten, ins Leere laufen. Lediglich bei den Sahara-Imazighen, den Tuareg *(at-tawarik* = die "ohne Weg") ist ein Alphabet, das *tifinagh* in Gebrauch; sie haben eine schriftlich fixierte Literatur, vor allem Poesie.

Vor diesem Hintergrund interessiert uns die Frage nach der Herkunft des *tifinagh*. Die Vorfahren der Imazighen sprachen "Libysch" und wurden von den pharaonischen Ägyptern "Libyer" genannt.[1]

Das heutige *tifinagh*, von den Tuareg *tamashak* genannt, ist in seiner alten Form erhalten geblieben. Es handelt sich dabei um das alte libysche oder libysch-punische Alphabet, das in ganz Nordafrika in Gebrauch war, einschließlich der Kanarischen Inseln. Verständlich, dass sich regionale Varianten herausbildeten. In Tunesien und Ostalgerien wurde ein "orientalisches Alphabet" verwendet und in Westalgerien und Marokko das "okzidentale Alphabet". Letzteres bildet den Vorläufer des aktuellen *tifinagh*, das einige Zusatzzeichen gegenüber der orientalischen Variante aufweist. Das heutige marokkanische *tifinagh* besteht aus 40 geometrischen Zeichen, deren Symbole – Punkte, Quadrate, Dreiecke, horizontale und vertikale Punktlinien etc. – bisher noch nicht eindeutig entschlüsselt werden konnten.

1 Libyan was written with consonants towards the close of the prehistoric era, which means that each letter represented a sound. We know this thanks to a bilingual inscription - in Libyan and Punic characters - dedicating the mausoleum of Massinissa, the Imazighen ruler in Thugga (Tunesia) dating from 138 BC as well as other mortuary inscriptions on tombs.

1 Das Libysche wurde gegen Ende der Vorgeschichte mit Konsonanten dargestellt, was bedeutet, dass jeder Buchstabe für einen Ton stand. Wir wissen davon dank einer zweisprachigen Widmungsinschrift – libysch-punischer Schrift – aus dem Mausoleum des Imazighen-Herrschers Massinissa in Thugga (Tunesien) aus dem Jahre 138 v. Chr. so-

The *tifinagh* of the present day, called *tamashaq* by the Tuareg, has been preserved in its ancient form. This is the ancient Libyan or Libyan-Punic alphabet which was used throughout North Africa and even on the Canary Islands. It is only natural that regional variations evolved. An "Oriental alphabet" was used in Tunesia and eastern Algeria and an "Occidental alphabet" was used in western Algeria and Morocco. The latter was a precursor of the present-day *tifinagh*, which has added a few characters to the Oriental variant. The contemporary Moroccan *tifinagh* comprises 40 geometric characters, whose symbols - dots, squares, triangles, horizontal and vertical dotted lines, etc. - have hitherto not been definitively deciphered.

After the arrival of the Arabs, the Imazighen of Morocco continued to correspond in writing in *tamazight*; however, as a concession to the Muslim Arabs, the *tifinagh* was replaced with Arabic characters. Consequently, the geometric letters could not help but lose their original meaning and assume new aesthetic functions: they survived as ornament and as decoration in the decorative arts: as patterns on carpets and fabrics, as decoration on pottery and as models for silver jewelry. The "letters" were now partly given a new, magic content: they ward off harmful spirits - *jnoun* - and have apotropaic powers against the evil eye and malicious tongues. They also bring blessings and protection from disease.

Modern Imazighen who use *tifinagh* characters have lost all knowledge of the origins and meaning of these graphic symbols. Thousands of years of history have survived in *oral* form in legends and tales, poetry and proverbs, songs and dances. In interpreting these in the light of the meaning and origins of *tifinagh* decoration on textiles, one must realize that each hand-made and painted - e.g. with henna - piece of fabric represents a work of art and that its creator is an artist. Since she is working without referential back-up, without written traditions, she is left to her own resources entirely: her imagination and the treasure trove of tales handed down from her forebears. Knowledge of only a handful of *tifinagh* characters makes it possible to create proper names - for instance, those of medicinal herbs and signs of the zodiac (see fig. p. 26 and Cat. no. 32).

In addition, social events such as dances and festivals can be represented in abstract form by multiple paratactic arrangement - in straight lines or in circles - of one or more letters. The letter "Z" as the sign for "human beings" (see fig. p. 27 and Cat. no. 19) is today the symbol of the Imazighen political movement, without, however, constituting a violation of the Old Testament ban on images, which was reconfirmed in Islam.

The *haik* of the *fqîh* (Cat. no. 32) is painted, among other things, with the names of therapeutic herbs in *tifinagh* signs. This detail shows the term *zaitoun*, which, in the Feija dialect, means "olive tree".

Der *haik* des *fqîh* (Kat.-Nr. 32) ist u.a. mit Namen von Heilkräutern in *tifinagh*-Schriftzeichen bemalt. Das Detail zeigt den Begriff *zaitoun*, was im Feija-Dialekt "Olivenbaum" bedeutet.

References:
Bertrand 1977, Camps 1961, Camps 1987, Chaker 1984, Galand 1979
Gsell 1929, Ibn Khaldûn 1890, Maçais 1946

Periodicals:
Awal 2, 1986, *Etudes et Documents Berbères* 2, 1987, *Tifinagh* 9, 1996, *Tifawt* 4, 1994

Marokkos Imazighen haben nach Ankunft der Araber ihren Schriftverkehr in *tamazight* beibehalten, allerdings, als Konzession an die muslimischen Araber, das *tifinagh* durch arabische Schriftzeichen ersetzt. So blieb es nicht aus, dass die geometrischen Buchstaben ihre ursprüngliche Bedeutung verloren und in neue ästhetische Funktionen schlüpften: Sie überlebten als Ornament und als Dekor im Kunstgewerbe: als Teppich- und Stoffmuster, als Keramikschmuck und als Vorlage für Silberschmuck, wobei die "Buchstaben" teilweise neue magische Inhalte bekamen: sie weisen schädigende Geister – *jnoun* – ab, helfen gegen böse Blicke und Zungen, sie bringen aber auch Segen und schützen vor Krankheit.

Die heutigen Imazighen, die sich der *tifinagh*-Zeichen bedienen, haben das Wissen um Herkunft und Bedeutung dieser graphischen Symbole völlig verloren. Ihre Jahrtausende alte Geschichte hat in *oraler* Form in Legenden und Erzählungen, in Poesie und Spruchweisheiten, in Liedern und Tänzen überlebt. Bei der Interpretation von Bedeutung und Herkunft der *tifinagh*-Dekorationen ist es wichtig, sich klar zu machen, dass jedes von Hand hergestellte und – z.B. mit Henna-Farbe – bemalte Textil ein Kunstwerk darstellt und seine Schöpferin eine Künstlerin ist. Da sie ohne Netz, d.h. ohne schriftliche Überlieferungen arbeitet, ist sie ausschließlich auf ihre Phantasie und den überlieferten Erzählschatz der Alten angewiesen. Die Kenntnis von nur einer Handvoll von *tifinagh*-Zeichen erlaubt es, Namen – z.B. von Heilpflanzen und Sternzeichen – zu kreieren (siehe Abb. S. 26 und Kat.-Nr. 32).

Außerdem können gesellschaftliche Ereignisse, wie Tänze und Feste in abstrakter Form durch das vielfache Anreihen – geradlinig oder in Kreisform – von einem oder mehreren Buchstaben dargestellt werden. Der Buchstabe "Z" als Zeichen für Menschen (siehe Abb. S. 27 und Kat.-Nr. 19), wobei nicht gegen das alttestamentarische Bilderverbot, erneuert durch den Islam, verstoßen wird, ist heute zum Symbol für die politische Imazighen-Bewegung geworden.

Literatur:
Bertrand 1977, Camps 1961, Camps 1987, Chaker 1984, Galand 1979, Gsell 1929, Ibn Khaldûn 1890, Maçais 1946

Zeitschriften:
Awal 2, 1986, *Etudes et Documents Berbères* 2, 1987, *Tifinagh* 9, 1996, *Tifawt* 4, 1994

The *tifinagh* sign for 'Z' changes into a dancing figure (detail of *haik* Cat. no. 19).

Das *tifinagh*-Zeichen "Z" verwandelt sich zu einer tanzenden Figur (Detail aus dem *haik* Kat.-Nr. 19).

The people of the Anti-Atlas

Die Menschen im Anti-Atlas

Textiles represent one of many possibilities of cultural expressions. In the following the culture and history of population groups of the Anti-Atlas, the Jebel Siroua and the Jebel Sarhro will be briefly outlined.

Textilien sind eine von vielen kulturellen Ausdrucksmöglichkeiten. Der folgende Beitrag beleuchtet die Kultur und Geschichte der Bevölkerungsgruppen des Anti-Atlas, des Jebel Siroua und des Jebel Sarhro.

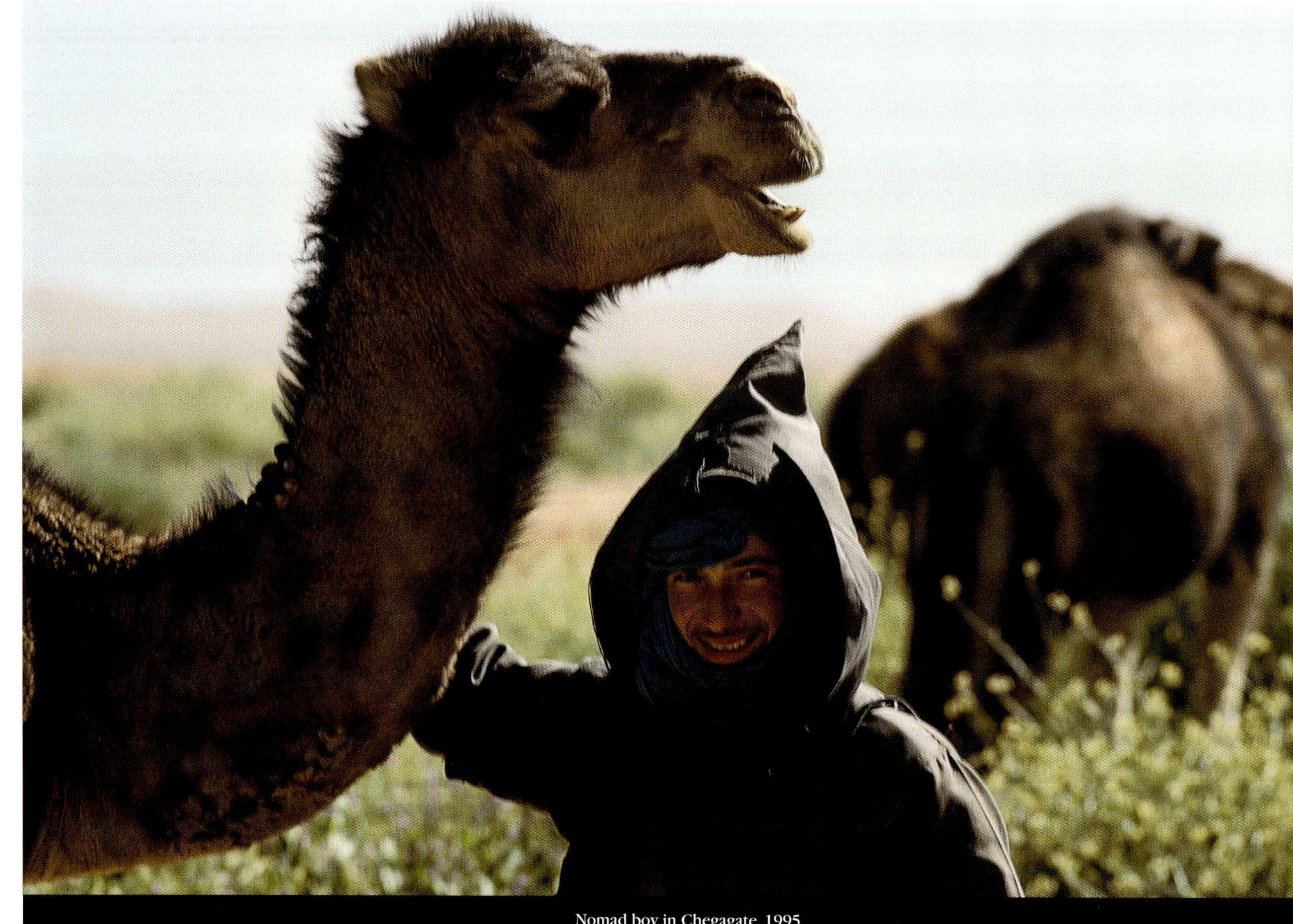

Nomad boy in Chegagate, 1995

Nomadenjunge in Chegagate, 1995

The Chleuh in the Anti-Atlas

The Chleuh are one of three Berber (Imazighen) main groups. In 1967 Hoffmann estimated the Chleuh population in Morocco at roughly three million. For approx. 3000 years they have inhabited the western High Atlas in southern Morocco as well as the Anti-Atlas with the Jebel Siroua and the Sous plain. They are divided into numerous subgroups with their own tribal names. The language of the Chleuh is the Berber *taschelheit*, which is subdivided into three regional dialects.[1] Unlike the nomadic way of life practized by the Aït Atta in the eastern part of the Anti-Atlas - the Jebel Sarhro - the Chleuh are sedentary, residing in one settled community, where they cultivate their territory in a subsistence economy. Islamisation of this population group seems to have taken place by about 1000 AD. Nevertheless, a Berber social structure was preserved intact, primarily in the Anti-Atlas, on into the 20th century. Islam and the indigenous animism fused.

Social equality is a characteristic trait of the mountain Chleuh. Nonetheless, the following classes or rather estates can be distinguished: the feudal aristocracy (e.g., the high *caïds*, whose social status corresponds to feudal lords in western Europe); the religious upper class, the *chorfa* (who claim descent from the Prophet) and the *marabouts* (saints and scholars); the *amma* (the commons); the *haratin* (descendants of the indigenous black people and freed slaves, mostly smiths and craftsmen, who formed the underclass, as it were); the Jews (also a lower class) and - earlier - slaves as well (most of them from the old kindom of Sudan).

Families are structured on patriarchal lines, society is stringently hierarchically ordered in groups or even castes with varying degrees of influence. For all that, the Chleuh are a society which can be said to be democratically organized to a great extent.

Several family bands are united (Bernard G. Hoffmann speaks of "districts" in this connection) to form a tribe which bears a name of its own, is distinguished by a more or less uniform culture and inhabits a particular territory yet rarely represents a political unit (thus the Feija discussed here).

Die Chleuh im Anti-Atlas

Die Chleuh sind eine der drei Berber- (Imazighen-) Hauptgruppen. Hoffmann schätzte die Chleuh-Bevölkerung in Marokko 1967 auf rund drei Millionen Menschen. Sie bewohnen seit ca. 3000 Jahren den westlichen Hohen Atlas im Süden Marokkos, den Anti-Atlas mit dem Jebel Siroua sowie die Sous-Ebene. Sie teilen sich auf in zahlreiche Gruppen mit eigenen Stammesnamen. Die Sprache der Chleuh ist das berberische *taschelheit*, welches sich in drei regionale Dialekte aufteilt.[1] Im Unterschied zur nomadischen Lebensweise der Aït Atta im östlichen Teil des Anti-Atlas – dem Jebel Sarhro – bleiben sie an einem Ort und bearbeiten ihren Lebensraum so, dass sie dort ihr Auskommen finden. Die Islamisierung dieser Bevölkerungsgruppe scheint sich bis um 1000 n. Chr. vollzogen zu haben. Dennoch hat sich gerade im Anti-Atlas eine Berber-Sozialstruktur bis ins 20. Jahrhundert intakt erhalten. Islam und ursprünglicher Animismus wurden miteinander verschmolzen.

Die Gleichstellung der verschiedenen sozialen Schichten ist ein charakteristischer Zug der Berg-Chleuh. Gleichwohl werden die folgenden Klassen unterschieden: die feudale Aristokratie (z.B. hohe *caïds*, deren Position den Feudalherren in Westeuropa entspricht), die religiöse Oberschicht der *chorfa* (welche für sich die Abkunft vom Propheten in Anspruch nehmen) und *marabouts* (Heilige und Gelehrte), die *amma* (das gemeine Volk), die *haratin* (Abkömmlinge der ursprünglich einheimischen Schwarzen und freien Sklaven, meist Schmiede und Handwerker, die sozusagen die Unterklasse bilden), die Juden (ebenfalls eine Unterklasse), und früher auch Sklaven (meist aus dem alten Sudan).

Die Familien sind patriarchalisch geführt, die Gesellschaft ist streng hierarchisch in Gruppen oder gar Kasten mit unterschiedlichem Einfluss strukturiert. Dennoch sind die Chleuh eine Gesellschaft, die hochgradig demokratisch organisiert ist.

Mehrere zusammengeschlossene Familienverbände (Bernard G. Hoffmann spricht von "districts") bilden einen Stamm, der einen eigenen Namen trägt, durch eine mehr oder weniger einheitliche Kultur geprägt ist, ein bestimmtes Gebiet bewohnt, selten aber eine politische Einheit darstellt (so z.B. die hier behandelten Feija).

1 *Shilba* is spoken in the western High Atlas, in the lower Sous Valley and in the region between the Anti-Atlas and the Saguia el-Hamra. *Es-Susi* is indigenous to the upper Sous. *Drawa* is spoken on the southern slopes of the Anti-Atlas, in the High Atlas and to the north and west of the Drâa river.

1 *Shilba* wird im westlichen Hohen Atlas, im unteren Sous-Tal und in der Region zwischen dem Anti-Atlas und der Saguia el-Hamra gesprochen. *Es-Susi* ist im oberen Sous heimisch. *Drawa* wird an den südlichen Hängen des Anti-Atlas, im Hohen Atlas sowie westlich und nördlich des Drâa-Flusses gesprochen.

Östlicher Anti-Atlas, Drâa-Tal und Jebel Sarhro: Beraber in der Mehrheit

Im Unterschied zu den Chleuh-Gruppen im zentralen Anti-Atlas pflegt der zur Beraber-Gruppe zählende Stamm der Aït Atta, welcher im Jebel Sarhro lebt, traditionell eine halbnomadische Lebensweise. Im Ursprung handelt es sich bei den Berabern um ein Hirtenvolk, welches Schafe, Ziegen und Dromedare auf die je nach Jahreszeit ergiebigsten Weiden führt. Im Winter leben sie in ihren festen Dörfern oder in Zelten auf der Südseite des Sarhro. Verwandte der Aït Atta sind jene Beraber-Stämme, welche auch die Berggebiete Zentralmarokkos, den östlichen Hohen Atlas und den Mittleren Atlas bewohnen.

Die Formen des Teilnomadentums werden weitgehend bestimmt vom Charakter des permanenten Wohnsitzes. Ihre Dörfer haben befestigte Gemeinschaftsspeicher sowie urbares Land in der Umgebung. In der Vorsahara wird diese Idee auf das ganze Dorf ausgedehnt; daraus sind Wehrdörfer *(ksar)* entstanden, welche die bäuerlichen Teile des Stammes beherbergen, während der nomadisierende Teil die meiste Zeit des Jahres in Zelten verbringt.

The eastern Anti-Atlas, the Drâa Valley and the Jebel Sarhro: Berabers in the majority

Unlike the Chleuh groups in the central Anti-Atlas, the Aït Atta tribe, which belongs to the Beraber group and lives in the Jebel Sarhro, traditionally pursues a semi-nomadic way of life. The Berabers were originally pastoral nomads who led sheep, goats and dromedaries to the best seasonal pasturage. In winter they lived in their settled villages or in tents on the southern side of the Sarhro. Related to the Aït Atta are the Beraber tribes who also inhabit the mountainous regions of central Morocco, the eastern High Atlas and the Middle Atlas.

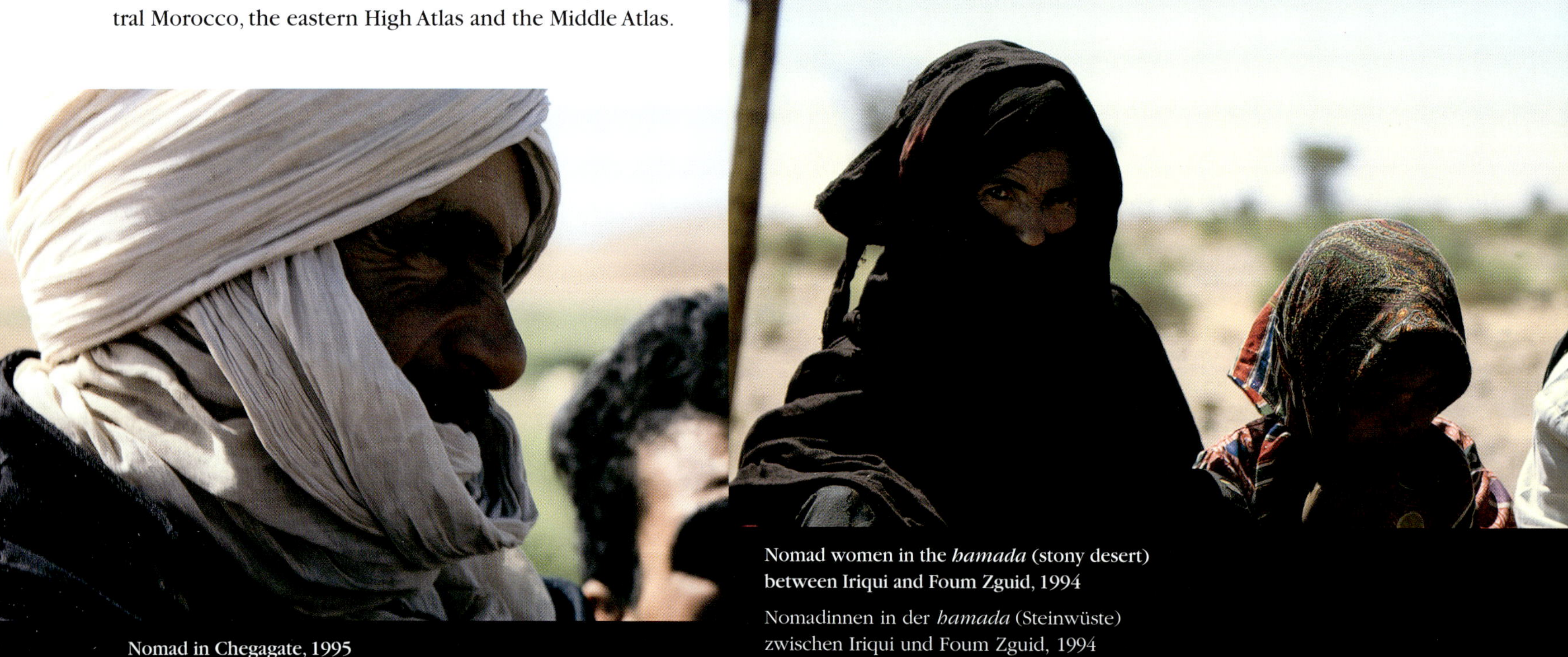

Nomad in Chegagate, 1995

Nomade in Chegagate, 1995

Nomad women in the *hamada* (stony desert) between Iriqui and Foum Zguid, 1994

Nomadinnen in der *hamada* (Steinwüste) zwischen Iriqui und Foum Zguid, 1994

The forms assumed by the semi-nomadic way of life are largely determined by the character of peoples' permanent place of residence. Such villages have fortified communal granaries as well as arable land in the immediate vicinity. In the pre-Sahara this idea is extended to include the entire village; from it fortified villages *(ksar)* developed which house those of the tribe engaged in sedentary agriculture while the nomadic part spends most of the year in tents.

The Drâa Valley, an important north-south corridor with palmeries extending continuously for 100 kilometers, is home to a blend of populations. In addition to the strongly represented Chleuh and Aït Atta, there are other Berber groups here as well as formerly nomadic Arabs, sedentary Arabs, dark-skinned *harar* and *haratin*. In addition, many Jews lived in the region until the end of the Protectorate.

References:
Brett/Fentress 1996, Hoffmann 1967, Laoust 1993,
Riser 1984, Spillmann 1931

Das Drâa-Tal, ein wichtiger Nord-Süd-Korridor, mit ununterbrochenen Palmengärten auf einer Strecke von 100 Kilometern, beherbergt ein Gemisch verschiedener Bevölkerungsgruppen. Neben den stark vertretenen Chleuh und Aït Atta, leben hier weitere Berber-Gruppen, ehemals nomadisierende Araber, sesshafte Araber, dunkelhäutige *harar* und *haratin*. Bis zum Ende des Protektorates lebten auch viele Juden in der Region.

Literatur:
Brett/Fentress 1996, Hoffmann 1967, Laoust 1993
Riser 1984, Spillmann 1931

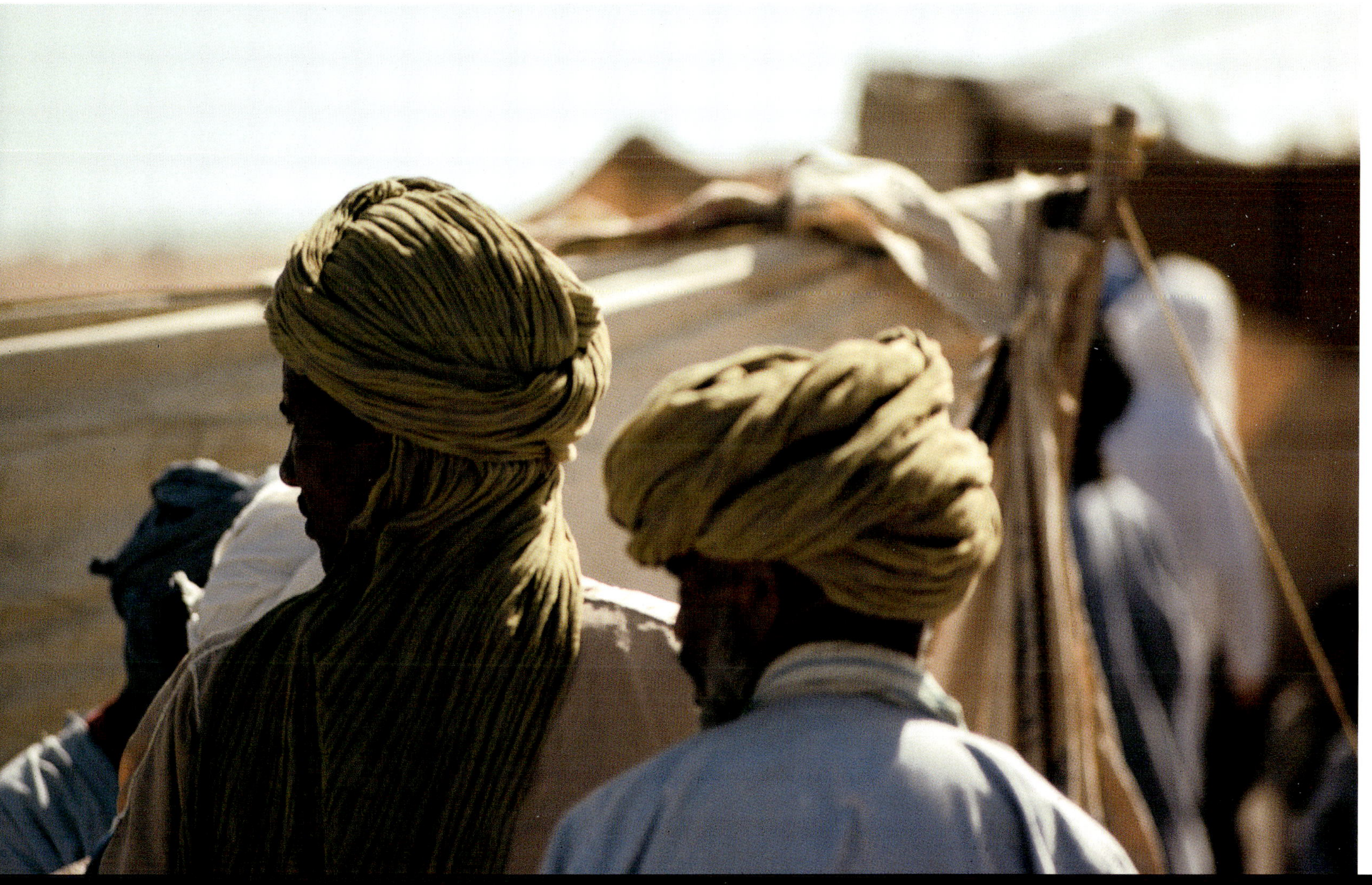

People of all groups meet at the weekly market in Mhamid in the lower Drâa Valley, 1992

Am Wochenmarkt in Mhamid, unteres Drâa-Tal, kommen Menschen aller Gruppen zusammen, 1992

The Feija

Die Feija

The present study focuses on the Feija and their textiles. Tribal customs and living conditions in this remote region have formed its people and influenced the techniques and materials as well as the design and character of their textiles.

Die Feija und ihre Textilien bilden den zentralen Gegenstand der vorliegenden Untersuchung. Die Gepflogenheiten des Stammes und die Lebensumstände in der abgelegenen Region prägen die Menschen und beeinflussen die Techniken und Materialien sowie die Gestaltung und den Charakter der Textilien.

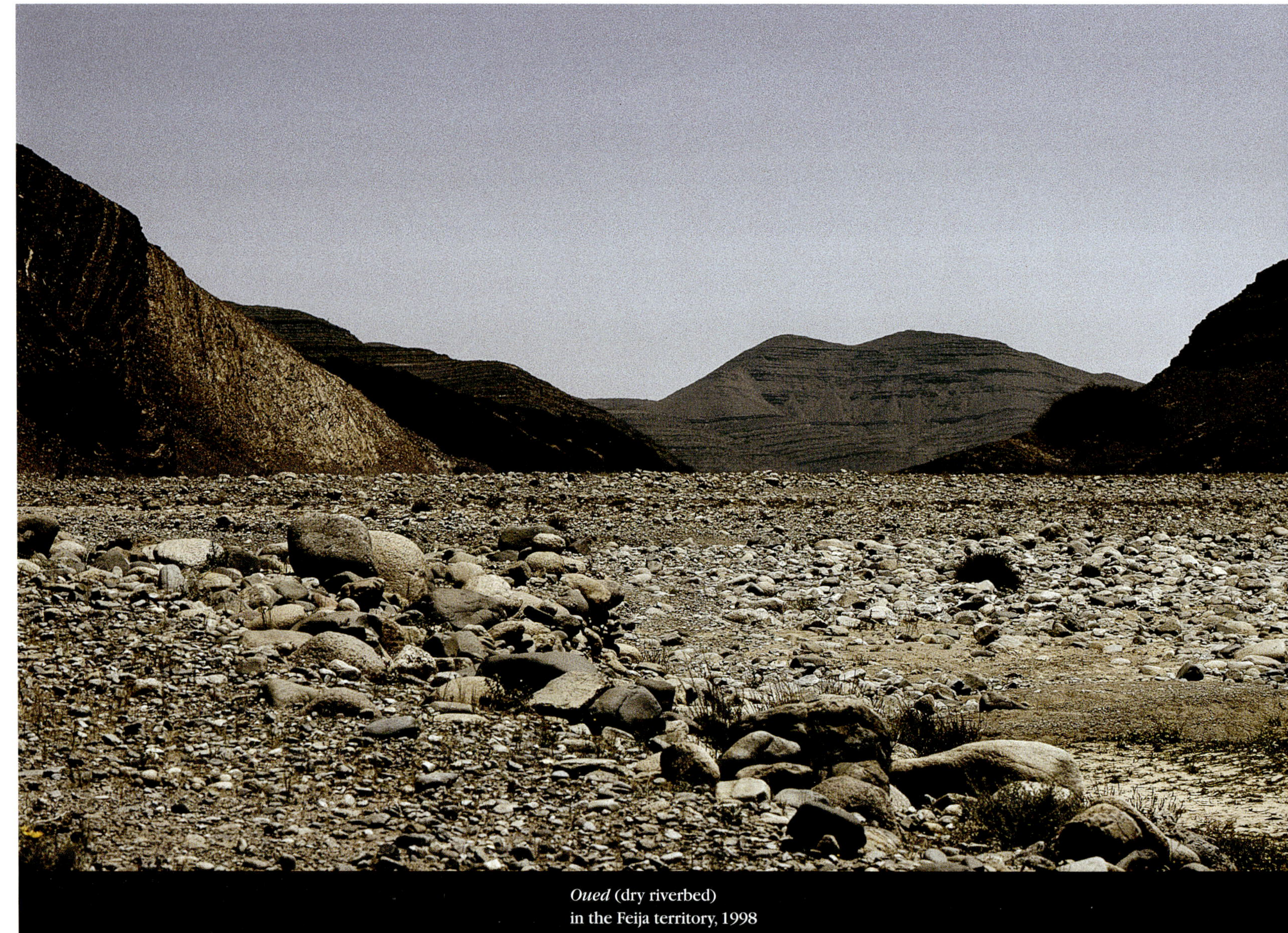

Oued (dry riverbed) in the Feija territory, 1998

Oued (trockenes Flussbett) im Feija-Gebiet, 1998

The Feija and their tribal territory

When one considers that the first telephone was not installed in a private home in Imi n'Tatelt, the largest town in the region, until 2000, that diesel-driven generators in the towns only produce electricity for an hour in the evening and that the road running from north to south was not surfaced with asphalt until 2001, one has some idea of how the Feija lived until very recently. Consequently, the scanty information on the region to be gleaned from one of the few writings on it available at all, a remarkably vivid description penned in his travel diary of 1904/05 by the Marquis de Segonzac, sounds astonishingly modern:

"13th February: The plain, the northern edge of which we are following, is bare and flat; one sees arid gorges. A legend which was related to us only serves to emphasize the solitude. The land of the Feija, it goes, was once a vast, green virgin forest teeming with beasts of prey; one day one of these beasts of prey devoured a saint's son. The saint cursed the region. The virgin forests disappeared, the rivers retreated into gorges and the wild animals fled ..."

After several days' journey under armed escort and many an adventure, Segonzac has this to say:

"27th February: For the last three hours of our journey we walked entirely in the dark to reach Iligh, shut up like a drum within its walls, at 9 o'clock in the evening. We set up camp by the gate after the guard laconically announced: 'It is too late.'

28th February: Iligh is a large village built of mudbrick. The dwellings are spacious but appear squalid. The gardens, however, are fertile and the scent of almond blossom fills the air. The hearths are 250 in number, there are just as many rifles and the *jemaa* has 12 members; no taxes are levied. This independence can be explained by the following circumstance. Iligh is the market-place for Arab and Berber tribes: Oulad Jellal, Zenaga, Ounzin (and others). Therefore, Iligh is neutral territory - a safe, thriving trading post. [...] The various races and castes live in disharmony yet the prevailing insecurity unites them. At present, for instance, two consanguineal Arab tribes are at war with one another and each has formed an alliance with a Berber tribe - one with the Aït Ounzin, the other with the Zenaga.

We should have liked to remain longer in Iligh but we nearly perished of starvation; under the pretext of there already being 70 'guests' in the village, we were only granted a bowl of couscous and a sheaf of corn." [1]

1 From: Segonzac 1910, p. 118 f. (translated from the French).

Die Feija und ihr Stammesgebiet

Bedenkt man, dass im Jahre 2000 das erste Telefon in einem Privathaus in Imi n'Tatelt, dem größten Ort des Gebiets, installiert wurde, dass in den Ortschaften ein Dieselgenerator nur während einer Abendstunde Strom liefert und dass erst 2001 die Asphaltierung der Nord-Süd-Verbindung in Angriff genommen wurde, so gewinnt man eine Vorstellung davon, wie sich das Leben der Feija bis in die jüngste Zeit abspielte. Daher wirken die wenigen Informationen, die über das Gebiet in der Literatur überhaupt zu finden sind, entnommen aus dem sehr anschaulich geschriebenen Reisetagebuch des Marquis de Segonzac von 1904/05, erstaunlich aktuell:

"13. Februar: Die Ebene, deren Nordrand wir folgen, ist nackt und flach, man sieht ausgetrocknete Schluchten. Die Verlassenheit wird noch unterstrichen durch eine Legende, die uns erzählt wurde. Das Land der Feija, hieß es, war ein riesiger, grüner Urwald, in dem es von Raubtieren wimmelte; eines dieser Raubtiere verschlang eines Tages den Sohn eines Heiligen. Dieser verfluchte die Region. Die Urwälder verschwanden, die Flüsse zogen sich in die Schluchten zurück und die wilden Tiere flüchteten ..."

Einige Tage unter starkem Geleitschutz und viele Abenteuer weiter heißt es bei Segonzac dann:

"27. Februar: Die letzten drei Stunden unseres Weges marschierten wir in völliger Dunkelheit und erreichen um 9 Uhr 30 die hermetisch verschlossenen Mauern von Iligh. Wir errichten unser Lager neben dem Tor, nachdem der Wächter lakonisch verkündete: 'Es ist zu spät.'

28. Februar: Iligh ist ein großes Dorf, in Lehmarchitektur errichtet. Die Häuser sind geräumig, wirken aber armselig. Die Gärten dagegen sind fruchtbar und der Duft von Mandelblüten erfüllt die Luft. Man zählt 250 Feuer, ebenso viele Gewehre und die *jemaa* hat 12 Mitglieder; es werden keine Steuern erhoben. Die Unabhängigkeit erklärt sich aus folgender Tatsache. Iligh ist der Marktort für arabische und berberische Stämme: Oulad Jellal, Zenaga, Ounzin (und andere). Daher ist Iligh neutrales Gebiet – ein sicherer, blühender Handelsplatz. [...] Die verschiedenen Rassen und Kasten leben in schlechtem Einvernehmen, doch die herrschende Unsicherheit eint sie. Derzeit, zum Beispiel, sind zwei verwandte arabische Stämme miteinander im Krieg und jeder hat sich einen Berberstamm als Verbündeten genommen – die einen die Aït Ounzin, die anderen die Zenaga.

Wir hätten uns länger in Iligh aufhalten wollen, doch wir kamen vor Hunger fast um; unter dem Vorwand, es seien schon 70 'Gäste' im Dorf, hat man uns nur eine Schale Couscous und einen Arm voll Korn zugestanden." [1]

1 Aus: Segonzac 1910, S. 118 ff. (Übersetzung aus dem Französischen).

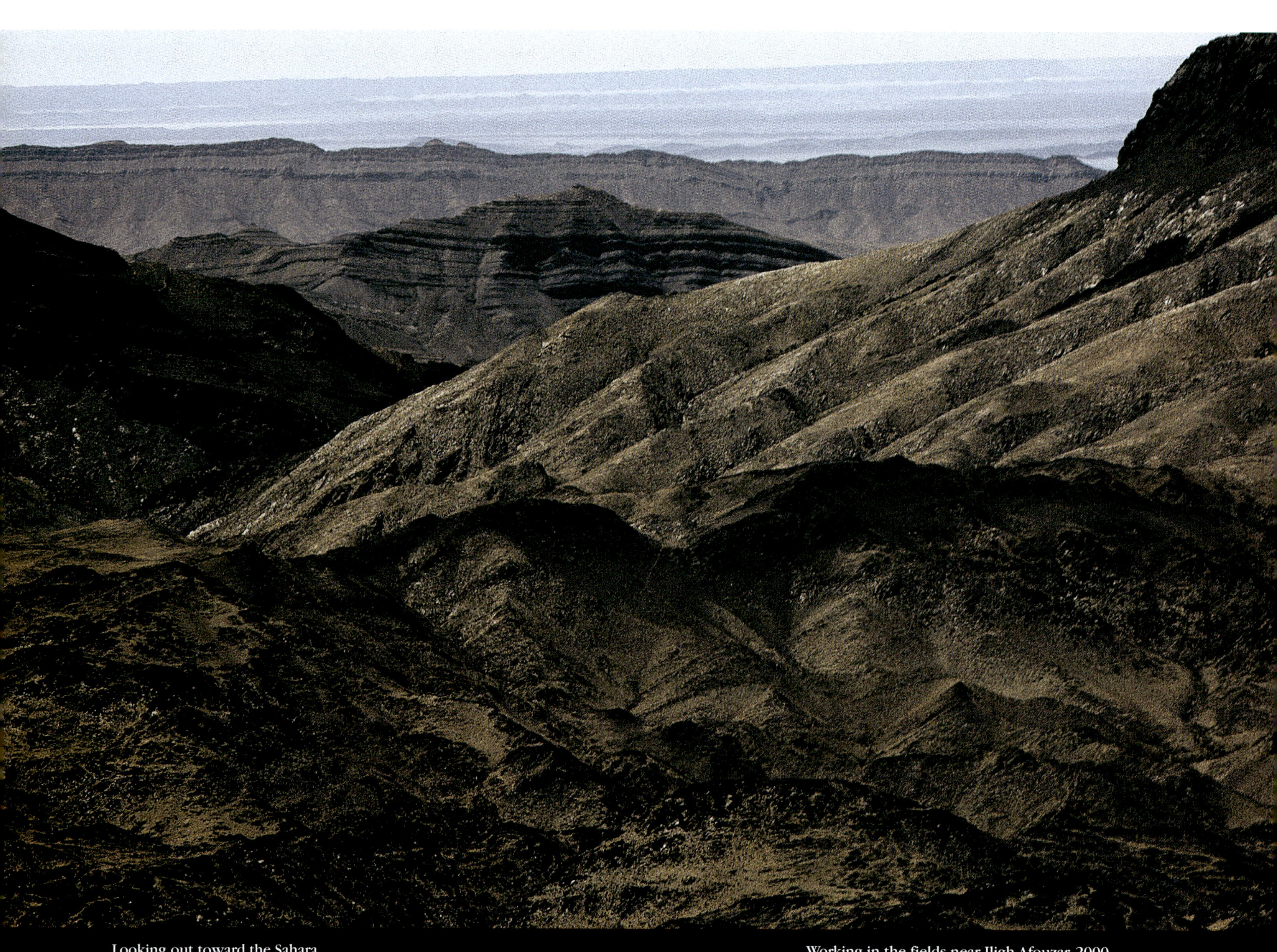

Looking out toward the Sahara over the rim of the Tagragra crater, 2000

Blick über den Kraterrand von Tagragra Richtung Sahara, 2000

Working in the fields near Iligh-Afouzar, 2000

Feldarbeit bei Iligh-Afouzar, 2000

The Feija tribe

According to the regional administration at Akka Irhèn, the Feija tribe numbered 15 000 persons in 1993. The Feija belong to the Oulad Jellal, among whom are also numbered the Ahl Tissint (to the south) and the Ahl Tata (to the west). The 1936 census carried out by the French colonial administration counts 4259 persons. There were 24 villages marked as belonging to the Feija. The population was entirely Muslim.[2] The language of the Feija is the Berber *tamazight*, with undertones from the Sous, where Arab tribes have also settled.

Crop yields from the fields and gardens are no longer sufficient to feed the population because it has greatly increased. The situation has been exacerbated by years of drought during which the oasis plantations have dried up and the topsoil has been lost. The men, therefore, often build up some small trade, become seasonal laborers at harvest-time in the Sous or work building roads. Agriculture at home is consequently often left to women and the elderly.

Der Stamm der Feija

Nach Informationen der Verwaltung in Akka Irhèn umfasste der Stamm der Feija im Jahre 1993 15 000 Personen. Die Feija gehören zu den Oulad Jellal, zu denen außerdem die Ahl Tissint (südlich) sowie die Ahl Tata (westlich) zählen. Die Volkszählung der französischen Protektoratsverwaltung ergab 1936 die Zahl von 4 259 Personen. Es wurden 24 Feija-Dörfer ausgewiesen. Die Bevölkerung bestand ausschließlich aus Muslimen.[2] Die Sprache der Feija ist das berberische *tamazight*, mit einer Färbung aus dem Sous, wo auch arabische Stämme ansässig sind.

Der Ertrag der Felder und Gärten reicht heute nicht mehr aus, die zahlenmäßig angewachsene Bevölkerung zu ernähren. Dies umso mehr als durch jahrelange Trockenheit Oasengärten verdursten und Humus verloren geht. Die Männer bauen daher oft einen kleinen Handel auf oder gehen als Saison-Erntehelfer in den Sous oder in den Straßenbau. Die Landwirtschaft zu Hause wird daher oft nur noch von Frauen und alten Menschen betrieben.

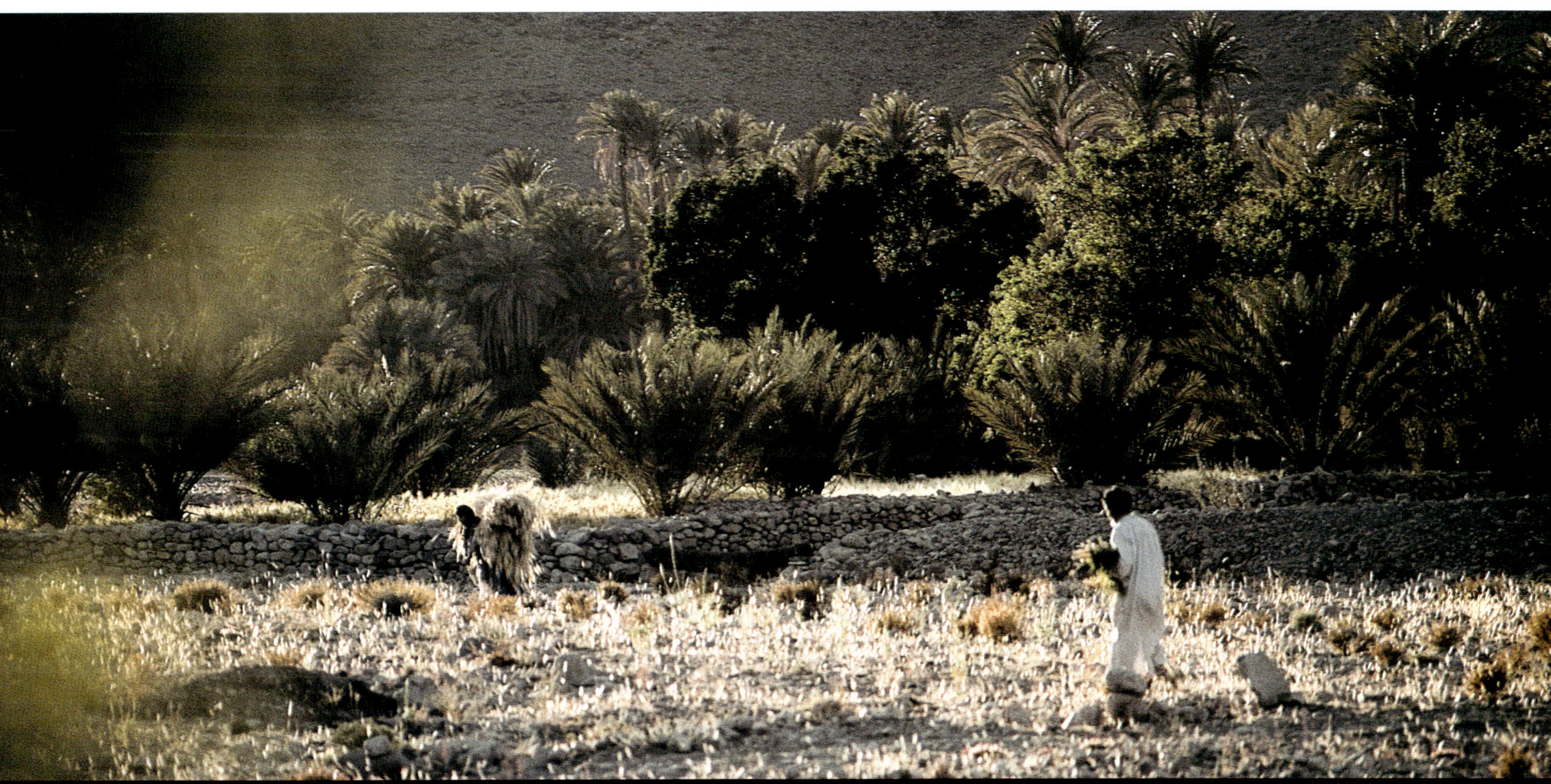

2 The circumstance that lovely silver jewelry with niello is made in the region is often cited as an indication that Jews also lived in the Feija territory since silversmiths and jewelry-makers were traditionally Jews. However, Jews only settled in Ouaouzguite territory in Taznaght and not among the Feija, where no Jewish community *(mellah)* existed. In *La vie juive au Maroc* (Muller-Lancet/Champault 1986), the nearest *mellah* is shown to be that al Tissint.

2 Ein Hinweis auf jüdische Bevölkerungsanteile im Feija-Gebiet wird zwar gerne abgeleitet aus der Herstellung von schönem, nielliertem Silberschmuck aus dem Gebiet, waren doch die Schmiede und Schmuckhersteller traditionell jüdischen Glaubens. Doch waren solche nur im Gebiet der Ouaouzguite in Taznaght ansässig, nicht aber bei den Feija, wo keine jüdische Gemeinde *(mellah)* existierte. In *La vie juive au Maroc* (Muller-Lancet/Champault 1986) ist als nächstgelegene *mellah* jene von Tissint verzeichnet.

Feija villages –

village life and the immediate vicinity

In order to avoid settlement of fertile land, the Feija villages are situated as close as possible to the edges of the palm groves, plantations and fields but not in them. There are cisterns and water basins with wells *(aghror)* in the plantations. Water is brought up in leather bags from depths of up to 15 meters by an ox or dromedary. To avoid evaporation, fields are usually irrigated at night.

Some villages in the Feija territory are mainly inhabited by Sektana or Zenaga who have immigrated from neighboring regions. These villages consist primarily of stone houses with balconies. The division into rooms corresponds roughly to what is found throughout rural Morocco: a gate leads into an open inner courtyard with three or four large rooms giving on to it.

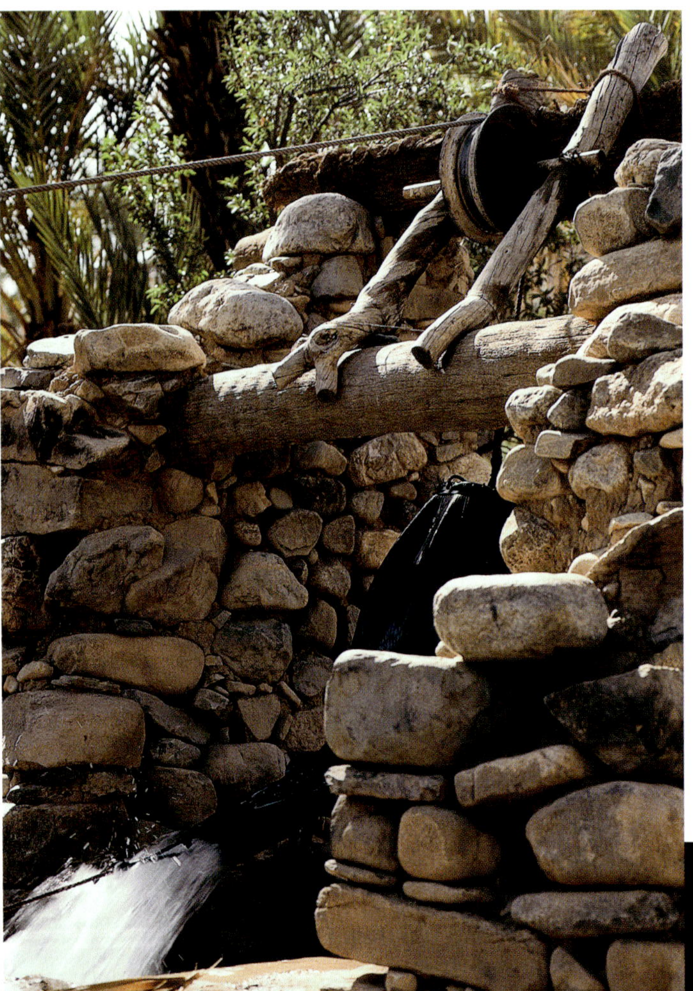

Die Feija-Dörfer –

Dorfleben und nähere Umgebung

Um kein fruchtbares Land zu verbauen, liegen die Dörfer der Feija so nahe wie möglich am Rand der Palmenhaine, Gärten und Felder, jedoch nicht in ihnen. In den Gärten befinden sich Zisternen und Wasserbecken mit Ziehbrunnen *(aghror)*. Aus einer Tiefe von bis zu 15 Metern wird das Wasser in einem Ledersack von einem Ochsen oder Dromedar heraufgezogen. Der geringeren Verdunstung wegen erfolgt die Bewässerung der Felder bevorzugt in der Nacht.

In manchen Dörfern des Feija-Gebiets lebt eine Mehrheit von aus den Nachbargebieten zugewanderten Sektana oder Zenaga. Diese Dörfer bestehen hauptsächlich aus Steinhäusern mit Loggien. Ihre Raumaufteilung entspricht ungefähr jener, die man überall im ländlichen Marokko antrifft: Ein Tor führt in einen offenen Innenhof, aus dem man in drei bis vier große Räume gelangt.

In den Dörfern, die von den Feija bewohnt werden, sind die Häuser flacher. Bevorzugtes Baumaterial ist Lehm. Balkone kennt man nicht, doch das Flachdach dient als Terrasse. Durch eine große Haustüre gelangt man in einen Vorraum von ca. 3 x 4 Metern Größe. Dies ist der soziale Mittelpunkt des Familienlebens. Tagsüber, wenn die Frau des Hauses anwesend ist, steht die Türe offen. Man tritt einen Schritt ein, ruft die Hausälteste beim Namen bzw. nennt die Namen in der Ordnung der Hierarchie. Dann wartet man, bis die Hausherrin kommt. Der Gast darf sich hier einfach niederlassen – ein Tongefäß mit frischem Wasser steht stets bereit. Hier wird auch gemeinschaftlich der Webstuhl aufgebaut, mit den Nachbarinnen zusammen gewoben, und hier wird – damit kein Neid aufkommt – einsehbar für die Vorbeigehenden ein geschächtetes Tier aufgehängt.

In villages inhabited by Feija, the houses are lower. Here the material of preference is mudbrick. There are no balconies but the flat roofs serve as patios. An antechamber measuring approx. 3 x 4 m is reached through a large front door. This room is the social focus of family life. During the day, when the lady of the house is at home, the door is left open. One steps in, calls the oldest person in the house by name or lists the names in hierarchical order. Then one waits until the lady of the house arrives. Guests may make themselves at home here - a clay vessel containing fresh water is always provided for them. This is where looms are set up in a communal effort by the women of the family and neighbor women. Weaving is done together with the neighbor women and this is where an animal carcass is hung after butchering so that it is visible to passers-by - to allay envy, should it arise.

The inner courtyard on to which the antechamber gives is small, occasionally roofed over, invariably plastered with clay and decorated with symbols executed in whitewash or spatters of whitewash. Two kitchens at least give on to the court - a dairy kitchen and a baking kitchen, where bread is also baked. In addition, from here one reaches several little storerooms, where provisions are stored in huge pottery jars sunk half-way into the dirt floor.

One or two steep sets of stairs lead to the upper floor, which is subdivided into a surprisingly large number of small rooms. Almost every member of the family is allocated a tiny room of his or her own. There is also a larger sitting-room on this floor in which guests are received.

References:

Census 1936, Flamand 1959, Hoffmann 1967, Muller-Lancet/Champault 1986, Segonzac 1910

Der sich von dem Vorraum aus öffnende Innenhof ist klein, manchmal überdacht, immer mit Lehm verputzt und mit weißen Kalksymbolen oder Kalkspritzern dekoriert. Am Innenhof liegen mindestens zwei Küchen – eine Milchküche sowie die Ofenküche, in der auch Brot gebacken wird. Außerdem gelangt man von hier aus in mehrere, kleine Vorratsräume, wo riesige, tönerne Vorratskrüge etwa zur Hälfte in den Naturboden eingelassen sind.

Eine oder zwei steile Treppen führen ins Obergeschoss zu einer überraschend großen Zahl kleiner Räume. Fast jedes der Familienmitglieder verfügt über einen solchen kleinen Raum. Im Obergeschoss liegt außerdem ein größeres Zimmer, in dem Gäste empfangen werden.

Literatur:

Flamand 1959, Hoffmann 1967, Muller-Lancet/Champault 1986, Segonzac 1910, Volkszählung 1936

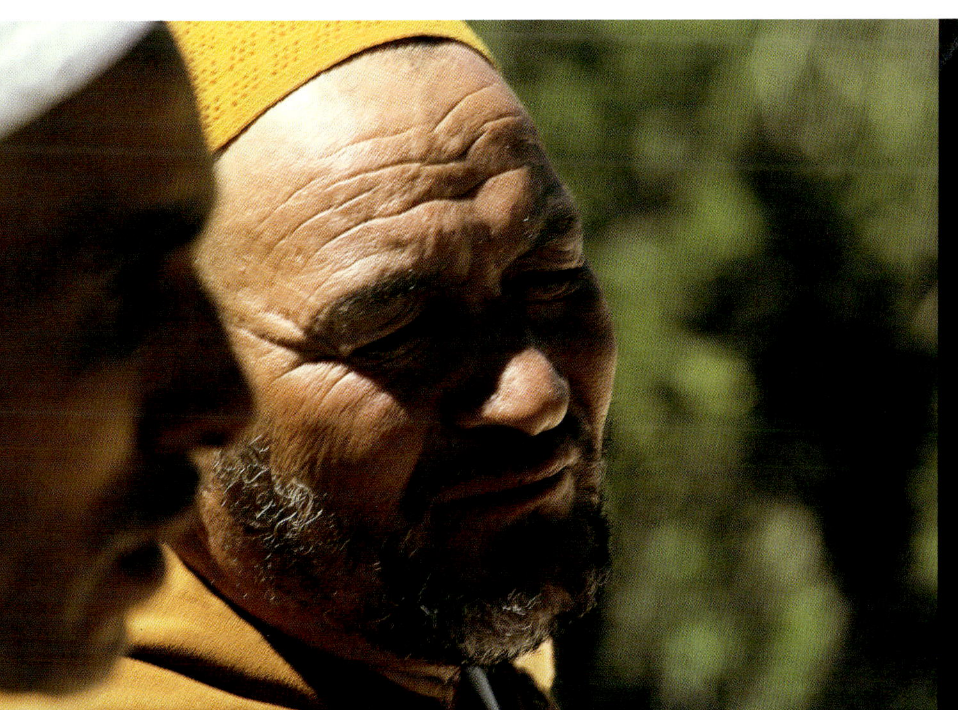

Hassan from Erkoune, *cheikh* and leader of prayers, 2000

Hassan, *cheikh* und Vorbeter in Erkoune, 2000

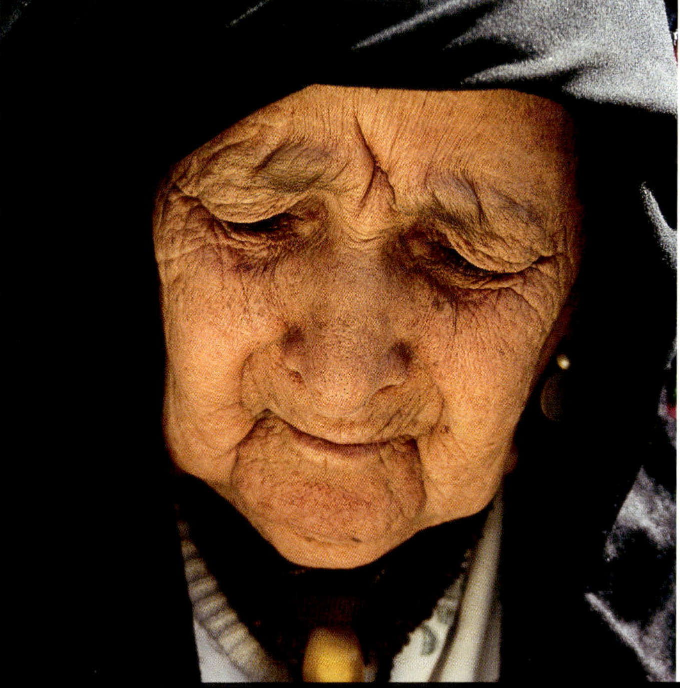

Hadja from Afouzar; she is the eldest of her family, 2000

Hadja aus Afouzar, Familienälteste, 2000

Die Feija und der Islam

Einer der wichtigsten Schlüssel zum Verständnis der Kultur der Feija in ihrem abgeschiedenen Gebiet liegt in der Bedeutung von Koranschule und Grabmal des Heiligen Si Mohand ou Yâacoub in Imi n'Tatelt. Sitten und Gebräuche im Zusammenhang mit dem islamischen Heiligtum und der damit verbundenen Glaubenswelt finden direkten Niederschlag in den auf den Textilien der Feija aufgemalten Motiven.

The Feija and Islam

One of the major keys to understanding the culture of the Feija in their remote territory is realizing the importance of the educational institution and the tomb of the saint Si Mohand ou Yâacoub in Imi n'Tatelt. Customs and observances associated with the Islamic shrine and the beliefs linked with it are directly reflected in the motifs painted by the Feija on their textiles.

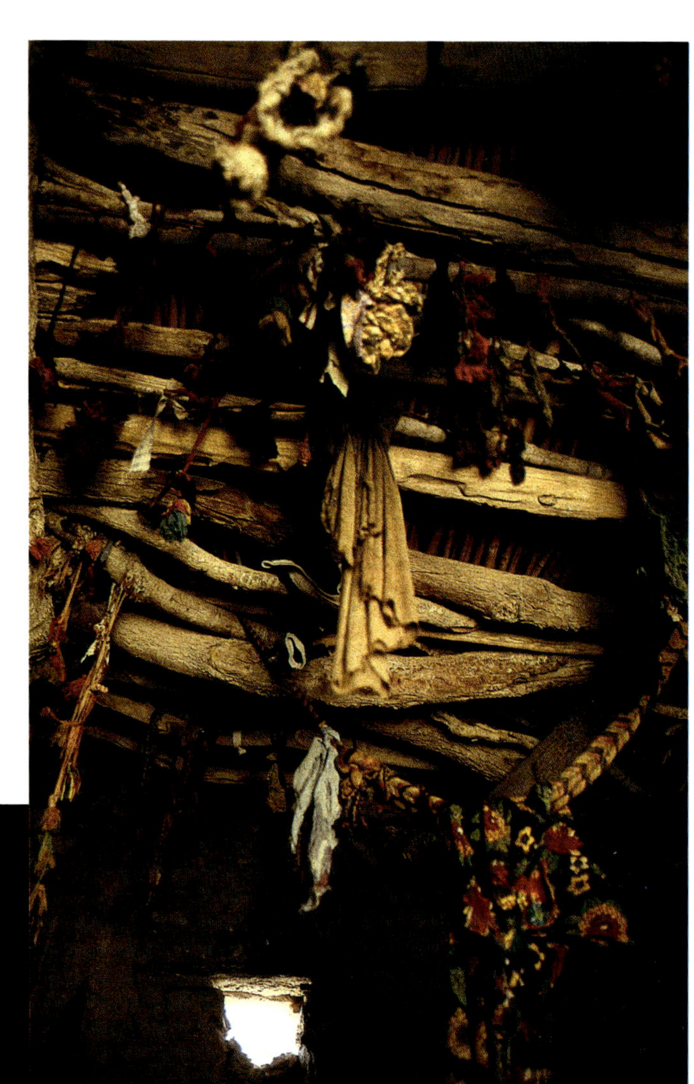

The interior of a saint's tomb *(marabout)* in a tiny oasis near Chegagate, *Hamada* du Drâa: worshippers attach scraps of cloth, woollen yarn or amulets to the ceiling above the grave or leave mementos of their visit such as coins, candles and pieces of sugar, 1994

Inneres einer Grabstätte *(marabout)* in einer winzigen Oase bei Chegagate, Hamada du Drâa: An der Decke über dem Grab befestigen die Gläubigen Stoffstücke, Wollfäden, Amulette oder lassen Erinnerungsgegenstände wie Münzen, Kerzen und Zuckerstücke als Zeichen ihres Besuchs zurück, 1994

Religion and superstition

The Berbers, and with them the Feija, are Muslims yet many more ancient, animist elements lie in the deeper layers of their religious awareness. In Morocco, and indeed throughout the North African Maghreb, special religious observances have evolved from this syncretism and from influences that have come from both the Arab and the African segments of the population. They are expressed in Maghrebine maraboutism (veneration of *marabouts*), in Islam and in animism, a blend of religion and superstition peculiar to the Maghreb. A great many saints are venerated. Their tombs are shrines at which worshippers pray, express wishes and attain *baraka*, blessed virtue.

In the faith adhered to and practised by the Berbers and, therefore, that of the Feija, every thing and every deed has psychic significance: *baraka* (blessed virtue) is inherent in natural substances and natural phenomena and on its reverse side - "taboo" or "the evil eye". The deleterious effects of "the evil eye" can be warded off or at least weakened by *baraka*. *Baraka* is, therefore, also inherent in textiles and the implements used to make them: in the wood of the loom, in the wool that is woven, in herbs used for medicinal purposes and dyestuffs and - especially - in henna, the herb of paradise. In addition, Berber religion recognizes the existence of both good and evil spirits: Djinns (*djin*; plural: *djinnun*, or also: *jnoun*).

Glaube und Aberglaube

Die Berber, und damit auch die Feija, sind zwar Muslime, doch liegen in den tieferen Schichten viele ältere, animistische Elemente. In Marokko bzw. im ganzen nordafrikanischen Maghreb haben sich aus dieser Mischung sowie aus den Einflüssen der arabischen und afrikanischen Bevölkerungsteile spezielle Glaubenspraktiken herausgebildet. Sie finden ihren Ausdruck im maghrebinischen Marabutismus, in dem Islam und Animismus, Glaube und Aberglaube ineinander verwoben sind. Man verehrt unzählige Heilige. Ihre Gräber sind Orte für das Gebet, wo man Wünsche hinträgt und wo man die *baraka* genannte Segenskraft erlangt.

In der Glaubenswelt der Berber und damit auch in jener der Feija besitzt jedes Ding und jede Verrichtung eine Seele: Natürlichen Substanzen wie auch Naturphänomenen wohnt *baraka* (Segenskraft) oder – im Gegenteil – "Tabu" oder "böser Blick" inne, wobei die Wirkung des "bösen Blicks" durch *baraka* abgewendet oder zumindest abgeschwächt werden kann. *Baraka* ist somit auch in den Textilien und ihren Herstellungswerkzeugen: im Holz des Webstuhls, in der Wolle, in Heil- und Färbekräutern und – ganz besonders – im Paradieskraut Henna. Außerdem existieren in der Glaubenswelt der Berber gute und böse Geister, die Dschinnen (*djin;* Mehrzahl: *djinnun*, oder auch: *jnoun*).

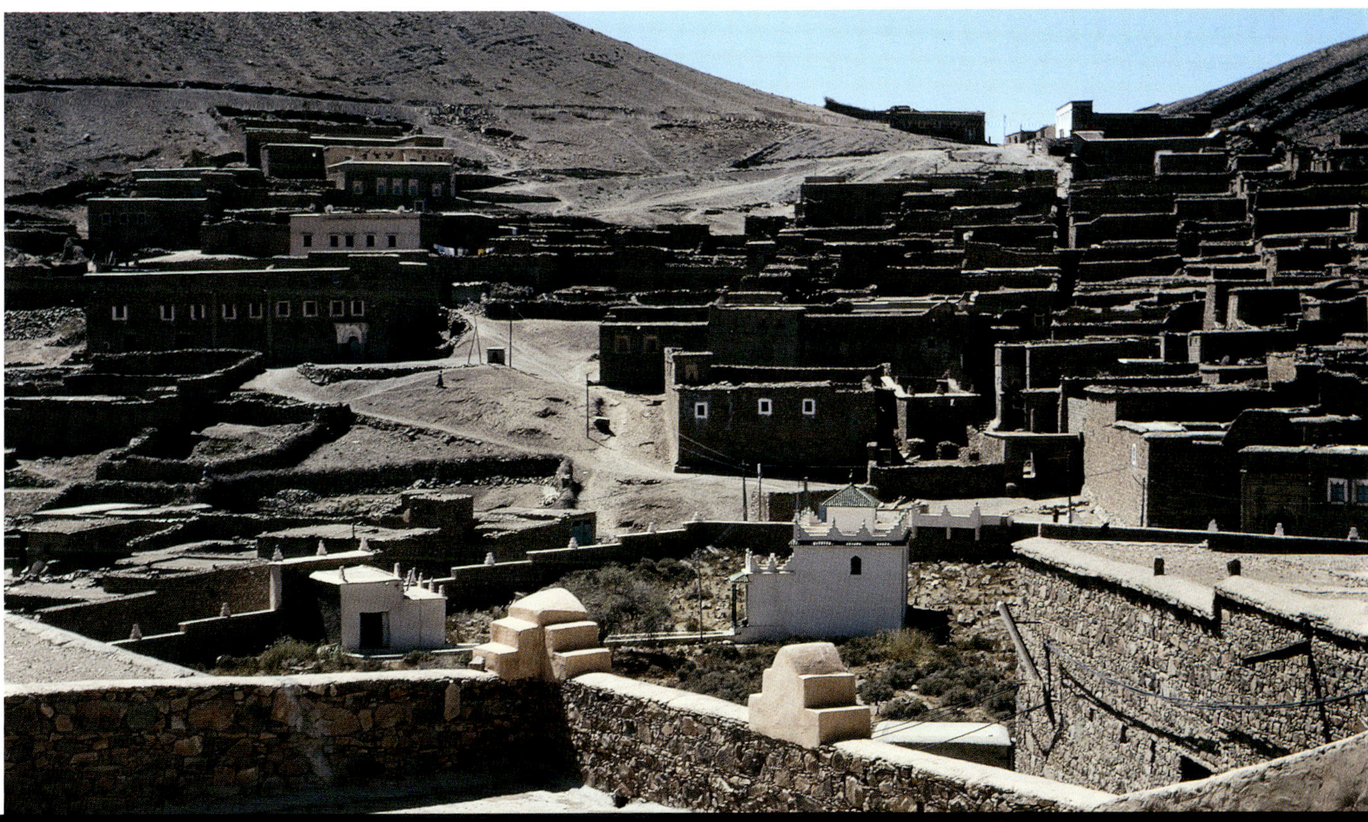

Imi n'Tatelt in Feija territory with the tomb shrine *(marabout)* of the saint Beni Yâacoub (building with the green roof), 2000

Imi n'Tatelt im Feija-Gebiet mit dem Grabmal *(marabout)* des Heiligen Beni Yâacoub (Gebäude mit dem grünen Dach), 2000

Beni Yâacoub, the saint of Imi n'Tatelt

Si Mohand ou Yâacoub or Beni Yâacoub, as he is popularly called, is regarded as the founder of the educational institution *(zaouia)* at Imi n'Tatelt, the most important settlement in the Feija territory. Saints in the Moroccan sense of the term are *chorfa* (pl. of *cherif*) - descendants of the Prophet - who have attained holiness through having lived exemplary and pious lives. Their holiness, the efficacy of their *baraka*, is enhanced after their deaths; the supernatural blessed virtues are inherent in their tombs *(marabout)*, their relics and their descendants. This is equally true of Si Mohand ou Yâacoub, except that he was a *chorfa* of Berber rather than Arab descent (see "The Chorfa", p. 42). Beni Yâacoub must have been an important preacher, healer and teacher even before he reached Imi n'Tatelt. He was one of a community of seven holy men in Taroudannt. Their school was called *Carrefour des amis saints* (Crossroads or Forum of the Holy Friends) and is now known as *Sidi ou Sidi*. It is not known when Beni Yâacoub came to Imi n'Tatelt and how long his tenure there lasted.

Unlike so many Moroccan saints, Si Mohand ou Yâacoub is the subject not only of oral reports but also of a historic text written by a contemporary of his. Fawad du Tamanart, a disciple of Beni Yâacoub's and Cadi in Taroudannt at the close of the reign of the Saadite El Mansour (1578-1602/03), wrote a corpus of texts in the Berber language which was translated into Arabic during his lifetime.[1] It reveals that Beni Yâacoub was of Berber Sektana descent. He received the classical education of his time. His inclination to asceticism was what induced him to choose such a barren and arid spot as Imi n'Tatelt as the site of his educational institution. He performed miracles and educated pupils in the teachings of the Koran. Like all *marabouts* he founded his own *zaouia* (educational institution): first, exactly on the border between two tribal territories and, second, at a strategically and commercially important spot on a caravan route. According to this text, he died in 1555 AD, which seems plausible.

1 The corpus of texts was translated into French by Colonel Justinard and published under its original title: *Fawad al Jamma Bi Isnadi Ououmi al Oumma* (cf. the discussion of the translation by Henri Terrasse in *Hespéris* 1954, vol. XLI, p. 286).

Beni Yâacoub, der Heilige von Imi n'Tatelt

Si Mohand ou Yâacoub oder Beni Yâacoub, wie er im Volk genannt wird, gilt als Gründer der Koranschule *(zaouia)* von Imi n'Tatelt, der wichtigsten Siedlung im Gebiet der Feija. Heilige im marokkanischen Sinne sind *chorfa* (Mz. von *cherif*) – Abkömmlinge des Propheten – welche ihre Heiligkeit durch ein beispielhaftes, religiöses Leben erhalten. Ihre Heiligkeit, die Wirksamkeit ihres *baraka*, verstärkt sich nach ihrem Tod; die übernatürliche Segenskraft wohnt ihrem Grabmal *(marabout)*, ihren Reliquien und ihren Nachfahren inne. Das gilt auch für Si Mohand ou Yâacoub, nur war er nicht *chorfa* arabischer sondern berberischer Herkunft (siehe "Die Chorfa", S. 42). Beni Yâacoub muss schon vor seiner Ankunft in Imi n'Tatelt ein bedeutender Prediger, Heiler und Lehrer gewesen sein und war Teil einer Gemeinschaft von sieben heiligen Männern in Taroudannt. Ihre Schule nannte sich *Carrefour des amis saints*, heute bekannt unter dem Namen *Sidi ou Sidi*. Wann Beni Yâacoub nach Imi n'Tatelt kam und wie lange er dort wirkte, ist ungewiss.

Im Unterschied zu einer Vielzahl marokkanischer Heiliger liegen zu Si Mohand ou Yâacoub aber nicht nur mündliche Berichte vor, sondern ein von einem Zeitgenossen verfasster historischer Text. Fawad du Tamanart, Schüler Beni Yâacoubs und Kadi in Taroudannt am Ende der Regierungszeit des Saaditen El Mansour (1578-1602/03), verfasste eine Textsammlung in berberischer Sprache, welche noch zu seinen Lebzeiten ins Arabische übersetzt wurde.[1] Daraus geht hervor, dass Beni Yâacoub von den berberischen Sektana abstammte. Er genoss die für seine Zeit klassische Ausbildung. Sein Hang zur Askese ließ ihn das karge und wasserarme Gebiet um Imi n'Tatelt als Ort für seine Koranschule wählen. Er bewirkte Wunder und bildete Koranschüler aus. Wie alle *marabouts* gründete auch er seine *zaouia* erstens genau auf der Grenze zweier Stammesgebiete und zweitens an einem strategisch wie kommerziell wichtigen Punkt einer Karawanenroute. Als Todesjahr gibt diese Schrift das Jahr 1555 unserer Zeitrechnung an, was glaubwürdig erscheint.

The holy places of Imi n'Tatelt

The building housing the educational institution *(zaouia)* still dominates the skyline of Imi n'Tatelt (see fig. p. 119). A square structure, it has several storeys and is constructed of dry walls built up in layers of flat, finely hewn stone slabs without mortar. A ramp-like structure leads up to the *zaouia*, beginning before the walls surrounding it and leading to the building through a large door which resembles the entrances to mosques.

The interior of the *zaouia*, as reliable local informants tell it (infidels are not granted access to it), now looks as follows: a large prayer room with ancient wooden doors and old wooden chests as well as storerooms and guest-rooms like those in a caravanserai, the entire building roofed over by a terrace. The roof terrace functions as an open-air mosque at the Feast of the Sacrifice of the Lambs celebrating Abraham's piety in being willing to sacrifice his son *(ait el kebir)*. The side of the terrace facing the mountain is on a level with a road from which grain or sacks of goods can be unloaded directly into the storerooms just below.

Relics of the saint are said to be in the *zaouia* even today: a *bournus*, a pair of his shoes, an arrow and a bow, a bag of gazelle leather and a pilgrim's staff These relics are housed apart in a special room and the *chorfa* (descendants of the saint) bring them out on the occasion of the feast of consecration, which lasts for two weeks in spring *(moussem)*, so that the faithful may attain *baraka* by touching them.

The educational institution possesses domains in various regions of Morocco, especially in the Sous. The revenue of the educational institution derives from the sale of agricultural produce as well as the rents paid by farmers, legacies and donations. In the early 20th century, the Marquis de Segonzac described the educational institution at Imi n'Tatelt as one of the richest and most powerful of its kind in southern Morocco. He reported that goods were delivered to it from all parts of Morocco, Algeria and the Sahara.

Die heiligen Stätten von Imi n'Tatelt

Das Gebäude der Koranschule *(zaouia)* dominiert auch heute noch das Ortsbild von Imi n'Tatelt (siehe Abb. S. 119). Der Bau ist rechteckig, mehrgeschossig und besteht aus Trockenmauern. Diese wiederum sind aus flachen und feinen Steinplatten geschichtet. Der Aufgang zur *zaouia* erfolgt über einen rampenartigen Zugang, welcher schon vor den Mauern beginnt und durch ein großes Tor, ähnlich den Toren zu den Moscheen, in das Gebäude führt.

Das Innere der *zaouia*, so berichteten zuverlässige Informanten vor Ort (Ungläubigen ist der Zugang verwehrt), hat man sich heute wie folgt vorzustellen: ein großer Gebetsraum mit uralten Holztüren und alten Holztruhen, zudem Vorrats- und Gasträume wie in einer Karawanserei, darüber eine Dachterrasse, die das ganze Gebäude überdeckt. Sie dient beim Lammopferfest *(ait el kebir)* als Freilichtmoschee. Bergseitig liegt die Terrasse auf gleicher Höhe mit einer Zufahrtstraße, von der aus Korn oder Säcke mit Waren direkt in die darunter liegenden Vorratsräume gekippt werden können.

Noch heute sollen sich Reliquien des Heiligen in der *zaouia* befinden: Ein *bournus*, ein Paar Schuhe, ein Pfeil und ein Bogen, ein Sack aus Gazellenleder und ein Wanderstab. Diese Reliquien sind in einem gesonderten Raum untergebracht, und die *chorfa* (Nachfahren des Heiligen) nehmen sie anlässlich des zweiwöchigen Weihefestes im Frühjahr *(moussem)* hervor, damit die Gläubigen durch ihre Berührung *baraka* erlangen können.

Zur Koranschule gehören Ländereien in verschiedenen Gegenden Marokkos, namentlich im Sous. Die Einkünfte der Koranschule setzen sich zusammen aus den Verkäufen der Landwirtschaft aber auch den Pachtzinsen der Bauern, aus Legaten und Schenkungen. Marquis de Segonzac beschrieb die Koranschule in Imi n'Tatelt zu Beginn des 20. Jahrhunderts als eine der reichsten und mächtigsten des marokkanischen Südens. Sie erhalte Güter aus allen Teilen Marokkos, Algeriens und der Sahara.

The Chorfa – descendants of the saint

The *chorfa* resident in Imi n'Tatelt are descendants of Beni Yâacoub.[2] It is a privilege to be *chorfa* and descendant of Beni Yâacoub including all the social injustice that is still widely and noticeably prevalent. Roughly 100 *chorfa* families, often comprising only four to six members, still live in Imi n'Tatelt and benefit from their privileged status. Their family connections and economic interests extend far and wide in Morocco.

The houses the *chorfa* live in are dry-wall structures like those of the educational institution. There are only a few windows to admit sufficient light in the stairwells. These *chorfa* houses resemble castles: towers, arched entrances, dark covered ways and granaries *(agadir)* are an integral part of each complex of this kind. Dark covered ways lead to ancient rooms that tend to be rather small but boast high ceilings. Wooden doors, columns and traces of murals glimmer faintly in the gloom.

Die Chorfa – Nachfahren des Heiligen

Die in Imi n'Tatelt ansässigen *chorfa* sind Abkömmlinge von Beni Yâacoub.[2] *Chorfa* und Nachfahre von Beni Yâacoub in Imi n'Tatelt zu sein ist ein Privileg, auch mit allen für uns heute sichtbaren sozialen Ungerechtigkeiten. Rund 100 *chorfa*-Familien, welche oft aus nicht mehr als vier bis sechs Personen bestehen, leben heute noch in Imi n'Tatelt und profitieren von ihrer privilegierten Stellung. Ihre familiären Bande und ihre wirtschaftlichen Interessen erstrecken sich über weite Gebiete Marokkos.

Die Häuser der *chorfa* sind aus denselben Trockenmauern erbaut wie die Koranschule. Fenster sind nur wenige eingelassen; sie dienen lediglich der Erhellung von Treppenhäusern. Die *chorfa*-Häuser gleichen Burgen: Türme, Torbögen, dunkle Laubengänge und Vorratsburgen *(agadir)* gehören zu jedem Häuserkomplex. Durch die dunklen Lauben gelangt man in uralte, eher kleine aber hohe Räume. Holztüren, Säulen und Spuren alter Wandbemalungen liegen im Dämmerlicht.

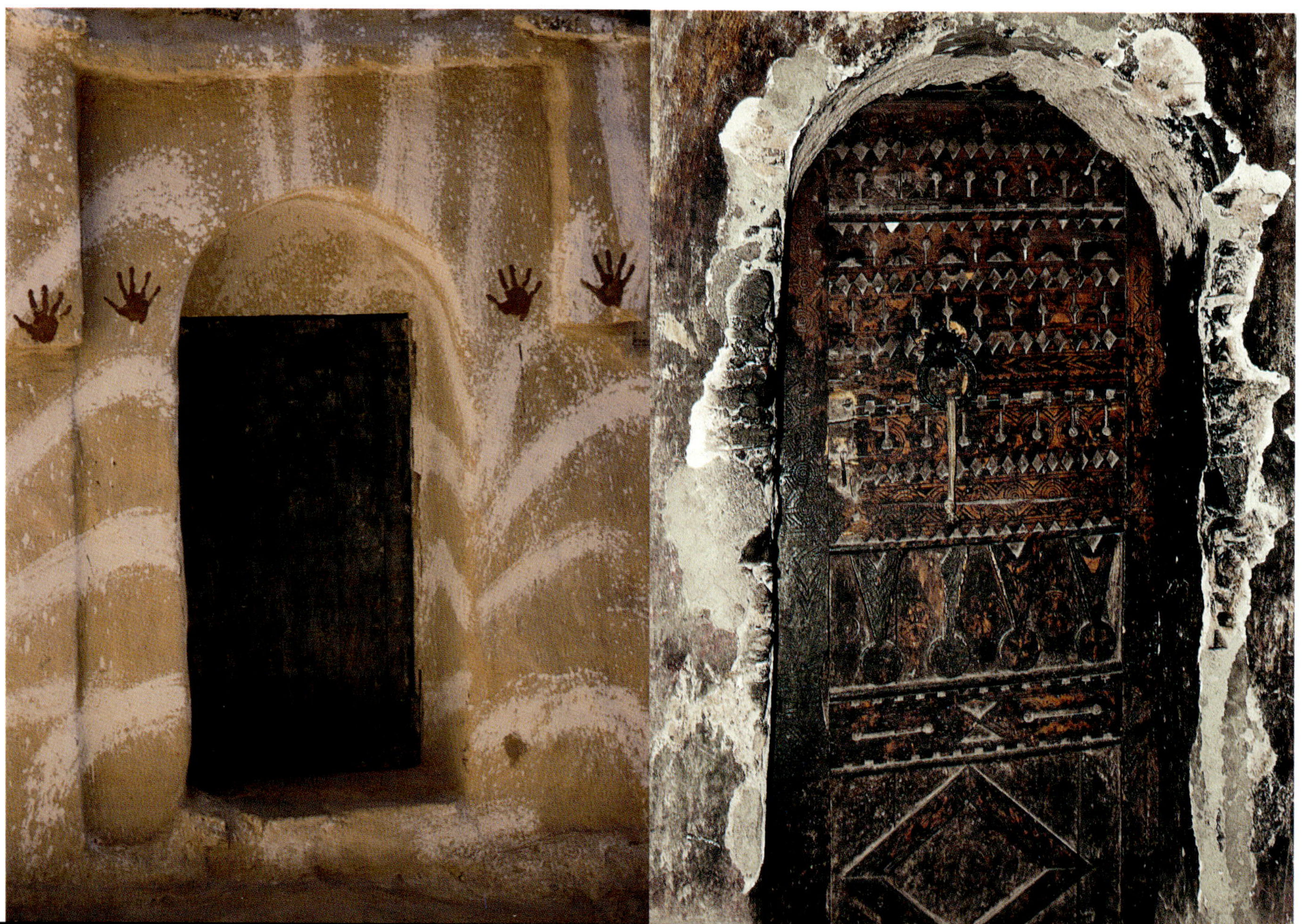

Imi n'Tatelt. The door of a *chorfa* dwelling with spatters of whitewash and the imprints of hands in henna, 1998

Imi n'Tatelt. Wooden door inside a *chorfa* house dating from the 16th century, 2000

Moussem – the feast of consecration

Once a year, during the two-week feast of consecration in spring *(moussem)*, farmers, tradesmen and craftsmen deliver their produce and products at the educational institution or pay their rent. The revenues are collected by a particular *chorfa* family chosen on the basis of a complicated rotation system. The head of the *chorfa* family collects the contributions and compensates farmers or craftsmen for their labors in produce or money. In addition, these farmers and craftsmen may stay free of charge at the educational institution. By working for it and paying contributions to it people attain *baraka*.

An important *moussem* of course attracts local tradesmen and others from farther away to Imi n'Tatelt. A *souq* is set up along the high street, where the locals and visitors can stock up on anything they might need for the year: millstones, agricultural implements, water-pistols, cheap sequins and jewelry for the women, bolts of cloth, footballs, second-hand clothing and carpets from Tazenaght or Sidi Mokhtar.

The annual *moussem* is also an occasion for jugglers, magicians, healers, specialists in herbal cures, prophets and Koran scholars to gather at Imi n'Tatelt - most of them come from the immediate vicinity. The essay that follows deals with such Koran teachers and healers or *fqîh*.[3]

References: Segonzac 1910, Topper 1984/1991

Moussem – das Weihefest

Jährlich einmal, während des zweiwöchigen Weihefestes im Frühjahr *(moussem)*, liefern Bauern, Händler und Handwerker ihre Produkte der Koranschule ab oder zahlen ihre Pacht. Als Einnehmer fungiert eine in einem komplizierten Rotationssystem bestimmte *chorfa*-Familie. Das Oberhaupt der *chorfa*-Familie nimmt die Leistungen entgegen und entschädigt Bauern oder Handwerker für ihre Leistungen durch Naturalien oder Geld; außerdem ist ihr Aufenthalt als Gast der Koranschule kostenlos. Durch die Arbeit und die Abgaben für die Koranschule erringen die Menschen wiederum *baraka*.

Natürlich zieht ein großes *moussem* einheimische und fremde Händler nach Imi n'Tatelt. Es wird entlang der Hauptstraße ein *souq* aufgebaut, wo die ansässige und angereiste Bevölkerung sich mit dem eindecken kann, was das Jahr über gebraucht wird: Steinmühlen, landwirtschaftliche Geräte, Wasserpistolen, billige Pailletten und Schmuck für die Frauen, Meterware, Fußbälle, Secondhand-Bekleidungsstücke, Teppiche aus Tazenaght oder aus Sidi Mokhtar.

Anlässlich des jährlichen *moussem* geben sich auch Gaukler, Magier, Heiler, Kräuterkundige, Wahrsager und Korangelehrte ein Stelldichein in Imi n'Tatelt – meist stammen sie aus der nahen Umgebung. So auch der im folgenden Beitrag beschriebene Korangelehrte und Heiler, der *fqîh*.[3]

Literatur: Segonzac 1910, Topper 1984/1991

2 *Chorfa* is, in Islamic countries, actually the term for the descendants of the Prophet. This also holds for Morocco although, in this westernmost Islamic country, the term is applied more broadly to include the caste of religious aristocracy. No fewer than five groups are termed *chorfa* in addition to the *cherifat* from the Tafilalt Valley. In Morocco *chorfa* may be both Arabs and Berbers, as exemplified by Beni Yâacoub and his descendants. The status of the *chorfa* within the complex social structure of Morocco is a privileged one yet within this caste itself there is a hierarchy of the groups comprising it.
For more on this:
Westermarck 1926, Hoffmann 1967, Brett/Fentress 1996, Meier 1992.

2 *Chorfa* ist im islamischen Raum eigentlich die Bezeichnung für Nachfahren des Propheten. Das trifft auch für Marokko zu, doch ist im westlichsten islamischen Land die Auslegung für die Kaste des religiösen Adels breiter. Nicht weniger als fünf Gruppen führen die Bezeichnung *chorfa*, dazu kommen noch die *cherifat* aus dem Tafilalt-Tal. *Chorfa* können in Marokko nicht nur Araber sondern auch Berber sein, wie das Beispiel von Beni Yâacoub und seinen Nachfahren zeigt. Die Stellung der *chorfa* innerhalb der komplexen Gesellschaftsstruktur Marokkos ist privilegiert, doch existiert innerhalb der Kaste eine Hierarchie unter den beteiligten Gruppen.
Weiterführende Literatur:
Westermarck 1926, Hoffmann 1967, Brett/Fentress 1996, Meier 1992.

3 The Tissint oasis situated by the Drâa riverbed on the southern fringes of the Feija territory is, according to Remco Ensel, famous far and wide for its *hartani*, who are experts in the healing properties of medicinal herbs. Trained healers, among them the village *chorfa-fqîh*, write amulets. These may be worn against the skin in specified places or may be positioned at strategic spots in a house. Cf. Ensel 1999.

3 Die Oase Tissint, am Südrand des Feija-Gebiets am Lauf des Draâ-Flussbettes gelegen, ist laut Remco Ensel für ihre heilkräuterkundigen *hartani* weithin bekannt. Gebildete Heiler, darunter der *chorfa-fqîh* des Dorfes, schreiben Amulette. Diese können an bestimmten Stellen auf der Haut getragen werden, oder man platziert sie an strategischen Punkten im Haus. Vgl. Ensel 1999.

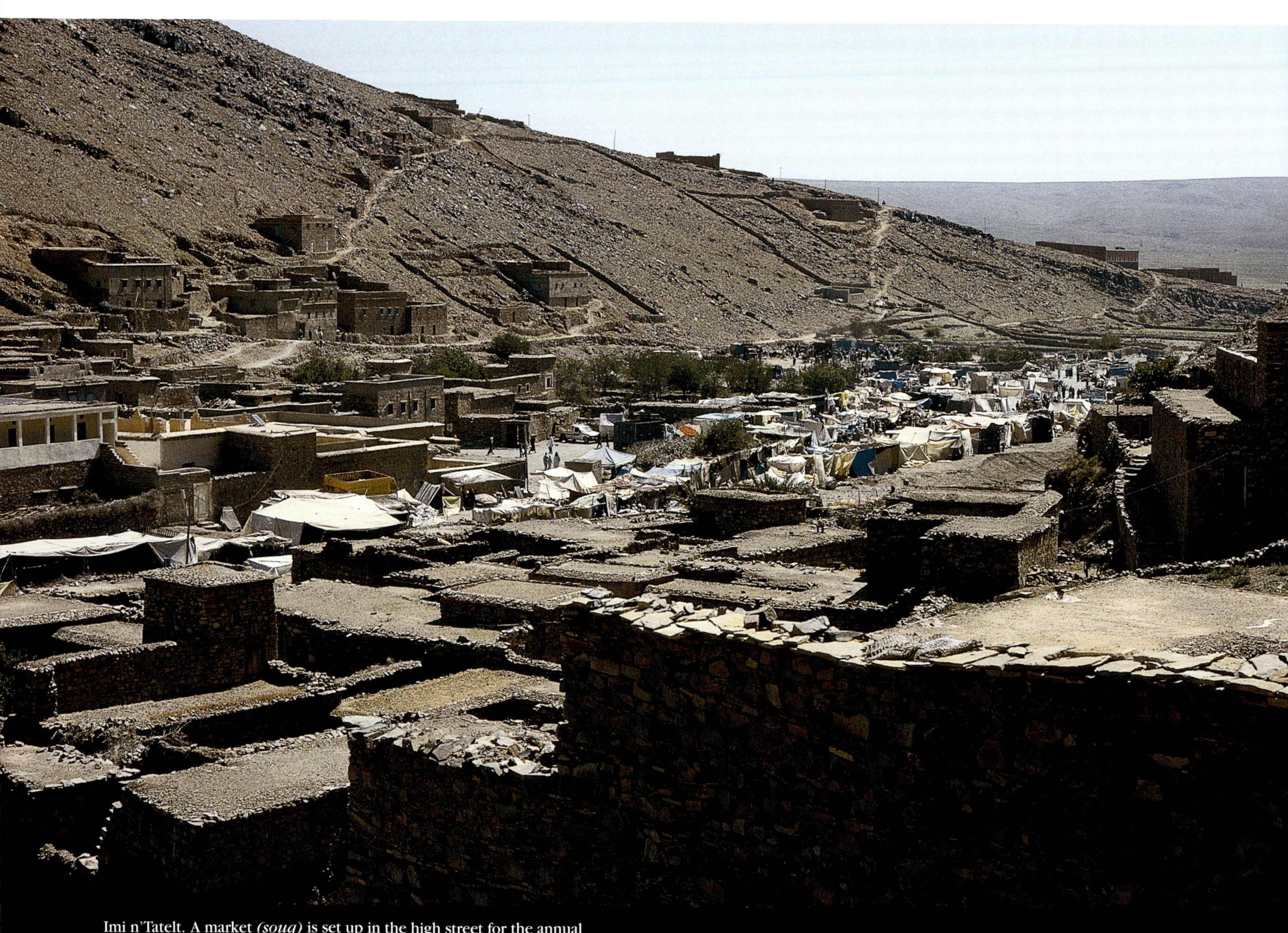

Imi n'Tatelt. A market *(souq)* is set up in the high street for the annual feast of consecration *(moussem)* in honour of the saint Beni Yâacoub, 1998

Imi n'Tatelt. Zum jährlichen Weihefest *(moussem)* des Heiligen Beni Yâacoub wird in der Hauptstraße ein Markt *(souq)* abgehalten, 1998

Traditional popular medicine and the fqîh

Edward Badeen

The Arab Islamic world is a reservoir of traditions in healing that have come from a variety of peoples, religions and civilizations. These are traces left by ancient peoples who once lived where Islam is now the dominant religion. There they lived and were active in taking over scholarship and translated texts from neighboring countries and adjoining cultural regions. This is why traditional popular Islamic medicine incorporates elements adopted from the following ancient cultures: Beduin, ancient Arab, ancient Egyptian, Mesopotamian, ancient Persian, Greco-Roman, ancient Syrian, early Berber, Jewish and Christian as well as indigenous African and others.

The medicines used include plants, minerals and parts of animals and minor surgical operations are performed. Magic signs, number combinations, magic squares, magic and ceremonial formulae as well as religious elements are also used.[1] In all the above, pre-Islamic practices are identifiable, some of them recommended by the Prophet Muhammad and added to by him[2], as well as those of other peoples and cultures. These holistic traditions of healing body, mind and soul embrace sorcery of all types as well as astrology, numerology, imitative magic based on the belief that "like produces like" etc.

Verses from the Koran, the sayings of the Prophet, prayers of supplication, the names of God[3] and many more similar elements place the whole within an Islamic framework, lending it particular significance for the population of this region molded by Islam because they often leave a deep and lasting impression on patients.

1 Cf. Badeen 2000, pp. 56-60 and 187f.

2 This is contained in the books entitled *Aṭ-Ṭibb an-nabawī (Prophetic Medicine)*. As an example of this a book of the same title should be mentioned, which was written by Šamsaddīn Muḥammad b. Abī Bakr b. Ayyūb az-Zurʿī ad-Dimašqī Ibn Qayyim al-Ǧawziyya (d. 751/1350) (ed. Muḥammad Karīm b. Saʿīd Rāǧiḥ, Beirut 1983/1992).

3 See AL-ASMĀʾ AL-ḤUSNĀ : "The most Beautiful Names" in EI, vol. 1, p. 714.

Die traditionelle Volksmedizin und der Fqîh

Edward Badeen

Der arabisch-islamische Raum ist ein Sammelbecken heilkundlicher Traditionen verschiedener Völker, Religionen und Zivilisationen. Es sind die Spuren alter Völker, die im Bereich der heutigen islamischen Welt lebten und wirkten und Gelerntes und Übersetztes von benachbarten Nationen und angrenzenden Kulturgebieten übernahmen. In der Heilkunde der traditionellen islamischen Volksmedizin finden sich deswegen unter anderem beduinisch-altarabische, altägyptische, mesopotamische, altpersische, altindische, griechisch-römische, altsyrische, altberberische, altjüdische, altchristliche und schwarzafrikanische Elemente.

Als Heilmittel werden nicht nur Pflanzen, Mineralien und Tierteile verwendet und kleine chirurgische Operationen durchgeführt, sondern auch Zauberzeichen, Zahlenkombinationen, magische Quadrate, Zauberformeln und zeremonielle sowie religiöse Elemente werden eingesetzt.[1] Darin sind zum Beispiel vorislamisch-beduinische Praktiken zu erkennen die teilweise vom Propheten Muhammad weiter empfohlen und ergänzt wurden[2], aber auch solche anderer Völker und Kulturen. Diese für Körper, Seele und Geist bestimmten Heiltraditionen umfassen magische Praktiken aller Richtungen sowie Astrologie, Numerologie, Analogiezauber usw.

Koranverse, Prophetensprüche, Bittgebete, Gottesnamen[3] und dergleichen mehr verleihen dem Ganzen einen islamischen Rahmen und haben eine besondere Bedeutung für die Bevölkerung dieses islamisch geprägten Gebietes, weil sie oft einen tiefen und wirkungsvollen Eindruck auf die Patienten machen.

1 Vgl. Badeen 2000, S. 56-60 und 187f.

2 Das findet man in Büchern, die den Titel *Aṭ-Ṭibb an-nabawī (Die prophetische Medizin)* tragen. Als Beispiel sei hier ein Buch mit demselben Titel erwähnt, das von Šamsaddīn Muḥammad b. Abī Bakr b. Ayyūb az-Zurʿī ad-Dimašqī Ibn Qayyim al-Ǧawziyya (gest. 751/1350) verfasst wurde (Hrsg. Muḥammad Karīm b. Saʿīd Rāǧiḥ, Beirut 1983/1992).

3 Siehe AL-ASMĀʾ AL-ḤUSNĀ – "The most Beautiful Names" in EI, Bd. 1, S. 714.

Unlike the classic *fakīh*[4], who is regarded as a lawyer and specialist in Islamic law, *fqīh* is a designation in Morocco with two principal meanings. The first refers to a man who knows the Koran by heart and is well versed in the tradition of the Prophet Muhammad. A man thus designated has often been educated in an establishment maintained by a religious brotherhood *(zāwiya = zaouia)* and afterwards teaches the Koran and Islamic tradition to small children at a Koran school. The second use of the term is as follows. If a *fqīh* of the first category wishes to work as a healer, he goes - according to Mustapha Akhmisse - to a secret school in the Sous[5], where he must liberate himself from all earthly concerns.[6] There he remains in seclusion until he has attained the realm of the Djinn.[7] Here he chooses a servant (*ḫidim*; in written Arabic: *ḫādim*), who from then on will never leave him. After associating himself with his Djinn, he may not meet any human beings for a period of 101 days. During this time he lives on dates, unleavened barley bread and milk. He must burn a mixture of salt, meadow rue, alum and sloughed-off skin of snake on waking and before going to sleep. On the last day of seclusion he lights a candle and looks into a mirror, where he will usually see the face of his Djinn servant. Now he is a consecrated healer.[8]

The *fqīh* or *ṭāleb* represents a class of traditional healers highly respected in Morocco. The *ṭubīb*[9], however, who is often illiterate, tends to be spoken of disparagingly by well educated Moroccans as ignorant.

The traditional healing practised by the *fqīh* in Morocco embraces several fields of popular medicine. There are *fqīhs* who specialize in homeopathy, dentistry and minor surgery etc. This means that a *fqīh* can establish a practice or surgery at a particular place where he sees patients at specified hours in his consulting room or he can make house visits.

Since the aetiology of pathological states, such as the harmful effect of black magic, demons or djinns[10], the "evil eye"[11] or maledictions and curses[12], cannot always be ascertained, a healer cannot rely entirely on medicinal herbs and conventional medicine. He must also deploy powers of healing which penetrate deep into the soul of the patient and thus on their own identify the agents of disease, eliminate them and restore good health.

Anders als der klassische *fakīh*[4], der als Jurist und guter Kenner der islamischen Jurisprudenz gilt, hat das Wort *fqīh* in Marokko zwei Hauptbedeutungen. Die erste ist: ein Mann, der den Koran auswendig kennt und die Tradition des Propheten Muhammad gut gelernt hat. Oft ist er in einer Niederlassung einer religiösen Bruderschaft *(zāwiya = zaouia)* ausgebildet worden und unterrichtet dann an einer Koranschule, den Koran und die islamische Tradition an kleine Kinder. Die zweite sieht wie folgt aus: Will sich ein *fqīh* der ersten Kategorie als Heiler betätigen, so geht er – laut Mustapha Akhmisse – an eine Geheimschule im Sous[5], wo er sich von all dem, was ihn mit dem Diesseits verbindet, befreien muss.[6] Dort begibt er sich in Klausur, bis er in die Welt der Dschinnen[7] gelangt. Hier wählt er sich einen Diener (*ḫidim*; auf Schriftarabisch: *ḫādim*), der ihn fortan nie mehr verlässt. Nach der Verbindung mit seinem Dschinn darf er für die Dauer von 101 Tagen keinen Menschen mehr treffen. Seine Nahrung während dieser Zeit besteht ausschließlich aus Datteln, hefelosem Gerstenbrot und Milch. Er muss eine Mischung aus Salz, Wildraute, Alaun und Schlangenhaut sowohl beim Erwachen als auch beim Schlafengehen brennen lassen. Am letzten Tag seiner Klausur zündet er eine Kerze an und schaut in einen Spiegel, wo er dann normalerweise das Gesicht seines Dschinni-Dieners sieht. Nun ist er ein eingeweihter Heiler.[8]

Der *fqīh* oder *ṭāleb* gehört zu der geachteten Kategorie der traditionellen Heiler Marokkos. Der *ṭubīb*[9] hingegen, der oft nicht lesen und schreiben kann, wird bei gut ausgebildeten Marokkanern oft abschätzig zu den Unwissenden gezählt.

Die traditionelle Heilmedizin des *fqīh* in Marokko umfasst mehrere Gebiete der Volksheilkunde. Man findet Spezialisten unter den *fqīhs* wie Homöopathen, Dentisten oder Chirurgen für kleinere Eingriffe usw. Demzufolge kann ein *fqīh* eine feste Praxis haben, feste Sprechstunden an verschiedenen Orten abhalten oder auch Hausbesuche machen.

Da die Krankheitserreger nicht immer dingfest gemacht werden können, wie z.B. die schädliche Wirkung durch schwarze Magie, dämonische Geister oder Dschinnen[10], den "bösen Blick"[11] oder Verwünschungen und Verfluchungen[12], kann sich der Heiler nicht ausschließlich auf Heilkräuter und herkömmliches medizinisches Wissen stützen, sondern muss auch Heilkräfte anwenden, welche tief in die Seele des Kranken eindringen und so die Krankheitserreger selbsttätig identifizieren, eliminieren und den gesunden Zustand wiederherstellen können.

Such healing methods are often various combinations of efficacious powers. Among them are the greatest or most sublime name of God, the totality of the names of God, passages or verses from the Koran, prayers of supplication to prophets and saints, the names of the archangels and Djinn princes, magic formulae written in identifiable or unidentifiable alphabets and hieroglyphs, mysterious magic signs - lines, circles, crosses, pentagrams and hexagrams magic triangles, squares and rectangles with one or more subdivisions - figurative representations of human beings and animals that may or may not be identifiable, etc., etc. (cf. "The haik of the fqîh", p. 130).

If the desired result is obtained, this has come about in a way which is often incomprehensible to the Western way of thinking prevailing in the 21st century. Nevertheless, it may be comparable to the therapeutic effect of placebos, hypnosis, suggestion and autosuggestion.

Since there are so few physicians trained in modern academic medicine, the people of Morocco at large set great store by the *fqīh*. What is important in all this is that the *fqīh* views the human being as a unity of mind, body and soul tied into a social and religious context. This holistic standpoint dramatically raises the success rate.

Es sind oft Kombinationen aus verschiedenen wirkungsmächtigen Kräften. Dazu gehören der größte oder großartigste Name Gottes, die Gesamtheit der schönen Gottesnamen, Koransuren und -verse, Bittgebete von Propheten und Heiligen, Namen von Erzengeln und Dschinnenfürsten, magische Formeln die in identifizierbaren oder auch unidentifizierbaren Alphabeten und Hieroglyphen geschrieben sind, mysteriöse Zauberzeichen, Striche, Kreise, Kreuze, Penta- und Hexagramme, ein- und mehrzellige magische Dreiecke, Quadrate und Rechtecke, erkennbare und nicht erkennbare Figuren von Menschen und Tieren und vieles mehr (vgl. "Der Haik des Fqîh", S. 130).

Wird die erwünschte Wirkung erzielt, so ist sie für die westliche Mentalität des 21. Jahrhunderts oft unverständlich, jedoch vielleicht vergleichbar mit der heilenden Wirkung von Placebos, Hypnose, Suggestion und Selbstsuggestion.

Aus Mangel an Ärzten mit moderner medizinischer Ausbildung setzen die einfachen Leute in Marokko große Hoffnungen auf einen *fqīh*. Wichtig bei alldem ist dass der *fqīh* den Menschen als Einheit von Körper, Seele und Geist versteht, eingebunden in sein soziales und religiöses Umfeld, was die Erfolgsquote drastisch erhöht.

4 See "FIḲH" in EI, vol. 2, p. 887 f.
5 In southern Morocco. Cf. "al-Sūs al-aḳṣā" in EI, vol. 9, p. 899.
6 An important principle leading to inner enlightenment *(via purgativa)* among Islamic mystics *(Ṣūfis)*. "Then follows association with translunary beings [...] in the realm of spirits and angels." Badeen 1999, p. 19.
7 On Djinns see Badeen 2000, p. 57 and p. 60.
8 Akhmisse 1985, p. 43.
9 In modern classical Arabic the word *Ṭabīb* means "physician."
10 On Djinns *(Jnūn)* in Morocco see Westermarck 1926, vol. 1, pp. 262-413.
11 Ibid., pp. 414-478.
12 Ibid., pp. 479 f.

4 Siehe "FIḲH" in EI, Bd. 2, S. 887 ff.
5 In Südmarokko. Vgl. "al-Sūs al-aḳṣā" in EI, Bd. 9, S. 899.
6 Ein wichtiges Prinzip auf dem Weg der inneren Läuterung *(via purgativa)* bei den islamischen Mystikern *(Ṣūfis)*. "Dann erfolgt der Umgang mit den translunaren Wesen [...] in der Welt der Geister und der Engel." Badeen 1999, S. 19.
7 Über Dschinnen siehe Badeen 2000, S. 57 und 60.
8 Akhmisse 1985, S. 43.
9 Im modernen Hocharabisch bedeutet das Wort *Ṭabīb* Arzt.
10 Über Dschinnen *(Jnūn)* in Marokko siehe Westermarck 1926, Bd. 1, S. 262-413.
11 Ebenda, S. 414-478.
12 Ebenda, S. 479 ff.

Wool and weaving among the Feija

Wolle und Weben bei den Feija

Undyed wool is generally used for both warp and weft in Feija weaving. The standard of workmanship and material revealed in earlier pieces (before 1940) is outstanding and often equal to that of the much vaunted highland weavings from the Jebel Siroua. The Feija use goat's hair for flatwoven carpets, heavy blankets and the burnous. All other materials are bought in from outside because they have never been produced in Feija territory.

Die Feija-Textilien bestehen zumeist aus ungefärbter Wolle für Kette und Schuss. Die Verarbeitungs- und Materialqualität der älteren Stücke (vor 1940) ist hervorragend und den vielgepriesenen Hochlandqualitäten aus dem Jebel Siroua oft ebenbürtig. Ziegenhaar verarbeiten die Feija in Webteppichen, schweren Decken und Burnussen. Alle anderen Materialien wurden und werden nicht im Gebiet der Feija erzeugt und daher von außen zugekauft.

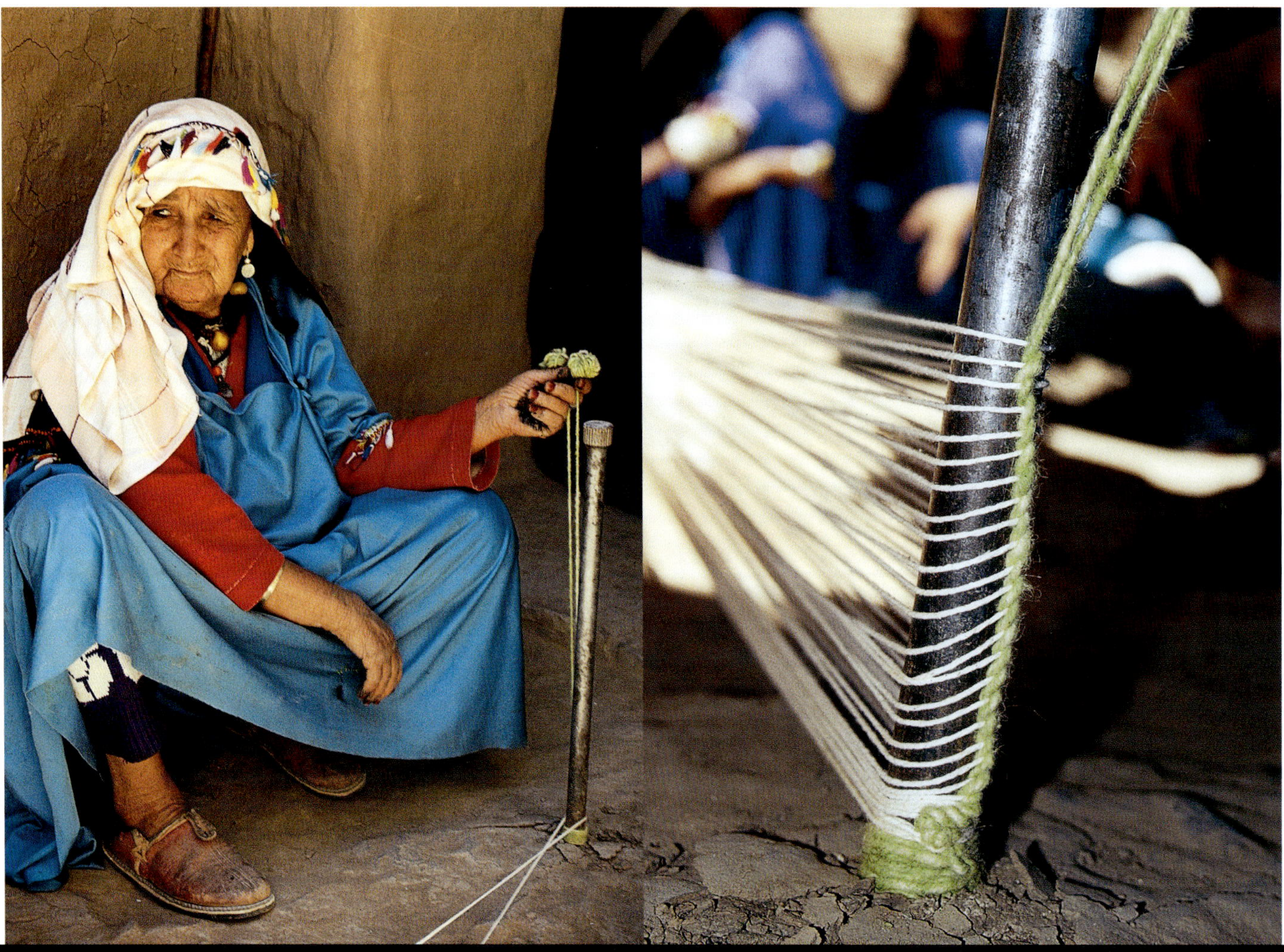

The Feija have their own distinctive weaving practices. The women here are showing how a loom is set up: a large blanket is to be woven. Hadja supervises the beginning of the cross, 2000

The warp being prepared, 2000

Die Kette entsteht, 2000

There are more goats than sheep in the Feija territory due to both topography and vegetation. Nevertheless, the textiles discussed here are woven mainly of wool.

The women of the families or village communities ensure that each of them has enough wool and goat's hair for weaving. They exchange wool and goat's hair instead of selling them to each other. Camel hair is bought from nomads who pass through the area at regular intervals. Spinning goes on everywhere and at all times even while walking and is done by men as well as women. Wool yarn dyed in various colors is bought at the *souq*, as is cotton thread, which is needed for the warp, for decorative wefts or tapestry woven motifs on weavings.

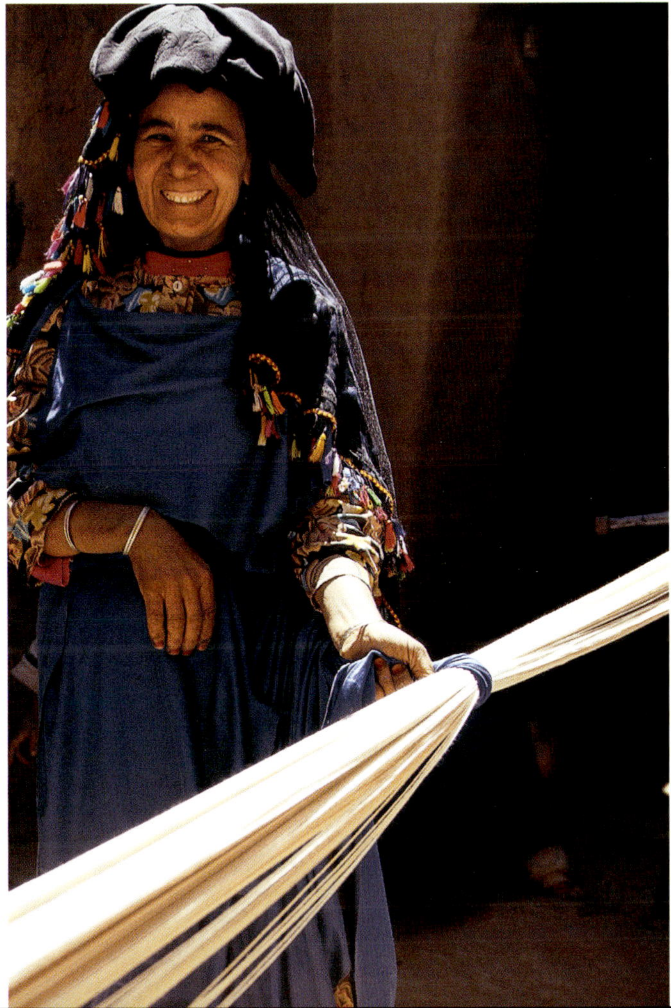

The warp is ready, 2000

Die Kette ist fertig, 2000

Entsprechend der Topographie und Vegetation des Feija-Gebiets ist der Bestand an Ziegen höher als jener an Schafen. Dennoch bestehen die hier besprochenen Textilien weitgehend aus Wolle.

Die Frauen in den Familien- oder Dorfgemeinschaften sorgen dafür, dass jede von ihnen über genügend Wolle und Ziegenhaar für ihre Webproduktion verfügt. Man verkauft sich nicht gegenseitig Wolle oder Ziegenhaar, sondern tauscht. Kamelhaar wird von den regelmäßig durchs Gebiet ziehenden Nomaden zugekauft. Gesponnen wird überall und jederzeit, auch wenn man unterwegs ist, und auch von den Männern. Farbige Wolle wird auf dem *souq* erstanden, ebenso Baumwolle, welche für die Kette, für Zierschüsse oder Einwirkungen in die Textilien verwendet wird.

Die Feija weben ausschließlich für den Eigenbedarf. Gewoben wird während der sehr warmen oder während der kalten Monate, auch während des Fastenmonats *ramadan*. Während wenigen Zeiten darf nicht gewoben werden: Nie vor einem großen Fest (und auch nach einem Fest beträgt die Wartezeit eine Woche), niemals kurz vor einer Niederkunft, nie vor dem nahen Erntetermin, nicht vor dem Dreschen und nicht vor dem Hammelfest *(ait el kebir)*. Die Gründe für diese "Tabu-Zeiten" sind handfest: Vor, während und nach ihnen ist man anderweitig beschäftigt. Einmal begonnen, muss ein Gewebe in einem Zug fertiggestellt werden, da es ansonsten kein *baraka* hat.

Gemeinsam kommt man beim Weben viel schneller voran, und manche Arbeit ist von einer Person alleine gar nicht zu bewältigen. Alle Generationen sind am Vorgang beteiligt. Jede Weberin bringt ihre Muster und Ideen ein. Wie viele Frauen an welchem Webvorgang beteiligt sein sollen, ist stark ritualisiert, und die Arbeit wird von ganz bestimmten Sprüchen und Liedern begleitet.

The Feija weave entirely for their own use. Weaving goes on during the very hot months as well as the cold ones and even during *ramadan*, the month of fasting. There are a few times at which weaving is prohibited: it is not permitted before an important festival (nor for a week afterwards), never shortly before a birth nor when harvest-time approaches or threshing is going on and not before the Feast of the Sacrifice of the Lambs *(ait el kebir)*. The reasons for these "taboo periods" are practical ones: before, during and after such periods of prohibition people are occupied with other important tasks. And, once begun, a textile must be completed without interruption or it will not have any *baraka*.

Weaving communally accelerates the process considerably and, after all, some tasks are too much for one person to handle alone. All generations participate. Each woman weaving contributes patterns and ideas. How many women may participate in which stage of the weaving process has been ritualized and these observances are accompanied by specific sayings and songs.

Fünf Frauen stellen zusammen die Kette her, während zwei weitere – ältere und besonders erfahrene Weberinnen – an den beiden Kettenden sitzen und überwachen, dass sich keine Fehler einschleichen. Wiederum fünf Frauen besorgen das Aufziehen der Kette auf die zwei Kettbäume und schieben die Stöcke in das Fadenkreuz. Es handelt sich dabei um alte, gleichmäßig dicke Oleanderstöcke; um eine ausgeglichene Spannung der Kette zu garantieren, sind diese Oleanderstöcke niemals länger als 80 bis 100 cm. Dies wiederum führt dazu, dass die Kette eines normalerweise etwa 160 cm breiten Gewebes auf zwei getrennten Ketten zu je etwa 80 cm hergestellt wird. Zwei Frauen besorgen das Senkrechtstellen der Kette.

Sämtliche notwendigen Maße werden mit der Handspanne, mit der Elle oder mit den ausgebreiteten Armen bestimmt. Unzählige verschiedene Schlingen und Knotenarten kommen zum Einsatz. Nie sieht man Messer oder Schere. Erst wenn ein Gewebe vom Kettbaum geschnitten wird, kommt das Messer des Hausherrn zum Einsatz. Die Hausherrin borgt es bei ihm für diesen Zweck und gibt es danach sofort wieder zurück. Ein abgebauter Webstuhl wird von einer sorgfältigen Weberin an einem trockenen, dunklen, luftdurchfluteten Ort aufbewahrt; die Hölzer werden regelmäßig eingeölt.

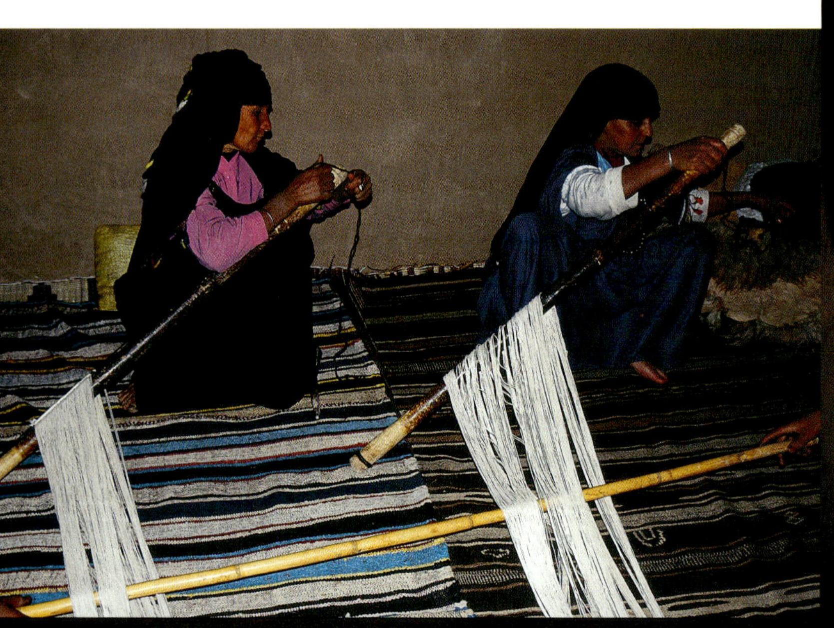

The warp is mounted on the warp beams, 2000

Die Kette wird auf die Webbäume montiert, 2000

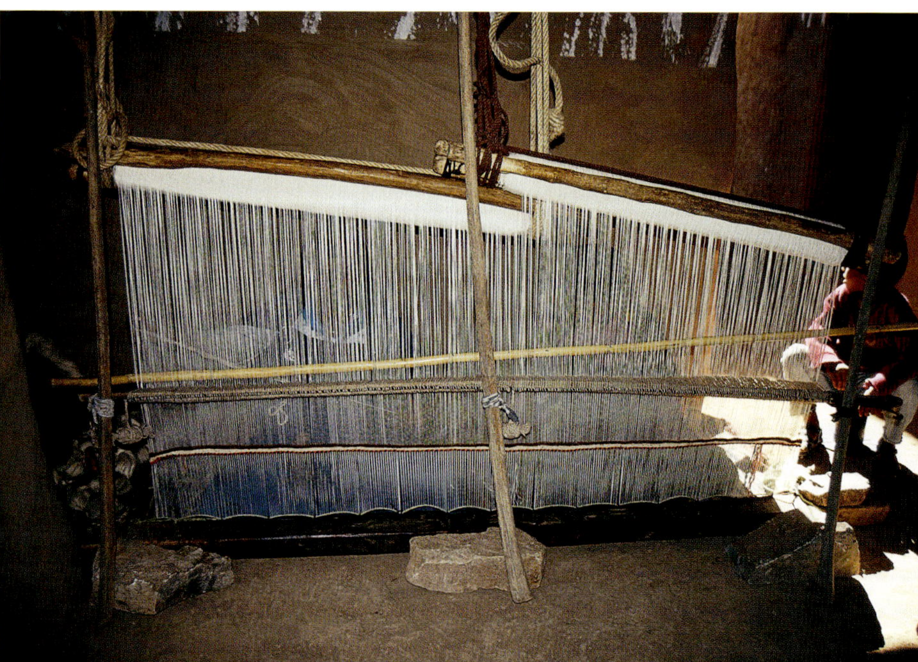

The warp beam is a two-piece one: a distinctively Feija type. The loom set up in the antechamber of the house, 2000

Der Webbaum besteht aus zwei Teilen; eine Besonderheit bei den Feija. Der im Vorraum des Hauses aufgebaute Webstuhl, 2000

Five women work jointly to prepare the warp while two more - older and particularly experienced weavers - sit at both ends of the warp to ensure that no errors creep in. Five more women deal with stretching the warp on the two warp beams and push the heddle rods into the cross. The rods are old oleander twigs of uniform thickness; to guarantee uniform warp tautness, the oleander twigs may never be longer than between 80 and 100 cm. This in turn causes the warp of a textile which is usually about 160 cm wide to be stretched on to two sheds, each of them about 80 cm in width. Two women ensure that the warp is in the vertical.

Calculation of all measurements needed are based on the distance from the tip of the thumb to the tip of the little finger when the fingers are spread, on the yardstick or on the distance between the fingertips when the arms are stretched out. Innumerable different loops and types of knots are used. Knives or scissors are conspicuous by their absence while all this is going on. Not until a weaving is to be cut from the warp beam does the lady of the house use a knife. She borrows one from her husband for this purpose and returns it to him immediately afterwards. A careful weaver stores her loom after it has been disassembled in a dry, dark place; the wood is regularly oiled.

The actual work of weaving is usually done by two people, with weavers being relieved as often as necessary. Among the Feija women, it is up to the lady of the house to determine the patterns and their sequence. Men who happen to pass by are expected to make suggestions about color schemes.

Good wishes uttered by people entering a house and greeting its occupants are transferred as *baraka* to what is being woven there. The greatest dangers for a textile, on the other hand, are the envy and ill-will which may result from a vehement dispute arising while weaving is going on. The more women participating in the weaving process the less likely this is to happen because everyone sees what is going on and what they will have from it when it is finished. Should the lady of the house be prevented from weaving for a whole day, a textile loses its *baraka* and this is supposed to bring bad luck. In such a case the village *fqîh* is summoned to the house. He is charged with freeing the weaving from the "evil eye" and starting it off propitiously again. This takes place with the aid of magic formulae, incense, prayers and divine service celebrated with the lady of the house.

Die eigentliche Webarbeit erfolgt fast immer zu zweit, wobei häufige Ablösungen erwünscht sind. Bei den Feija-Frauen bestimmt die Hausherrin alleine die Muster und ihre Abfolge. Vorbeikommenden Männern fällt die Rolle zu, einen Farbwunsch zu äußern.

Gute Wünsche beim Eintritt ins Haus und bei Begrüßungen übertragen sich als *baraka* auf das Gewebe. Die größten Gefahren für ein Gewebe hingegen sind Neid und Missgunst, etwa wenn sich während des Webens ein heftiger Streit entspinnt. Sind viele Frauen am Webvorgang beteiligt, ist die Gefahr geringer, weil jede sieht, was getan wird und was man anschließend besitzt. Auch wenn die Hausherrin einen ganzen Tag verhindert ist zu weben, verliert ein Gewebe sein *baraka*, und das soll Unglück bringen. Es wird dann der *fqîh* des Dorfes herbeigerufen. Er hat die Aufgabe, das Gewebe vom "bösen Blick" zu befreien und wieder auf einen guten Weg zu bringen. Dies geschieht mit Hilfe von Zauberformeln, Weihrauch, Gebeten und einer Andacht gemeinsam mit der Hausherrin.

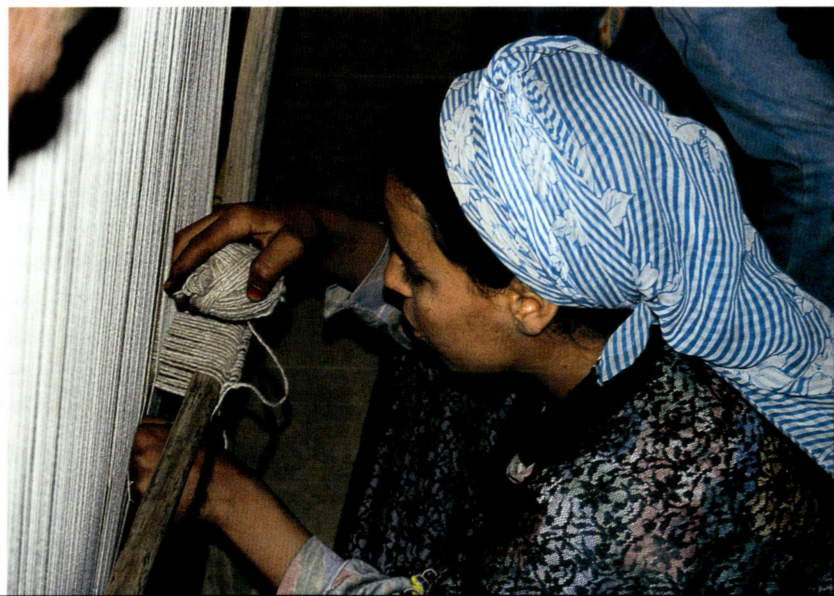

A daughter of the house stabilizing the cross, 2000

Eine Tochter der Hausherrin stabilisiert das Fadenkreuz, 2000

The blanket which was woven while we were present is over three meters long. It took about a dozen women to weave it and it was finished in a week's time. It takes three women about ten days to finish a flatwoven rug.

Nowadays the Feija women make blankets, flatwoven rugs and bags as well as *jellabahs*, *bournous'* and wedding blankets. Blankets which are used as beddings are made of soft wool, with the warp usually cotton, and show stripes in colored wool yarn from the *souq*. Common motifs are the comb motif as well as lentil-shaped patterns. Pattern bands are also woven in, for which the following terms are used: "scissors" *(tozline)*, "crouch" *(tiskobrine)*, "teeth" *(toukhssine)* and "harrow" *(tighamriouine)*.

Before 1920 a wider variety of textiles was produced, including woman's wrappers and headscarves. It took about ten days to weave a woman's wrapper or a wedding blanket if three women worked on it. After 1920 black and blue cloth for making women's clothing was sold by the bolt. Textile colors thus changed from light natural shades to the dark and blue tones which nowadays are so widespread throughout southern Morocco.[1]

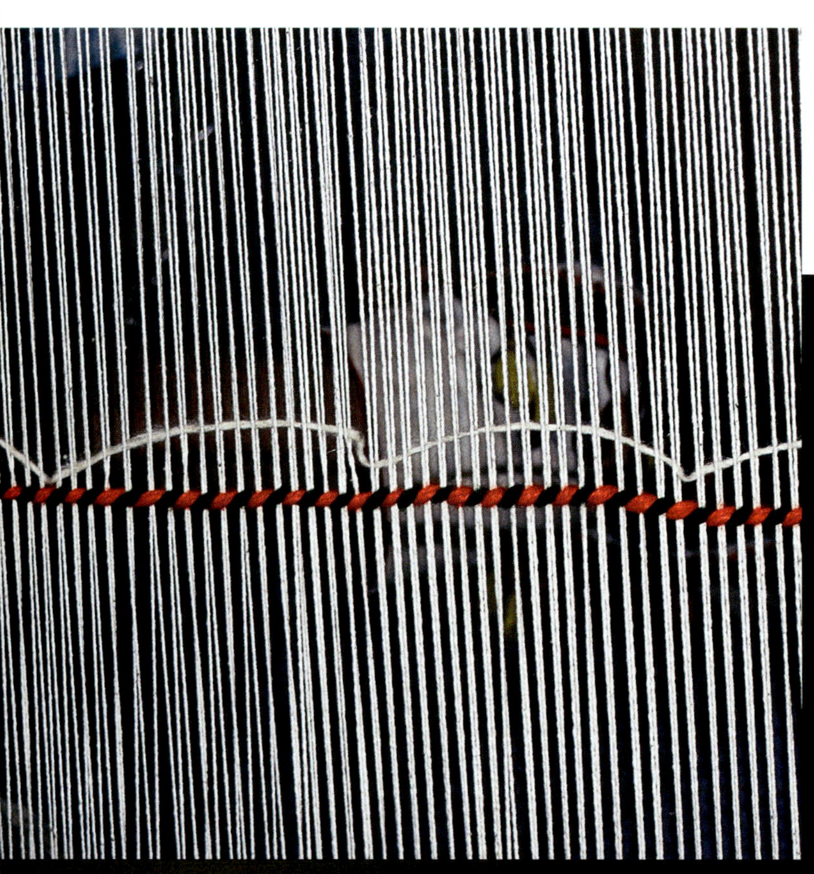

The warp and the heading cord are stretched, 2000

Die Leitkordel und der erste Schuss sind eingelegt, 2000

Die Decke, welche während unserer Anwesenheit gewoben wurde und über drei Meter lang ist, beschäftigte rund ein Dutzend Frauen während einer Woche. Für das Weben eines flachgewobenen Teppichs benötigen drei Frauen etwa zehn Tage.

Die Feija-Frauen stellen heute Decken, Webteppiche und Säcke her, sowie *jellabahs*, *bournous'* und Hochzeitsdecken. Solche, die als Schlafdecken verwendet werden, bestehen aus weicher Wolle, meist auf Baumwollkette, und zeigen Streifen aus farbiger Wolle vom *souq*. Gängige Motive sind das Kammmotiv sowie linsenförmige Gebilde. Es werden auch Musterbänder eingewoben, die zum Beispiel mit den Begriffen "Schere" *(tozline)*, "kauern" *(tiskobrine)*, "Zähne" *(toukhssine)*, "Egge" *(tighamriouine)* benannt sind.

Bis 1920 war das Sortiment größer und umfasste außerdem Wickel- und Kopftücher. Die Webzeit eines naturhellen Wickeltuchs oder einer Hochzeitsdecke betrug bei einer Beteiligung von drei Frauen rund zehn Tage. Nach 1920 setzte sich schwarze oder blaue Meterware für die Frauenbekleidung durch und veränderte das Erscheinungsbild von den hellen Naturfarben hin zu den dunklen, blauen, welche heute in ganz Südmarokko verbreitet sind.[1]

1 André Adam reports: "In the oases of the Jebel Bani there must have been a trade in indigo-dyed cotton cloth from the (old) Sudan for a very long time. As early as 1850 de Foucault mentions a degree of class-consciousness which was expressed in the wearing of clothing made of Khent. This cloth was particularly popular with women in Tissint. When the French Protectorate was established, blue-dyed cloth was immediately imported from England via Mogador; this cloth was considerably less expensive. In the oases of the Jebel Bani the change was quickly made to this lighter-weight fabric whereas in the less accessible mountainous regions the heavier-weight wool cloth prevailed longer." *Hespéris* 1952, pp. 460-485 (translated from the French).

1 André Adam berichtet: "In den Oasen am Jebel Bani muss es schon sehr lange einen Handel mit indigoblauen Baumwolltüchern aus dem (alten) Sudan gegeben haben. Schon de Foucault erwähnt 1850 einen gewissen Klassendünkel, der sich darin ausdrückt, dass man Kleider aus Khent trug. Besonders beliebt war dieses Tuch bei den Frauen in Tissint. Mit der Errichtung des französischen Protektorats wurde sofort blaugefärbte Baumwolle aus England über Mogador importiert; diese Ware war entschieden preisgünstiger. In den Jebel Bani Oasen wurde rasch auf diese leichteren Gewebe umgestellt, während sich in den weniger zugänglichen Berggebieten die schwereren Wollgewebe länger hielten." *Hespéris* 1952, S. 460-485 (Übersetzung aus dem Französischen).

When asked about the making of the old, finely woven headscarves, Feija women impart the following information: such headscarves were woven by women working alone, which took at least two weeks. This was confirmed by an old woman who was a master weaver.

The unpainted wedding blanket, in Berber *tahdicht*, is still part of a bride's dowry in the early 21st century. The *tahdicht* is made of light natural-colored wool and may have cotton shots; it measures approx. 150 cm in width and may be between 300 and 350 cm long. In the old days there was a lighter fabric for weddings that took place in summer and a heavier one for winter nuptials. Now only the heavier variant is made.

We are indebted to:
Frieda Sorber, curator of textiles and costumes,
Antwerp Fashion Museum, Wynegem, Belgium

Über die Herstellung der alten, feinen Kopftücher befragt, gaben die Feija-Frauen folgende Auskunft: Diese Kopftücher wurden von einer einzelnen Weberin gewoben; sie benötigte dafür mindestens zwei Wochen; dies bestätigte auch eine alte Meisterweberin.

Die unbemalte Hochzeitsdecke, in Berber *tahdicht*, gehört auch zu Beginn des 21. Jahrhunderts noch zum Brautschatz. Der *tahdicht* besteht aus naturheller Wolle und kann Baumwollschüsse aufweisen, er ist ca. 150 cm breit und 300 bis 350 cm lang. Früher existierte ein leichteres Gewebe für die Hochzeit im Sommer und ein schweres für den Winter. Heute wird nur noch die schwere Variante hergestellt.

Dank an:
Frieda Sorber, Kuratorin für Textilien und Kostüme,
Mode Museum Antwerpen, Wynegem, Belgien

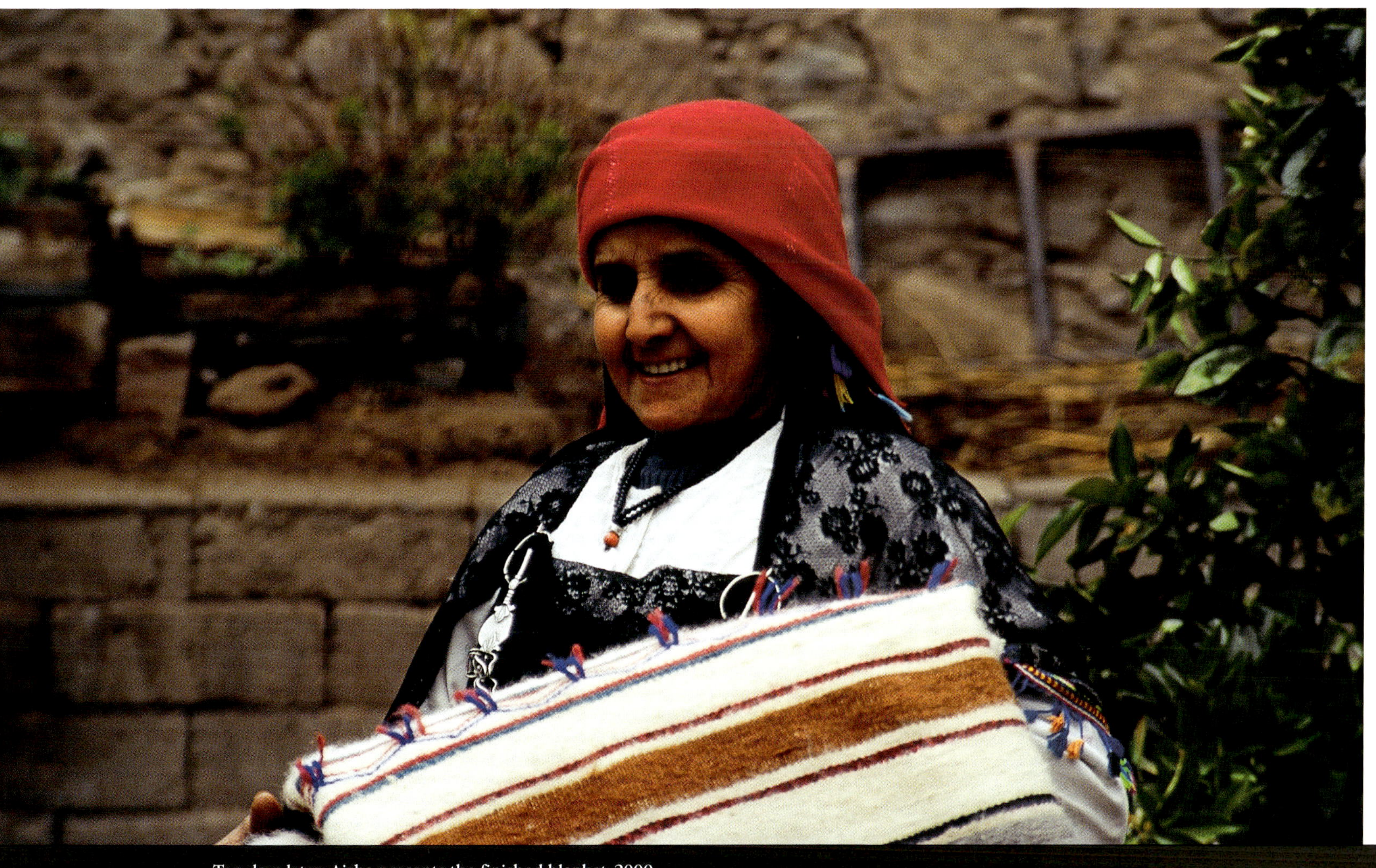

Ten days later: Aisha presents the finished blanket, 2000

Zehn Tage später: Aischa präsentiert die fertige Decke, 2000

Henna

Markus Ritter

Widespread in Europe and Asia, henna has been cultivated since ancient times. It enjoys high status in European and Asian ethnobotany because so many parts of the plant can be used and they have such a wide variety of uses. Henna is used throughout the Islamic world nowadays; in eastern and central Asia it is also grown in numerous non-Islamic cultures. Several remarkable properties of the henna plant evidently led to it being simultaneously "discovered" and put to use at a very remote time in the past.

Henna

Markus Ritter

Henna ist eine alte, in Eurasien weit verbreitete Kulturpflanze. Die Vielfalt der gebräuchlichen Pflanzenteile und der Verwendungszwecke geben dieser Pflanzenart einen herausragenden Rang in der euro-asiatischen Ethnobotanik. Henna ist heute im ganzen islamischen Raum in Gebrauch, in Ost- und Zentralasien zudem auch in vielen nicht-islamischen Kulturen. Einige auffällige Eigenschaften dieser Pflanze führten dazu, dass Henna schon in frühester Zeit offenbar in mehreren Kulturen parallel "entdeckt" und verwertet worden ist.

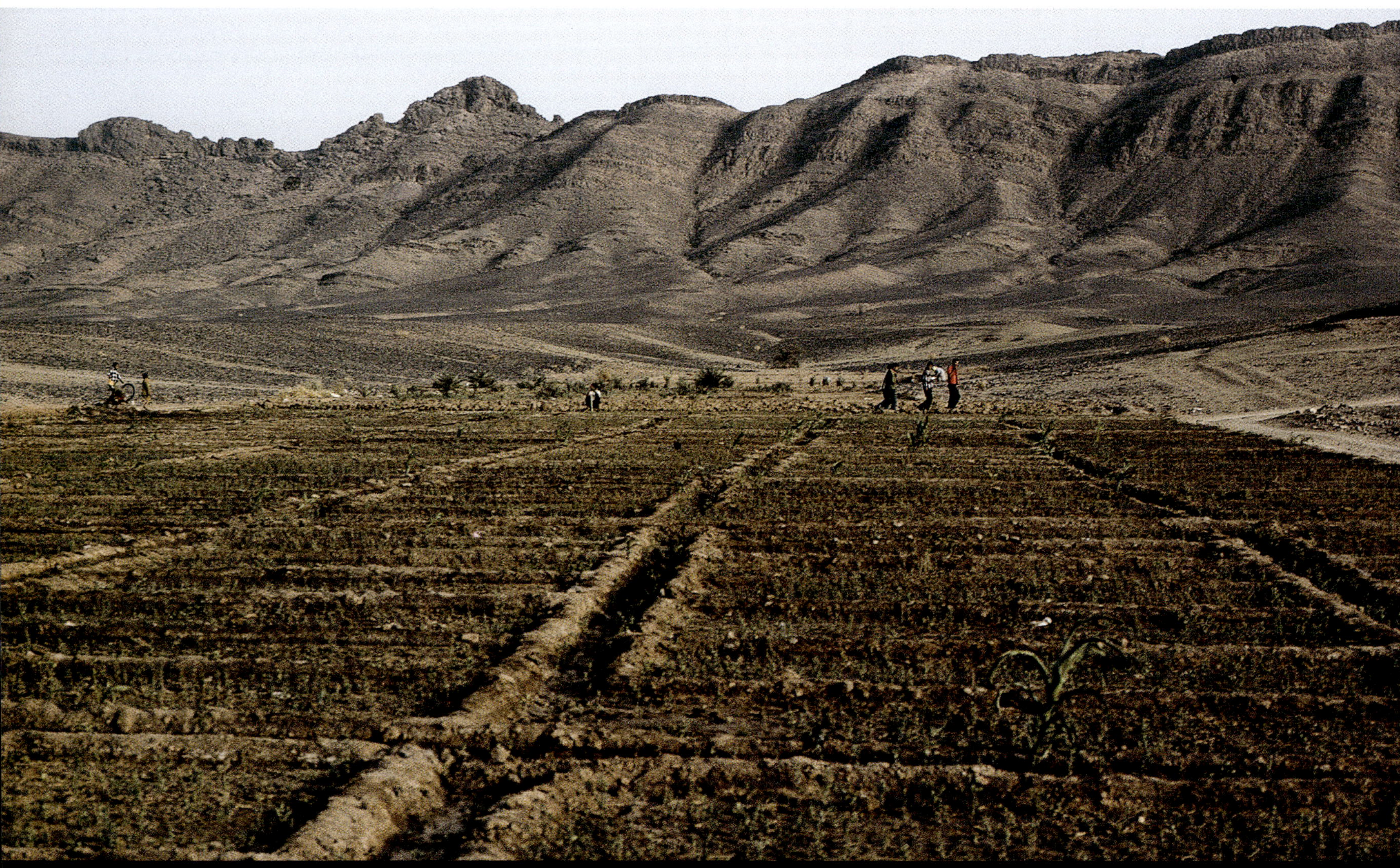

Henna cultivated under irrigation in the stony desert *(hamada)*, away from the village, 2001

Henna, cultivated since ancient times

The order Amyridaceaae (which includes myrrh, used in incense), to which the henna plant is related, embraces an unusually large number of plants used for flavoring and medicinal purposes. The henna plant (Lawsonia inermis L.) especially unites a great many interesting characteristics and, among the plants to which it is closely related, is unique in this (see "Botanical description", p. 60). The appearance of the henna plant can vary considerably yet all varieties belong to a single species.

Not enough is known about the endemic range of the henna plant. Even the natural habitat of the species has not been satisfactorily (in earlier specialist publications) described. Prairie and steppes with thorny scrub[1] are known as its habitat.

The geographical origins of this domesticated plant and the time and place in which it was first cultivated have always been a subject of dispute in specialist publications. Its origins have been variously located from Persia to India. Cultivation of it must have set in very early in antiquity. In all likelihood, the plant originated in southern central Asia because this region is important as the center from which the domestication of so many European and Asian plants, importantly also, the cultivation of plants used for food, spread.[2]

Henna is known to have been cultivated in late antiquity in the areas inhabited by at least three of the great ancient civilizations: Egypt, India and Persia.[3] The henna plant is not, however, native to the Maghreb. Presumably the Arabs introduced the henna plant to this region, where it probably did not grow in antiquity.[4] Al-Idrisi (1100-1165) mentions that henna was cultivated in Morocco in the 12th century. Today henna is grown in southern Morocco. Until only a few decades ago at least, it was grown in the region of Azemmour, the northernmost point of cultivation throughout its range. It must have been introduced there from the Sous by the Shtuka. In the Maghreb henna requires intensive irrigation.[5]

1 Rübel 1930.
2 Vavilov 1951; Hawkes, 1983; Hawkes 1991.
3 Hegi 1926, p. 747 f.; Schweppe 1992, p. 20; Garcia 1992, p. 37.
4 Knapp 1973. p. 468.
5 Knapp 1973, p. 468; also: Kerner/Hansen 1913, vol. 3, p. 322 (refers to Jordan).

Henna, eine uralte Kulturpflanze

Die Ordnung der Weihrauchgewächse (Myrtales), zu dessen Verwandtschaftskreis der Hennastrauch gehört, umfasst eine ungewöhnlich große Zahl von Gewürz- und Heilpflanzen. Der Hennastrauch (Lawsonia inermis L.) vereinigt besonders viele interessante Eigenschaften auf sich und steht auch in seinem Verwandtschaftskreis ganz einzigartig da (siehe "Botanischer Steckbrief", S. 60). Der Hennastrauch ist in seiner Gestalt relativ stark variabel, umfasst aber nur eine einzige Art.

Die natürliche Verbreitung des Hennastrauches ist ungenügend bekannt. Auch der natürliche Standort der Art wird – in der älteren Literatur – nicht befriedigend umschrieben. Steppenwiesen und Dornstrauch-Steppenwüsten[1] sind als Lebensräume bekannt.

Die geographische Herkunft der Kulturpflanze und der Zeitraum und Zeitpunkt der ersten Kultivierung ist in der Literatur stets strittig geblieben. Von Persien bis Indien werden Herkunftsgebiete genannt. Die Kultivierung muss bereits im frühen Altertum erfolgt sein. Ein Ursprungsgebiet im südlichen Zentralasien ist recht wahrscheinlich, weil dieser Raum ein bedeutendes Ursprungszentrum vieler euro-asiatischer Kulturpflanzen, insbesondere auch von Nahrungspflanzen, darstellt.[2]

Henna ist im späteren Altertum in mindestens drei alten, großen Kulturräumen bekannt: in Ägypten, Indien und Persien.[3] Im Maghreb hingegen ist der Hennastrauch nicht einheimisch. Es ist anzunehmen, dass die Araber den Hennastrauch eingeführt haben, wo er wohl im Altertum noch nicht vorkam.[4] Al-Idrisi (1100-1165) erwähnt die Kultur von Henna in Marokko im 12. Jahrhundert. Heute wird Henna im Süden Marokkos angebaut. Zumindest noch bis vor einigen Jahrzehnten wurde es bis in die Gegend von Azemmour, dem nördlichsten Vorkommen der Art in ihrem gesamten Verbreitungsgebiet, angebaut, wo es wohl von den Shtuka aus dem Sous eingeführt worden ist. Henna braucht im Maghreb eine intensive Bewässerung.[5]

1 Rübel 1930.
2 Vavilov 1951; Hawkes 1983; Hawkes, 1991.
3 Hegi 1926, S. 747 f.; Schweppe 1992, S. 20; Garcia 1992, S. 37.
4 Knapp 1973, S. 468.
5 Knapp 1973, S. 468, auch: Kerner/Hansen 1913, Bd. 3, S. 322 (hier auf den Jordan bezogen).

Henna is used in southern Morocco (and generally in the Maghreb) in several ceremonial rites. In southern Morocco "a high degree of *baraka* is attributed to it."[6] A henna ceremony is known within the context of Moroccan marriage rites.[7] But henna also is loaded with important connotations in association with other *rites de passage* marking the different stages of life.[8] The essence of the plant is regarded as ambivalent. On the one hand, henna guards - if used properly - against dangers and impurity yet it can also cause them. Only if it has been properly prepared can it achieve the positive effect desired. Noxious properties emanate from the plant itself and even dried henna leaves. That is why henna is always grown in the Drâa Valley apart from the village fields in a separate plantation.[9]

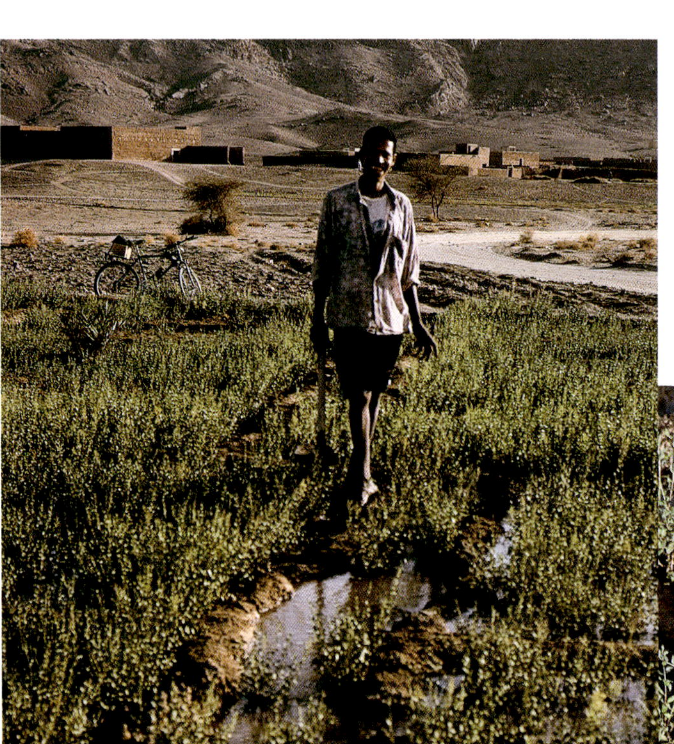

Irrigation water for the fields, 2001

Wasser wird zu den Feldern geleitet, 2001

Henna wird in Südmarokko (und generell im Maghreb) in mehreren zeremoniellen Riten verwendet. In Südmarokko wird ihm "reichlich *baraka* zugesprochen".[6] Bekannt ist die Henna-Zeremonie im Rahmen der marokkanischen Hochzeitsriten.[7] Aber auch in anderen *rites de passage* (Lebensabschnittsriten) besitzt Henna gewichtige Konnotationen.[8] Dabei gilt das Wesen der Pflanze als ambivalent. Henna schützt zwar – bei sachgemäßer Anwendung – einerseits vor Gefahren und Unreinheit, es kann aber andererseits auch Ursache davon sein. Erst durch die sachgemäße Präparation erlangt es die erzielte positive Wirkung. Die Pflanze selbst und auch noch die getrockneten Blätter breiten unheilvolle Wirkungen aus. Deshalb befinden sich die Hennakulturen im Drâa-Tal stets außerhalb der Dorfflur in einem separaten Geviert.[9]

The young plants must be watered often, 2001

Die jungen Sträuchlein müssen oft bewässert werden, 2001

A multiplicity of names

Henna bears a remarkably wide range of names in the cultures in which it is cultivated. Gustav Hegi lists about 20 names for it from the main European and Asian languages alone.[10] This suggests that the various useful properties of henna have been noticed as positive by the peoples of several different cultures.

In some cultures, names are known for each different part of the plant or for its different uses. In Arabic, for instance, there are names for the leaves: *yaranna* and *rakun/irkan*. Other names designate the flowers: *faghiya/faghw*. A perfumed oil made from henna is called *duhn-al-faghw*. The Berber also distinguish between the flowers *(lwerd)* and the whole plant *(tifidas)* in their use of nomenclature.

An overwhelming majority of these many names refer to the flower. Its lovely scent was proverbial even in antiquity. Muhammad praises the enchanting flowers of the henna plant in numerous hadiths. *Copher* is an old name for the flowers in the Song of Solomon. Other names for the flowers are *cyper* and Ligustrum Aegypticum.

The name in general use today, "henna", is derived from Persian *henni*.[11] This is also an indication that it may have originated in the lands under Persian sway. We must assume that, in the Persian civilization of late antiquity (and in the regional states that followed it up to the Sassanids), *henni* was invested with extraordinary significance. The Muslim Arabs probably took over the use of the henna plant from the Persians. With the spread of Islamic culture, henna was disseminated across the world.

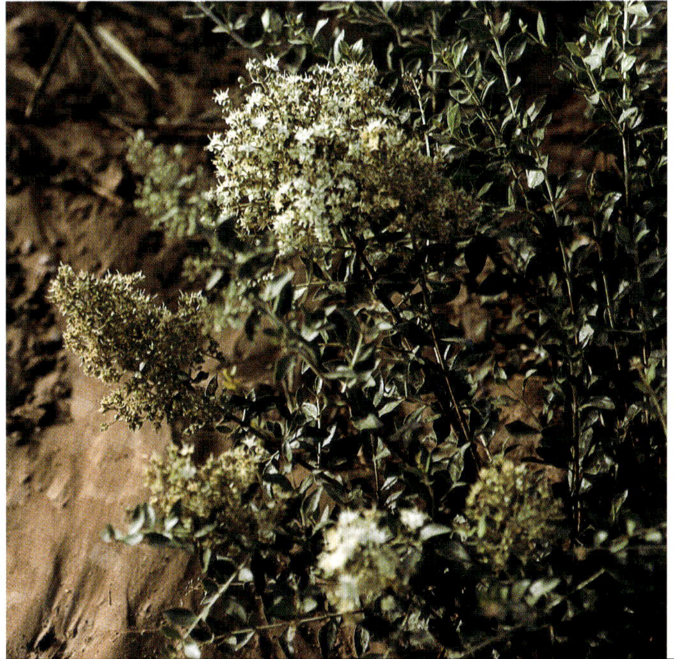

Henna flowers and seed-cases are on the plant at the same time.
The soil must consist of equal parts of clay and sand, 2001

Vielfalt der Namensgebung

Henna trägt eine auffallende Vielfalt von Eigennamen in den Kulturen des Gesamtverbreitungsgebietes. Gustav Hegi zählt rund 20 Eigennamen aus euro-asiatischen Kultursprachen auf.[10] Dies deutet darauf hin, dass die unterschiedlichen nützlichen Eigenschaften von Henna der Bevölkerung in mehreren Kulturen positiv aufgefallen sind.

In einigen Kulturen sind Namen für jeweils unterschiedliche Pflanzenteile oder Verwendungszwecke bekannt. In der arabischen Sprache gibt es z.B. Namen für Blätter: *yaranna* und *rakun/irkan*. Weitere Namen betreffen die Blüten: *faghiya/faghw;* ein parfümiertes Öl aus Henna heißt *duhn-al-faghw*. Auch die Berber unterscheiden die Blüten *(lwerd)* mit einem Eigennamen von der Pflanze als Ganzes *(tifidas)*.

Besonders viele der zahlreichen Eigennamen beziehen sich auf die Blüte. Der wunderbare Blütenduft ist schon im Altertum sprichwörtlich. Mohammed lobt in zahlreichen Hadithen die bezaubernden Hennablüten. Kopher ist ein alter Name für die Blüten im Hohelied Salomonis *(copher)*. Auch *cyper* und Ligustrum Aegypticum sind Namen für die Blüten.

Der heute gebräuchliche Name "Henna" geht auf den persischen Namen *henni* zurück.[11] Dies ist auch ein Hinweis auf den Ursprung im persischen Großraum. Wir müssen annehmen, dass in der persischen Kultur des späten Altertums (und in lokalen Nachfolgestaaten bis auf die Sassaniden) *henni* eine herausragende Bedeutung hatte. Die muslimischen Araber müssen wohl den Gebrauch des Hennastrauches von den Persern übernommen haben. Mit der islamischen Kultur hat sich Henna später in der ganzen Welt ausgebreitet.

The use of the plant in various civilizations

Henna can be used for an astonishing variety of purposes. This is one of the reasons why there are so many names for it. Its best known use is as a natural dyestuff. Combined with all sorts of alkalis, it can be used to paint the skin or dye hair, leather goods and, more rarely - this is what is particularly of interest in the present connection - textiles.[12] Even in ancient civilizations there were other substances from which red dyes could be produced. Henna was at first unknown in China, where Impatiens balsamica was used instead.[13] It is interesting that the dyestuff used there also contained Lawson, the dyestuff of henna. In India the insect Coccus lacca produced a red dyestuff rivaling henna.[14] The ancient Greek physician Ctesias (ca. 400 BC) praises in *Persika* the red dyestuff produced from henna ("Persian dyestuff") as

Verwendung der Pflanze in verschiedenen Kulturen

Henna eignet sich für eine erstaunlich große Vielfalt von Verwendungszwecken. Dies ist auch eine der Ursachen für die vielfältigen Namen. Die Verwendung als Färbemittel stellt die bekannteste Anwendung dar. Stets unter Zusatz von unterschiedlichsten Alkalien werden eingefärbt: Haut, Haare, Lederwaren, seltener, und das ist in diesem Zusammenhang besonders interessant, auch Textilien.[12] Henna steht bereits in den alten Kulturen in Konkurrenz zu anderen Rotfarbstoffen. In China kennt man Henna zunächst nicht, sondern verwendet Impatiens balsamica.[13] Dieses enthält interessanterweise ebenfalls Lawson als Farbstoff. In Indien ist die Lackschildlaus (Cochenille) eine Konkurrenz zu Henna.[14] Der griechische Arzt Ktesias (um 400 v. Chr.) zieht in seinem Werk *Persika* die Cochenille der Henna ("persischer Farbstoff") als "vorzüglicher" vor. Im neuzeitlichen Europa stellt

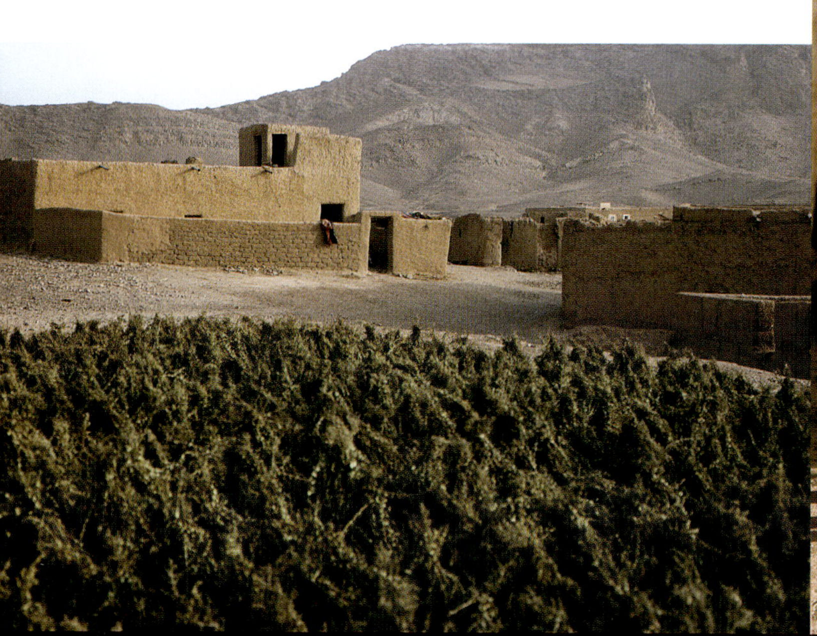

The leaves and the stems from which dye is made are bound in sheaves and laid out to dry at the edge of the village, 2001

Die Blätter und Stängel, die den Farbstoff liefern werden zu Büscheln zusammengebunden und am Dorfrand zum Trocknen ausgelegt, 2001

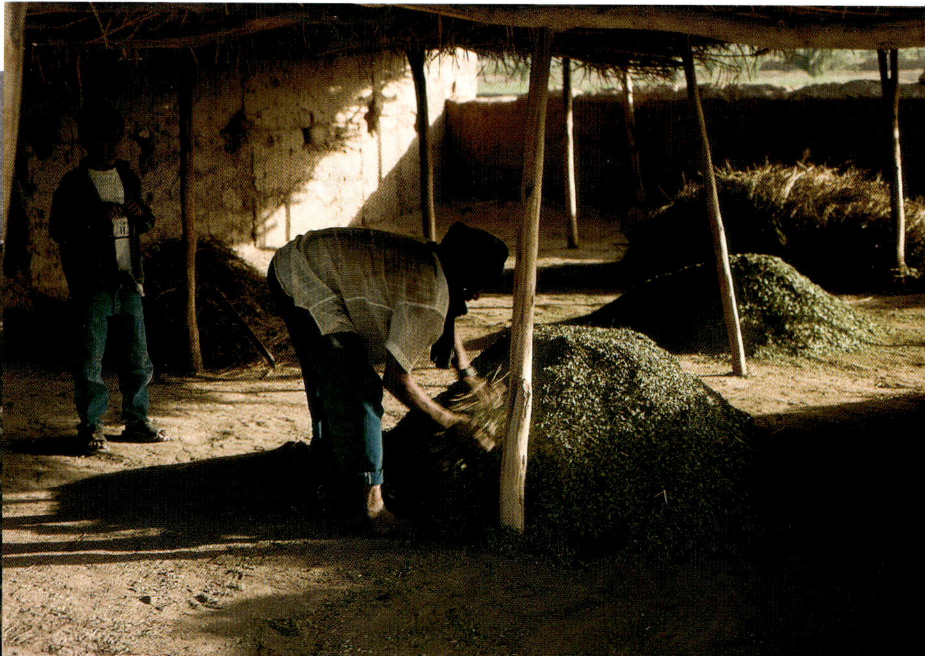

Henna leaves are removed from the stem by being hit gently and turned, 2001

Sanftes Abschlagen und Wenden trennt die Hennablätter von den Stängeln, 2001 "excellent". In post-medieval Europe the red dyestuff extracted from the root of the false alkanet (Alkanna tinctoria) represented strong competition for henna. For several centuries it was often confused or equated with henna. Since false alkanet thrives throughout southern Europe, it was highly prized as an alternative to henna from the 16th/17th centuries. The natural dyestuff produced from false alkanet is chemically related to that found in henna. In addition, madder (Rubia tinctorum) and safflower (Carthamus tinctorius) grow everywhere henna thrives and also are competitive alternatives to it.[15]

die Färbende Ochsenzunge (Alkanna tinctoria) eine große Konkurrenz für Henna dar. Über mehrere Jahrhunderte wird sie oft mit Henna verwechselt oder ihr gleichgesetzt. Da sie im ganzen südeuropäischen Raum gut gedeiht wird sie seit dem 16./17. Jahrhundert als Alternative zu Henna angepriesen. Alkanna enthält ebenfalls einen Farbstoff, der chemisch mit dem Lawson von Henna verwandt ist. Überall im Verbreitungsgebiet von Henna sind außerdem Krapp und Färberdisteln (Carthamus) Alternativen und Konkurrenten des Farbstoffes Henna.[15]

Aus den Henna-Blüten wurden außerdem – ebenfalls schon seit dem Altertum – wohlriechende Salben und Öle[16] sowie Parfüms[17] hergestellt. Die Verwendung von Henna als Arzneimittel ist zwar heute nicht mehr sehr gebräuchlich, war aber schon im Altertum bekannt. Dioskurides empfiehlt die Blätter gegen Soor, Karbunkel und Verbrennungen, die Blüten, mit Essig auf die Stirn gerieben, gegen Kopfschmerzen. In Marokko wird Henna zusammen mit Artemisia-Arten als Fiebermittel eingesetzt.[18] Eine ideale Voraussetzung für die medizinische Anwendung von Blütenessenzen des Hennastrauches in der arabischen Medizin ist deren Wohlgeruch. Mild wirkende, angenehm schmeckende und wohlriechende Arzneien werden von den Arabern im Gegensatz zur griechisch-römischen (und der modernen) Medizin bevorzugt.[19]

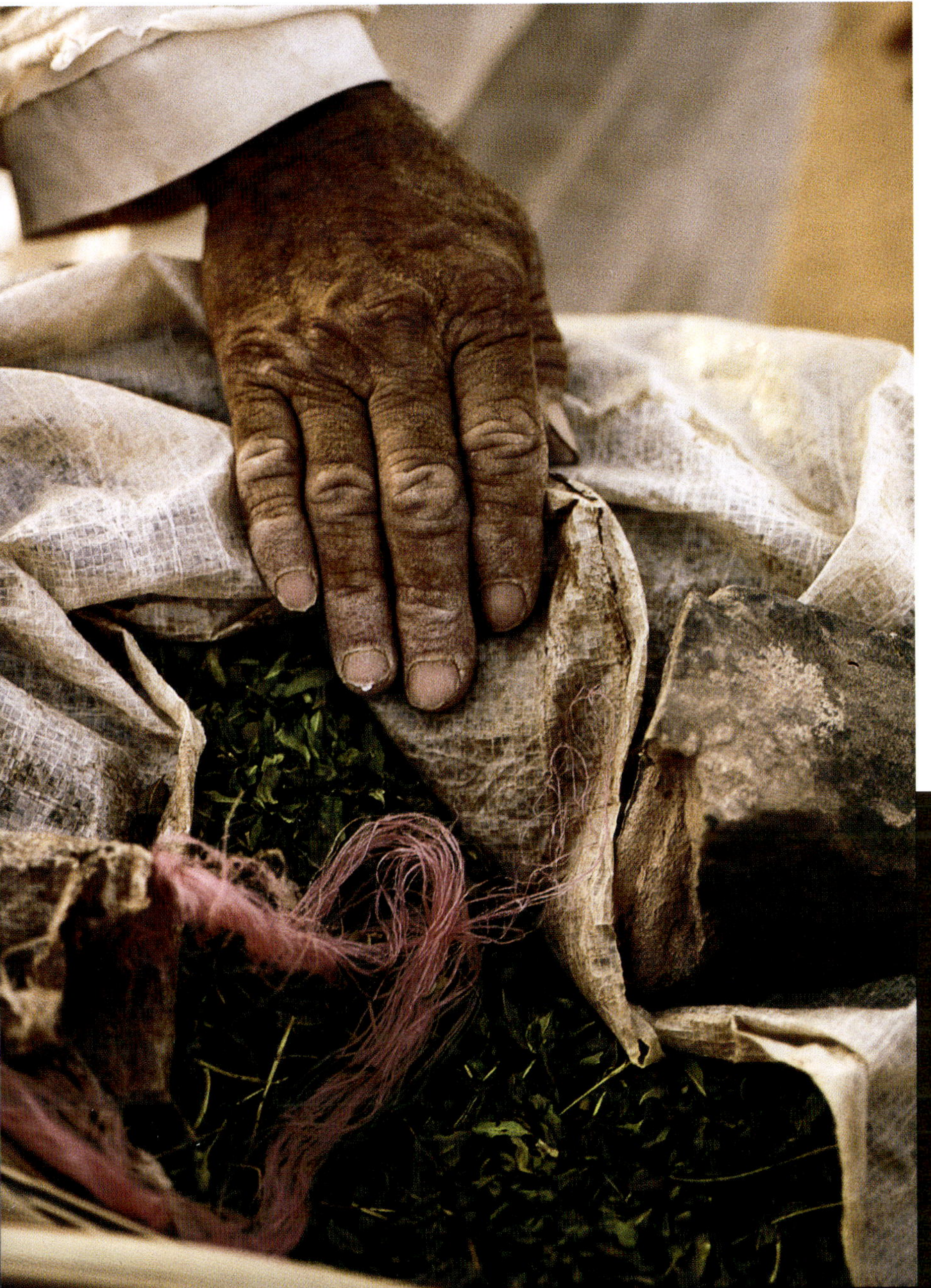

A 50 kg bag of henna costs – depending on its quality when harvested – approx. 1000 MAD, 2001

12 "Zenaga in the Anti-Atlas", in: Rainer 1999, p. 42; allegedly not used as a carpet dyestuff in Algeria: Rikli/Schröter 1912, p. 129.
13 Schweppe 1992, p. 38.
14 Schweppe 1992, p. 276.
15 Schweppe 1992.

12 "Zenaga im Anti-Atlas", in: Rainer 1999, S. 42; in Algerien angeblich nicht als Teppichfarbstoff verwendet: Rikli/Schröter 1912, S. 129.
13 Schweppe 1992, S. 38.
14 Schweppe 1992, S. 276.
15 Schweppe 1992.
16 Rikli/Schröter 1912, S. 131.
17 Garcia 1992, S. 66.
18 Schneider 1974; Garcia 1992, S. 70/71.
19 Kessler 2001, S. 24 ff.

Aromatic unguents and oils[16] as well as perfumes[17] have been made from henna - also since antiquity. Henna is now seldom employed medicinally but this use of the plant was known in antiquity. Dioscurides recommends henna leaves as a cure for thrush, carbuncle and burns and the flowers, rubbed on to the forehead with vinegar, as a headache remedy. In Morocco henna is used, together with some species of the genus Artemisia (wormwood, southernwood), as a remedy for fever.[18] What made the use of henna-flower essences so ideal for the purposes of Arab medicine was that they are so fragrant. Unlike Greco-Roman medicine (and in Europe on into the modern era), Arab medicine preferred mild, pleasant-tasting and aromatic medicaments.[19]

Judging by the standard lists of relevant reference works, pharmacological research into the medicinal substances contained in the henna plant is far from exhaustive. In the most recent publications, the antibacterial, antifungal, anaesthetic, antihaemorrhagic (stopping the flow of blood), nematicidal (combatting roundworm: ascariasis) and even the antituberculous properties of henna extracts are being studied.

The importance of henna, even though it has been used for so many different purposes for thousands of years in such diverse cultures, is still underestimated. In this sense henna is, in fact, one of the most intriguing plants known.

Die pharmakologische Forschung über Wirkstoffe des Hennastrauches ist, wenn man die einschlägigen Literaturlisten konsultiert, keineswegs abgeschlossen. Antibakterielle, antifungale, anaesthetische, antihaemorragene (blutstillende), nematizide (Fadenwürmer bekämpfende) und tuberkulostatische Wirkungen von Henna-Gehaltstoffen werden in neusten Publikationen untersucht.

Die Bedeutung von Henna ist, trotz der Jahrtausende alten und den je nach Kultur unterschiedlichen Anwendungen, immer noch unterschätzt. In diesem Sinne ist Henna eines der faszinierendsten Gewächse überhaupt.

16 Rikli/Schröter 1912, p. 131.
17 Garcia 1992, p. 66.
18 Schneider 1974; Garcia 1992, pp. 70-71.
19 Kessler 2001, p. 24 f.

Henna: Botanical description

Ethereal oils are characteristic of the (lysigenous) secretory leaves of the Myrtaceæ in the narrower sense (Weberling/Schwantes 1972, p. 103). There are examples of this among the various species (nearly 700) comprising the genus of Eucalyptus as well as the clove used as a household spice and oil and the eponymous Mediterranean myrtle.

Henna (Lawsonia) belongs to the family (formerly called natural order) of Lythraceæ. This family includes about 500 species in 24 genera, for the most part herbs. Within the family of Lythraceæ, Lawsonia belongs to the tribe of Nesaeeæ and, within it in turn, is closely related to the subtribe of Lagerstroemiinæ. Subsumed under 3 genera, this subtribe comprises a small number of Asian woody perennials. The largest genus is Lagerstroemia comprising roughly 30 species, among them the Lagerstroemia indica L. tree, which is popular in southern Europe as a late blooming park tree. Orias, the second genus, comprises a single species, which is widespread in central Asia. The genus Lawsonia is also monotypic, that is, with a single species: the henna plant, Lawsonia inermis, or Egyptian Privet. It occurs, however, in different forms and varies quite considerably.

Henna: Ein botanischer Steckbrief

Für die Myrtaceen im engeren Sinn sind ätherische Öle in (lysigenen) Sekretblättern charakteristisch (Weberling/Schwantes 1972, S. 103). Beispiele finden sich unter den Eucalyptusarten (fast 700 Arten), bei der Gewürznelke und bei der namengebenden, mittelmeerischen Myrte.

Henna (Lawsonia) gehört zur Familie der Blutweiderichgewächse (Lythraceae). Diese Familie mit rund 500 Arten in 24 Gattungen umfasst überwiegend Kräuter. Innerhalb der Familie Lythraceae gehört Lawsonia in den Tribus Nesaeeae und dort in den engen Verwandtschaftsbereich des Subtribus Lagerstroemiinae. Dieser Subtribus umfasst in drei Gattungen eine kleine Zahl asiatischer Holzgewächse. Die größte Gattung ist Lagerstroemia mit rund 30 Arten, darunter die in Südeuropa als spätblühender Parkbaum beliebte Indische Lagerströmie (Lagerstroemia indica L.). Orias, die zweite Gattung, umfasst bloß eine einzige Art welche in Zentralasien verbreitet ist. Die Gattung Lawsonia ist ebenfalls monotypisch mit der einzigen Art, dem Hennastrauch Lawsonia inermis. Diese ist allerdings ziemlich vielgestaltig und relativ stark variabel.

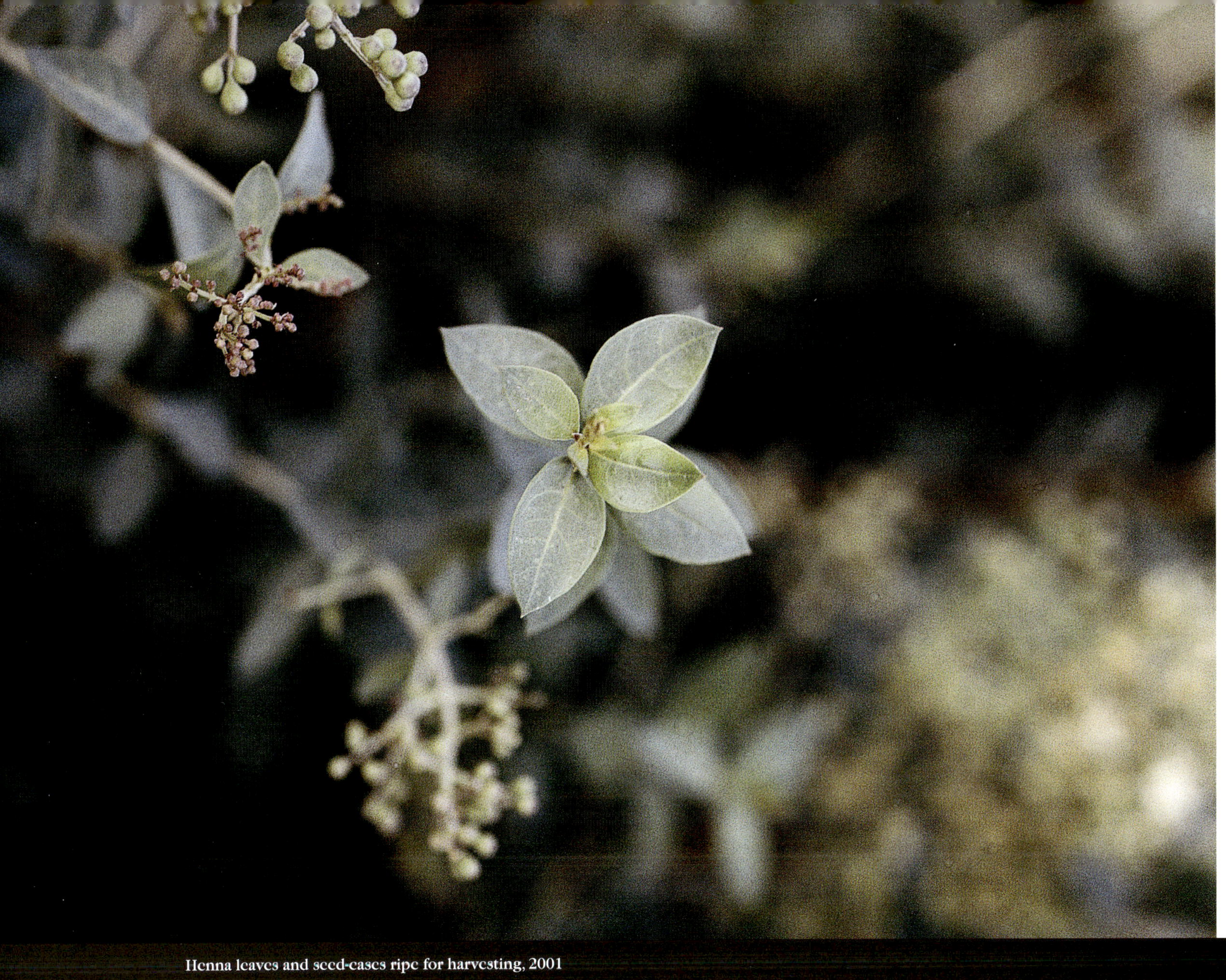

Henna leaves and seed-cases ripe for harvesting, 2001

Erntereife Hennablätter sowie Samenkapseln, 2001

Henna is a deciduous shrub, which grows to a height of from 2 to 6 metres. In appearance it recalls ligustrum (privet) yet its shoots can also be thorny. The deciduous leaves are opposite in arrangement and lanceolate (narrow and tapering at both ends) in shape. The small tetramerous flowers stand on stalks in attractive panicles. The color range is from yellowish white to brick red and the musky scent resembles that of tea roses. The corolla petals are thick and wrinkled. The number of stamens varies (4) 8 (12); they are arranged in epipetalous (in front of the corolla petals) equal pairs, rarely also occurring in unequal pairs of 1 or 3, and are only slightly lower than the corolla petals. The calyx is shaped like a gyroscope, ultimately bowl-shaped, without any appendages. The fruit is a dry berry which is not dehiscent nor does it rupture in fibers. The seeds are small and angular; the pericarp is very spongy and swollen at the tip.

Linnaeus distinguished erroneously between two variant forms as species: inermis and spinosa. In reality, these are merely two different stages of maturity of the same species: inermis stands for the unripe, spinosa (with thorns) for the mature form. The third Latin name for the same species, L. alba, goes back to Lamarck but is no longer in use.

Henna ist ein laubabwerfender, 2 bis 6 Meter hoher Strauch. Der Wuchs erinnert an Liguster, doch kommen z.T. verdornte Kurztriebe vor. Die Laubblätter sind gegenständig, ihre Form ist lanzettlich. Die kleinen Blüten stehen in ansehnlichen Rispen, sie sind 4-zählig, ihre Farbe steigert sich vom Gelblichweiß bis ins Ziegelrot, der intensive Duft ist teerosenartig. Die Kronblätter sind dick und gerunzelt. Die Zahl der Staubblätter variiert (4) 8 (12), sie stehen paarweise, selten zu 1 oder 3 vor den Kronblättern und sind nur wenig tiefer als diese. Der Kelch ist kreiselförmig, zuletzt schüsselförmig, ohne irgendwelche Anhängsel. Die Frucht ist eine trockene, nicht aufspringende oder faserig zerreißende Beere. Die Samen sind klein und eckig. Die Samenschale ist an der Spitze stark schwammig aufgetrieben.

Linné unterschied irrtümlich zwei Varianten als Arten: inermis und spinosa In Wirklichkeit handelt es sich dabei bloß um zwei Altersstadien der gleichen Art: inermis steht für die jugendliche Form, spinosa (mit Dornen) für die Reifeform. Der dritte wissenschaftliche Name für die gleiche Art, L. alba, geht auf Lamarck zurück, ist aber heute nicht mehr gebräuchlich.

The henna-painted textiles of the Feija

Die hennabemalten Textilien der Feija

That fabric was hardly ever decorated in polychrome by means of complicated weaving techniques among the Feija but rather was mainly painted with henna has several implications. The process of painting is more spontaneous than weaving. Consequently, new elements and motifs could be taken up much more quickly. Moreover, henna might have been expensive yet the expenditure of using it were ultimately lower than those incurred when textile fibers were dyed in several colors.

Die Tatsache, dass Gewebe bei den Feija kaum mit komplizierten Webtechniken mehrfarbig dekoriert, sondern vorwiegend mit Henna bemalt wurden, führt zu einigen Schlüssen. Der Vorgang des Malens ist spontaner als jener des Webens. Neue Elemente und Motive konnten so viel schneller aufgenommen werden. Zudem ist Henna zwar kostbar, doch ist der Aufwand am Ende eher geringer als beim Einfärben von Fasern in mehreren Farben.

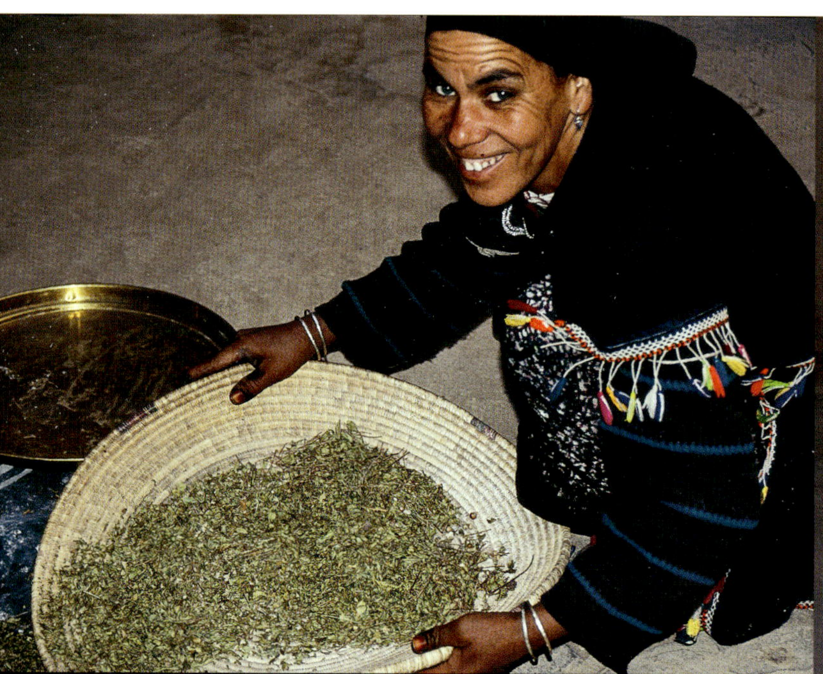

Winnowing henna leaves, 2000

Worfeln der Hennablätter, 2000

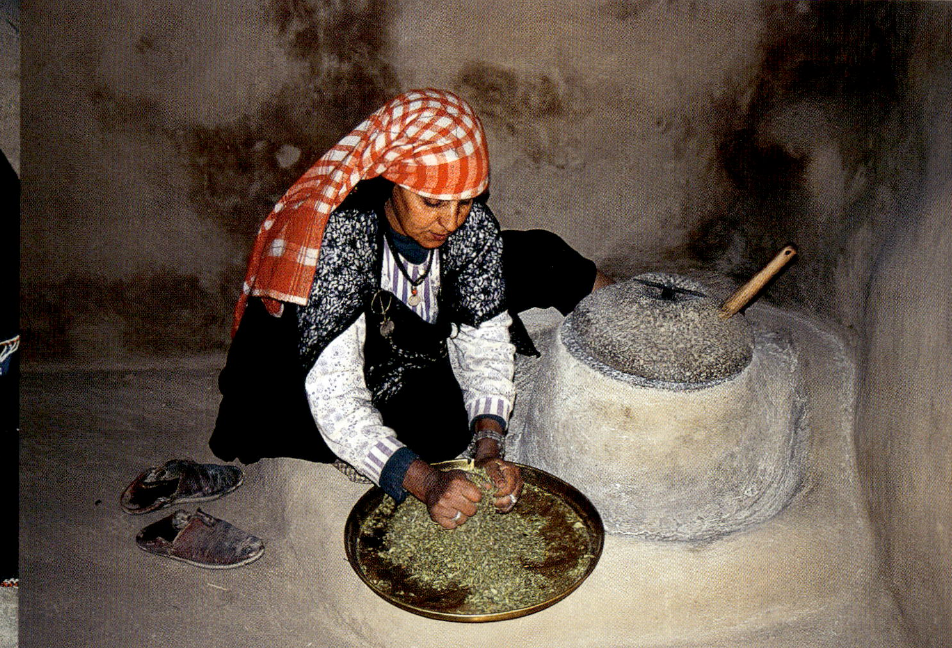

Aisha crushes the leaves in her hands before they are put into the grinding stone, 2000

Aischa zerdrückt die Blätter mit der Hand bevor sie in die Steinmühle gefüllt werden, 2000

1 Marie-Rose Rabaté (1996) reports that Feija jewelry from Imi n'Tatelt (this is probably the jewelry owned by *chorfa* women: editors' note) is particularly meticulously worked and original in design yet the little silver plates supporting the chains have been beaten to a considerably thinner thickness than they are among other tribes in the region. This clearly indicates that the costly material had to be dealt with very sparingly (presumably to reduce costs).

1 Marie-Rose Rabaté (1996) berichtet, dass der Feija-Schmuck aus Imi n'Tatelt (es handelt sich wohl um den Schmuck der *chorfa*-Frauen, Anm. d. Hrsg.) zwar besonders sorgfältig gearbeitet und eigenständig in der Gestaltung ist, jedoch die tragenden Silberplättchen wesentlich dünner ausgewalzt wurden als bei anderen Stämmen der Region. Dies ist ein deutlicher Hinweis darauf, dass mit dem kostbaren Material (wohl aus Gründen der Sparsamkeit) sehr vorsichtig umzugehen war.

The traditional dress worn by Feija women consists of a headscarf and a woman's wrapper. The cloth is either pinned with a fibula *(azarzay)* or held together by means of a red and green wool cord *(tassmarte)*, which is approx. 150 cm in length. With this dress are worn necklaces of a type which comes from the region of the oases on the Jebel Bani.[1]

Feija textiles are distinguished by an extraordinarily high standard of workmanship and materials as well as meticulous execution – their quality quite often surpasses that of fabrics made by other Chleuh tribes. Polychrome embroidered patterns, however, are rarely encountered among the Feija. When they occur, they are used sparingly. Patterns and motifs painted on with henna are the distinctive feature of Feija textiles. Presumably economic conditions were such in the remote region inhabited by the Feija that they were forced to restrict themselves to using this dyestuff. Henna, too, is ex-

Die traditionelle Kleidung bei den Feija besteht aus dem Kopftuch und dem Wickeltuch. Dieses wird entweder von einer Fibel *(azarzay)* oder einer ca. 150 cm langen, rotgrünen Wollkordel *(tassmarte)* zusammengehalten. Dazu werden Halsketten getragen, deren Typus aus dem Gebiet der Oasen am Jebel Bani stammt.[1]

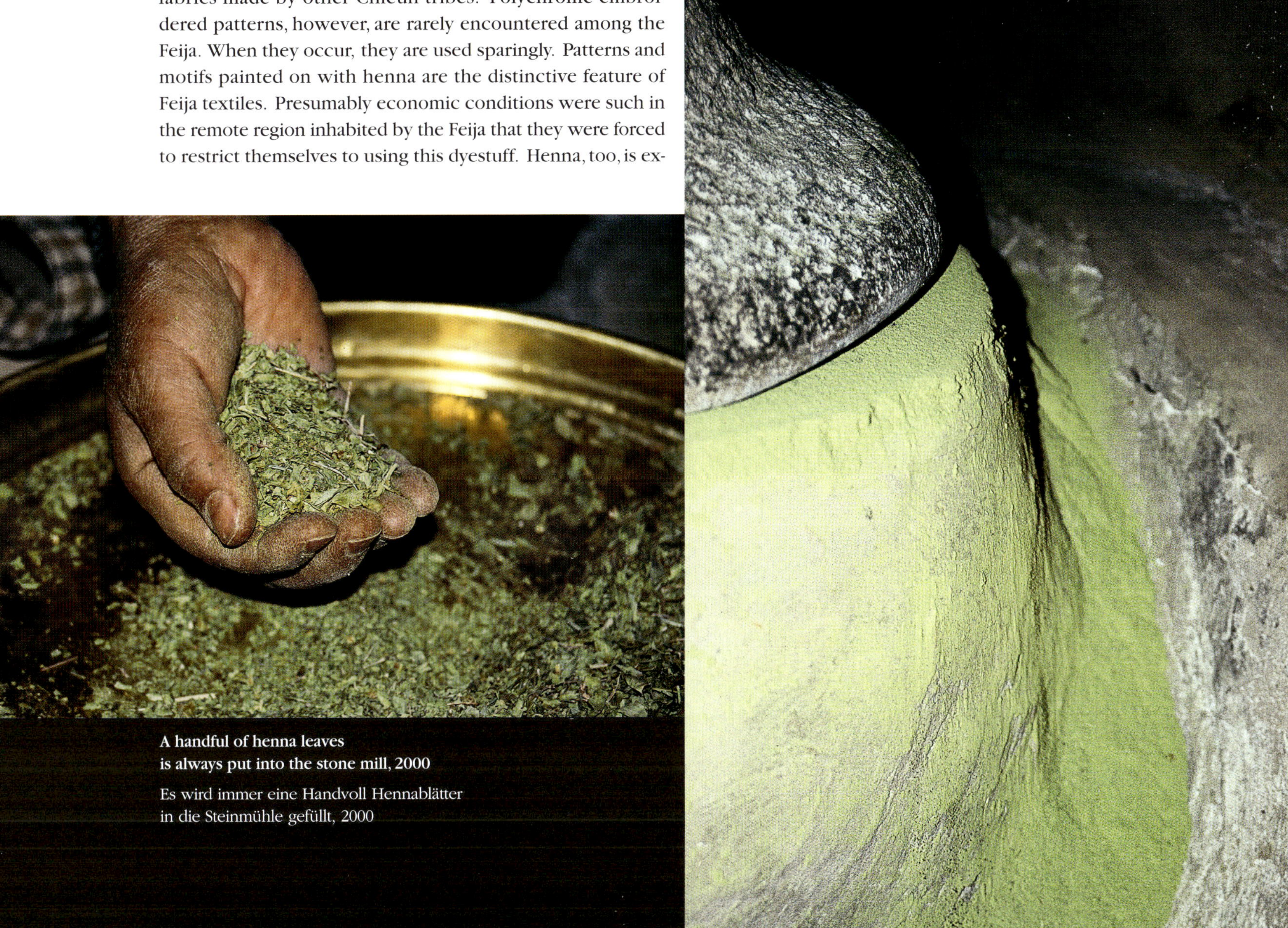

A handful of henna leaves is always put into the stone mill, 2000

Es wird immer eine Handvoll Hennablätter in die Steinmühle gefüllt, 2000

Henna comes from the quern as a fine powder, 2000

Henna kommt als feines Pulver aus der Mühle, 2000

pensive yet in the long run it was probably cheaper and less time-consuming to use it than to dye fibers in various colors. Any woman could paint with henna - without having recourse to the help of a dyer, who would have to be paid for his services. In the case of the Feija textiles this very limitation led to a particular quality and it was the spontaneous technique which made the distinctive motifs possible in the first place.

Die Feija-Textilien zeichnen sich durch ein ausgesprochen hohes Maß an Sorgfalt, Können und Materialqualität aus – ihre Feinheit übertrifft sogar manchmal jene der anderen Chleuh-Stämme. Farbig gewirkte Muster finden sich bei den Feija jedoch selten, und wenn, dann werden sie nur sparsam eingesetzt. Ihr Merkmal sind eben jene besonderen, mit Henna aufgemalten Muster und Motive. Es ist anzunehmen, dass die Beschränkung auf diese Färbemittel in den problematischen wirtschaftlichen Verhältnissen gründet, denen sich die Feija in ihrem abgelegenen Gebiet ausgesetzt sahen. Zwar war auch Henna kostbar, doch der zeitliche und finanzielle Aufwand dürfte geringer gewesen sein als beim Einfärben von Fasern in verschiedenen Farben: Jede Frau konnte mit Henna malen – ohne die Hilfe etwa eines zu entlohnenden Färbers. Im Falle der Feija-Textilien führte diese Beschränkung aber zugleich zu einer ganz besonderen Qualität, und die spontane Technik ermöglichte auch erst die besonderen Motive.

In den Hennabemalungen der Feija lassen sich Unterschiede zwischen Elementen aus der islamischen und der berberischen Kultur erkennen. Während die islamischen Elemente – selbst wenn sie aus dem Bereich des Marabutismus kommen – von Eingeweihten recht klar gedeutet werden können, ist es mit den frühen, animistischen Berberelementen wesentlich komplizierter. Anscheinend kann ein

Aisha, 2000

Aischa, 2000

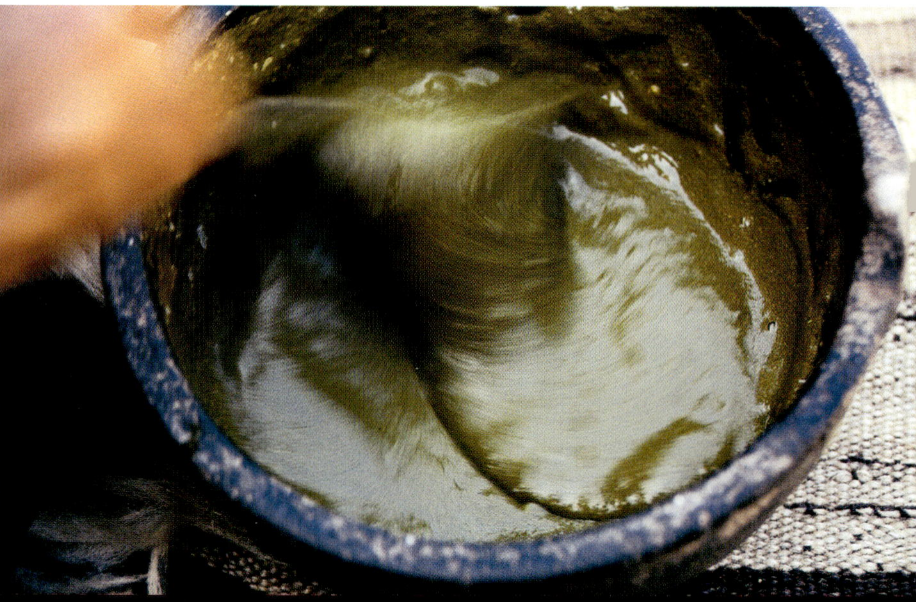

Aisha mixes pulverised henna with hot water to make a thick paste, 2000

Aischa rührt Hennapulver mit heißem Wasser zu einem dicken Brei an, 2000

2 Im Gebiet der Feija leben viele Angehörige von den Nachbarstämmen der Sektana und Zenaga. Auch sie bemalen ihre Gewebe mit Henna, doch sind die Motive ihrer Kopftücher von denen der Feija deutlich verschieden.

In the Feija henna paintings there are noticeable differences between elements taken from Islamic culture and Berber elements. Whereas the Islamic elements - even when they come from the marabout cult - can be interpreted quite easily by those in the know, the situation is far more complex where the early animistic Berber elements are concerned. Apparently a motif can have a special meaning for a family or even for one particular woman. Possibly also a group - for instance, a tribe, village or quite large region - may have agreed, as it were, on what the meaning of a motif or pattern was so that it became typical or was given a heraldic function. The Feija repertoire of patterns and motifs includes characters used in writing, some of which come from the *tifinagh* alphabet. These multilayered meanings will be individually dealt with in depth in the catalog.

Motiv für eine Familie oder für eine Frau eine jeweils eigene Bedeutung haben. Es ist außerdem möglich, dass sich eine Gruppe – zum Beispiel ein Stamm, Dorf oder größeres Gebiet – über die Bedeutung eines Motivs oder Musters sozusagen geeinigt hat, und dieses dann typisch wurde oder eine heraldische Funktion erhielt. Das Muster- und Motivrepertoire schließt Schriftzeichen ein, welche zum Teil aus dem *tifinagh*-Alphabet kommen. Im Katalog wird auf diese vielschichtigen Bedeutungen jeweils eingegangen.

Bei den Feija scheint schon die konsequente und fast ausschließliche Verwendung von Henna zur "Dekoration" ihrer Textilien eine Abgrenzung und damit eine Identifikationsfunktion gegenüber den Nachbarstämmen zu erfüllen, sind doch die Feija-Frauen nach derzeitigem Kenntnisstand die einzigen, welche Henna so vielfältig und so konsequent einsetzen.[2] Heute werden keine Textilien mehr im traditionellen Sinn mit Henna bemalt. Diese Tradition hatte um 1950 ihr Ende. Als letzte Textilien dieser Art entstanden bis etwa 1950 die Hochzeitsdecken *(tahdicht)*. Zu kommerziellen Zwecken haben die *chorfa*-Frauen seit ca. 1998 die Bemalung von Textilien mit Henna wieder aufgenommen, und es ist wahrscheinlich, dass unser Forscherinteresse sie dazu angeregt hat.

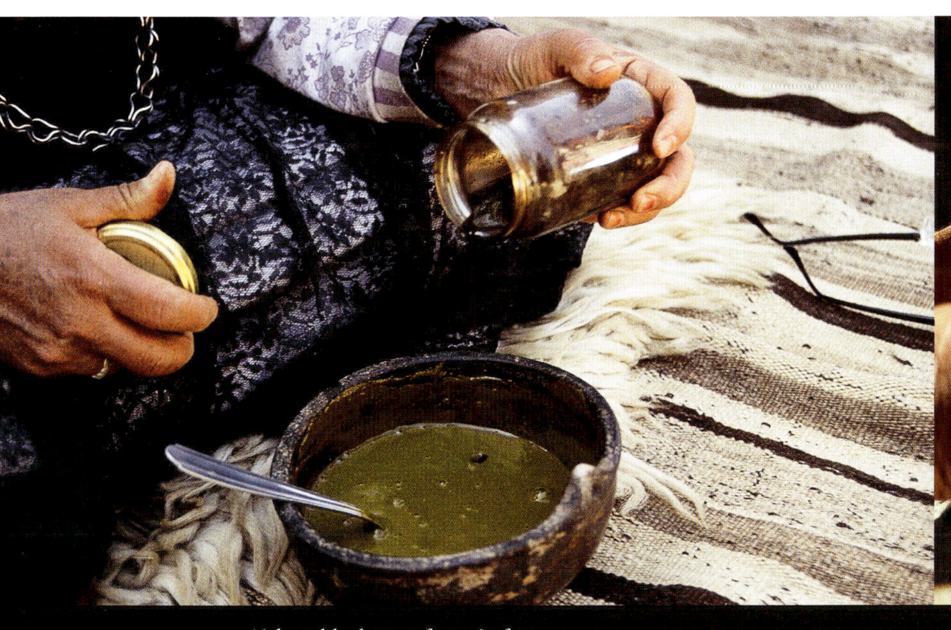

Aisha adds drops of tannin from pomegranate skins, 2000

Aischa gibt Gerbstoff aus Granatapfelschale tropfenweise hinzu, 2000

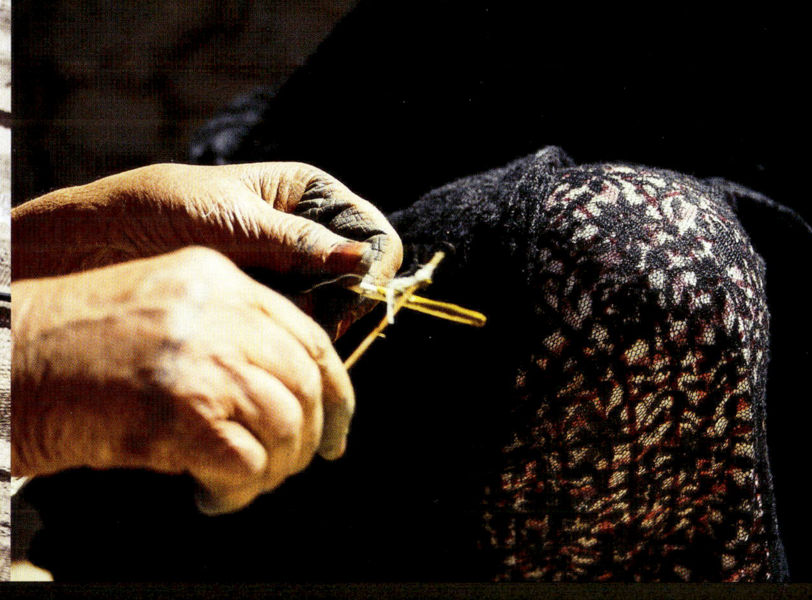

Wool is wrapped round a little stick to make a "brush", 2000

Ein Holzstöcklein wird mit Wolle umwickelt und dient als "Pinsel", 2000

Among the Feija the consistent and virtually exclusive use of henna for "decorating" textiles seems to represent a demarcation and, therefore, to fulfil an identification function distinguishing the Feija from neighboring tribes. Feija women are, after all, as far as is known at present, the only people known to have used henna with such prolific versatility and consistency.[2] Nowadays, however, textiles are no longer painted with henna in the traditional sense. This tradition came to an end in about 1950. The last textiles of this kind made up to that date were wedding blankets *(tahdicht)*. *Chorfa* women have again been painting textiles with henna since about 1998 for commercial purposes and it is highly likely that our interest in researching into these textiles is what has encouraged them to do so.

The old henna recipes are today no longer known with absolute certainty. Women who were older than 60 were, however, able to tell us the following when we visited: they remembered seeing their mothers paint textiles with henna. They also recalled that there were various different techniques of painting. Further, they knew that there used to be many different recipes for mixing henna and that these were different to those known today yet they were only able to provide vague information on these points. Women who still knew the old techniques were too old to continue practising them. One family was willing to demonstrate the techniques they knew of preparing henna and painting textiles with it. This demonstration was photographed and is reproduced here.

Die alten Henna-Rezepte sind heute nicht mehr mit Sicherheit bekannt. Frauen, die älter als 60 Jahre waren, konnten bei unseren Besuchen aber die folgenden Angaben machen: Sie erinnerten sich, dass sie ihre Mütter Textilien mit Henna bemalen sahen und dass es verschiedene Maltechniken gab. Ferner wussten sie, dass Henna früher nach verschiedenen Rezepten angerührt wurde und dass es andere Rezepte waren als die heute bekannten, doch konnten sie nur noch vage Informationen dazu liefern. Frauen, die noch die alten Techniken kannten, waren schon zu betagt, um sie noch auszuführen. Eine Familie war bereit, die ihnen bekannte Technik der Henna-Zubereitung und Textil-Bemalung vorzuführen; diese Demonstration wurde fotografisch festgehalten und ist hier wiedergegeben.

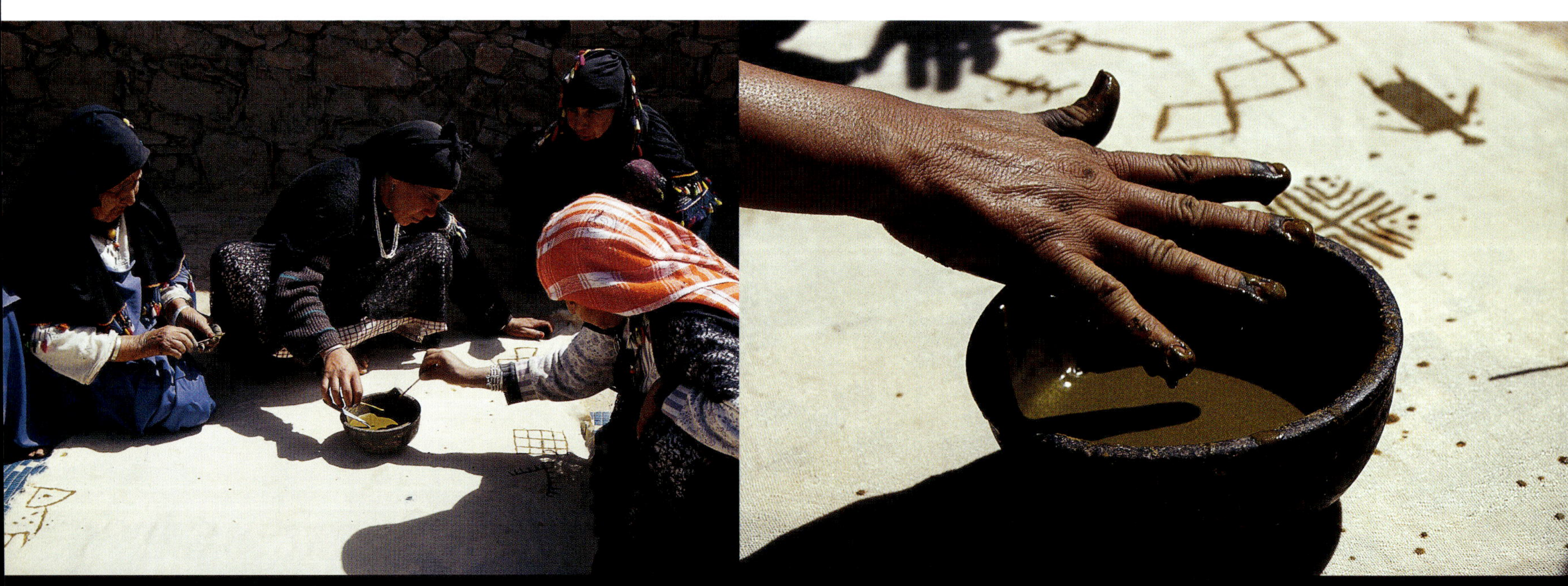

Three generations absorbed in a demonstration of painting, 2000

Aisha's hand turns into ...

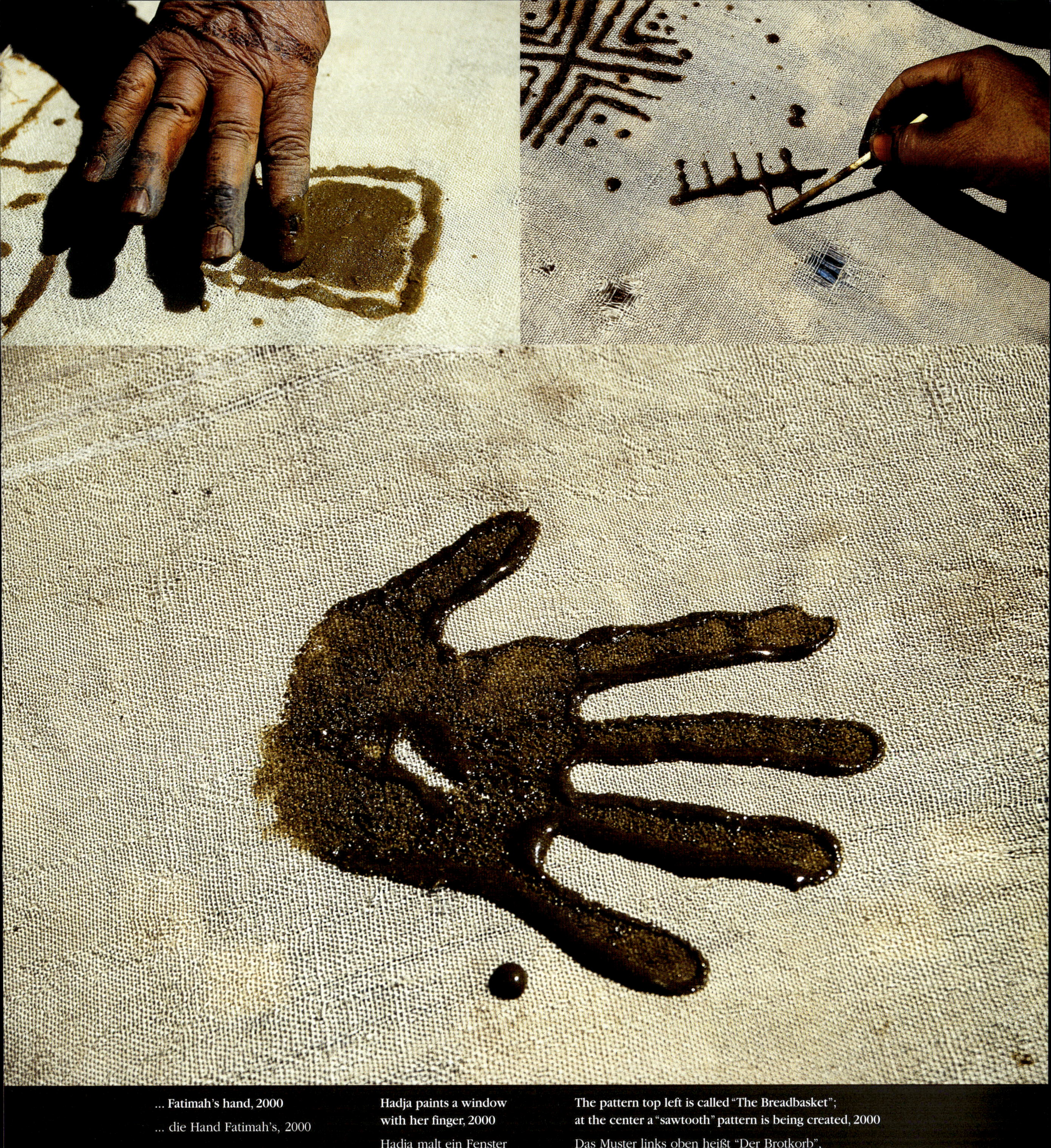

... Fatimah's hand, 2000

... die Hand Fatimah's, 2000

Hadja paints a window with her finger, 2000

Hadja malt ein Fenster mit dem Finger, 2000

The pattern top left is called "The Breadbasket"; at the center a "sawtooth" pattern is being created, 2000

Das Muster links oben heißt "Der Brotkorb", in der Bildmitte sind die "Zacken der Sichel" im Entstehen, 2000

Textiles from the Feija territory

In the follwing catalog the henna painted textiles of the Feija are arranged according to their place of origin. These weavings were documented on site in the makers' families and acquired there from them directly. Comparison with textiles made by their immediate neighbors, which are for the most part polychrome and executed in complex weaving and intricate techniques, shows how independently the Feija set about doing their henna paintings.

Jewish, Christian and Islamic symbols are encountered on some textiles. Both the Feija women and a *fqîh* invariably used motifs and symbols almost arbitrarily as long as they stood in some way for positive forces and energies. The original meanings of such motifs need not necessarily have been known to the weaver but use drew on the collective memory. Explanations of symbols and patterns, therefore, either derive from statements made by members of the indigenous population quoted in the following (and cited as such) or are based on the study by Edward Alexander Westermarck, *Ritual and Belief in Morocco*, London 1926.

In addition, the 1936 census is mentioned in several connections. The use of data from this census is based on the consideration that the census was carried out at about the same time as most of the textiles collected were made.

Together with the previous owners, we have been able to ascertain when the Feija pieces were made. Unless otherwise noted, the pieces presented here are in the editors' collection and the inventory numbers (Inv. no.) given refer to this collection.

Textilien aus dem Gebiet der Feija

Die hennabemalten Textilien der Feija sind im folgenden Katalogteil nach Herkunftsorten geordnet. Diese Gewebe wurden vor Ort bei den Familien der Hersteller dokumentiert und direkt erworben.

Vergleicht man sie mit Textilien benachbarter Chleuh-Stämme, deren Dekorationen überwiegend mehrfarbig und in komplizierten Web- und Wirktechniken ausgeführt sind, wird deutlich, wie eigenständig der Weg ist, den die Feija mit ihren Hennabemalungen gingen.

Verschiedentlich finden sich jüdische, christliche und islamische Symbole auf den Textilien. Sowohl die Feija-Frauen wie etwa auch ein *fqîh* verwendeten stets fast beliebige Motive und Symbole, solange sie nur in irgendeiner Art für positive Kraft und Energie stehen. Die ursprüngliche Bedeutung solcher Motive muss dem Anwender nicht zwingend bekannt gewesen sein, sondern wurde aus dem kollektiven Gedächtnis geschöpft. Für die Erklärung von Symbolen und Mustern werden daher im folgenden entweder Aussagen der einheimischen Bevölkerung zitiert (und als solche gekennzeichnet) oder es liegt die Studie *Ritual and Belief in Morocco*, London 1926, von Edward Alexander Westermarck zugrunde.

An mehreren Stellen ist außerdem die Volkszählung von 1936 erwähnt. Der Verwendung von Angaben aus dieser Volkszählung liegt die Überlegung zugrunde, dass diese in etwa zu der Zeit durchgeführt wurde, als auch die Mehrzahl der gesammelten Textilien hergestellt wurde.

Der Herstellungszeitpunkt der Feija-Stücke wurde gemeinsam mit den Vorbesitzern ermittelt. Wenn nichts anderes vermerkt ist, befinden sich die hier vorgestellten Stücke in der Sammlung der Herausgeber, auf die sich auch die angegebene Inventar-Nummer (Inv. no.) bezieht.

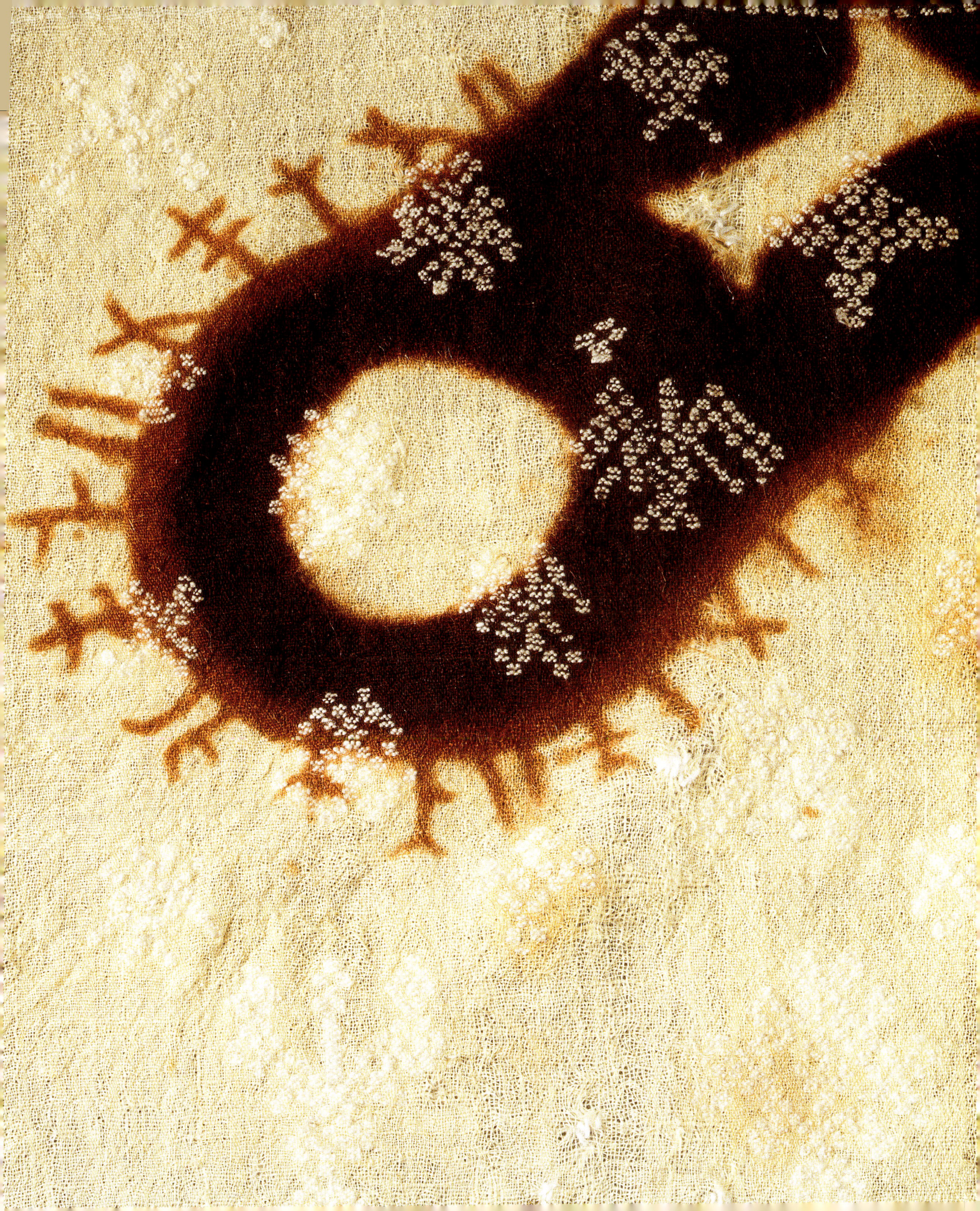

Aït Manesour

The 1936 census - incidentally, the first census taken in Morocco which is regarded as sufficiently accurate - assigns 488 Muslim inhabitants, distributed over three villages, to the Aït Manesour territory.

Coming from Akka Irhèn, one reaches Aït Manesour by going north on the *piste* (rough track) branching off from it. One then reaches a canyon-like valley which soon forks. At this almost magical place there are a great many Berber rock carvings, most of them dating from after 1000 BC. The Aït Manesour villages are deeper in the mountains in a beautiful setting. Even though they can only be reached by a rough track, at least one of these villages looks as if it were definitely receptive to modern civilization since there are quite few new buildings there. The other two villages, by contrast, are less accessible and have consequently retained their original character to quite an extent.

Aït Manesour

Die Volkszählung von 1936 – übrigens die erste Volkszählung in Marokko, die als hinreichend zuverlässig gilt – weist für die Fraktion von Aït Manesour 488 muslimische Einwohner aus, verteilt auf drei Dörfer.

Aït Manesour erreicht man von Akka Irhèn kommend, wenn man der östlich abzweigenden Piste nordwärts folgt. Man gelangt dann in ein canyonartiges Tal, welches sich bald gabelt. An dieser fast magisch wirkenden Stelle findet sich eine große Anzahl von Berber-Felsritzungen; die meisten sind wohl nach 1000 v.Chr. entstanden. Weiter in den Bergen liegen dann die Aït Manesour-Dörfer in reizvoller Landschaft. Wenn auch nur über eine Piste zu erreichen, scheint zumindest eines dieser Dörfer mit einer größeren Zahl von Neubauten durchaus an die moderne Zivilisation angeschlossen. Die beiden anderen Dörfer dagegen sind schwerer zugänglich und haben wohl daher ihren ursprünglichen Charakter einigermaßen bewahrt.

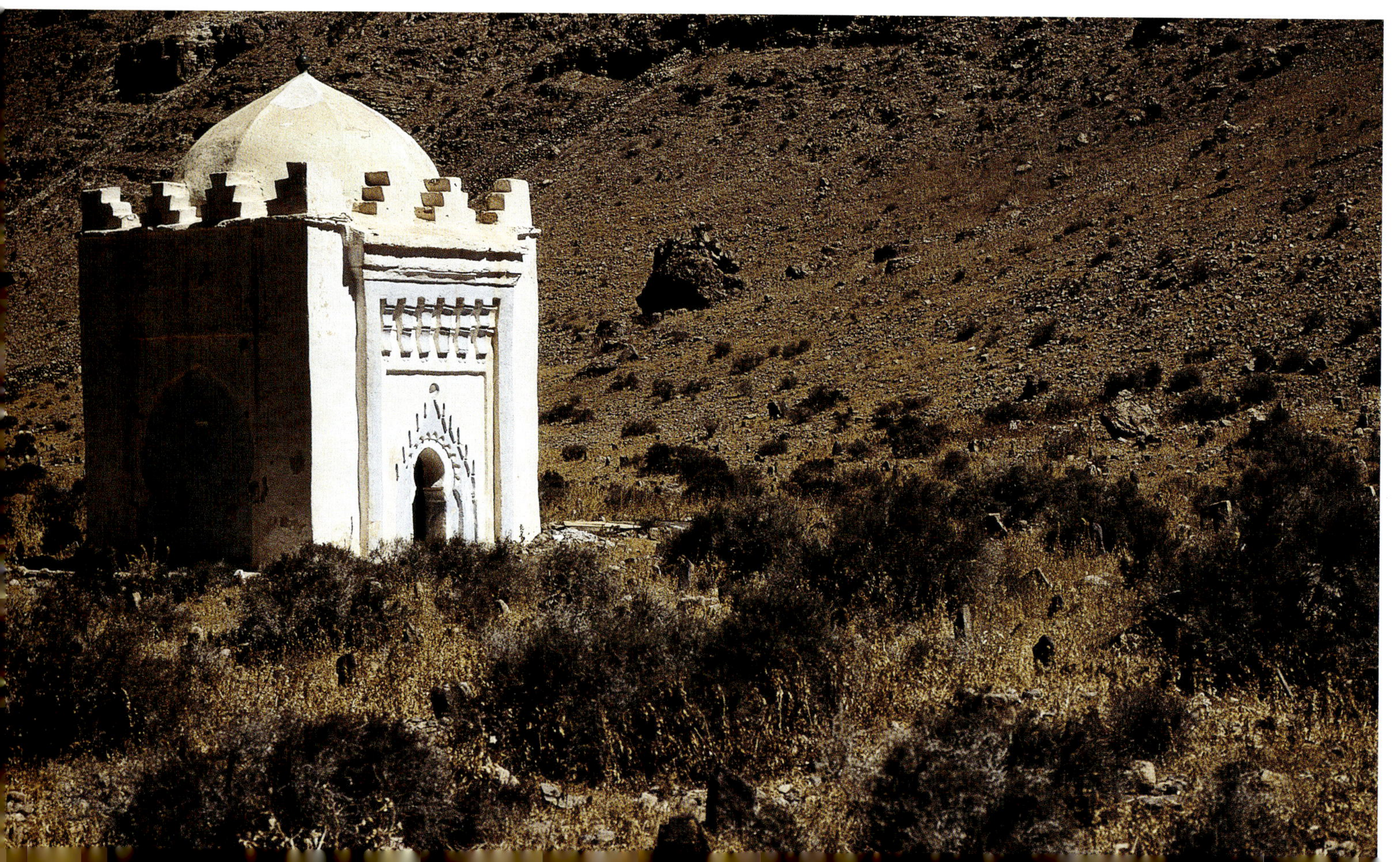

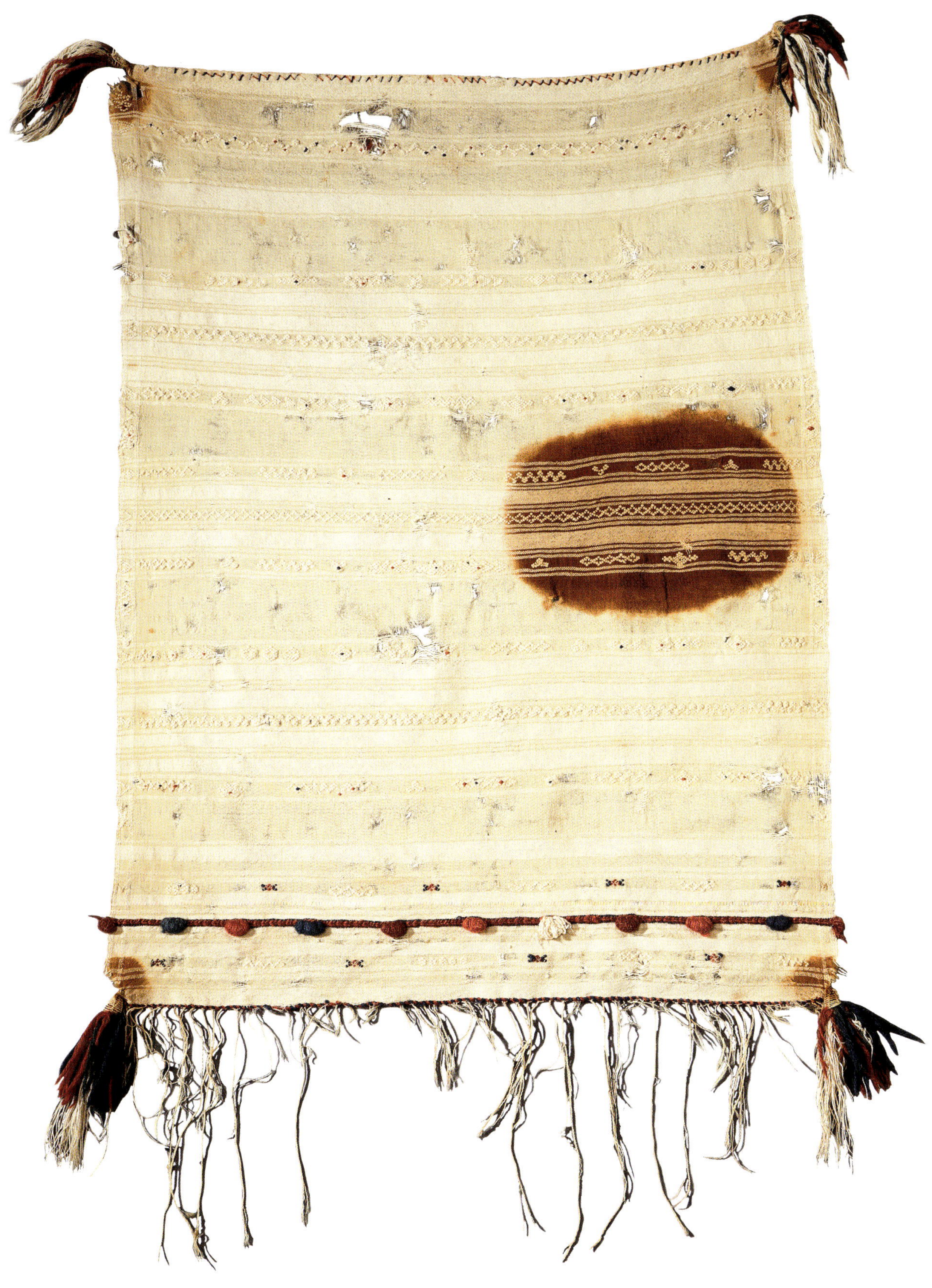

1 Adrar

Headscarf/Kopftuch, ca. 1920
Aït Manesour
100 x 60 cm, Inv. no. K 48

The henna oval recalls "The Prophet's Sandals" (cf. Cat. nos. 2 and 3). Similar pieces were encountered in Erkoune (see p. 92) and in Imi n'Tatelt (see p. 106).

Das Henna-Oval erinnert an die "Sandalen des Propheten" (vgl. Kat.-Nrn. 2 und 3). Ähnliche Stücke fanden sich auch in Erkoune (siehe S. 92) und in Imi n'Tatelt (siehe S. 106).

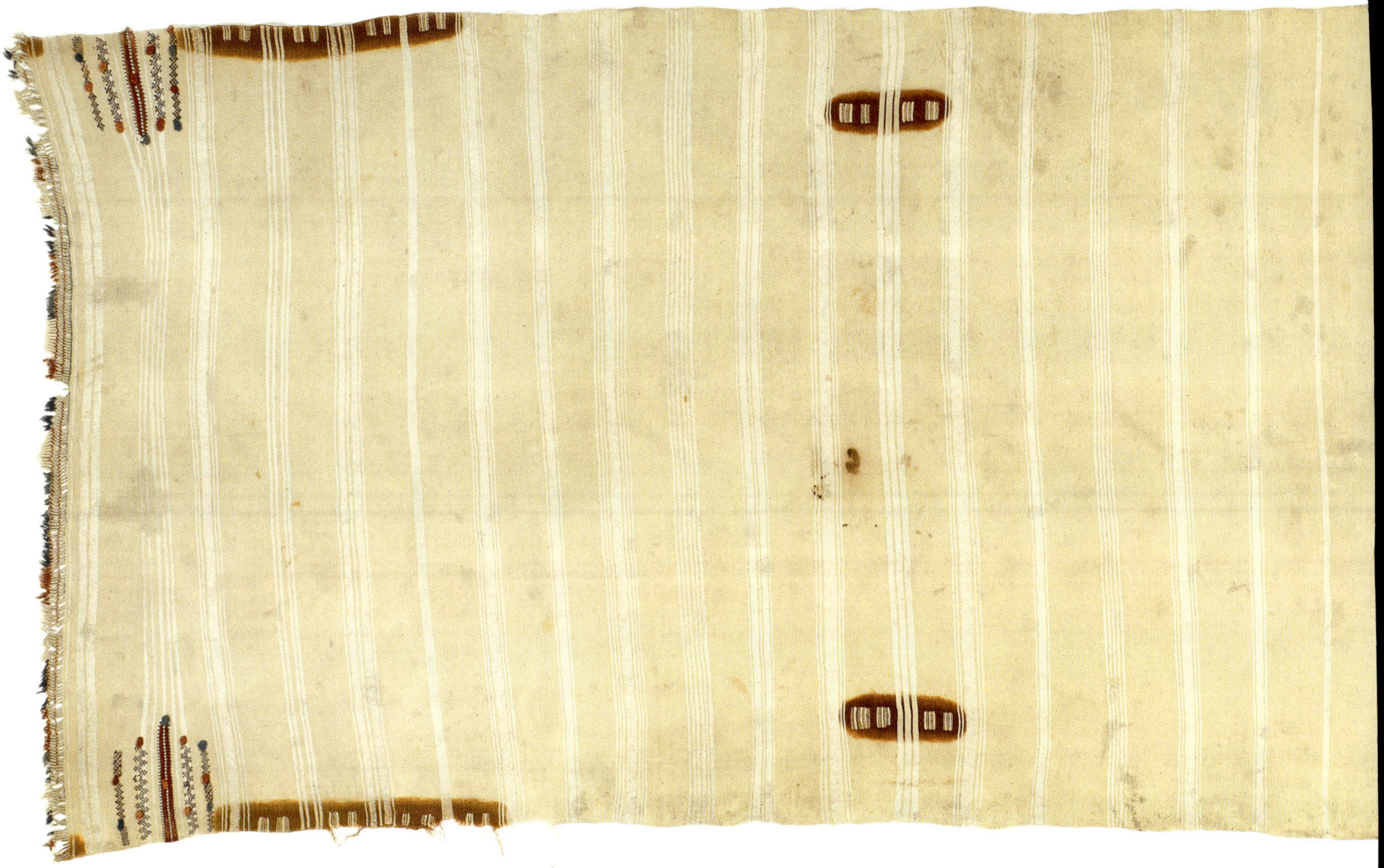

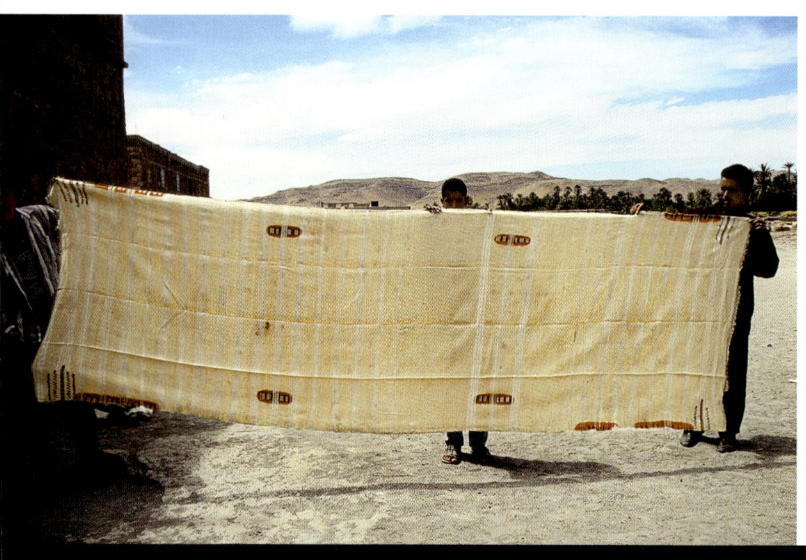

The maker was a Zenaga woman who was married in Aït Manesour. This explains deviations in the textile design from those Feija work: the number of white cotton weft threads is larger than usual; the corner motifs are polychrome and intricately brocaded and tapestry woven; the fringes are partly in color. The henna painting was designated by several of the persons questioned as "The Prophet's Sandals" (see on this "Tisfrioudine", p. 74).

Die Herstellerin war eine Zenaga-Frau, in Aït Manesour verheiratet. Dies erklärt Abweichungen in der Textilgestaltung im Vergleich zu denen der Feija: Die Zahl der weißen Baumwollschüsse ist größer als üblich; die Eckmotive sind mehrfarbig und in feiner Wirktechnik ausgeführt; die Fransen sind teilweise farbig. Die Hennabemalung wurde von mehreren dazu befragten Personen als "Sandalen des Propheten" bezeichnet (siehe hierzu "Tisfrioudine", S. 74).

Woman's wrapper *(haik)* Cat. no. 2, 2000

Wickeltuch *(haik)* Kat.-Nr. 2, 2000

2 Haik

Woman's wrapper/Wickeltuch, ca. 1930

Aït Manesour

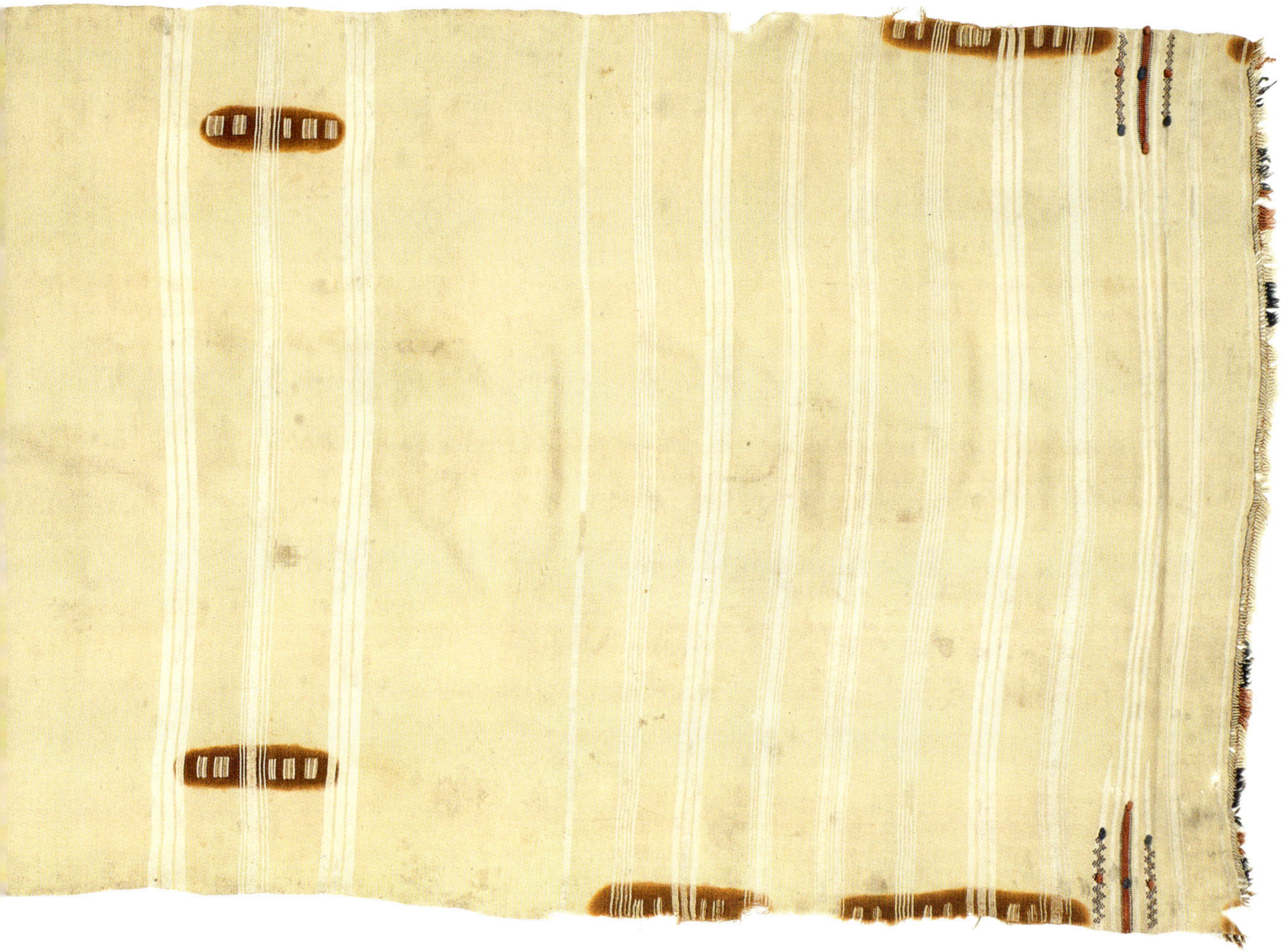

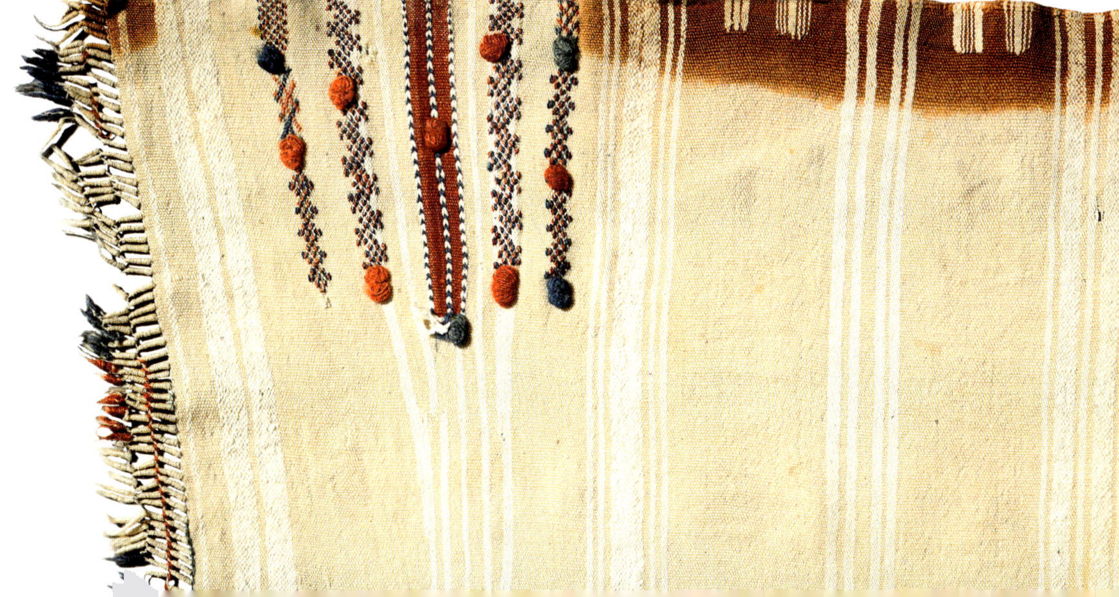

Tisfrioudine and Tisnassemine

One hour's walk distant from one another, the two villages are linked by a *piste* which crosses the Anti-Atlas from the north to run into the Feija territory. The 1936 census shows a population of 110 for Tisfrioudine and 163 for Tisnassemine, all Muslims.

Tisfrioudine, set in what is still hilly country, today comprises 72 households, which are made up of members of two main clans and their families. This amounts to a population of approx. 350. In the village there is a saint's tomb *(marabout)*; the saint venerated here is Sidi Boussalh. At the center of the village stands an impressive granary, an *agadir*, which is still partly in use.

Since we only found one example of the textiles dealt with here in Tisnassemine, we are discussing this village together with Tisfrioudine. The village of Tisnassemine is situated in the high plateau of the Feija territory. It comprises three Feija clans living in 82 households, amounting to a population of about 400. A large *agadir* is in a state of dilapidation.

Tisfrioudine und Tisnassemine

Die beiden Dörfer liegen ungefähr eine Wegstunde auseinander und sind durch eine Piste miteinander verbunden, die über den Anti-Atlas von Norden her in das Feija-Gebiet führt. Die Volkszählung von 1936 wies für Tisfrioudine 110, für Tisnassemine 163 Einwohner aus, allesamt Muslime.

Tisfrioudine, noch in den Hügeln gelegen, besteht heute aus 72 Haushaltungen, welche von zwei Hauptsippen und deren Familien bewohnt werden. Das entspricht etwa 350 Einwohnern. Im Ort befindet sich ein Heiligengrab *(marabout)*. Verehrt wird Sidi Boussalh. In der Dorfmitte steht ein imposanter Vorratsspeicher, ein *agadir*, der zum Teil heute noch in Gebrauch ist.

Da wir in Tisnassemine nur ein textiles Beispiel gefunden haben, behandeln wir das Dorf zusammen mit Tisfrioudine. Das Dorf Tisnassemine liegt in der Hochebene des Feija-Gebietes. Es umfasst drei Feija-Sippen in 82 Haushaltungen, was rund 400 Einwohnern entspricht. Ein großer *agadir* ist im Verfall begriffen.

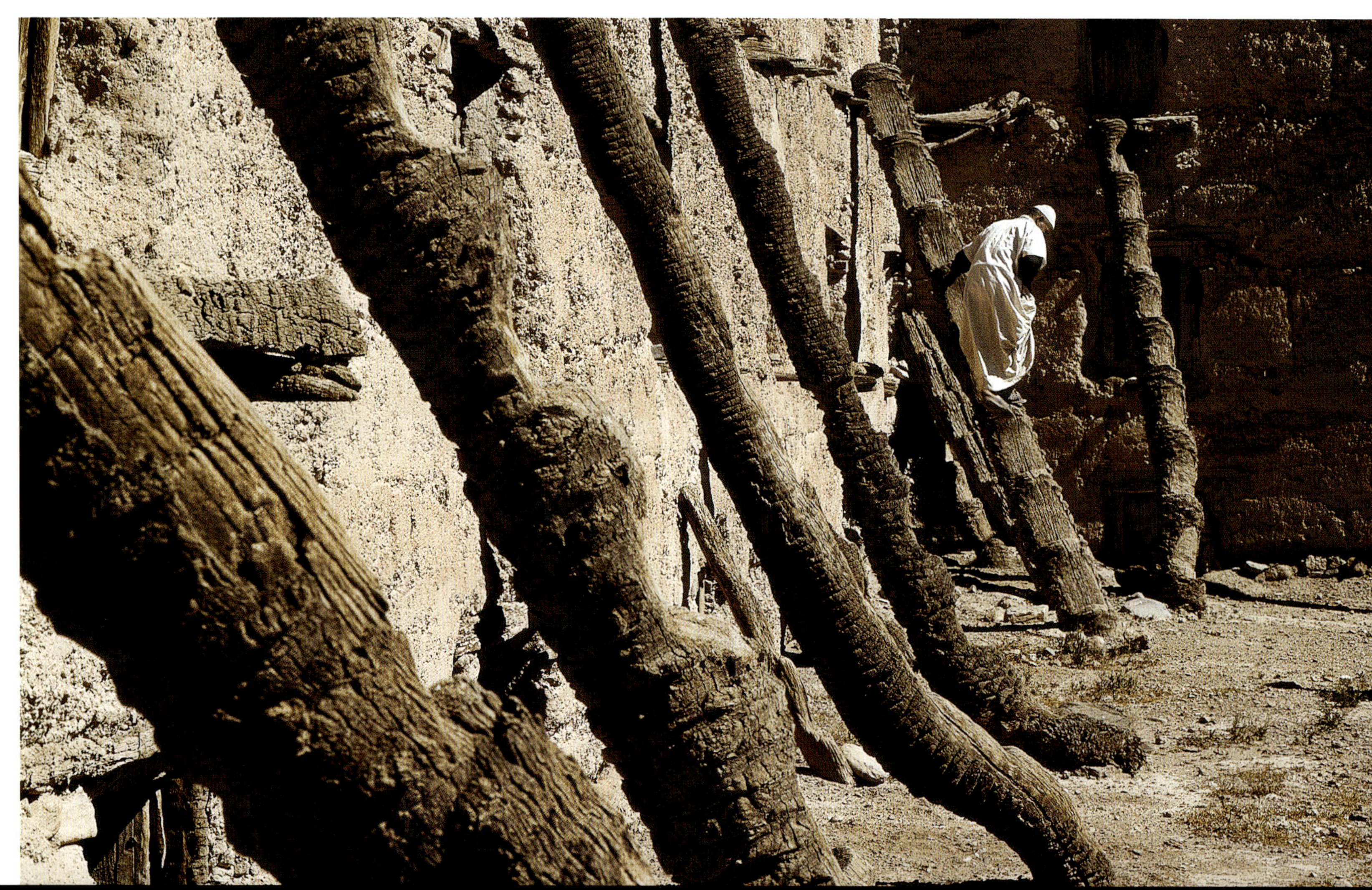

Befestigter Vorratsspeicher *(agadir)* in Tisnassemine, 2000

Fortified granary *(agadir)* in Tisnassemine, 2000

We were able to document *haiks* which contained motifs called "The Prophet's Sandals" by the Feija (cf. also Cat. no. 2). Jean Gabus notes on this motif: "The sandal motif is widespread among several Tuareg tribes on women's provision sacks. Among the Oullemmeden, a Tuareg *chorfa* caste, it is explicitly designated 'Les sandales du Prophète'. Rock carvings with this motif at various places in the Hoggar and near Tit bear witness to pre-Islamic times (Sahara Neolithic). The tombs in a necropolis in the Hoggar are sandal-shaped and bear the motif in the form of incisions." [1]

Uwe Topper adds on the Islamic context of the sandal motif: "A command issued by God in the Koran (Sura 20, verse 12) reads as follows: 'Verily I am thy Lord, therefore remove thy sandals! Verily art thou in the holy vale of Tuwa.' The tone of the exhortation has pleasant associations, for the request that one remove one's sandals means a gesture of welcome to Arabs, just as one might say to a guest: 'Sit down and make yourself at home! 'The figurative meaning of removing one's sandals is laying aside cares, especially cares about one's family and children." [2]

Moreover, the Feija tell the following story: among them something has persisted to the present day which is called "babouches peace". After negotiations have been satisfactorily concluded, men deliberately take off one of their own shoes and one of their opponent's. Amid the general laughter, the babouches are returned to their rightful owners and the men who have made peace with each other say: "Now I am on a good footing with you again."

Wir konnten Wickeltücher dokumentieren, deren Motive von den Feija als "Sandalen des Propheten" bezeichnet wurden (vgl. auch Kat.-Nr. 2). Jean Gabus schreibt über dieses Motiv: "Das Sandalenmotiv ist bei verschiedenen Tuareg-Stämmen auf Vorratssäcken der Frauen verbreitet. Bei den Oullemmeden, einer *chorfa*-Kaste der Tuareg, heißen sie ausdrücklich 'Les sandales du Prophète'. Zeugnis aus vorislamischer Zeit (Sahara-Neolithikum) sind Felsgravuren mit dem Motiv an verschiedenen Orten im Hoggar und bei Tit. Die Gräber eines Grabfeldes im Hoggar sind in Sandalenform gestaltet und tragen das Motiv in Form von Gravuren." [1]

Uwe Topper ergänzt zum islamischen Kontext des Sandalen-Motivs: "Im Koran (Sure 20, Vers 12) klingt ein Befehl Gottes so: 'Wahrlich, Ich bin dein Herr, darum zieh deine Sandalen aus! Wahrlich, du bist im heiligen Tale Tuwa.' Diese Anrede ist freundlich gestimmt, denn die Aufforderung zum Sandalenausziehen bedeutet dem Araber eine Geste des Willkommens, so wie man zu einem Gast sagt: 'Bleib hier und mach es dir bequem!' Die übertragene Bedeutung des Sandalenausziehens ist das Ablegen der Sorgen, besonders der Sorgen um die Familie und die Kinder." [2]

Die Feija erzählen außerdem folgende Geschichte: Bei ihnen gibt es bis auf den heutigen Tag den so genannten "Babouchen-Frieden". Nach Abschluss einer erfolgreichen Verhandlung ziehen die Männer absichtlich je einen eigenen und einen Schuh des Kontrahenten an. Unter Gelächter gibt man sich danach die richtigen Babouchen zurück und sagt dazu: "Jetzt stehe ich wieder auf gutem Fuße mit Dir."

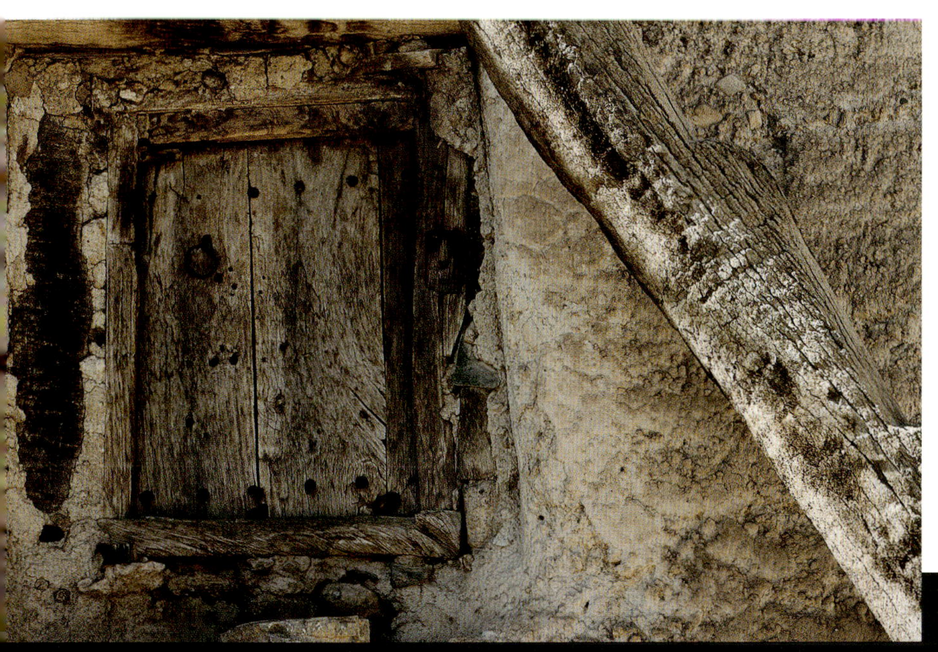

Door to the Tisnassemine *agadir*, 2000

Tür zu einer Vorratskammer im *agadir* Tisnassemine, 2000

1 Gabus 1982, p. 452.
2 Topper 1984/1991, p. 9.

1 Gabus 1982, S. 452.
2 Topper 1984/1991, S. 9.

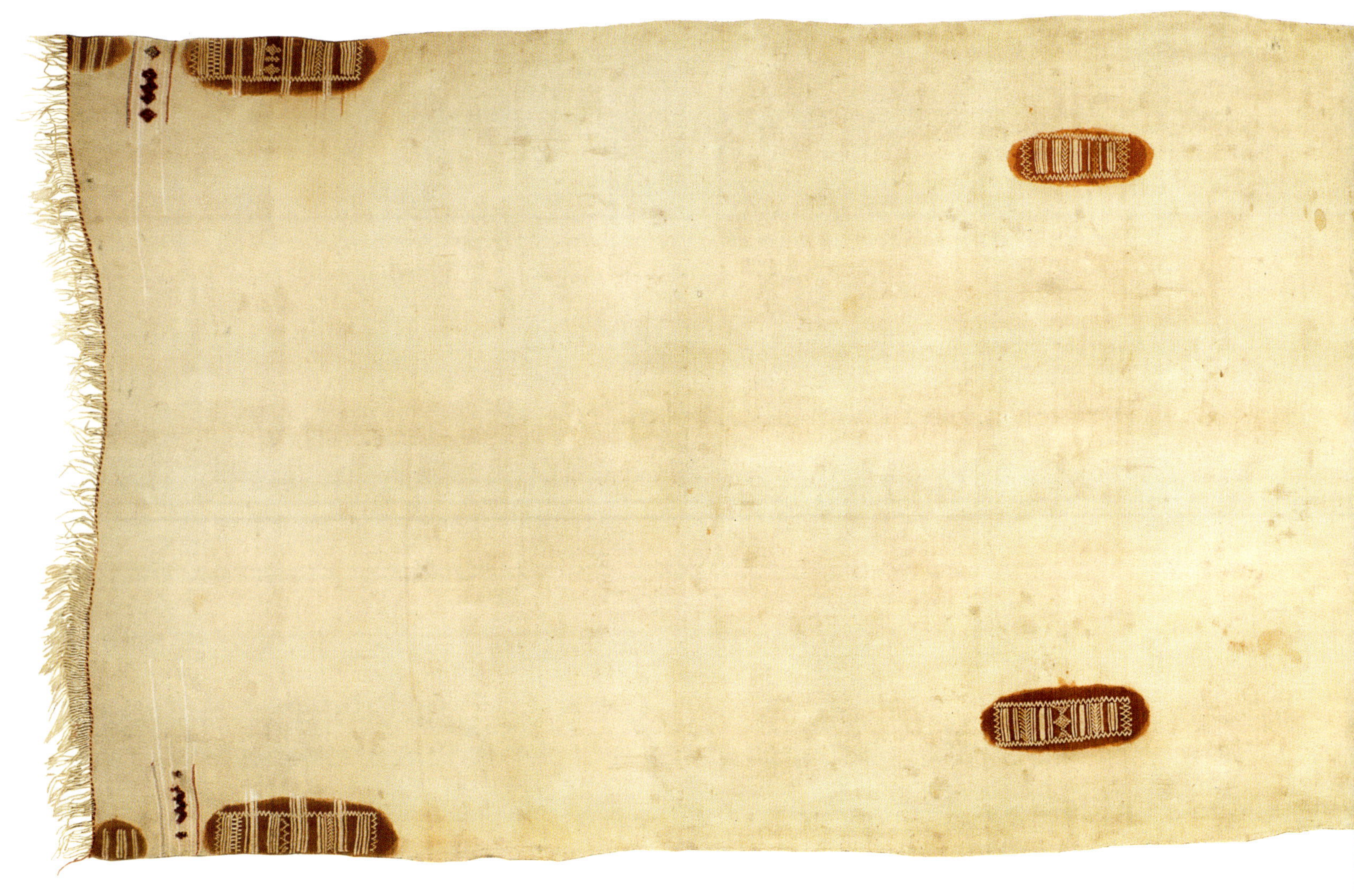

3 Haik

Woman's wrapper/Wickeltuch, ca. 1920-1930
Tisfrioudine
415 x 127 cm, Inv. no. K 129

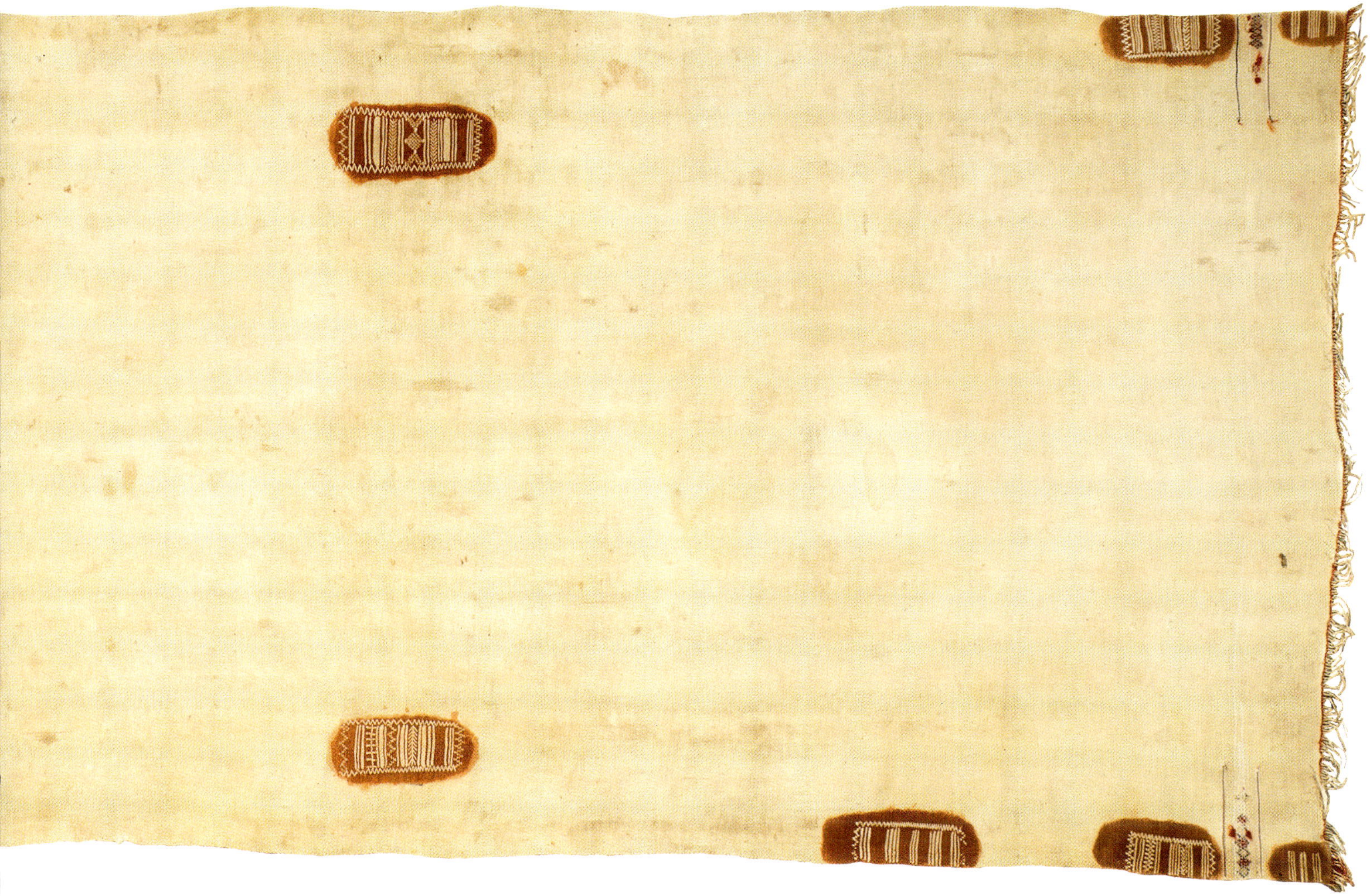

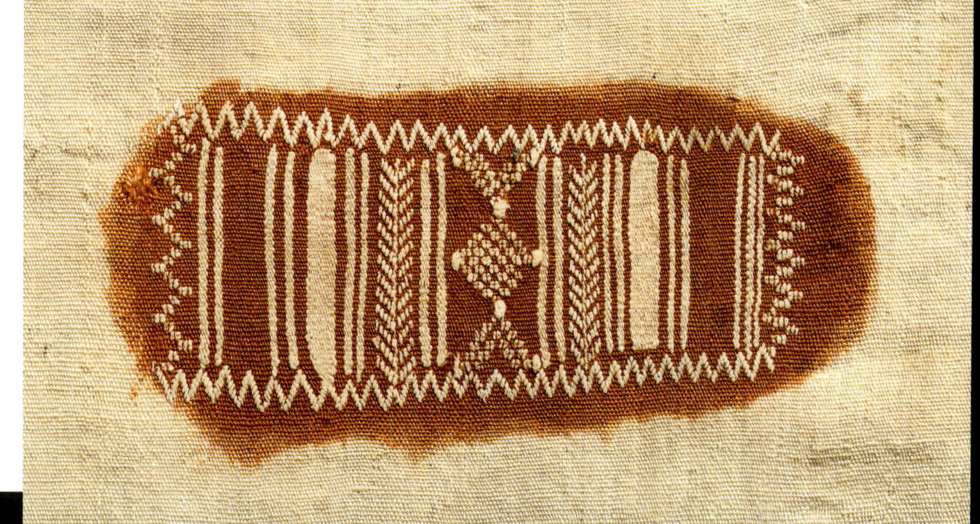

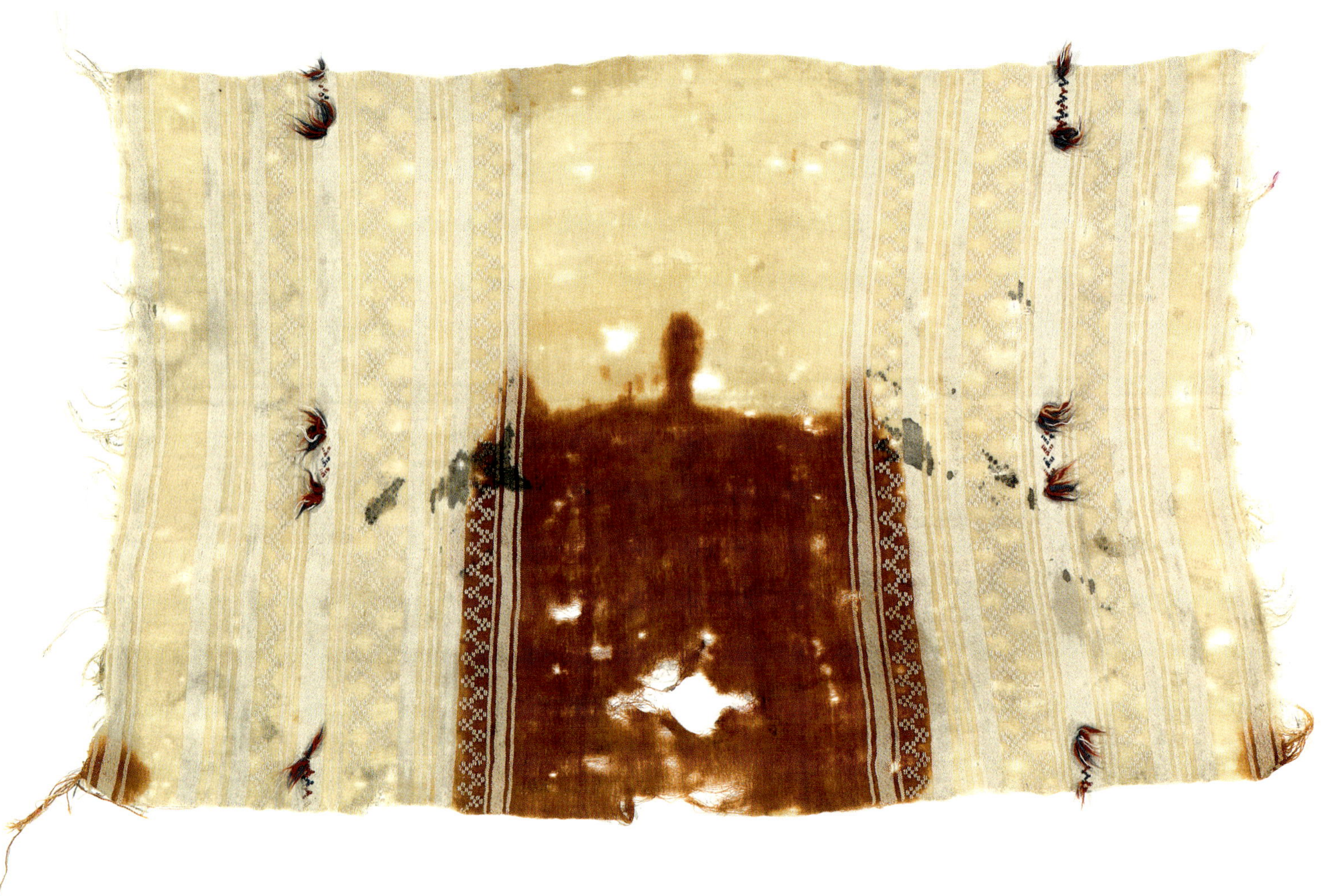

One of the most common motifs in the Feija territory is called *tismissine* and is perhaps the representation of a building (see also Cat. no. 15). However, the motif is worn by Sektana or even possibly also Zenaga women rather than Feija women. Additional tapestry woven pattern bands in white cotton into the earlier piece (Cat. no. 4); repeated applications of henna have the effect of biting, which is apparent here.

Eines der gebräuchlichsten Motive im Feija-Gebiet wird *tismissine* genannt, vielleicht die Repräsentation eines Gebäudes (siehe auch Kat. Nr. 15). Das Motiv wird jedoch nicht von Feija- sondern von Sektana- oder eventuell auch Zenaga-Frauen getragen. Im älteren Stück (Kat.-Nr. 4) sind zusätzliche Musterstreifen in weißer Baumwolle gewirkt; wiederholter Henna-Auftrag wirkt ätzend, wie hier sichtbar wird.

4 Adrar

Headscarf/Kopftuch, ca. 1900-1920
Tisfrioudine
104 x 63 cm, Inv. no. K 135

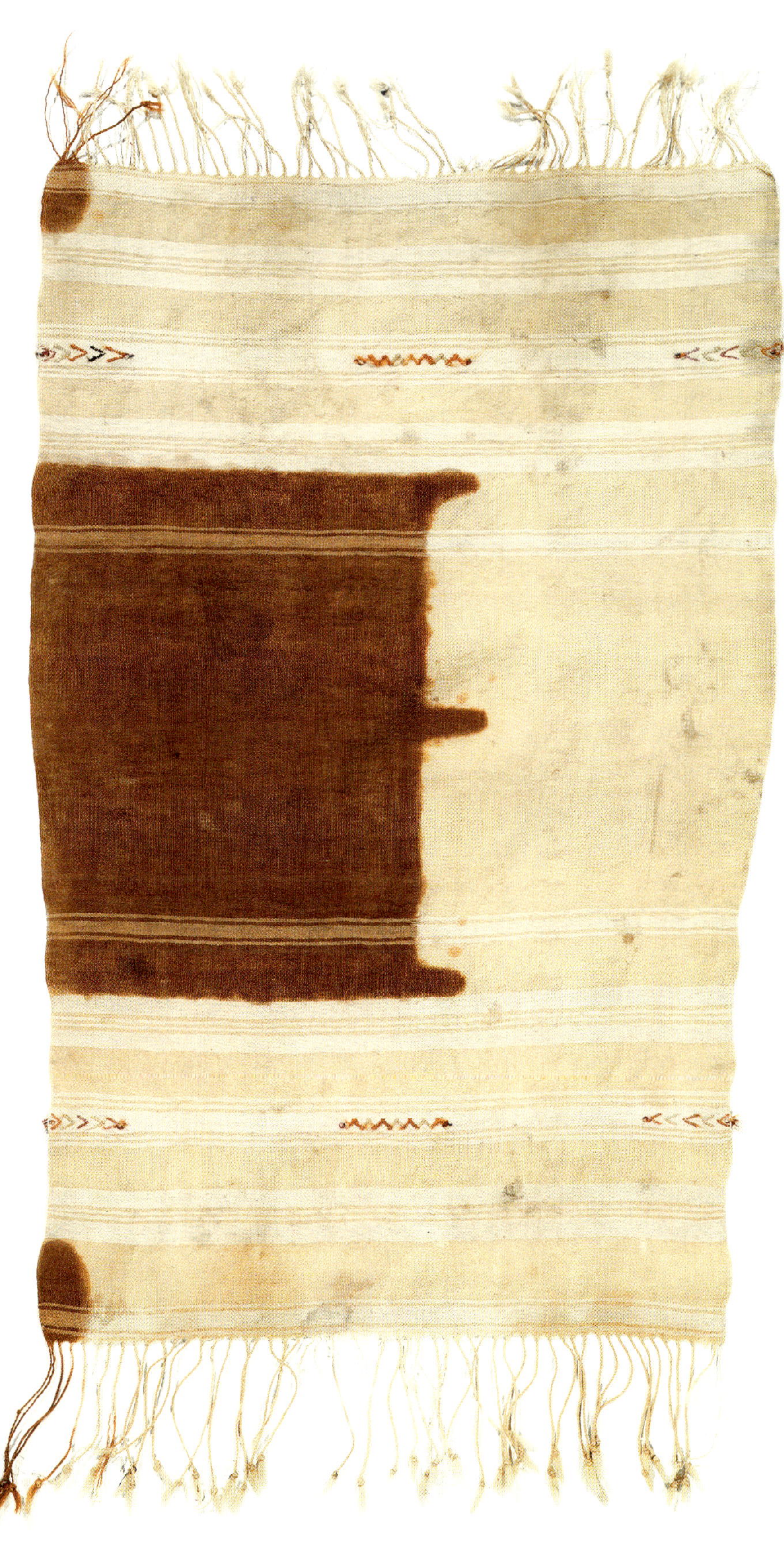

5 Adrar

Headscarf / Kopftuch, ca. 1940
Tisnassemine
110 x 60 cm, Inv. no. K 199

Iligh and Afouzar

This is a dual community with an old and a new section of the village. The 1936 census records a Muslim population of 462 for Iligh. The name of the village is supposed to mean "mouth", which suggests the presence of a spring.

Two Jewish clans are said to have lived in Iligh - locals persist in claiming that there was a Jewish community *(mellah)* here until 1956, with an active silversmith's workshop.[3] The painting on some of the textiles we have recorded was attributed to Jewish women. These statements, however, contradict both the evidence furnished by the census and the account provided by the Marquis de Segonzac, who traveled through the region in 1904. On the spot no traces could be found of a Jewish population (usually Jewish cemeteries at least would have be preserved).

"Afouzar" probably means "figs". It is a village of fairly recent date without any striking features except for its quite extensive and well-tended palmeries. Five clans live in Afouzar at 33 "hearths", which corresponds to a population of about 160. Near Afouzar, as far as we could ascertain, there used to be about five inhabited fortified Berber villages *(kasbahs)*, all of which have vanished. The 1936 census in fact records a considerably larger number of inhabited villages than can be found now.

Iligh und Afouzar

Es handelt sich um eine Doppelgemeinde mit einem alten und einem neueren Dorfteil. In der Volkszählung von 1936 sind für Iligh 462 muslimische Einwohner verzeichnet. Der Dorfname soll "Mund" bedeuten, was auf das Vorhandensein einer Quelle hinweist.

In Iligh sollen zwei Sippen jüdischen Glaubens ansässig gewesen sein – Einheimische beharren darauf, dass es hier bis 1956 eine jüdische Gemeinde *(mellah)* gegeben habe, in der eine Silberschmiede betrieben worden sei.[3] Bei einigen der von uns dokumentierten Textilien wurden deren Bemalungen jüdischen Frauen zugeschrieben. Die Aussagen widersprechen jenen der Volkszählung sowie dem Bericht von Marquis de Segonzac, welcher 1904 die Region bereiste. Vor Ort ließen sich keine Spuren jüdischer Bewohner finden (gewöhnlich erhalten sich zumindest die Friedhöfe).

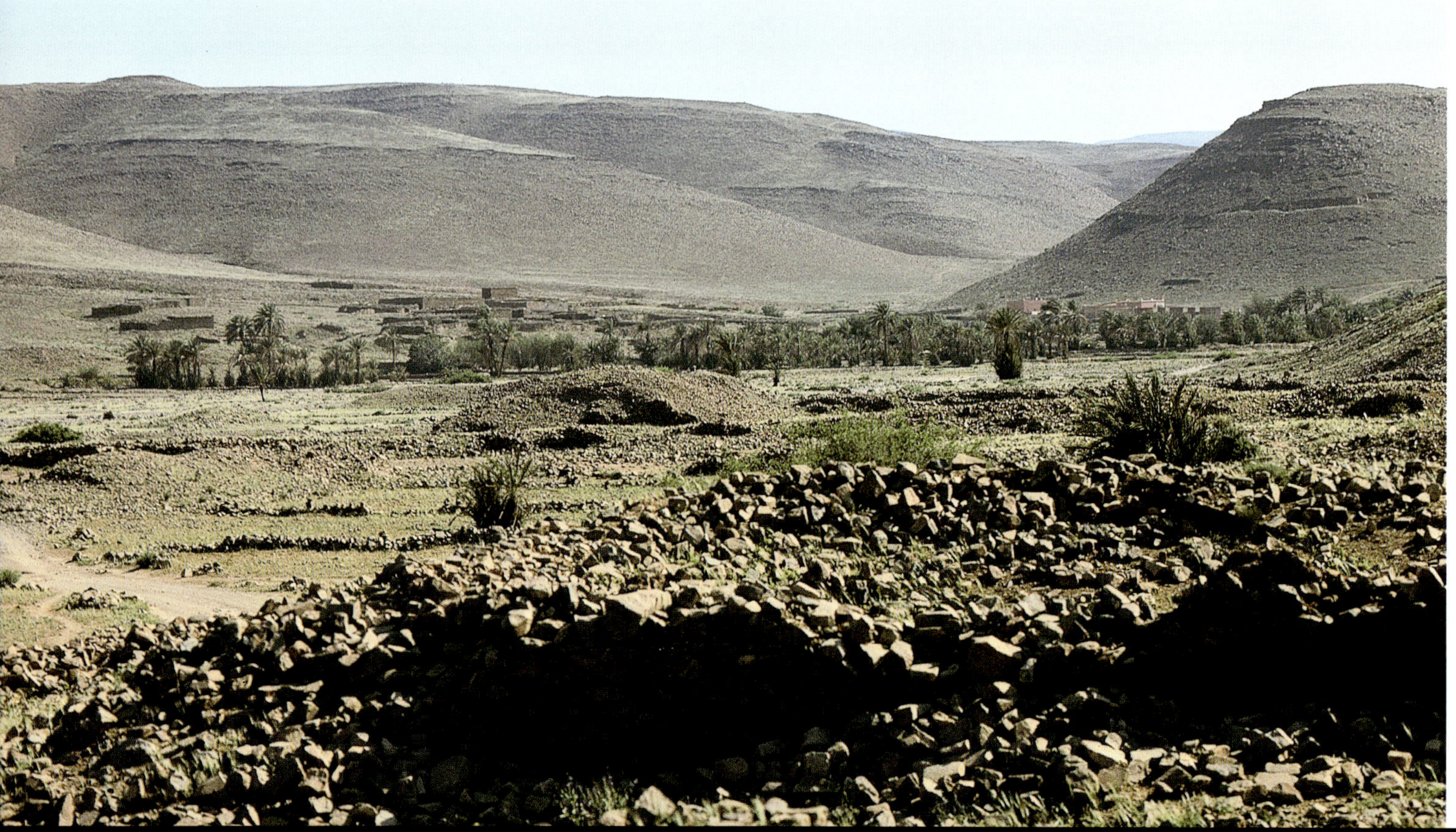

The village of Iligh. In the foreground ruined houses, supposedly a Jewish community *(mellah)*, 1998

Das Dorf Iligh. Im Vordergrund zerfallene Häuser einer angeblich jüdischen Gemeinde *(mehllah)*, 1998

At Iligh and Afouzar we first encountered a motif, of which there subsequently proved to be a high incidence, called by the locals *bouitri*. This is the typical Feija motif (cf. Cat. no. 6); however, it only occurred on headscarves *(adrar)* and this was equally true of other villages in the region. We were told two names for this motif: *bab* (gate) and *bouitri*. The Feija motif used here is simpler and more abstract than the *chorfa* version (cf. Cat. nos. 22-24); it may even occur as a mere sketchy figuration and the Feija representations of the moon are usually less clear.

The following features are typical of this *bouitri* type of headscarf: first, the motif is not centered; its two columns are at the beginning of the weaving and frequently on a baseline, which extends to the selvedge. Second, small signs in henna usually supplement the picture at the ends of a weaving. These signs looked like script to us and indeed they tally with characters in the *tifinagh* alphabet. Further, other distinctive features of these headscarves include several white cotton bands in cotton at the beginning and at the end there is a border with a tapestry woven pattern band in cotton. Finally, integral elements are a narrow red or purple stripe as well as colored individual knots in wool or silk. A cord and fringes finish off the weaving. The four corners are frequently embellished with tassels of colored or henna-dyed wool. The Feija headscarf is always an elongated rectangle.

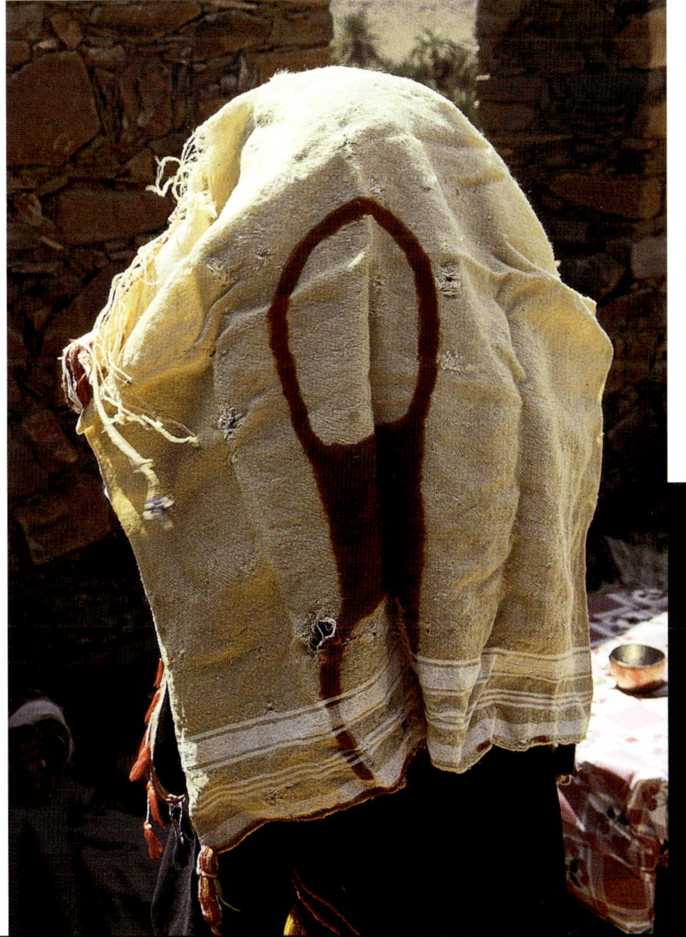

Afouzar bedeutet wahrscheinlich "Feigen". Es ist ein neueres Dorf ohne augenfällige Besonderheiten, wenn man von den recht ausgedehnten und bewirtschafteten Palmengärten absieht. Es leben fünf Sippen in 33 "Feuern" von Afouzar, was etwa 160 Personen entspricht. Unweit von Afouzar haben sich dem Vernehmen nach etwa fünf bewohnte Berberburgen *(kasbahs)* befunden, die allesamt verschwunden sind. Überhaupt weist die Volkszählung von 1936 eine ungleich größere Zahl bewohnter Dörfer aus, als heute vorzufinden sind.

In Iligh und Afouzar stießen wir zum ersten Mal, und dann gehäuft, auf ein Motiv, welches von der Bevölkerung als *bouitri* bezeichnet wurde. Es ist das typische Feija-Motiv (vgl. Kat.-Nr. 6); allerdings fand es sich nur auf den Kopftüchern *(adrar)*, auch in weiteren Dörfern der Region. Für das Motiv wurde außerdem die Bezeichnung *bab* (Tor) genannt. Das hier verwendete Feijamotiv ist gegenüber der *chorfa*-Version (vgl. Kat.-Nrn. 22-24) einfacher und stärker abstrahiert, eventuell auch auf ein Rumpfgebilde reduziert, und die Mond-Darstellungen sind bei den Feija meist weniger deutlich.

Merkmale dieses *bouitri*-Kopftuchtypus sind: Das Motiv ist nicht zentriert; seine beiden Säulen stehen am Anfang des Gewebes und häufig auf einer Basislinie, die an die Kante gerückt ist. Meistens wird das Bild durch kleine Hennazeichen an den Gewebeenden ergänzt. Uns erschienen diese Zeichen schriftartig, und tatsächlich haben sie im *tifinagh*-Alphabet Entsprechungen. Weiter gehören zu den Merkmalen dieser Kopftücher mehrere weiße Baumwollstreifen am Anfang und zum Ende hin eine Reihe mit einem Musterstreifen, in Baumwolle gewirkt. Schließlich sind ein schmaler, roter oder violetter Farbstreifen sowie farbige Einzelknoten aus Wolle oder Seide feste Bestandteile. Eine farbige Abschlusskordel und Fransen bilden das Ende des Gewebes. Häufig sind die vier Ecken mit Quasten aus farbiger oder mit Henna gefärbter Wolle verziert. Das Kopftuch der Feija ist immer länglich.

3 The name of the village of Iligh is said to be a generic name for Jewish villages. The Iligh situated near the city of Tiznit also had a Jewish population (Mann 2000). However, evidence that Jews lived among the Feija is lacking (see p. 35).

3 Der Dorfname Iligh soll grundsätzlich ein Name für jüdische Dörfer sein. Das nahe der Stadt Tiznit gelegene Iligh jedenfalls hatte jüdische Einwohner (Mann 2000). Beweise, dass Menschen jüdischen Glaubens bei den Feija ansässig waren, fehlen aber (siehe S. 35).

Headscarf for everyday wear *(adrar)* with gate *(bab)* or *bouitri* motif, 2000

Alltagskopftuch *(adrar)* mit Tor-*(bab-)* oder *bouitri*-Motiv, 2000

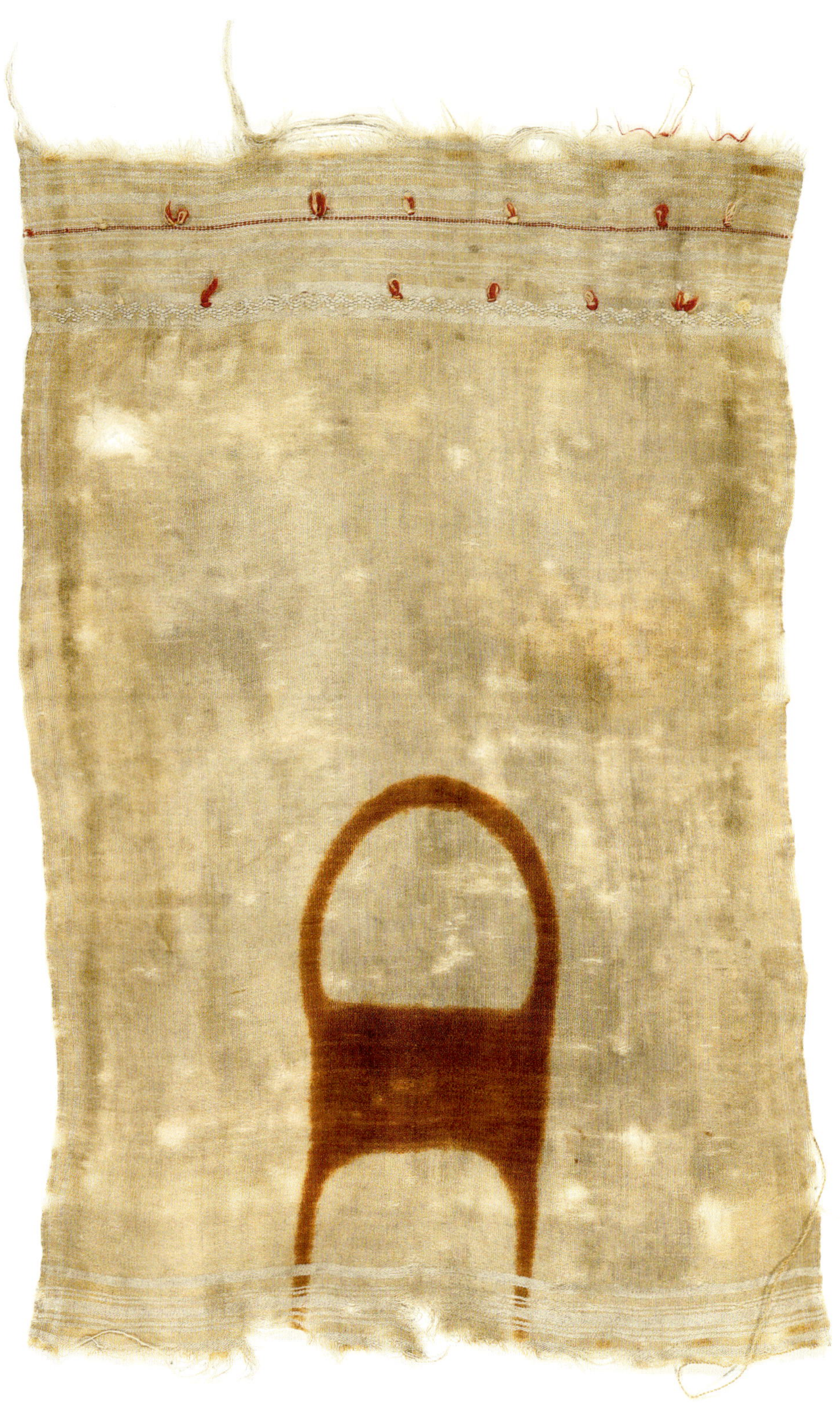

This headscarf originally belonged to the grandmother of the previous owner, who was about 90 years old in 1998.

Das Kopftuch gehörte ursprünglich der Großmutter der letzten Besitzerin, die ihrerseits 1998 etwa 90 Jahre alt war.

6 Adrar

Headscarf/Kopftuch, ca. 1890
Iligh

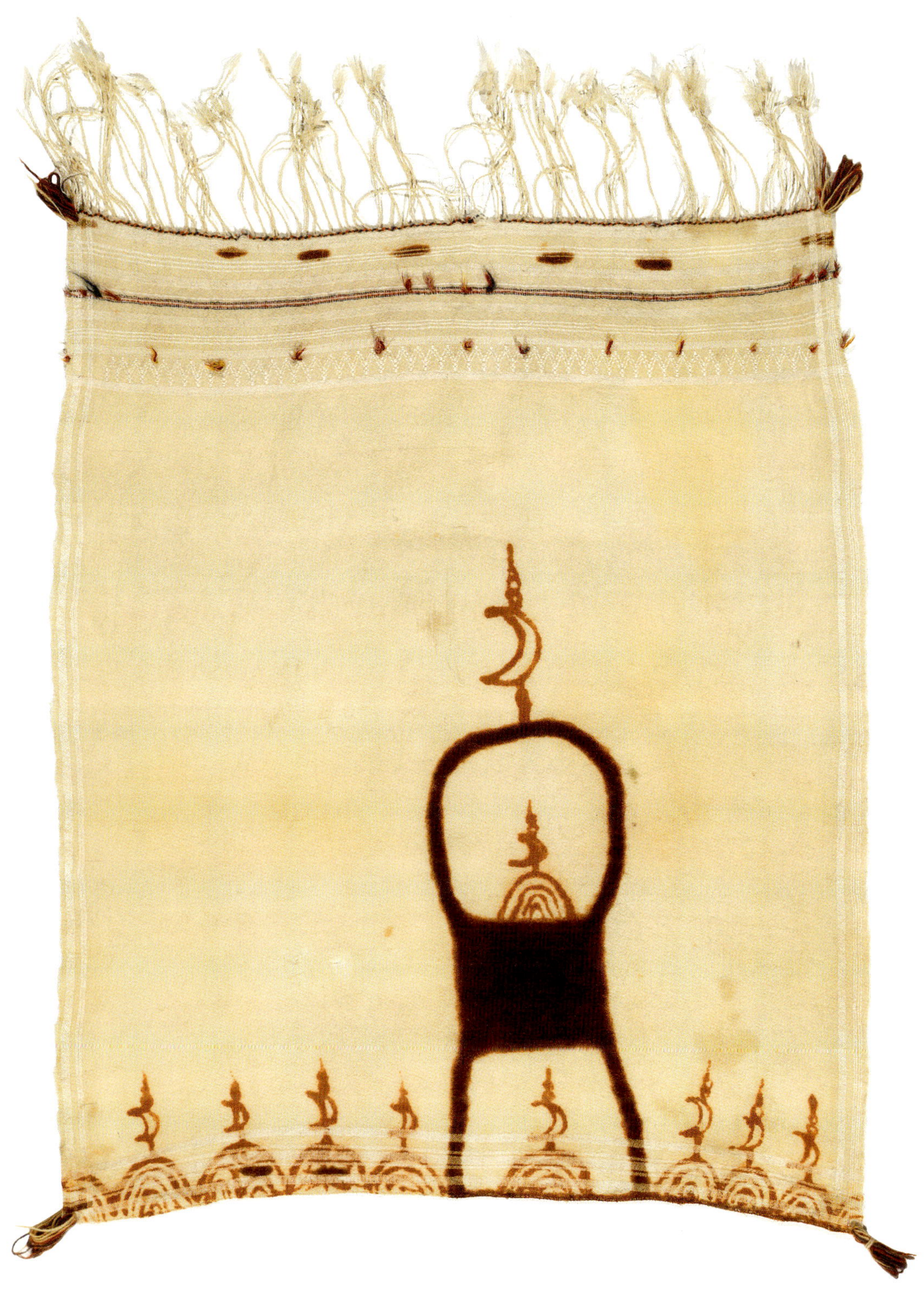

A headscarf for everyday wear was turned into a wedding *adrar* by the addition of henna-painted decorations. Chains of dome-like motifs were added to the *bouitri* main motif. They are each surmounted by a half moon, probably to represent the minaret of a mosque. Feija women, however, said that these were representations of mounds *(tumuli)* or wheat sheaves. When practically ordered in rows, they form a "path through a garden". In addition, the *bab* motif was painted over several times with henna, which amounts to an enhancement of *baraka*.

Durch nachträglich aufgemalte Hennadekorationen wurde aus einem Alltagskopftuch ein Hochzeits-*adrar*. Dem *bouitri*-Hauptmotiv wurden Ketten kuppelartiger Motive zugefügt. Sie sind von je einem Halbmond gekrönt, was wohl das Minarett einer Moschee darstellt. Laut Aussagen der Feija-Frauen sind es jedoch Erdhügel oder Korngarben. Aneinander gereiht ergibt sich ein "Weg durch die Gärten". Außerdem wurde das *bab*-Motiv mehrmals mit Henna übermalt, was einer *baraka*-Anreicherung gleichkommt.

7 **Adrar**

Headscarf/Kopftuch, ca. 1920
Afouzar-Iligh
120 x 80 cm
Inv. no. K 178

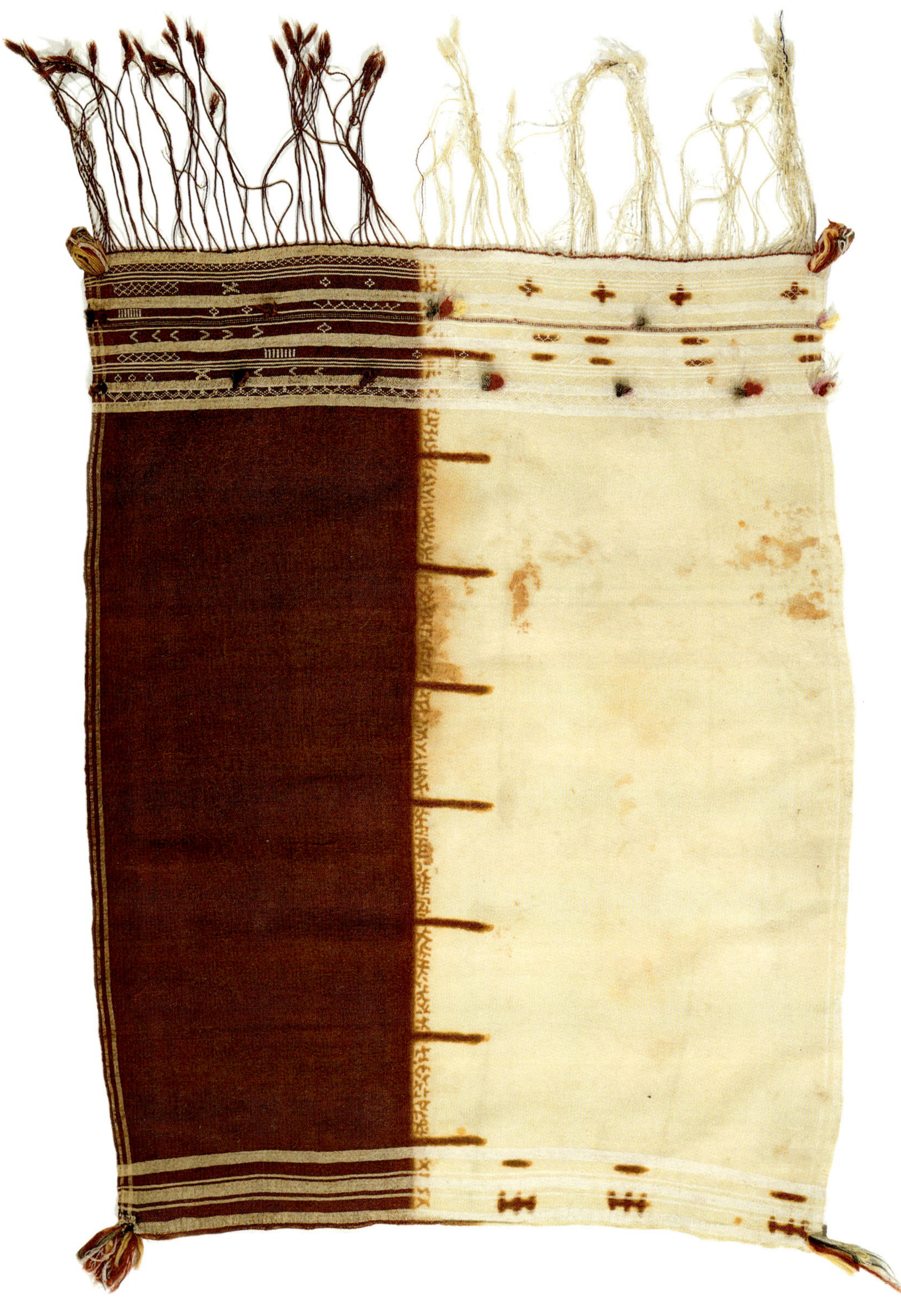

Yet another type of headscarf, technically identical in weave with Cat. no. 7, boasts henna painting which divides the weaving longitudinally yet not in the middle. This is a second Feija motif, known as "henna morte" *(tarioualte)*. The small tifinagh characters recall those of the *bouitri* type. Each of the patterns woven in white cotton has a name.

Ein weiterer Kopftuchtypus mit identischer Gewebestruktur wie bei Kat.-Nr. 7 hat eine Hennabemalung, welche das Gewebe zwar längs, jedoch nicht in der Mitte teilt. Es handelt sich um ein zweites Motiv der Feija, "Henna morte" *(tarioualte)* genannt. Die kleinen *tifinagh*-Zeichen erinnern an die des *bouitri*-Typus. Die weiß in Baumwolle gewirkten Muster haben jeweils eigene Bezeichnungen.

8 Adrar

Headscarf/Kopftuch, ca. 1930
Afouzar-Iligh
Fatimah Oumssri, b. 1930 (previous owner/Vorbesitzerin)
97 x 75 cm, Inv. no. K 202
Technical analysis/Strukturanalyse, p. 138

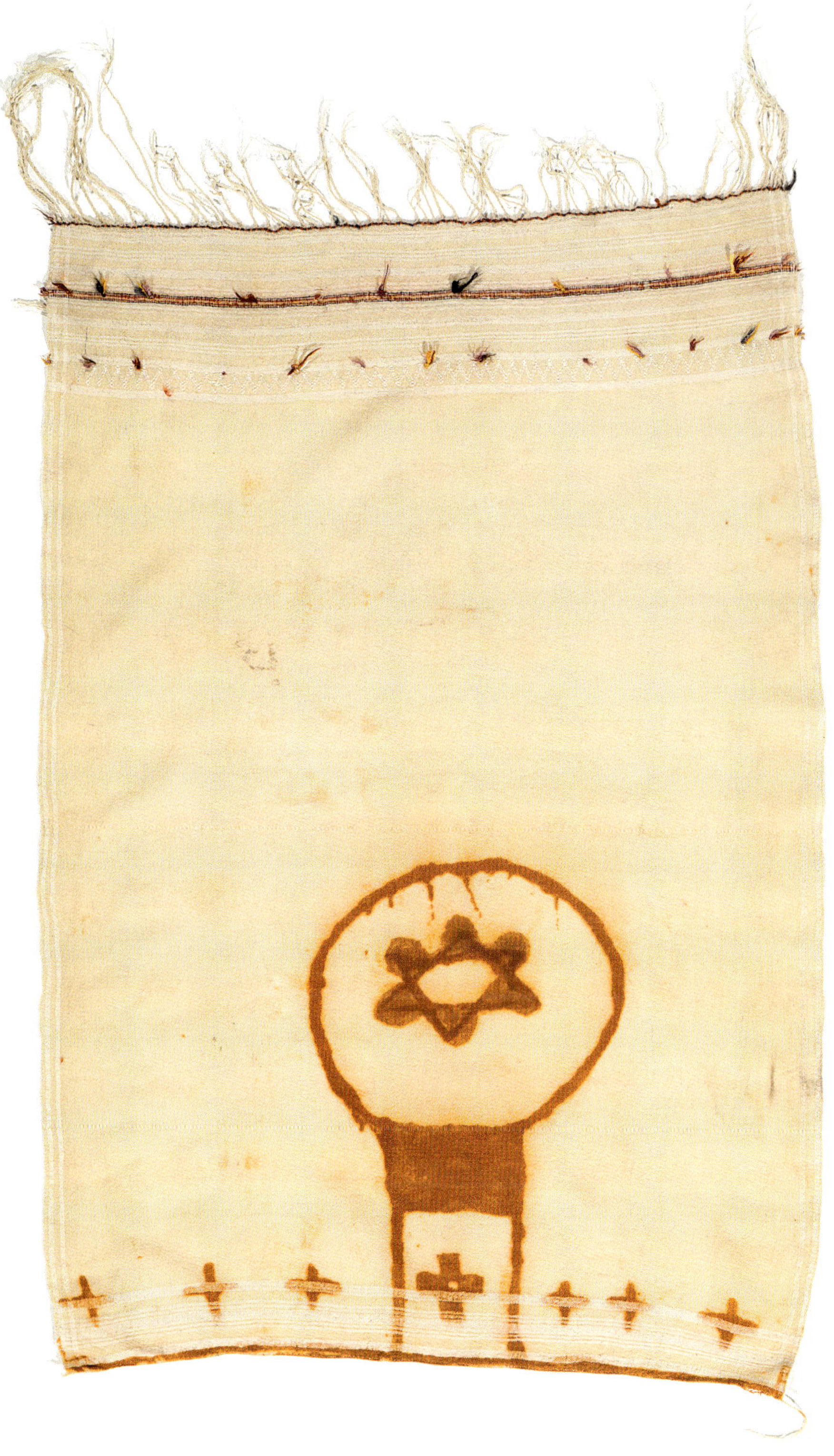

From the outset the painting was for nuptial purposes. The star of David looks almost like a flower in its circle. The cruciform motifs are probably *tifinagh* characters. The cross in the lower zone of the motif also represents the lucky number five (four arms and an eye at the center).

Die Bemalung erfolgte von Anfang an für Hochzeitszwecke. Im Kreis wird der Davidstern beinahe zu einer Blume. Bei den Kreuzmotiven handelt es sich wahrscheinlich um *tifinagh*-Zeichen. Das Kreuz im unteren Motivteil stellt auch die Glückszahl Fünf dar (vier Arme und ein Auge in der Mitte).

9 Adrar

Headscarf/Kopftuch, ca. 1940
Afouzar-Iligh
130 x 80 cm, Inv. no. K 177

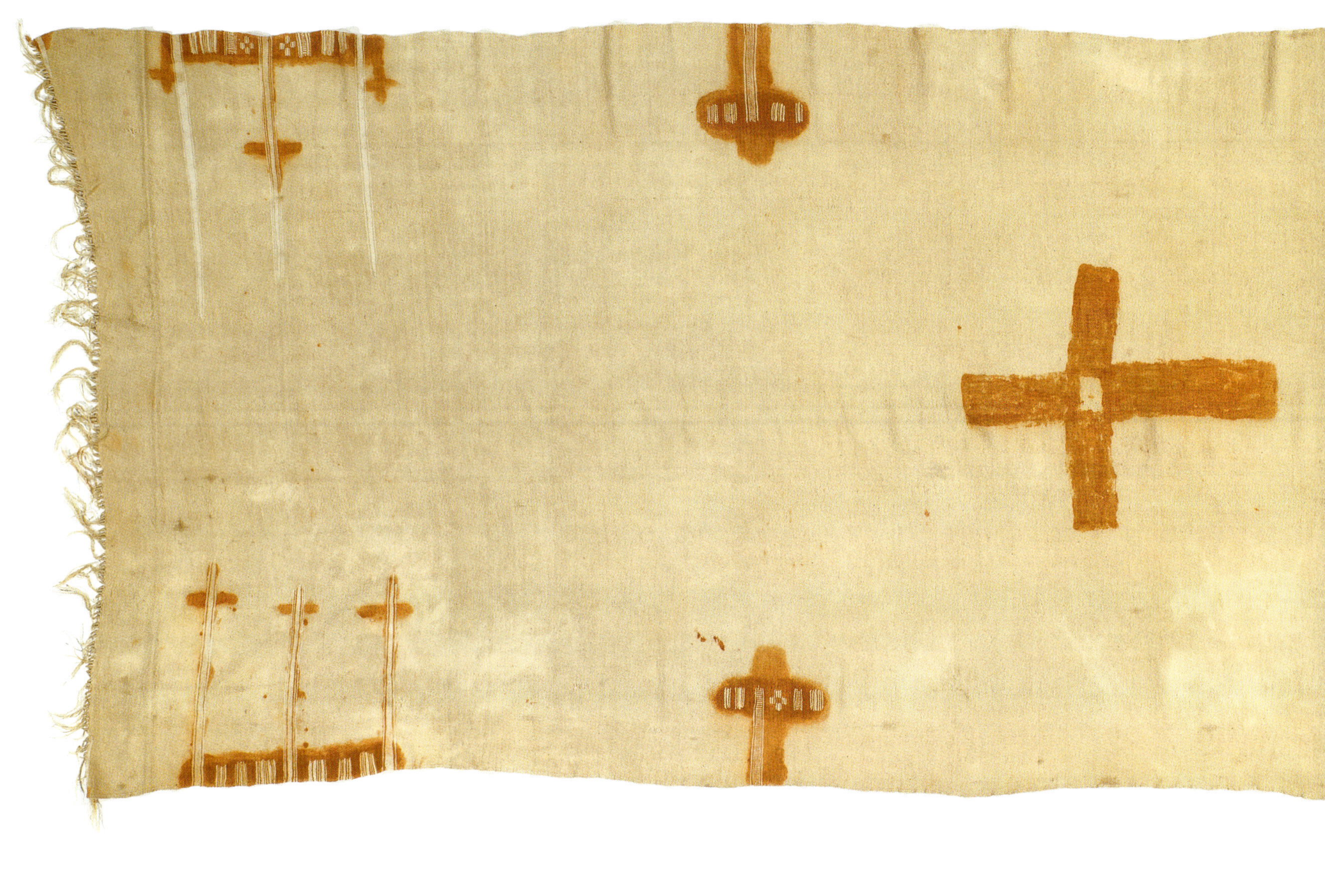

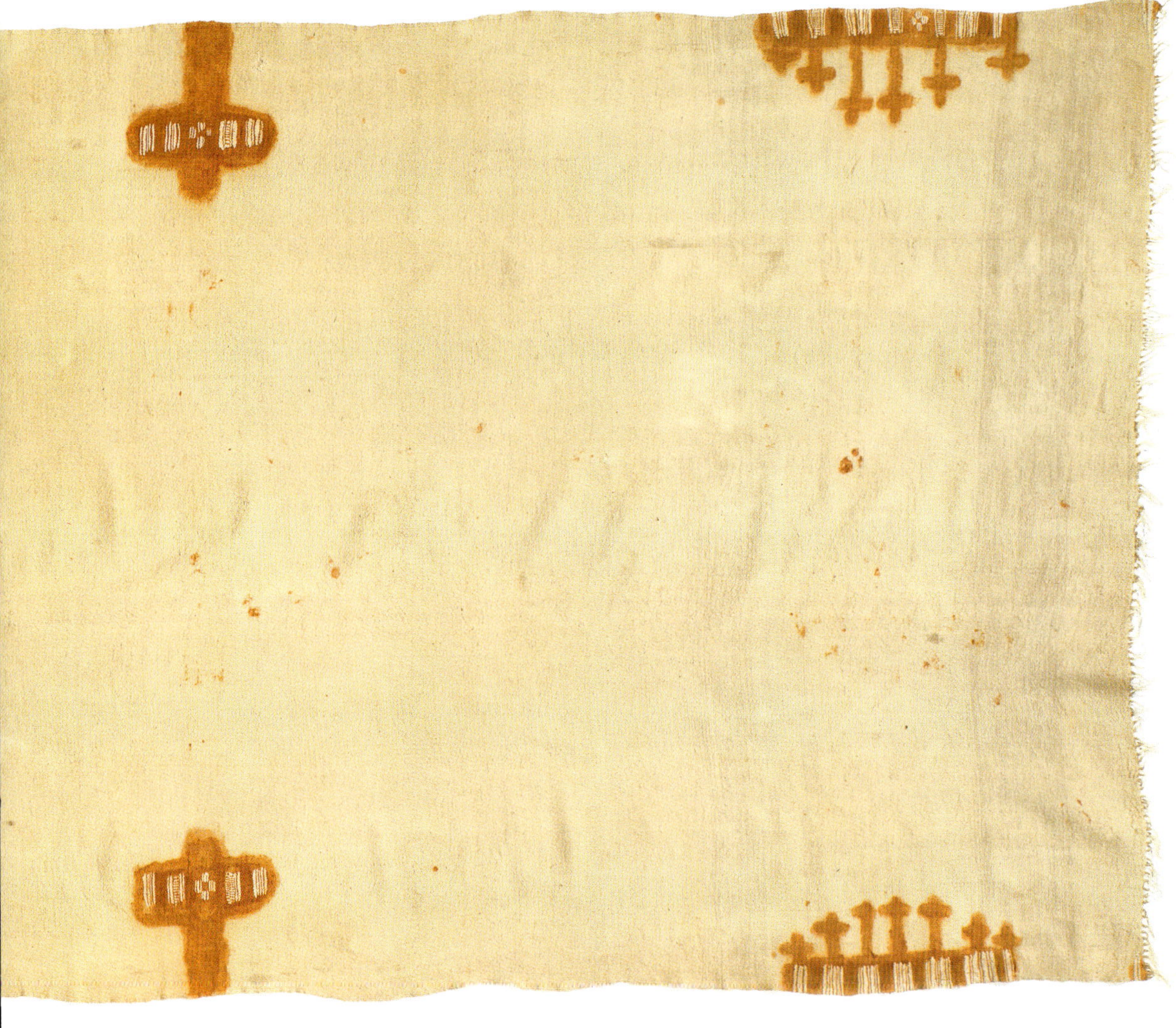

Although the arrangement of the elements on the cloth is typically Feija, their form has changed: we have already encountered the "Prophet's Sandals" on pieces from Aït Manesour (see Cat. no. 2) and Tisfrioudine (Cat. no. 3) yet here they have been changed into cruciform motifs. The cross with an eye represents the lucky number 5 – as it does on Cat. no. 9. This means it attracts the "evil eye" to itself and disperses it into the four directions of the wind (points of the compass), thus rendering it harmless.

Während die Anordnung der Elemente auf dem Tuch die für die Feija typische ist, hat sich ihre Form verändert: Den "Sandalen des Propheten" sind wir bereits in Stücken aus Aït Manesour (siehe Kat.-Nr. 2) und Tisfrioudine (Kat.-Nr. 3) begegnet, doch sind sie hier zu Kreuzformen umgestaltet. Das Kreuz mit dem Auge stellt – analog jenem auf Kat.-Nr. 9 – die Glückszahl Fünf dar, d.h. es zieht den "bösen Blick" auf sich, zerstreut ihn in die vier Windrichtungen und macht ihn so unwirksam.

10 Haik

Woman's wrapper/Wickeltuch, 1903
Afouzar-Iligh
410 x 140 cm, Inv. no. K 191

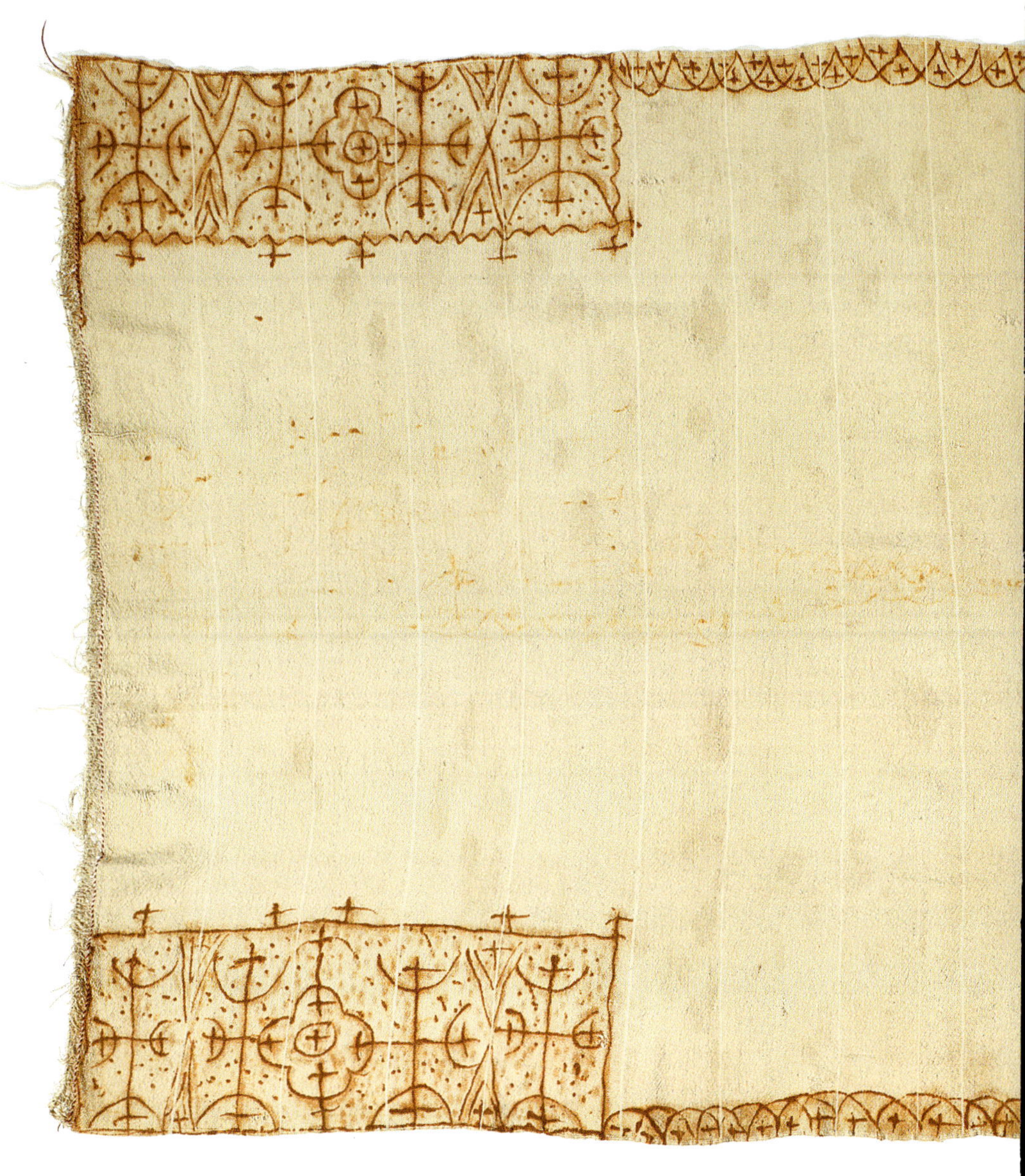

A light-weight blanket for a summer wedding, this one is painted on both sides. The patterned pictures of the cartouche-like corner motifs bear a certain resemblance to old Feija jewelry. Hill-like motifs line the selvedges (cf. also Cat. no. 7).

Eine Hochzeitsdecke in leichterer Qualität für den Sommer. Die Bemalung ist beidseitig. Die Musterbilder der kartuschenartigen Eckmotive haben eine gewisse Ähnlichkeit mit alten Schmuckstücken der Feija. Entlang der Kanten befinden sich hügelartige Motive (vgl. auch Kat.-Nr. 7).

11 Tahdicht

Wedding blanket/Hochzeitsdecke, 1933
Afouzar-Iligh
365 x 145 cm, Inv. no. K 35

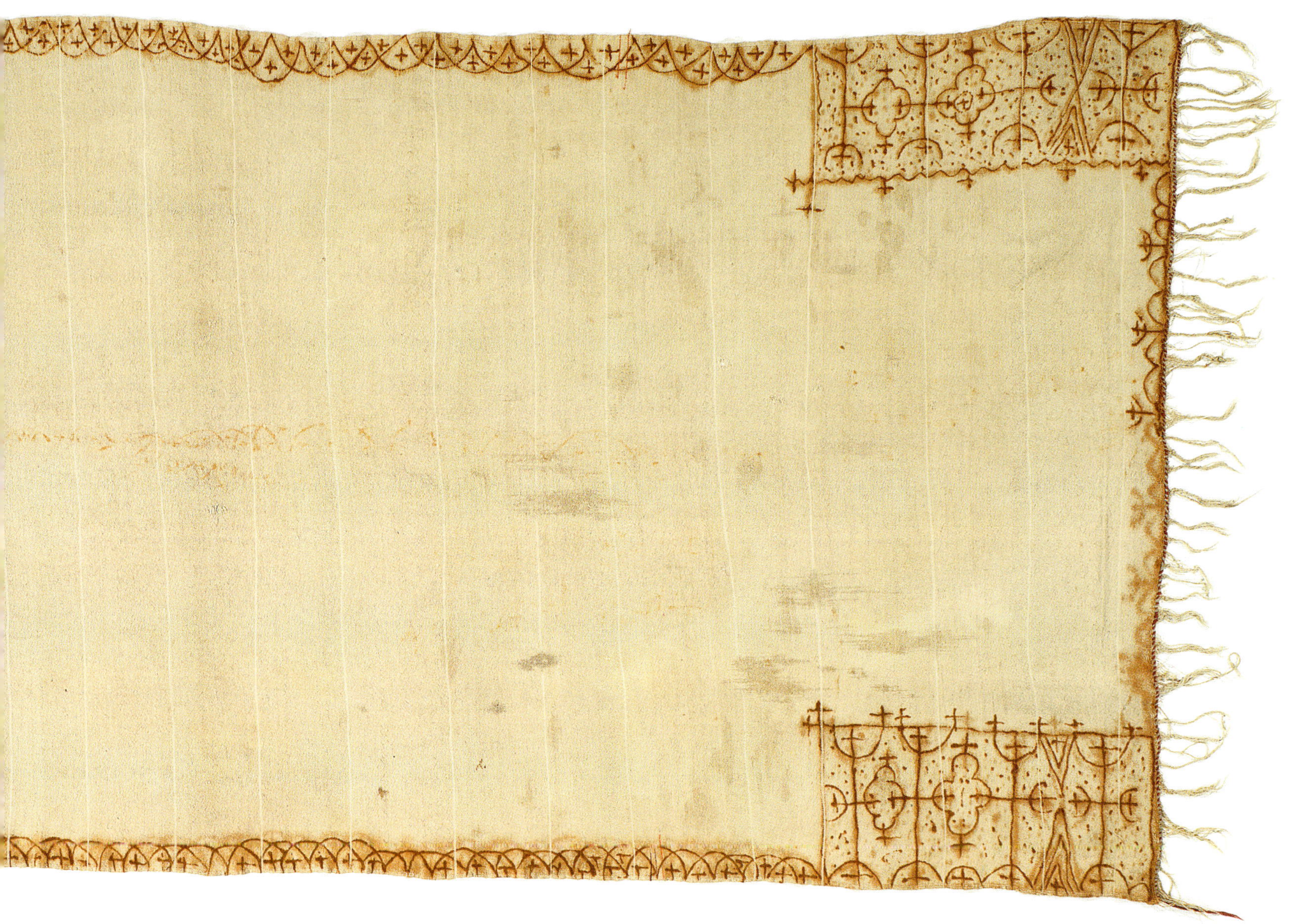

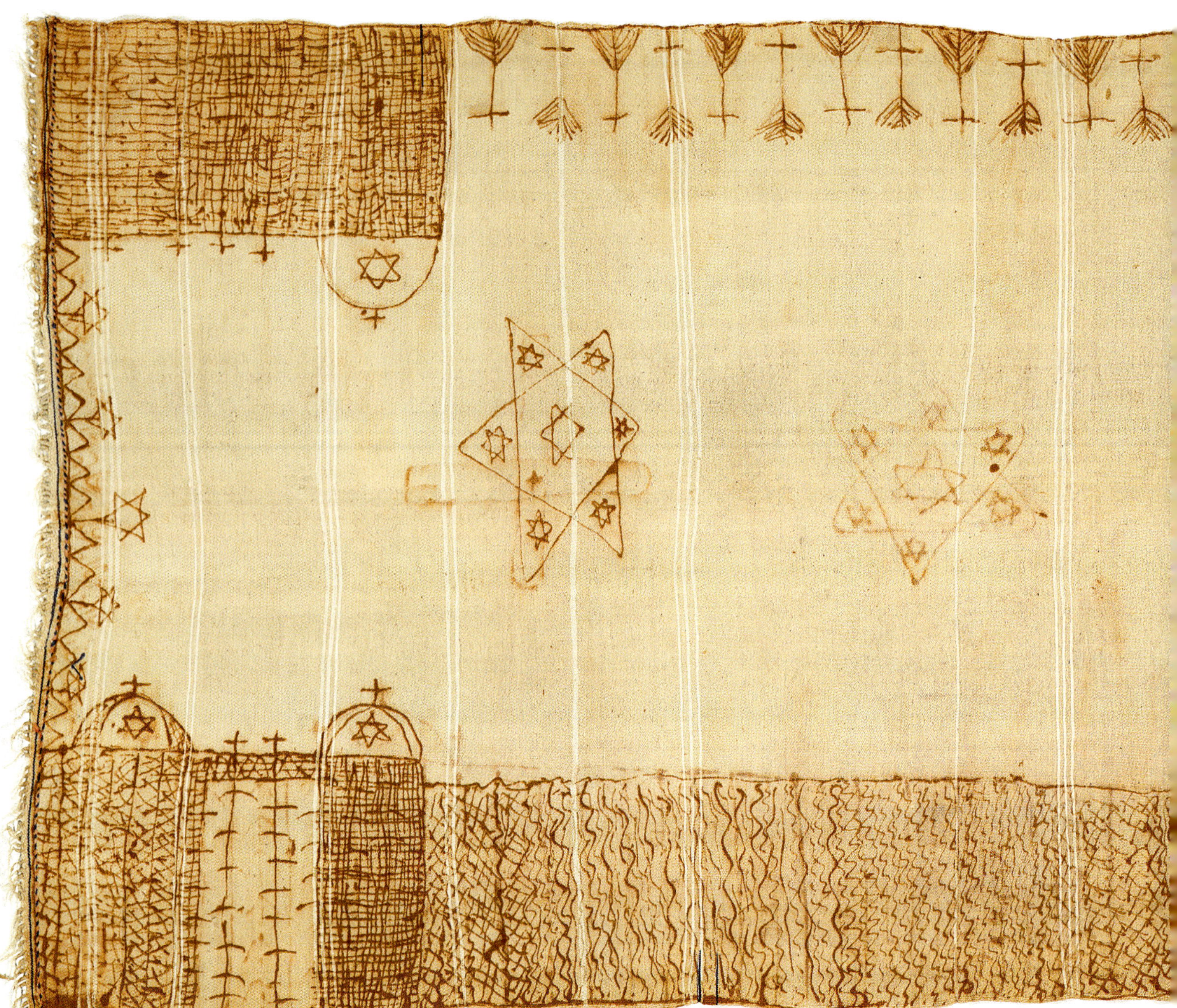

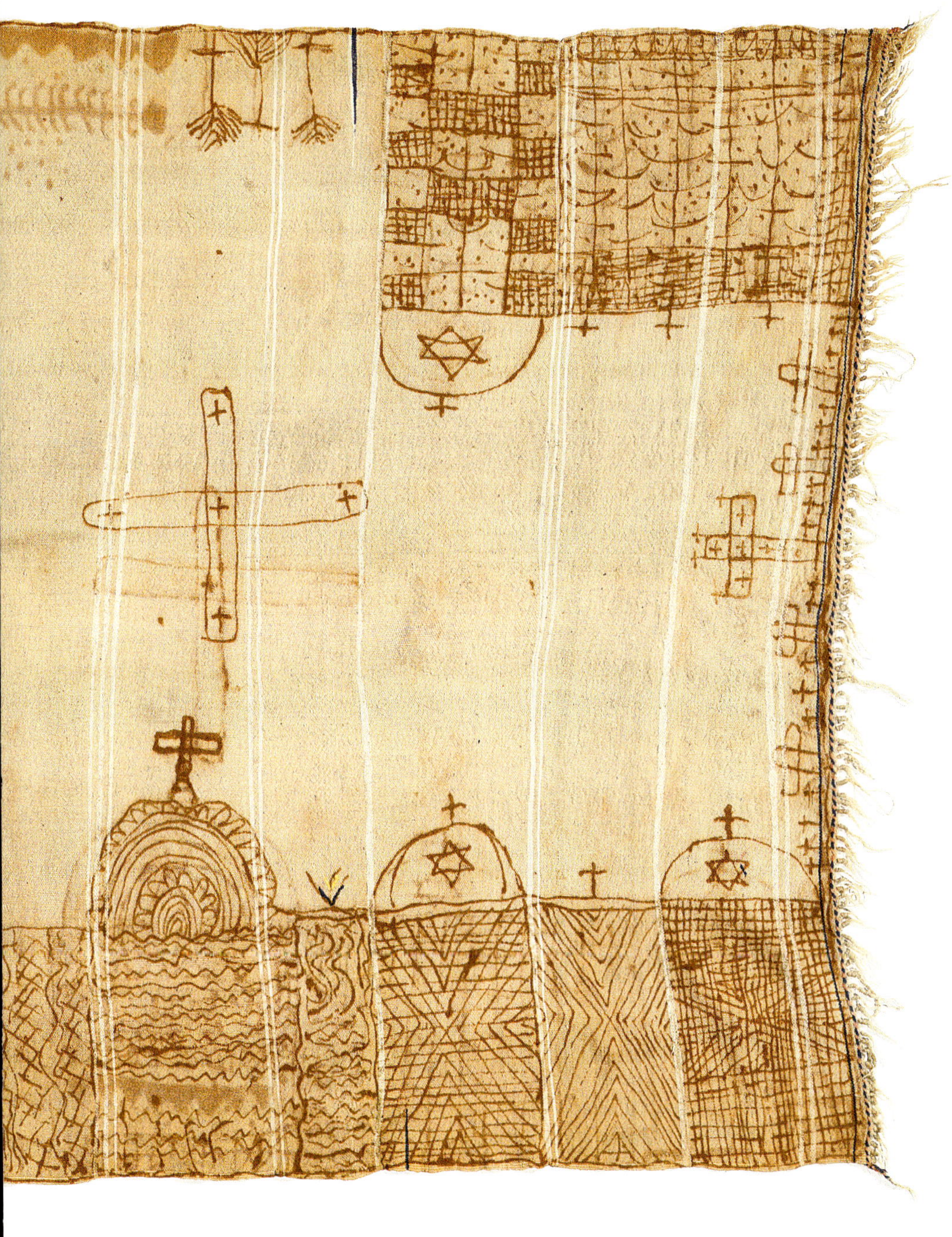

A heavy blanket for a winter wedding. The painting is different on the two sides. According to information imparted by Feija women, the two corner motifs represent the homes of the families from which the bride and groom came. The path through fertile palmeries or fields is represented along one selvedge. Mosques or *marabouts*, protected by a wall which is painted like Feija houses are probably represented on the opposite selvedge. In addition, a large number of beneficial and apotropaic signs are painted on the blanket.

Schwere Winterqualität. Vorder- und Rückseite mit unterschiedlicher Bemalung. Die beiden Eckmotive stellen nach Auskunft der Feija-Frauen die Heimstätten der Brautfamilien dar. Entlang einer Kante ist der Weg durch fruchtbare Palmengärten oder Felder dargestellt. An der gegenüberliegenden Kante dürften Moscheen oder *marabouts* dargestellt sein, geschützt von einer Mauer, welche ähnlich bemalt ist wie die Häuser der Feija. Zudem sind eine Vielzahl von Glücks- und Abwehrzeichen auf die Decke aufgemalt.

12 Tahdicht

Wedding blanket/Hochzeitsdecke, 1952
Afouzar-Iligh
283 x 142 cm, Inv. no. K 55

Erkoune

The Arabic name "Erkoune" means "corner" or "angle" – a reference to the situation of this village in a small, steep-sided fertile oasis valley. Hidden in the mountains between Imi n'Tatelt and Afouzar, Erkoune is in a really idyllic setting. The 1936 census recorded a population of only 42, entirely Muslim. Now four clans live there in 41 households. The patron saint of the village is Sidi Jâafar. A relatively large number of Zenaga and Sektana, who belong to the neighboring tribes, live in Erkoune.

Erkoune

Der arabische Name "Erkoune" bedeutet "Ecke" oder "Winkel" – ein Bezug zur Lage des Dorfes in dem kleinen, steilen, fruchtbaren Oasental. Zwischen Imi n'Tatelt und Afouzar hinter Bergen versteckt, ist Erkoune geradezu idyllisch gelegen. Die Volkszählung von 1936 ergab gerade einmal 42 Einwohner, ausschließlich Muslime. Heute sind vier Sippen in 41 Haushaltungen ansässig. Der Dorfheilige ist Sidi Jâafar. In Erkoune leben verhältnismäßig viele Zenaga und Sektana, Angehörige der Nachbarstämme.

Auf den Kuppen der umliegenden Berge liegen eine Speicher- und eine Wehrburg. Im Ort Erkoune selbst befindet sich hinter der Moschee ein weiterer *agadir*, wie die anderen ist er heute im Verfall begriffen. Die Häuser von Erkoune liegen an den beiden steilen und steinigen Abhängen des engen V-förmigen Tals über dem Palmengarten, welcher einigen Feldern entlang dem Flüsschen Schatten spendet. Besondere Steinkonstruktionen, die als Bienenhäuser dienen, weisen darauf hin, dass in Erkoune viel Honig erzeugt wird.

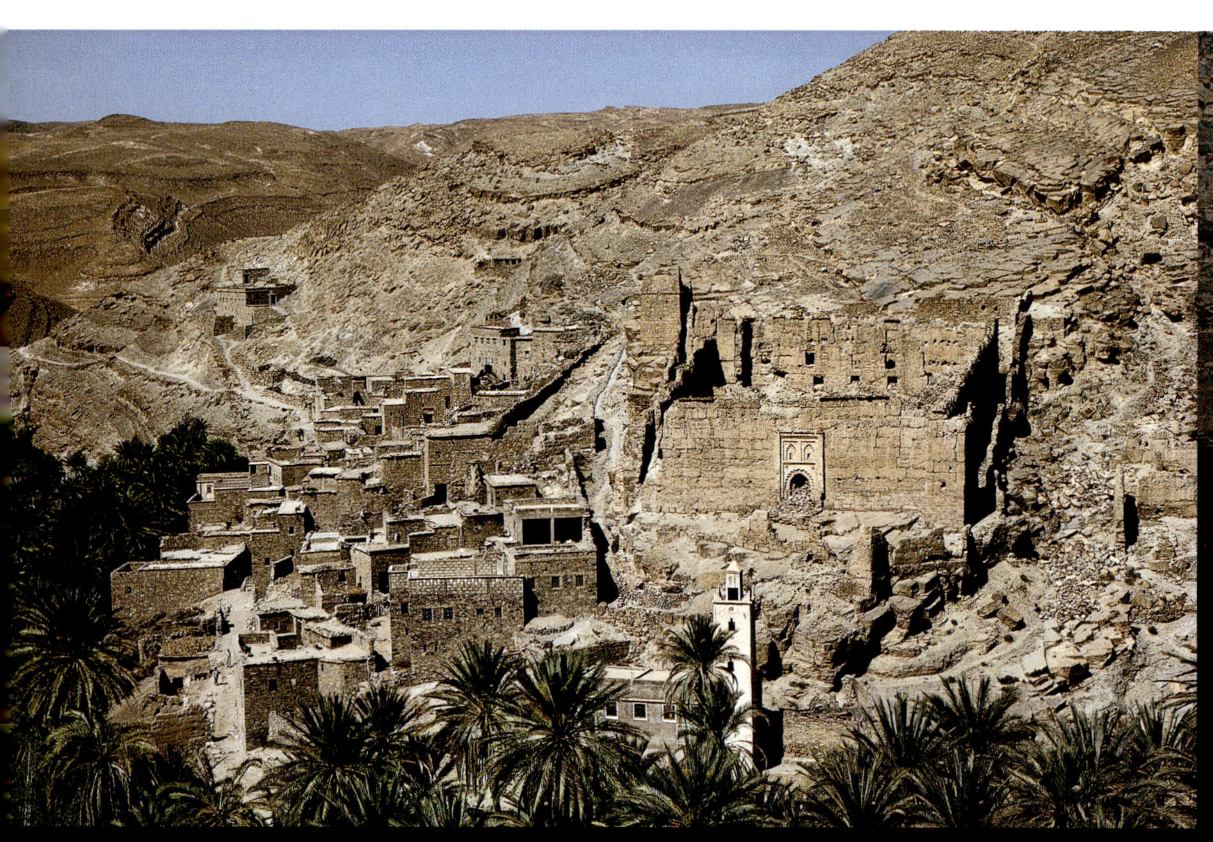

The village of Erkoune. The granary *(agadir)* is in ruins, 1999

Das Dorf Erkoune. Der Speicher *(agadir)* ist im Verfall, 1999

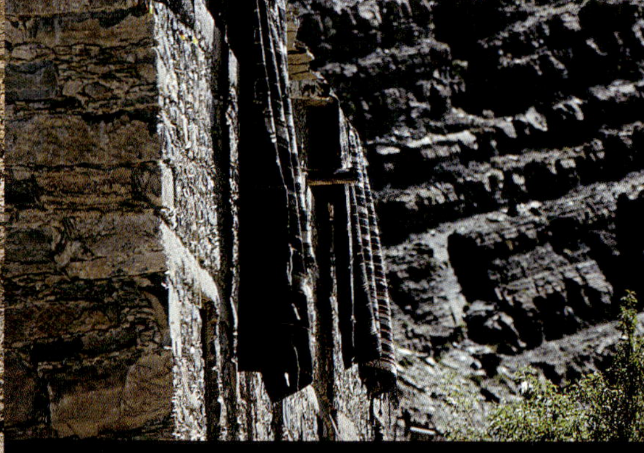

Hand-woven grain sacks are aired, 2000

Handgewobene Getreidesäcke werden gelüftet, 2000

A granary and a fortification crown the tops of the surrounding mountains. In the town of Erkoune there is another *agadir* behind the mosque; like the others it is now in ruins. The houses are set on the two steep slopes of the narrow V-shaped valley above the palmery, which shades several fields along the little river. Peculiar stone structures which are used as beehives show that a lot of honey is produced at Erkoune.

About half an hour's walk from Erkoune is the hamlet of Agouni, where two clans live in 13 households; the hamlet belongs to Erkoune. Some of the approx. 250 inhabitants are Sektana and Zenaga, Berbers who have migrated here from neighboring regions.

Etwa eine halbe Wegstunde entfernt liegt der Weiler Agouni mit zwei Sippen in 13 Haushaltungen; er gehört zu Erkoune. Ein Teil der insgesamt ca. 250 Bewohner sind Sektana und Zenaga, also zugewanderte Berber aus den benachbarten Gebieten.

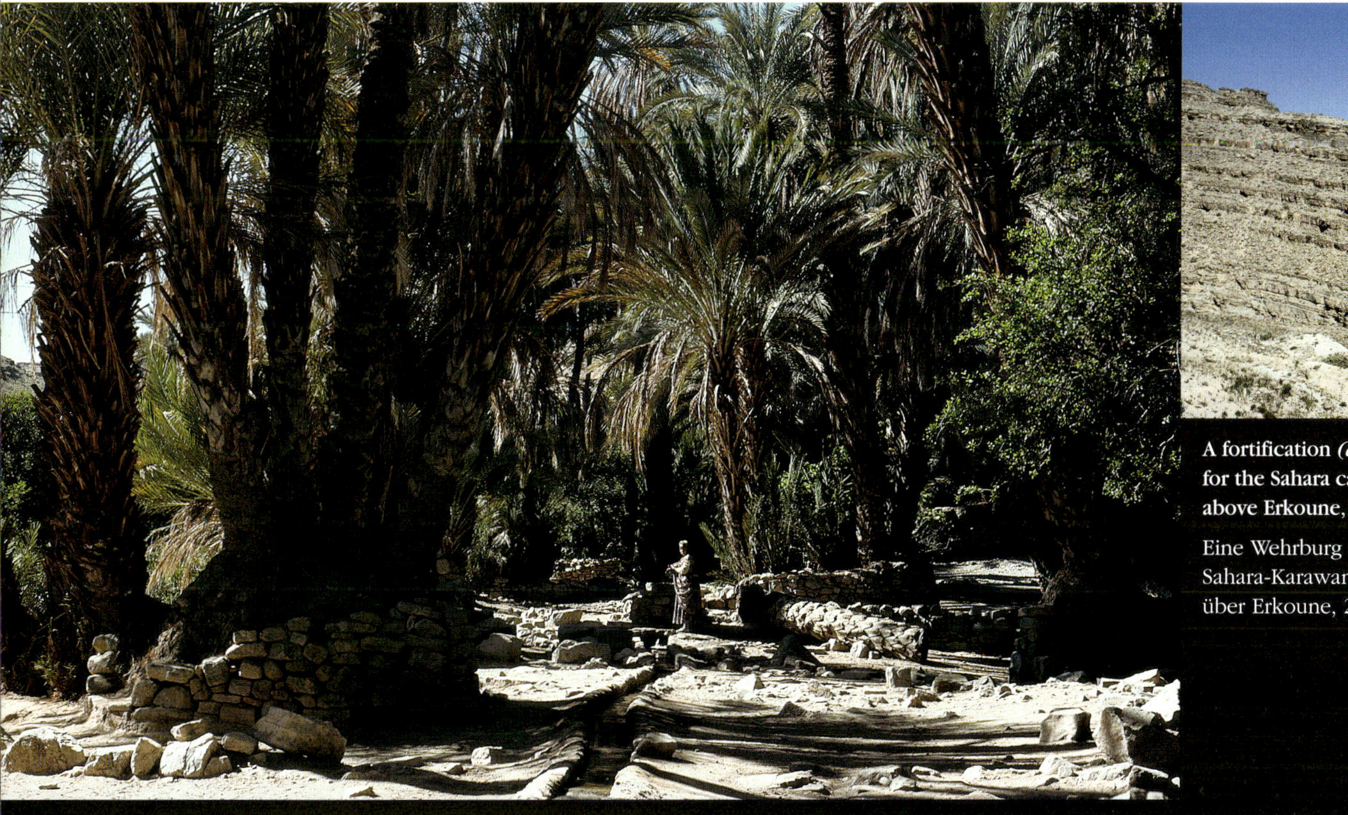

A fortification *(agadir romanni)* for the Sahara caravans on a mountain top above Erkoune, 2000

Eine Wehrburg *(agadir romanni)* für die Sahara-Karawanen auf einer Bergkuppe über Erkoune, 2000

In the Erkoune palmery, 2000

Im Palmengarten von Erkoune, 2000

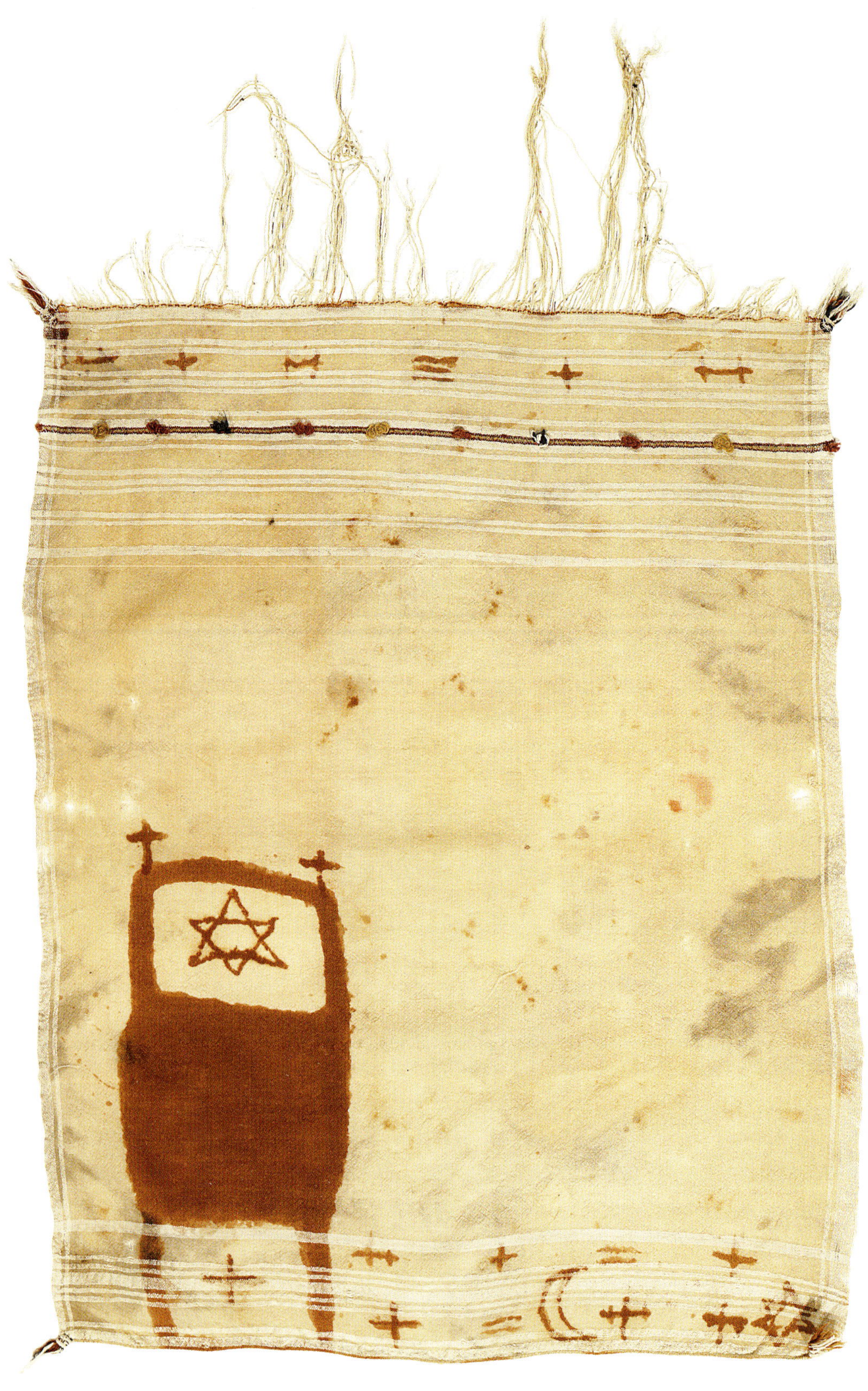

Although the *bouitri* or *bab* motif is slightly different to those from Iligh and Afouzar (see Cat. nos. 6, 7, 9), it is still recognizable as such. The piece reveals two generations of henna painting: the first for everyday use and a later one for a wedding. The *tifinagh* characters are interspersed with Arabic-Islamic symbols.

Das *bouitri*- oder *bab*-Motiv ist gegenüber denen aus Iligh und Afouzar etwas verändert (siehe Kat. Nrn. 6, 7, 9), bleibt jedoch erkennbar. Das Stück zeigt zwei Generationen der Henna-Bemalung: die erste für den Alltag, später eine zweite für eine Hochzeit. Zwischen die *tifinagh*-Zeichen mischen sich arabisch-islamische Symbole.

13 Adrar

Headscarf/Kopftuch, ca. 1910
Erkoune
120 x 75 cm, Inv. no. K 152

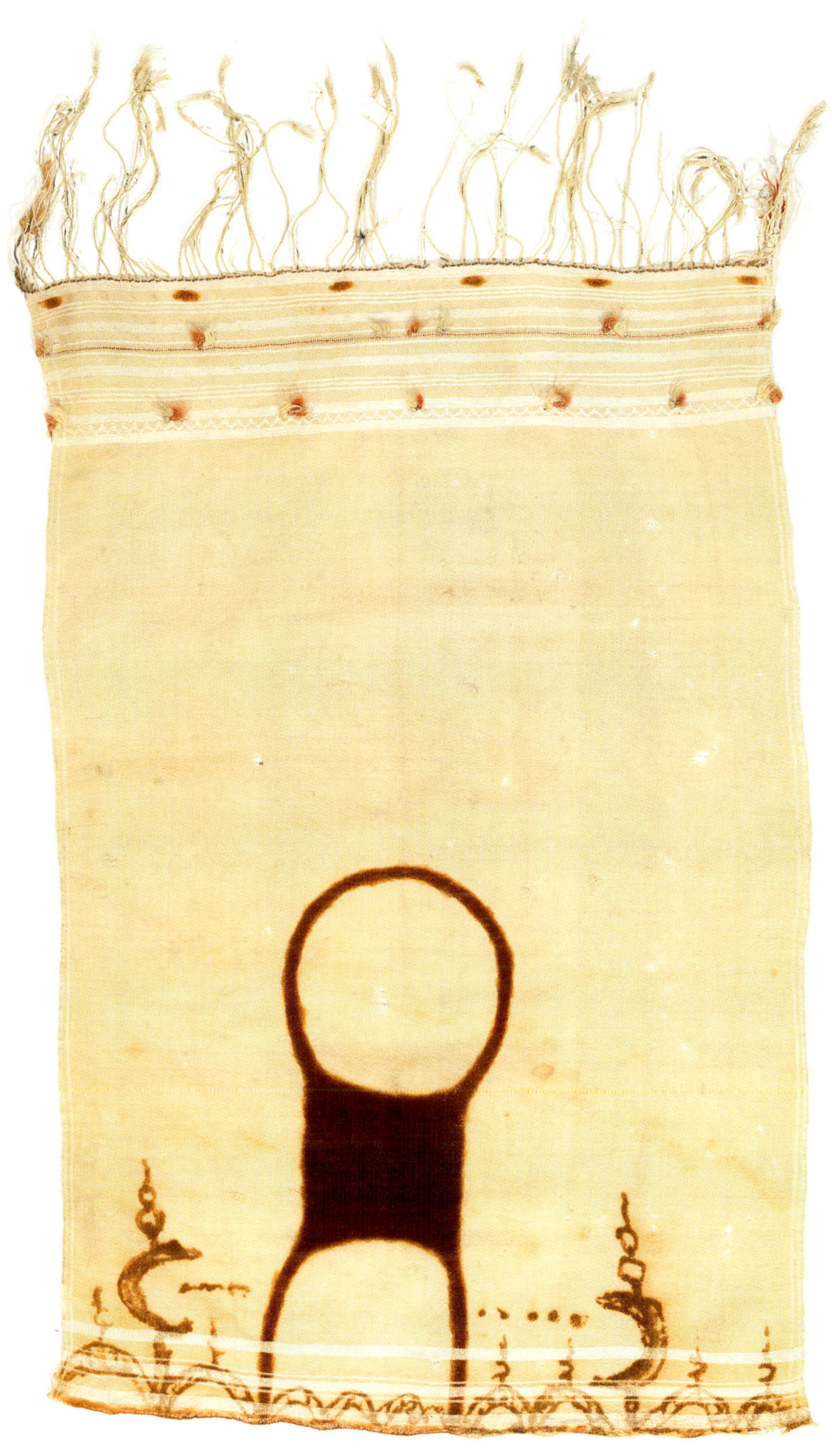

Corresponds to Cat. no. 7 from Afouzar. An *adrar* for everyday wear which was painted additionally for a wedding.

Entspricht Kat.-Nr. 7 aus Afouzar. Alltags-*adrar*, der für eine Hochzeit zusätzlich bemalt wurde.

14 Adrar

Headscarf/Kopftuch, ca. 1930
Erkoune
118 x 66 cm, Inv. no. K 181
Technical analysis/Strukturanalyse, p. 138

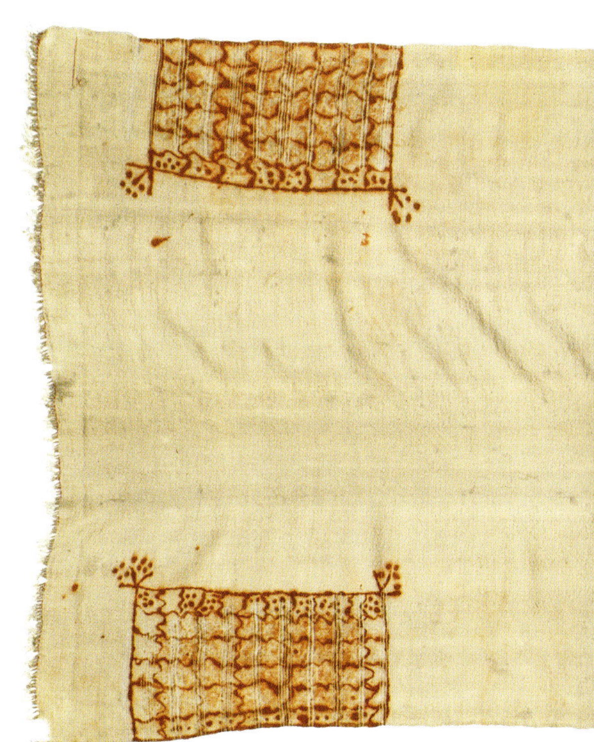

In the subdivision into fields typical of the area the *tismissine* motif used at Tisfrioudine and Tisnassemine (cf. Cat. nos. 4 and 5) occurs here. Both front and back are painted. The four inner *tismissine* motifs mark the place where the bride and groom stand facing each other at a particular point in the wedding ceremony. This cloth apparently had a dual function as clothing and as a ceremonial textile.

In der gebietstypischen Feldaufteilung begegnet man dem *tismissine*-Motiv von Tisfrioudine und Tisnassemine (vgl. Kat.-Nrn. 4 und 5) wieder. Vorder- und Rückseite des Tuches sind bemalt. Die vier inneren *tismissine*-Motive markieren den Ort, wo sich Brautleute bei einer bestimmten Hochzeitszeremonie gegenüberstehen. Anscheinend hat das Tuch eine Doppelfunktion als Kleidungsstück und als Zeremonialtextil.

15 Haik

Woman's wrapper/Wickeltuch, ca. 1920-1940
Erkoune, Sektana or Zenaga work/Sektana- oder Zenaga-Arbeit
Ben Daoud Elhassane (the family who previously owned it/Vorbesitzer-Familie)

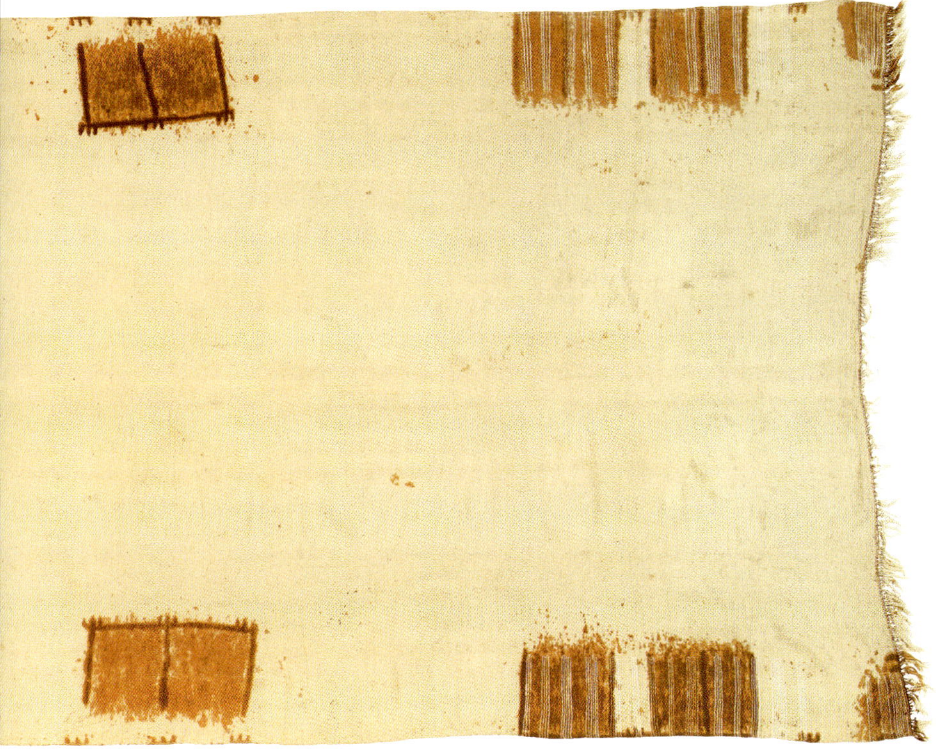

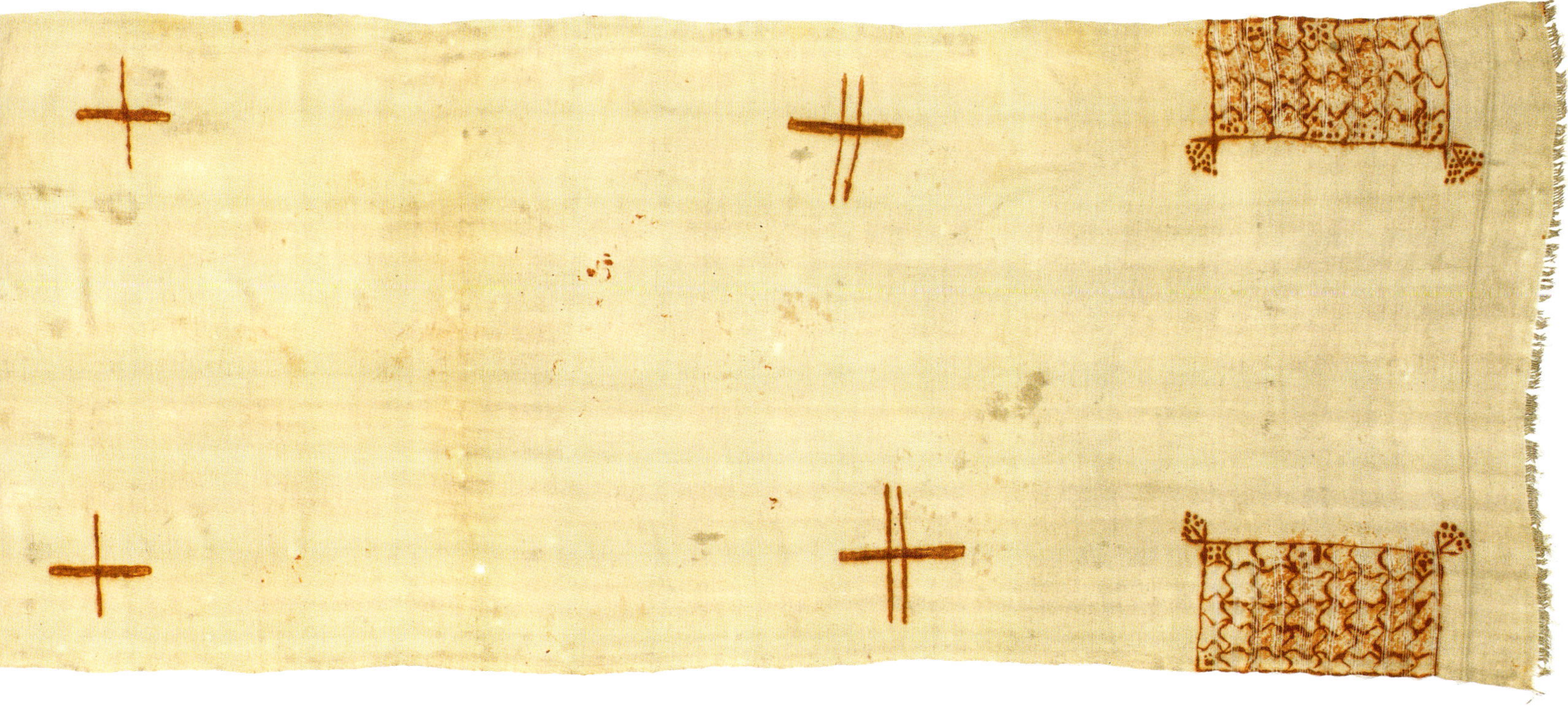

Our question as to whether the corner motifs represented the beehives of Erkoune was greeted with shouts of laughter. No answer to this question was forthcoming.

Unsere Frage, ob in den Eckmotiven die Bienenhäuser von Erkoune dargestellt seien, löste großes Gelächter aus. Eine Antwort auf diese Frage war nicht zu bekommen.

16 Haik

Woman's wrapper/Wickeltuch, ca. 1920
Erkoune
445 x 132 cm, Inv. no. K 144
Technical analysis/Strukturanalyse, p. 139

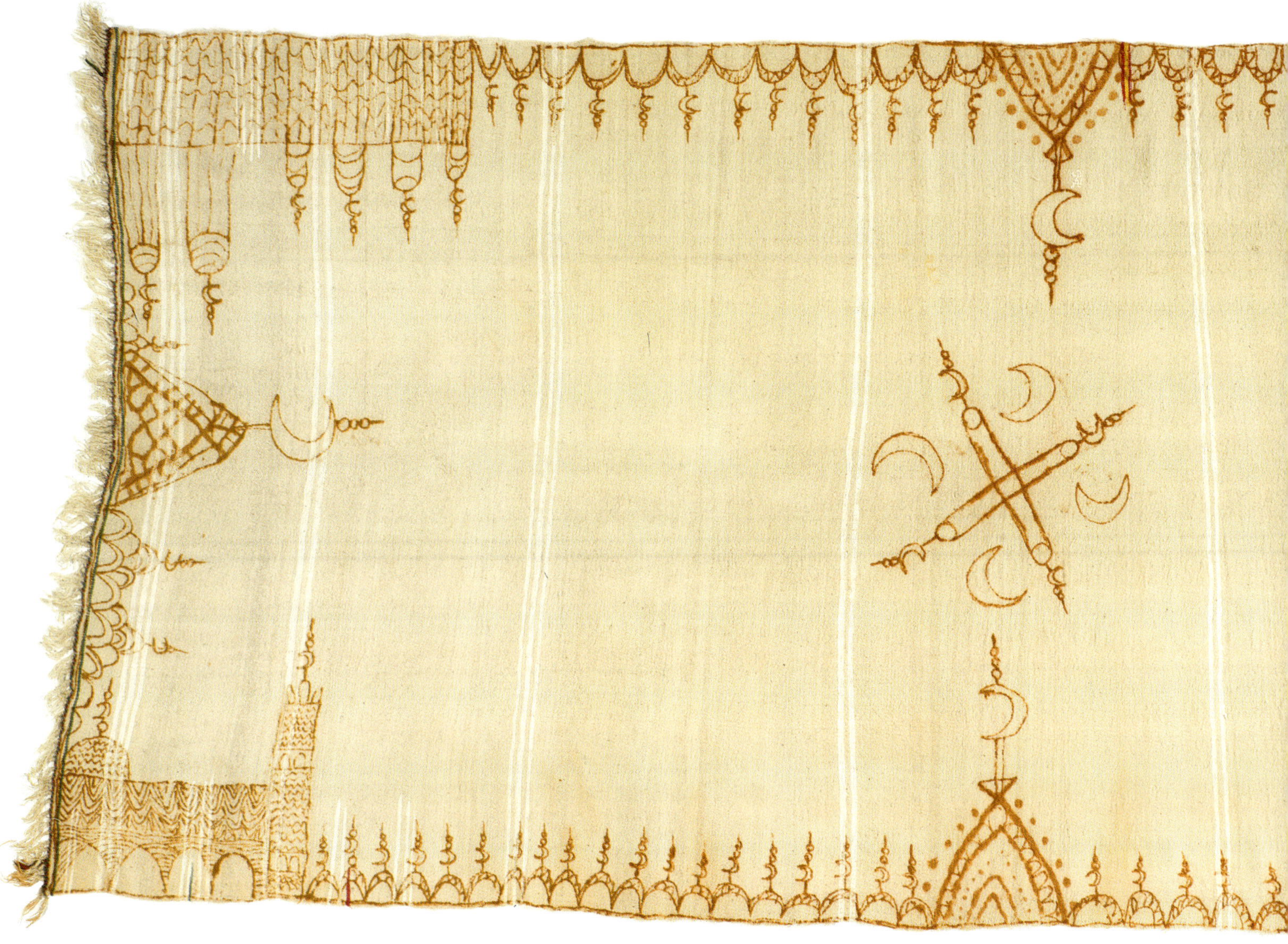

Heavy-weight for a winter wedding. Painted differently on the two sides. What is depicted overall is probably a village interpretation of the Mecca representation generally encountered throughout Islamic countries. Typical Feija features here are the selvedges of the weaving emphasized with henna, the short white and polychrome cotton shots and the arcade-like motifs lining the selvedges. The central motif was called the "Moon in the Four Seasons" ("La lune des quatre saisons") – a symbol of permanence and recurrence. The painting is simpler on the back. It consists merely in house motifs in the corners as well as a roof motif (?) at the ends and sides.

Schwere Winterqualität. Auf der Vorder- und Rückseite verschieden bemalt. Es dürfte sich insgesamt um eine dörfliche Interpretation der Mekkadarstellung handeln, wie sie im islamischen Raum gebräuchlich ist. Typisch für die Feija sind dabei die mit Henna betonten Gewebekanten, die kurzen weißen und farbigen Baumwollschüsse sowie die arkadenförmigen Motive entlang der Kanten. Das Zentralmotiv wurde als der "Mond in den vier Jahreszeiten" bezeichnet ("La lune des quatre saisons") – Symbol für Dauer und Wiederkehr. Die Bemalung der Rückseite ist einfacher gehalten. Sie weist lediglich Häusermotive in den Ecken sowie je ein Dachmotiv (?) an den Enden und Seiten auf.

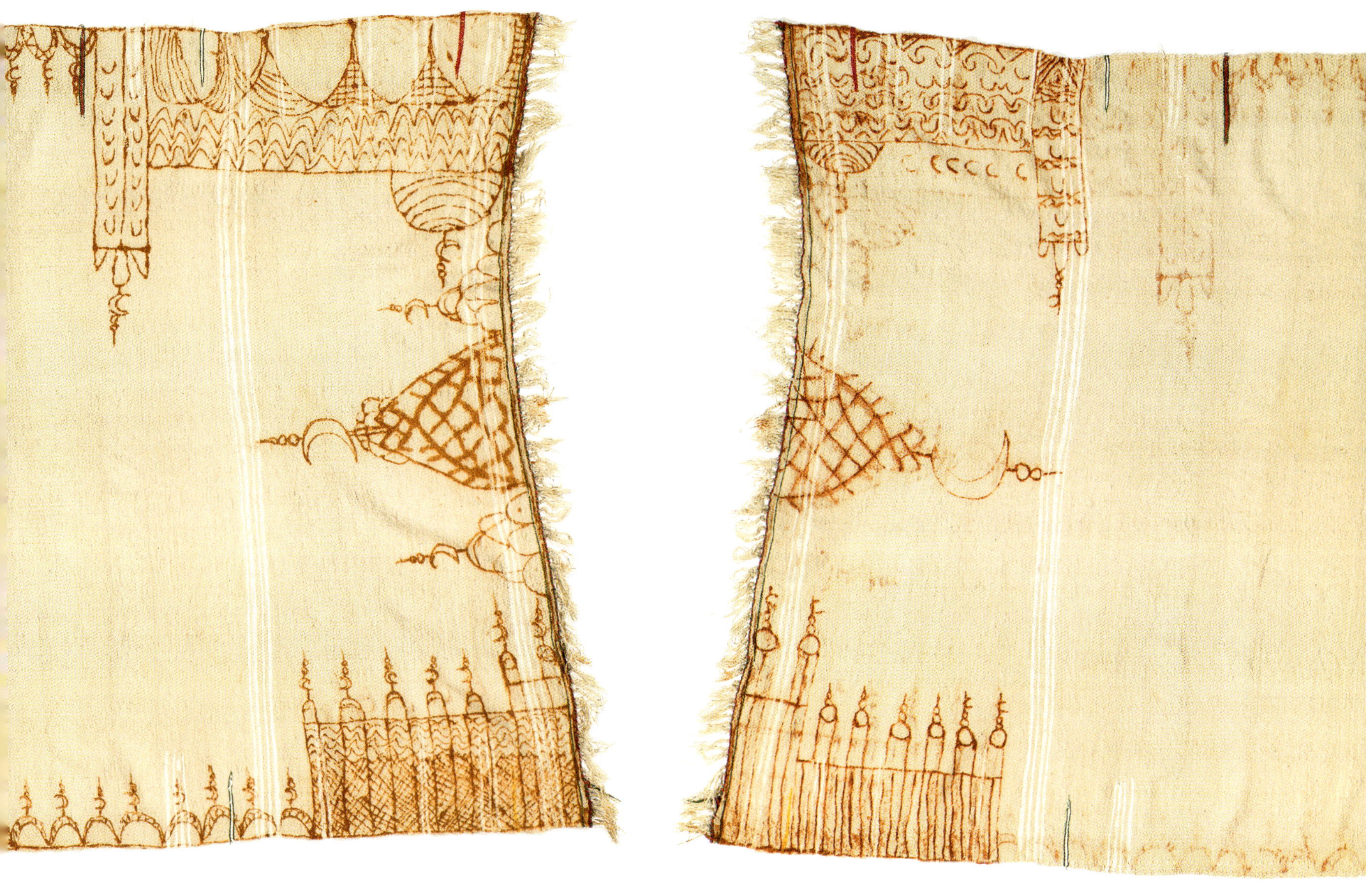

17 Back / Rückseite

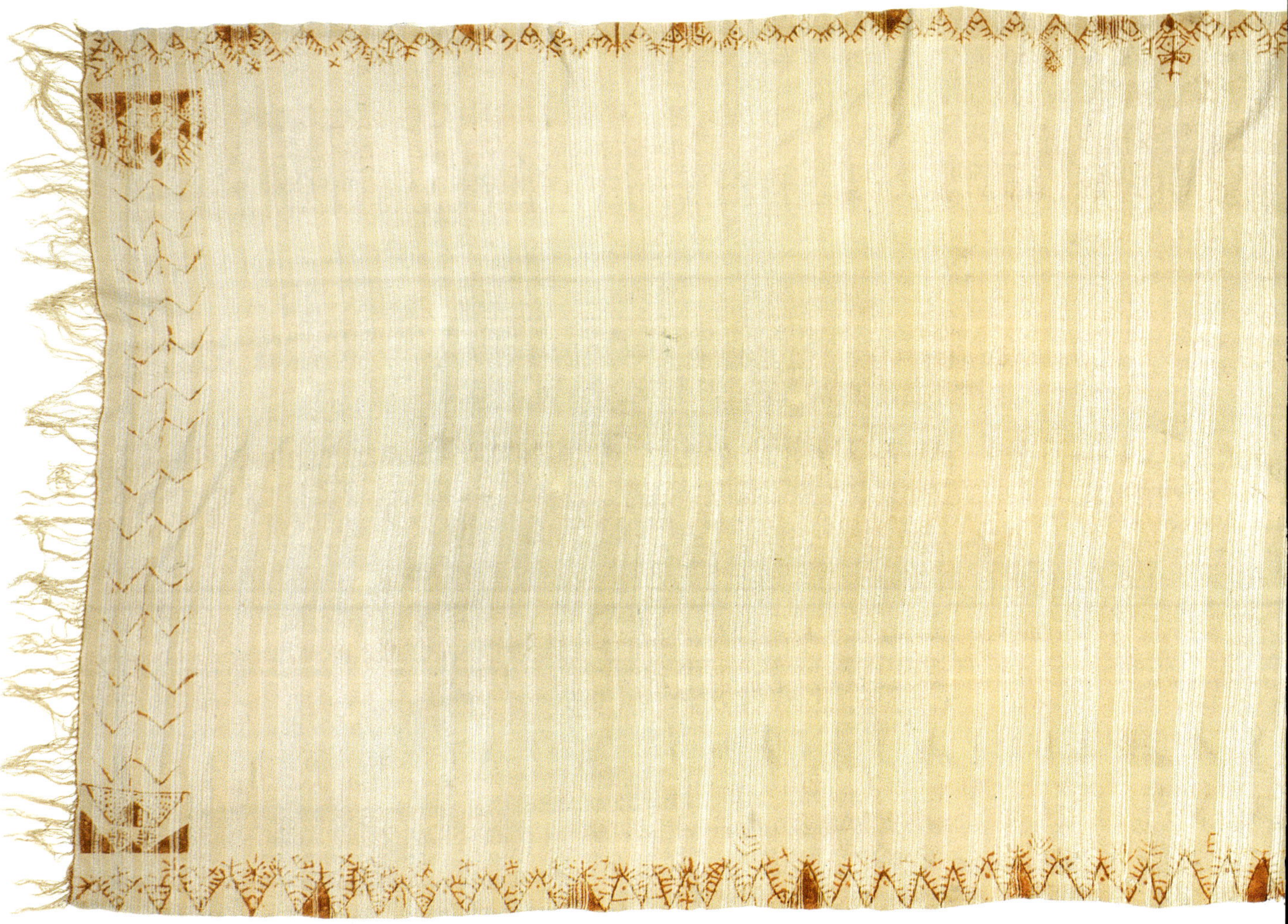

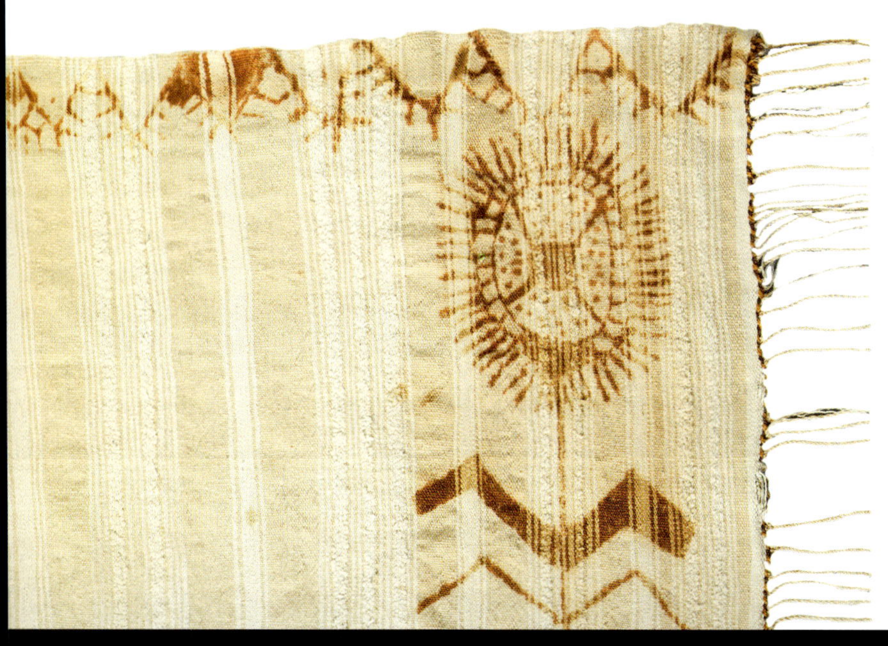

18 Detail

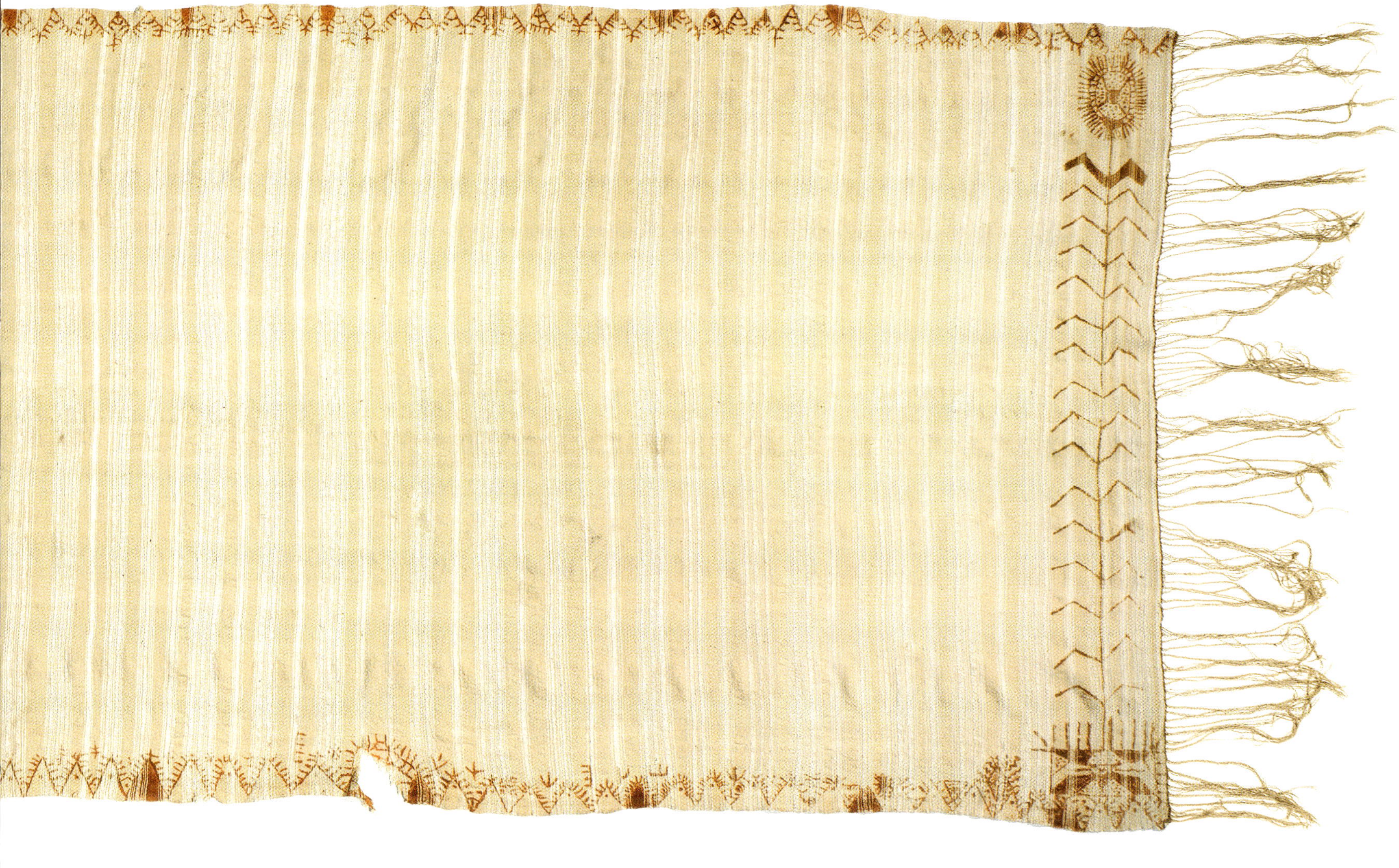

A long-stemmed flower or ear of barley painted at both ends; a sheaf motif decorates the selvedges. Representations of fields or gardens are popular motifs with the Feija. The following motifs in henna can be identified: the comb, scorpion, breadbasket, palm frond, sawtooth, carding-comb – all "positive" signs, many of them symbols of water and fertility.

An beiden Enden ist je eine langstielige Blume oder Gerstenähre aufgemalt, ein Garbenmotiv ziert die Kanten. Felder oder Gärtendarstellungen sind beliebte Feija-Motive. Folgende Hennamotive lassen sich identifizieren: Kamm, Skorpion, Brotkorb, Palmblatt, Zacken der Sichel, Wollkamm – insgesamt alles "positive" Zeichen, viele sind Symbole für Wasser und Fruchtbarkeit.

18 Haik

Woman's wrapper/Wickeltuch, ca. 1930
Erkoune
510 x 150 cm, Inv. no. K 193

19 Haik

Woman's wrapper/Wickeltuch, ca. 1900
Erkoune
462 x 147 cm, Inv. no. K 149

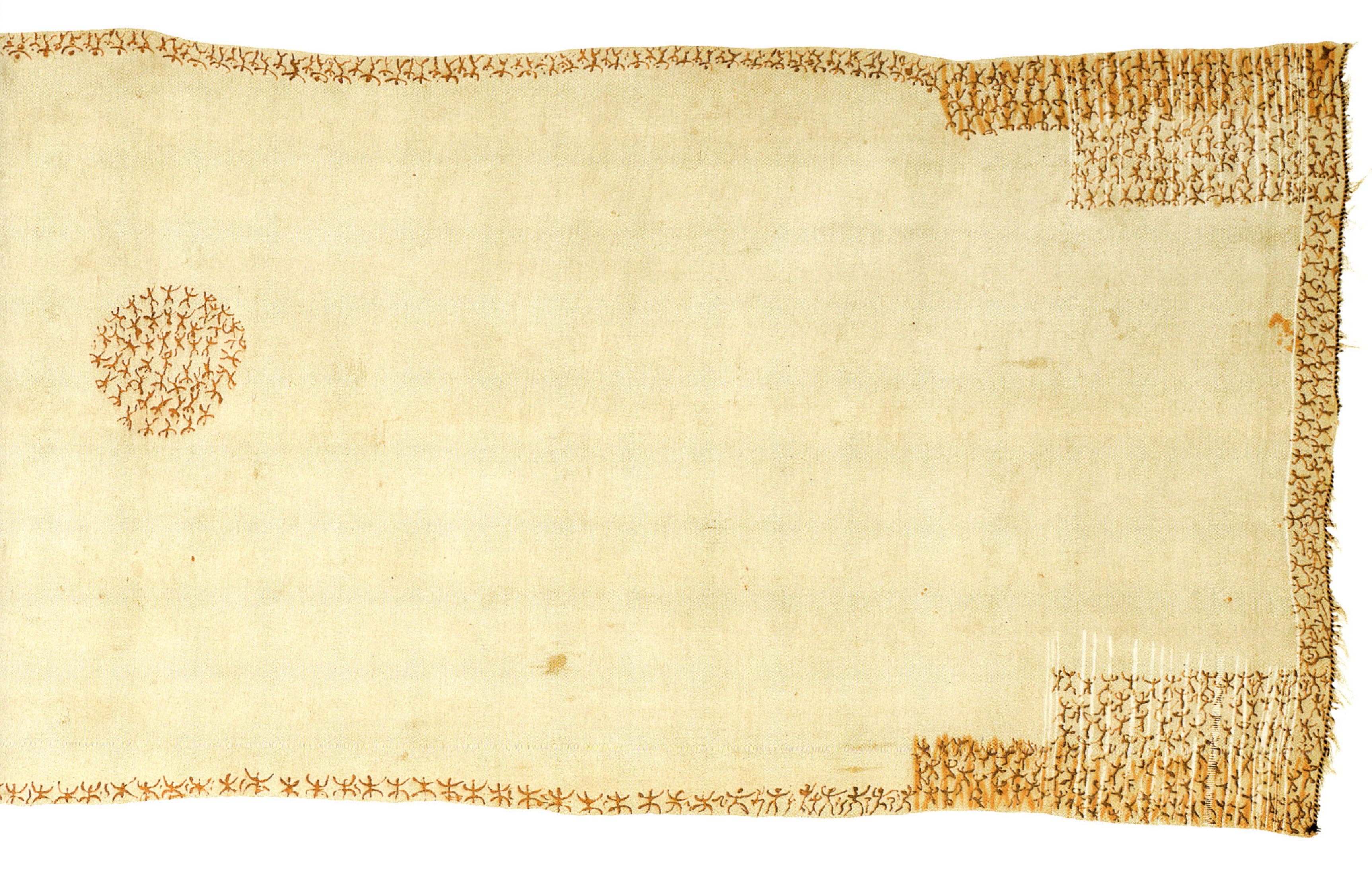

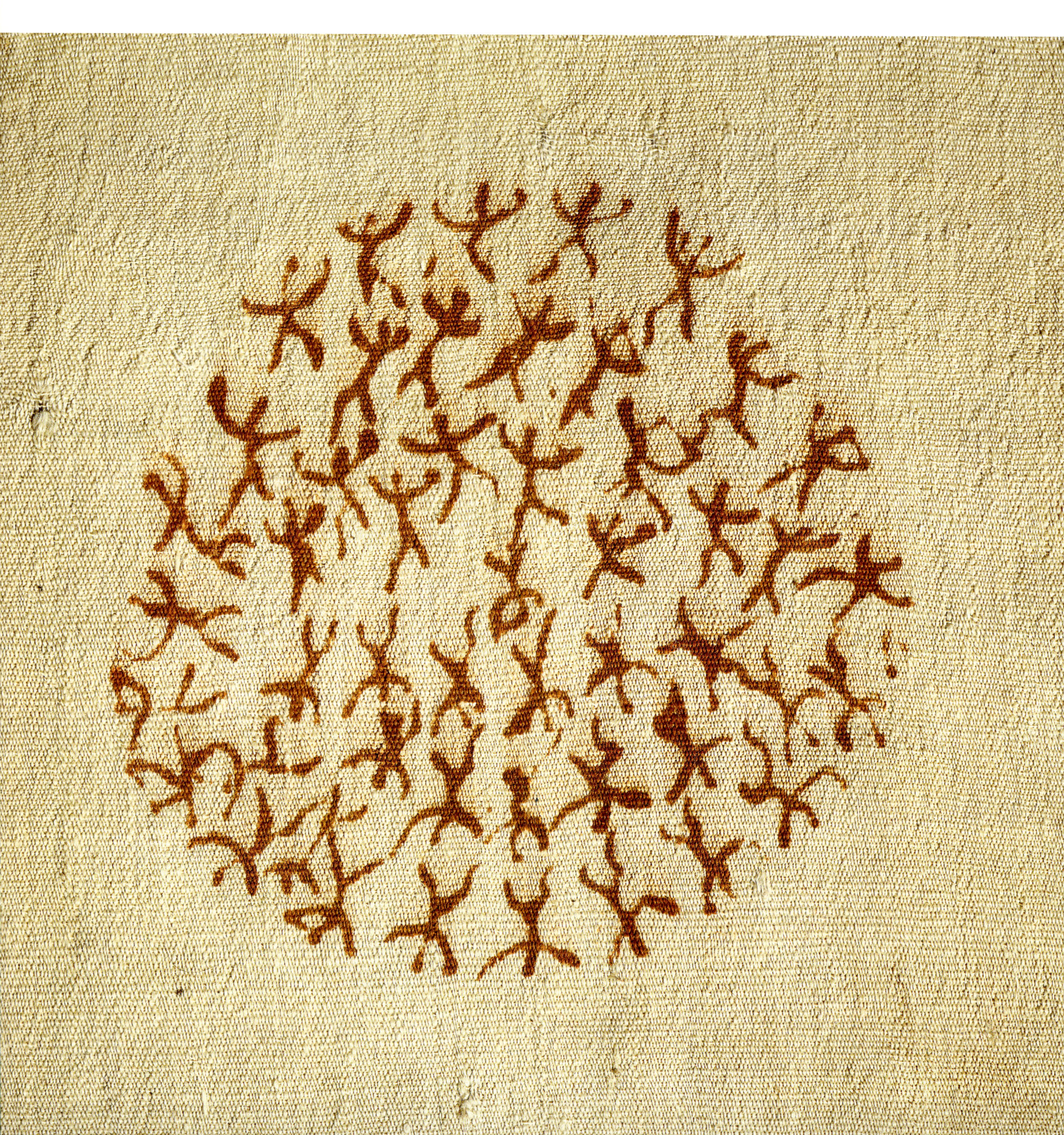

19 Central motif / Zentralmotiv

The front of the *haik* Cat. no. 19 is painted; the back is decorated with henna sprayed on. The painting was probably done by several women. The corner motifs are underlaid with white cotton shots. On our visits we were told that these represented the feet of dancing doves. There is, however, a character in the *tifinagh* alphabet for the value "Z", which corresponds in one form to this motif. This sign recurs in endless modification on the present weaving and assumes the appearance of dancing figures. Where the alphabet characters change into dancing figures other signs appear which correspond to "T", "I" and "S" in the *tifinagh* alphabet. The motif probably depicts a Feija dance - the *agoual* - although this could not be verified with absolute certainty. The representation on this woman's wrapper, however, suggests that dance scenes are represented both along the selvedges and in the corners as well as at the center. An invisible axis bisects the central motif and the feet of the figures on the two sides point in opposite directions. A particular phase of the dance may be represented. However, this arrangement may simply be the result of the two halves of the signs having been painted from one side or the opposite side.

It is not clear whether the women who painted it were aware that they were using a *tifinagh* character and changing it into a dancing figure (see on this also "The Imazighen and their Tifinagh", p. 22). This woman's wrapper seems to be a one-of-a-kind piece; even though the subdivision of the surface area is definitely typical of the territory, this cloth with its dance figures is probably unique. That it, too, was executed according to a design planned from start to finish is shown by the circumstance that the white cotton shots woven into the corners mark the surfaces of those motif combinations which were painted on later.

Die Vorderseite des *haik* Kat.-Nr. 19 ist bemalt, rückseitig ist Henna in Spritztechnik aufgetragen. Die Bemalung dürfte von mehreren Frauen ausgeführt worden sein. Die Eckmotive sind mit weißen Baumwollschüssen unterlegt. Es wurde uns bei Besuchen mitgeteilt, es seien die Füße tanzender Tauben dargestellt. Allerdings gibt es im *tifinagh*-Alphabet auch ein Zeichen mit dem Lautwert "Z", welches dem Motiv in einer Form entspricht; dieses Zeichen wird im vorliegenden Textil laufend abgewandelt und nimmt die Formen tanzender Figuren an. An den Übergängen von Schriftzeichen zu Tanzfiguren erscheinen weitere Zeichen mit Entsprechungen im *tifinagh*-Alphabet: "T", "I", "S". Das Motiv stellt vermutlich einen Tanz der Feija – den *agoual* – dar, doch konnte dies nicht mit letzter Sicherheit geklärt werden. Die Darstellung auf dem Wickeltuch legt aber nahe, dass sowohl entlang der Kanten als auch in den Ecken und im Zentrum Szenen des Tanzes dargestellt sind. Durch das Zentralmotiv verläuft eine unsichtbare Linie, und bei den Figuren zu beiden Seiten zeigen die Füsse gegeneinander. Es ist möglich, dass damit eine bestimmte Phase des Tanzes dargestellt wird; es kann aber ganz einfach auch davon herrühren, dass je eine Hälfte der Zeichen von einer bzw. von der Gegenseite her gemalt wurden.

Ob sich die Malerinnen bewusst waren, dass sie ein *tifinagh*-Zeichen verwendeten und dieses zu einer Tanzfigur verwandelten, bleibt unklar (siehe hierzu auch "Die Imazighen und ihr Tifinagh", S. 22). Es scheint sich bei diesem Wickeltuch um ein Ausnahmestück zu handeln; auch wenn die Aufteilung der Fläche durchaus gebietstypisch ist, dürfte das Stück mit den Tanzfiguren einmalig sein. Auch dieses Tuch beweist, dass seine Gestaltung von Anfang an durchgeplant war, bezeichnen doch die an den Ecken eingewobenen weißen Baumwollschlüsse die Flächen der später aufgemalten Motivkombinationen.

Imi n'Tatelt

The name "Imi n'Tatelt" means "place from which several springs flow". The settlement grew up round a saint's tomb and a Koran school (cf. "The Feija and Islam", p. 38). Consequently, the place looks more like a small town than a village.

The 1936 census records an entirely Muslim population of 485 for Imi n'Tatelt. Now the village has 202 households of approx. 5 persons each, which makes for a total population of about 1000. Of the households, 110 are Yâacoubi kinship (that is, they are *chorfa*), descendants of the local saint, Si Mohand ou Yâacoub. Zenaga comprise 28 of the households, members of a tribe whose territory borders the Feija territory to the east. Of the households, 45 are *issouqen* (descendants of black slaves) and 19 households are Feija.

Imi n'Tatelt

Der Name "Imi n'Tatelt" bedeutet "Ort, an dem mehrere Quellen entspringen". Die Siedlung ist um ein Heiligengrab und eine Koranschule entstanden (vgl. "Die Feija und der Islam", S. 38). Das Ortsbild entspricht daher eher dem eines kleinen Städtchens als dem eines Dorfes.

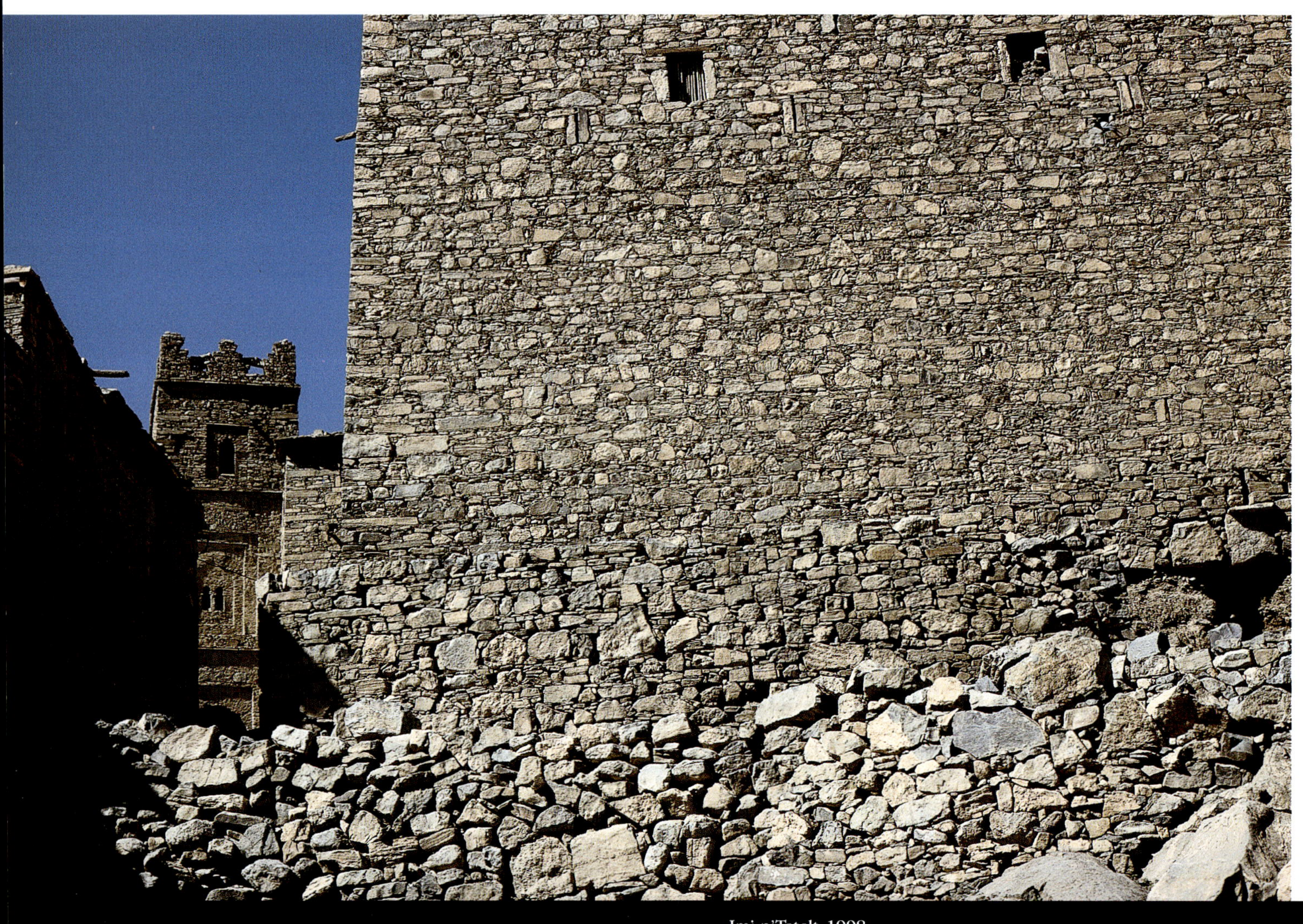

Imi n'Tatelt, 1998

Imi n'Tatelt, 1998

The oral tradition persists that there were Jews in this town yet only contradictory information on this is available.[4] The 1936 census conducted by the French Protectorate administration records only Muslims for the entire Feija tribal territory and no adherents to other religions.

The town is set as if camouflaged in a bend in the valley precisely on the border between the Feija and the Sektana tribal territories. Important links to other tribal territories lead through Imi n'Tatelt. A rough track *(piste)* runs from the northern edge of the village through Sektana territory to the Ida tribes clustered about the village of Igherm. Another track leads first over a high pasture and then through the crater of an extinct volcano to the provincial capital Tata and its extensive oasis. There are some Berber rock carvings (ca. 1000 BC) along the way, near Tagragra.

Die Volkszählung von 1936 weist für Imi n'Tatelt 485 Bewohner aus, ausschließlich Muslime. Heute zählt der Ort 202 Haushaltungen zu rund fünf Personen, etwa 1000 Einwohner insgesamt. 110 Haushaltungen sind von der Yâacoubi-Sippe (also von *chorfa*) bewohnt, Nachfahren des Ortsheiligen Si Mohand ou Yâacoub. In 28 Haushaltungen leben Zenaga, Angehörige eines Stammes, dessen Gebiet östlich an das Gebiet der Feija angrenzt. 45 Haushaltungen beherbergen *issouqen* (schwarze Nachfahren ehemaliger Sklaven) und weitere 19 sind Feija-Haushalte.

Hartnäckig hält sich in der mündlichen Überlieferung, dass es im Ort Juden gab, doch liegen widersprüchliche Informationen vor.[4] Die Volkszählung der französischen Protektoratsverwaltung von 1936 verzeichnet im ganzen Stammesgebiet der Feija ausschließlich Mohammedaner, keine Angehörigen anderer Religionen.

Der Ort liegt wie getarnt in einem Taleinschnitt und punktgenau auf der Grenze zwischen den Stammesgebieten der Feija und der Sektana. Durch Imi n'Tatelt führen wichtige Verbindungen in andere Stammesgebiete. Vom nördlichen Dorfausgang aus führt eine Piste durch das Sektana-Gebiet und zu den Ida-Stämmen um den Ort Igherm. Ein anderer Weg führt zunächst über eine Hochweide und anschließend durch den Krater eines erloschenen Vulkans in die Provinzhauptstadt und Großoase Tata. Auf dem Weg, bei Tagragra, befinden sich einige Berber-Felsritzungen (ca. 1000 v. Chr.).

Östlich von Imi n'Tatelt gehören noch zwei Täler zum Gebiet der Feija, danach folgt das Gebiet der Zenaga. Südlich von Imi n'Tatelt befinden sich Feija-Dörfer und drei wichtige Durchgänge in das Jebel Bani-Tal und in die offene Wüste. Als Knotenpunkt ist (oder war) der Ort also gut gelegen und gar nicht so abgeschieden, wie es zunächst den Anschein hat, wenn man sich der Siedlung von Norden her nähert.

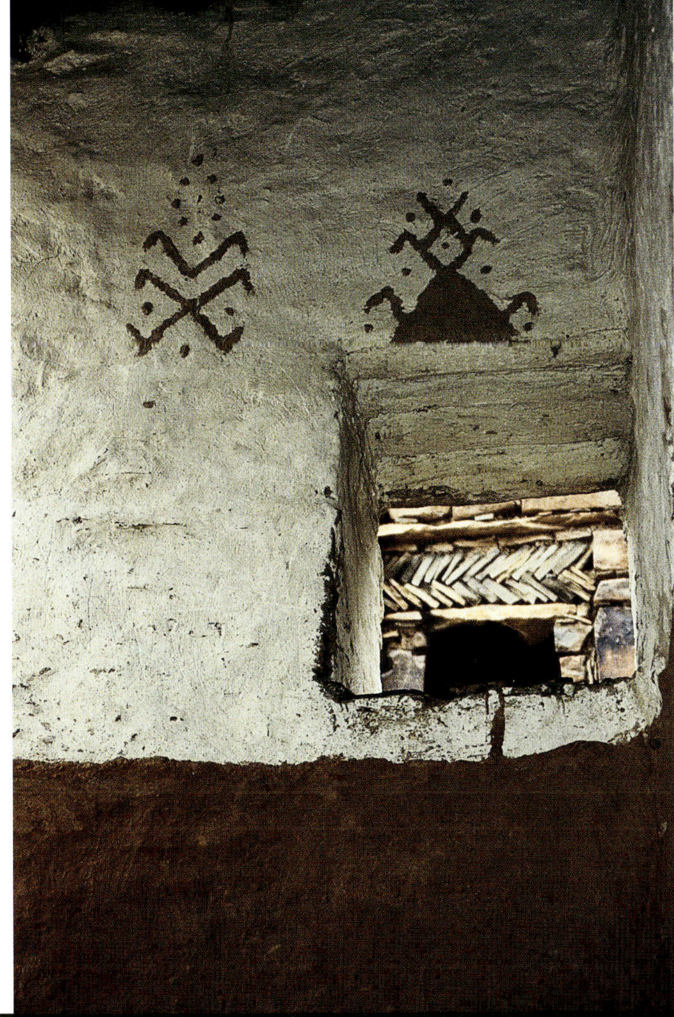

Imi n'Tatelt. Interior of a house, 2000

Imi n'Tatelt. Inneres eines Hauses, 2000

4 Marquis de Segonzac records explicitly: "La Zaouia compte 166 feux, dont 116 pour la seule postérité de Sidi Mohammed. Point de juifs, bien entendu, mais beaucoup de Haratin, serviteurs de la zaouia." (Segonzac 1910, p. 126).

4 Marquis de Segonzac erwähnt ausdrücklich: "La Zaouia compte 166 feux, dont 116 pour la seule postérité de Sidi Mohammed. Point de juifs, bien entendu, mais beaucoup de Haratin, serviteurs de la zaouia." (Segonzac 1910, S. 126).

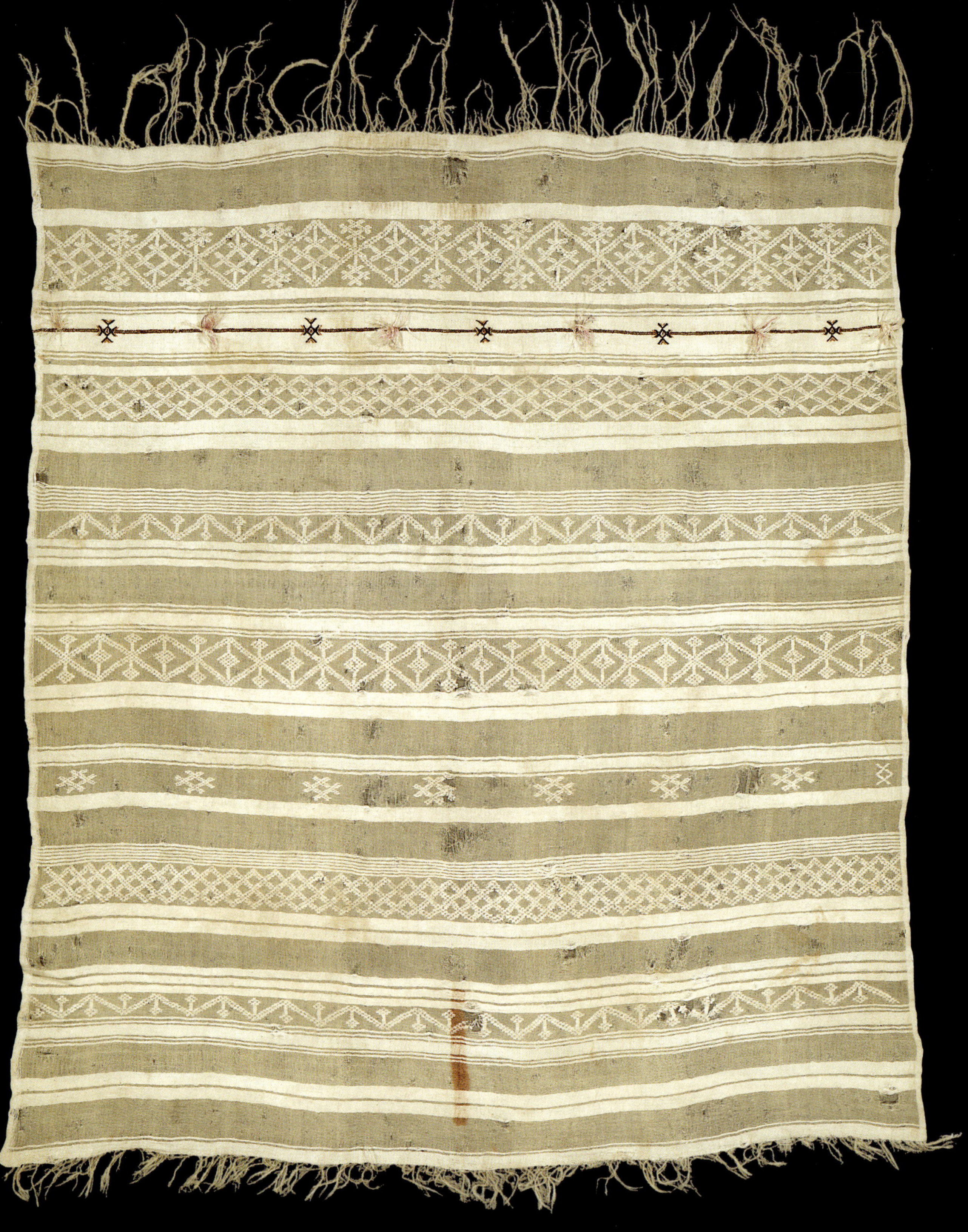

Both pieces are skillfully worked; the veil reveals consummate mastery of technique. The tapestry woven pattern bands in white cotton into the headscarf and the veil show many similarities. The local women were able to name each of these patterns and they also know what they mean. The isolated lozenge with double extensions of the sides, for instance, is called *itri*, meaning "star".

Die Ausführung beider Stücke ist gekonnt, beim Schleier meisterhaft. Die in weißer Baumwolle gewirkten Musterstreifen des Kopftuches und des Schleiers oder Umschlagstuches zeigen viele Übereinstimmungen. Die Frauen vor Ort können jedes dieser Muster benennen, und sie kennen auch seine Bedeutung. Zum Beispiel heißt die einzeln stehende Raute mit den doppelt fortgesetzten Seiten *itri* und bedeutet "Stern".

20 Veil/Umschlagtuch, Schleier

ca. 1910-1920
Imi n'Tatelt, Feija work/Feija-Arbeit
190 x 143 cm, Inv. no. K 122
Technical analysis/Strukturanalyse, p. 139

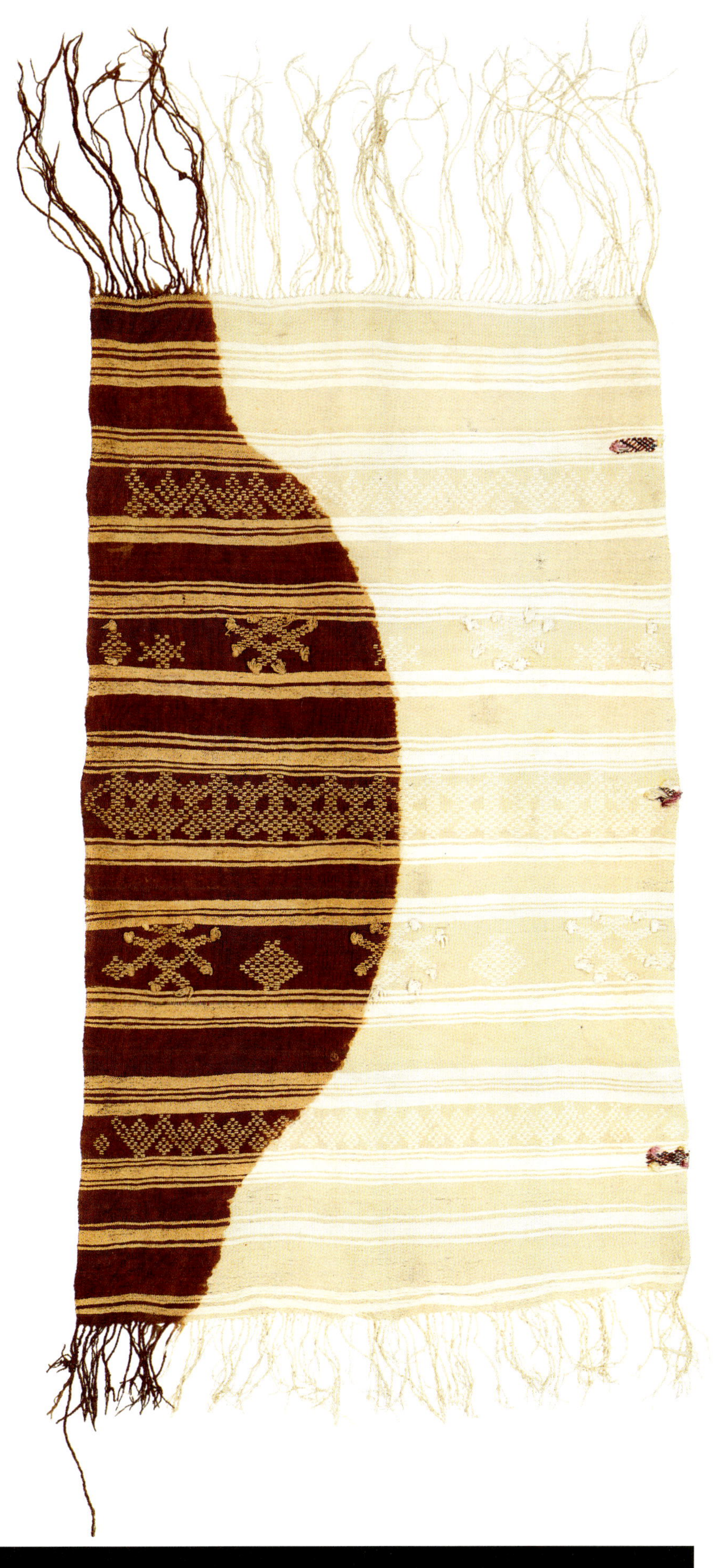

21 Adrar

Headscarf / Kopftuch, ca. 1930
Imi n'Tatelt, Feija work / Feija-Arbeit

Two valleys to the east of Imi n'Tatelt are still in Feija territory; then follows Zenaga territory. There are Feija villages south of Imi n'Tatelt as well as three important passes to the Jebel Bani Valley and the open desert. The town is (or was) well placed to be a junction nor was it so isolated as might appear when one approaches the settlement from the north.

Viewing Imi n'Tatelt from the highest point, one realizes that in the past far more towers soared upwards from it; only two have been preserved. The two large communal granaries *(agadir)* are in ruins. The *chorfa* quarter is situated on the western slopes of the mountain; on the eastern are the Koran school *(zaouia)*, the present-day administration buildings and scattered dwellings of the indigenous Feija. Belong them the residential sections of the Feija and the *haratin* sprawl along the main road.

The houses in which the Feija and the *haratin* live differ only in a few respects from those in other villages in Feija territory. There are, however, a few noteworthy peculiarities. A narrower road branches off the village street. A few paces down this second road there is a large gate, which was probably closed at night in the old days. It opens on to a small square, where the townspeople like to gather. From this square several small gates lead into dark arcades. It is through these that the entrances to the individual dwellings are reached. Between three and five houses share an arcade. The houses, walls and gateway arches are stone.

The house interiors for the most part resemble those in Feija villages. The water jars are larger and decorated with a spindle symbol; they are said to come from the Jebel Bani oases.[5] Moreover, the wall paintings are rather more sophisticated than in the villages: apart from the splashes of whitewash and hand prints, here there are representations of jewelry such as fibulae and chains as well as garlands, flowers and sun motifs. Compositions of lozenges, identical with those encountered on henna-painted woman's wrappers, are typical of the wall paintings found in Feija houses at Imi n'Tatelt. Light yellow and light blue feature in the wall paintings as well as chalk white and the natural color of clay.

Betrachtet man Imi n'Tatelt vom höchsten Punkt aus, wird klar, dass einst wesentlich mehr Türme in den Himmel ragten als die beiden heute noch erhaltenen. Die beiden großen Gemeinschaftsspeicher *(agadir)* sind im Verfall. An der westlichen Bergflanke liegt das Viertel der *chorfa*, am östlichen Bergabhang liegen die Koranschule *(zaouia)*, die Gebäude der heutigen Administration sowie einzelne Wohnhäuser der einheimischen Feija. Unterhalb davon erstrecken sich parallel zur Hauptstrasse die Wohnquartiere der Feija und der *haratin*.

Die Häuser der Feija und der *haratin* zeigen nur wenige Unterschiede zu denen in anderen Dörfern des Feija-Gebietes. Erwähnenswert sind kleine Besonderheiten: Von der Dorfstraße geht eine kleinere Straße ab, an welcher nach einigen Schritten ein großes Tor liegt, das früher wohl nachts verschlossen wurde. Das Tor führt auf einen kleinen Platz, dem Treffpunkt der Anwohner. Vom Plätzchen aus führen mehrere kleinere Tore in dunkle Laubengänge. Durch sie erreicht man die Eingänge der einzelnen Wohnhäuser, zwischen drei und fünf pro Laubengang. Häuser, Mauern und Torbogen sind in Steinarchitektur ausgeführt.

Das Innere der Häuser entspricht weitgehend jenen in den Dörfern der Feija. Die Wasserkrüge sind größer und mit einem Spindelsymbol geschmückt; sie sollen aus den Jebel Bani-Oasen kommen.[5] Auch sind die Wandbemalungen etwas raffinierter als in den Dörfern: Zusätzlich zu den Kalkspritzern und den Handabdrücken finden sich hier Schmuckdarstellungen wie Fibeln und Ketten sowie Girlanden, Blumen- und Sonnenmotive. Typisch für Feija-Häuser in Imi n'Tatelt sind Rautenkompositionen als Wandbemalungen, welche sich identisch auf den mit Henna bemalten Umschlagtüchern wiederfinden. Die Wandbemalungen sind nicht nur kalkweiß und lehmfarben, sondern zusätzlich auch hellgelb und hellblau.

5 See Grammet/De Meersman 1998, nos. 718 and 719.

5 Siehe Grammet/De Meersman 1998, Nrn. 718 und 719.

Chorfa textiles in Imi n'Tatelt

Except for the distinctively designed headscarves, *chorfa*[6] weavings do not have tapestry woven patterns. Except for the motifs painted on them in henna, the *chorfa* woman's wrappers, wedding blankets and other textiles are indistinguishable in other respects from those of the Feija. The woman's wrappers lack large corner motifs; the selvedges are painted with henna motifs instead.

Textilien der Chorfa in Imi n'Tatelt

Mit Ausnahme der besonders gestalteten Kopftücher ließen sich bei den *chorfa*[6]-Geweben keine gewirkten Muster feststellen. Ihre Umschlagtücher, Hochzeitsdecken und die anderen Textilien unterscheiden sich ansonsten in der technischen Struktur nicht von jenen der Feija, durchaus aber in den mit Henna aufgemalten Motiven. Bei den Wickeltüchern fehlen größere Eckmotive; stattdessen sind die Kanten mit Hennamotiven bemalt.

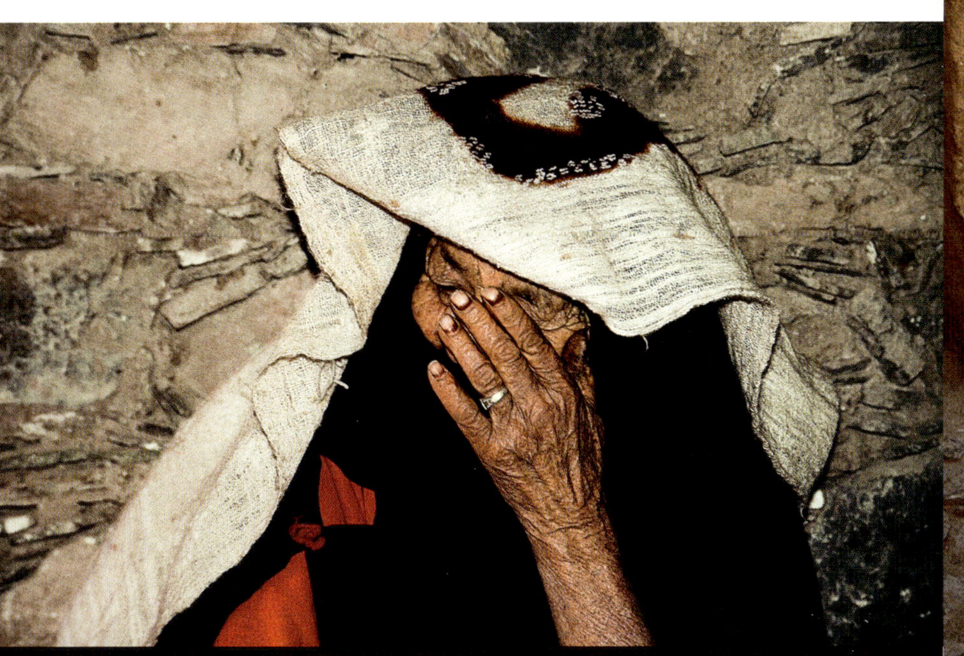

A centenarian demonstrates how the wedding headscarf *(adrar)* was worn by the *chorfa*, 2000

Eine Hundertjährige zeigt, wie das Hochzeitskopftuch *(adrar)* der *chorfa* getragen wurde, 2000

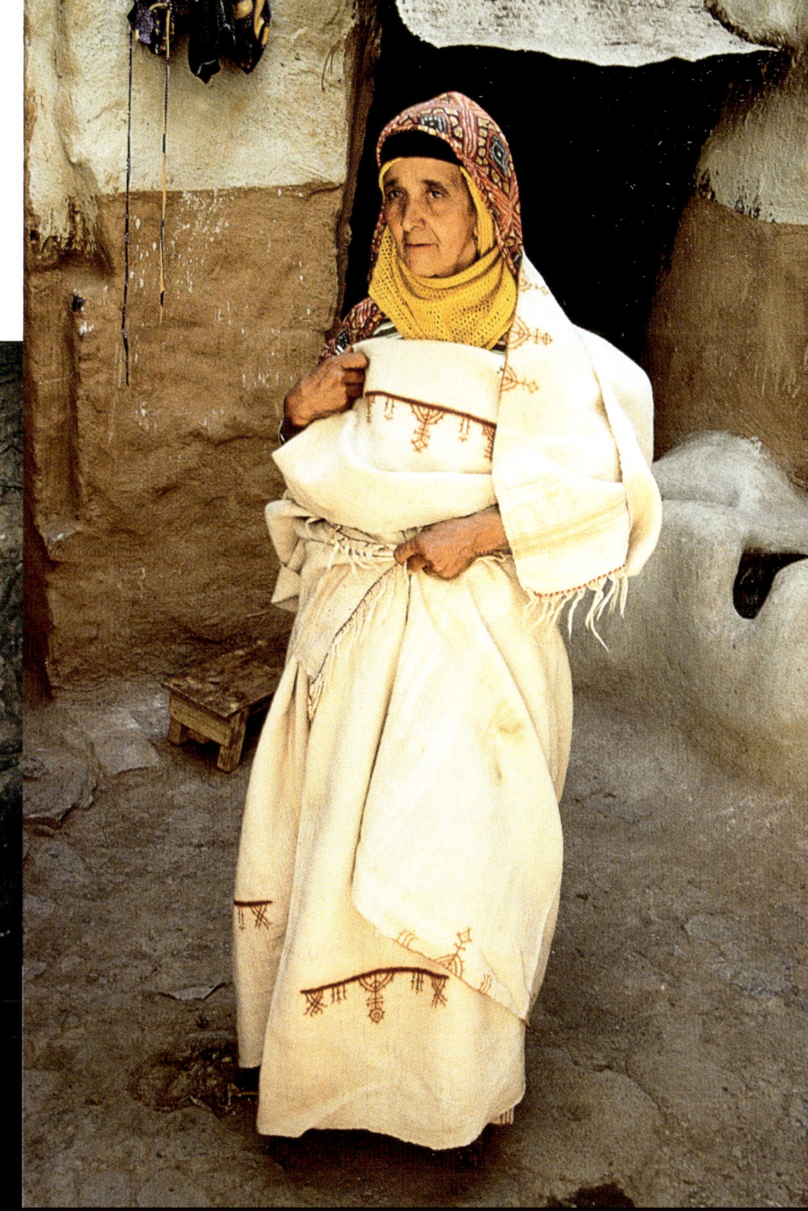

***Haik* (Cat. no. 25), draped about a *chorfa* woman, 2000**

Haik (Kat.-Nr. 25), umgewickelt von einer *chorfa*-Frau, 2000

6 **On the *chorfa* see "The Feija and Islam", p. 38.**

6 Zu den *chorfa* siehe "Die Feija und der Islam", S. 38.

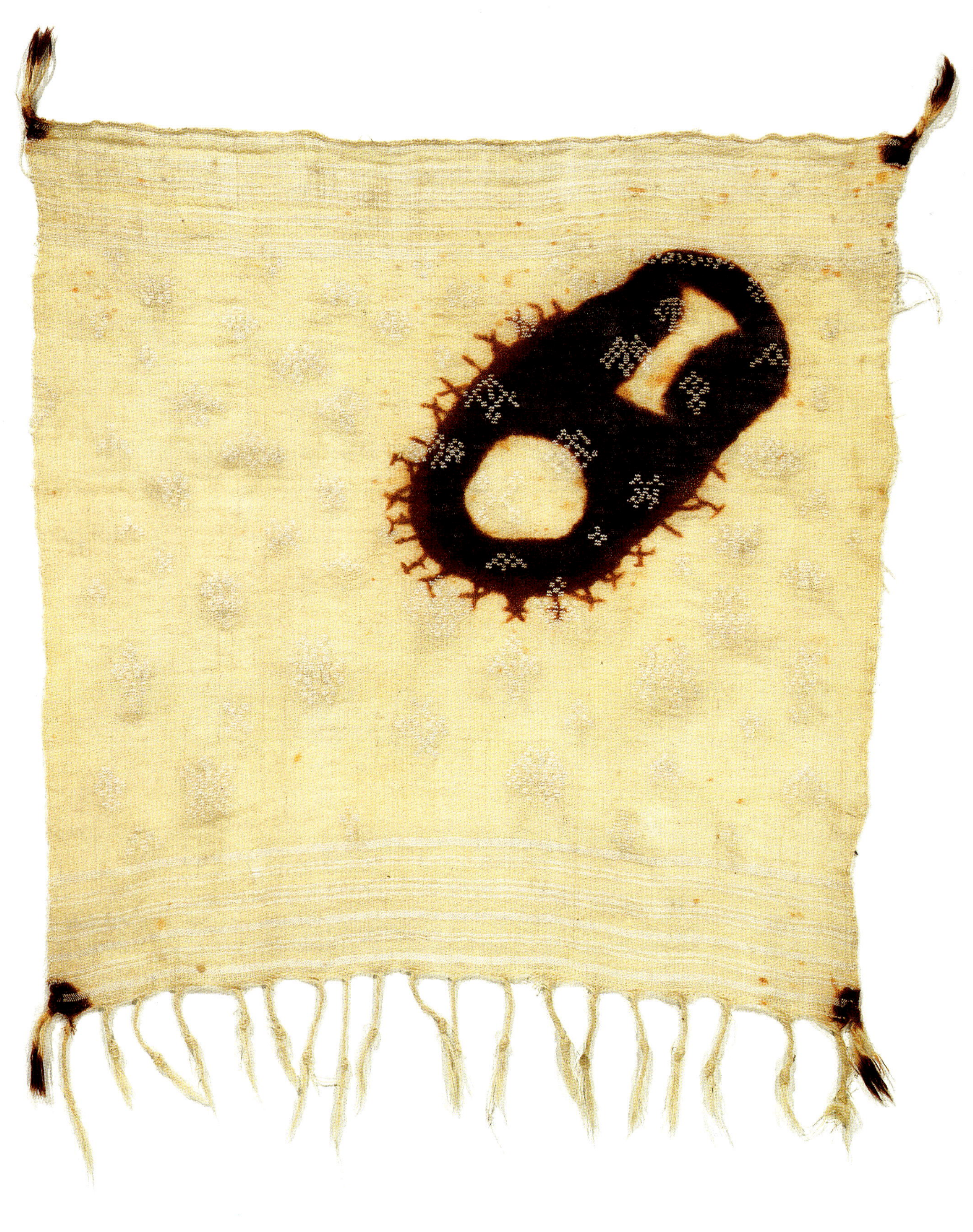

22 Adrar

Headscarf/Kopftuch, ca. 1950
Imi n'Tatelt, *chorfa* work/*chorfa*-Arbeit

Several local owners concur that the henna painting represents a symbol of heaven. A full moon symbol is reserved in the dark part as well as a concave form with two half moons. The concave form is invariably turned to the round form at an angle of 90° so that the horns of the crescent moon are turned to the sides and do not point up or down. This position is supposed to neutralize unfavorable effects: horns pointing upwards signalize piety, receptivity and joy; horns pointing downwards mean war, aggressiveness and battle. Both representations have been united in one form and are *adossée*, "turned back to back", as it were. The tapestry woven patterns in white cotton or wool in the dark henna ground are star symbols *(itri)*; these in turn bring good luck - the Berber cosmology assigns a star to every person. On some headscarves (e.g., Cat. no. 24) the tapestry woven patterns in white cotton have a deliberately reserved space for later painting with henna.

Various types of finishing are encountered along the contours of the henna forms. Type 1 (Cat. nos. 22 and 23): the shape is surrounded by characters as if from a script as they also appear in Feija henna paintings. These are probably *tifinagh* characters. Type 2 (Cat. nos. 23 and 24): the henna painting is applied twice or even more frequently to form a sort of lighter "halo" round the contour; thus the desire for rain and, concomitantly, fertility, is expressed.

Adrar with this decoration are made by the *chorfa* for weddings only. They remain with the mothers, who only lend them to their daughters for their weddings. After a wedding the *adrar* are returned to the mothers. This type of headscarf is almost square.

Nach übereinstimmenden Aussagen mehrerer Besitzerinnen vor Ort stellt die Hennabemalung ein Symbol für den Himmel dar. Im dunklen Teil sind ein Vollmond-Symbol sowie eine konkave Form ausgespart, welche zwei Halbmonde zeigt. Auf allen uns bekannten Kopftüchern steht die konkave Form um 90° zur runden gedreht, so dass die Spitzen der Mondsicheln nach den Seiten, und nicht nach oben oder unten zeigen; diese Stellung soll ungünstige Wirkungen neutralisieren: Zeigen die Spitzen nach oben, bedeutet dies Religiosität, Offenheit und Freude, zeigen sie nach unten, bedeutet dies Krieg, Aggressivität und Kampf. Man hat also beide Darstellungen in einer Form vereint und sozusagen "Rücken an Rücken" gestellt. Die im dunklen Hennagrund in weißer Baumwolle oder Wolle gewirkten Muster sind Sternsymbole *(itri)*, diese wiederum sind Glücksbringer – in der Glaubenswelt der Berber ist jedem Menschen ein Stern zugeordnet. Bei manchen Kopftüchern (z.B. Kat.-Nr. 24) sparen die weiß gewirkten Baumwollmuster absichtlich Platz für die spätere Hennabemalung aus.

Entlang der Kontur der Hennaform lassen sich verschiedene Ausführungstypen feststellen. Typ 1 (Kat.-Nrn. 22 und 23): die Form ist umgeben von schriftzeichenartigen Gebilden, wie sie auch in den Hennabemalungen der Feija vorkommen. Es dürfte sich um *tifinagh*-Zeichen handeln. Typ 2 (Kat.-Nrn. 23 und 24): Die Hennabemalung wird zwei- oder mehrmals aufgetragen und bildet um die Kontur herum eine Art helleren "Hof"; es wird damit dem Wunsch nach Regen und damit Fruchtbarkeit Ausdruck verliehen.

Adrar mit diesem Dekor werden von den *chorfa* ausschließlich für die Hochzeit hergestellt. Sie bleiben im Besitz einer Mutter, welche das Kopftuch ihrer Tochter ausschließlich für die Hochzeitstage ausleiht. Danach geht der *adrar* an die Mutter zurück. Dieser Kopftuchtypus ist beinahe quadratisch.

23 Adrar

Headscarf/Kopftuch, ca. 1950
Imi n'Tatelt, *chorfa* work/*chorfa*-Arbeit
100 x 91 cm, Inv. no. 198b
Simone Korolnik Jablonka, Tübingen

24 Adrar

Headscarf/Kopftuch, close of the 19th cent./ca. Ende 19. Jh.
Imi n'Tatelt, *chorfa* work/*chorfa*-Arbeit
ca. 93 x 83 cm
The Minneapolis Institute of Arts, Minneapolis, Minnesota, USA, Inv. no. 96.16

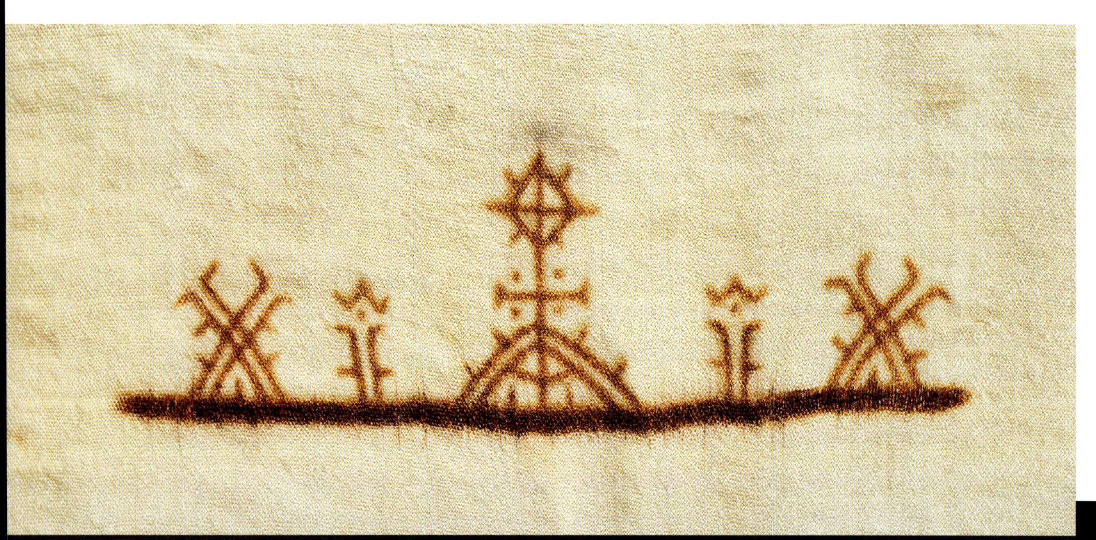

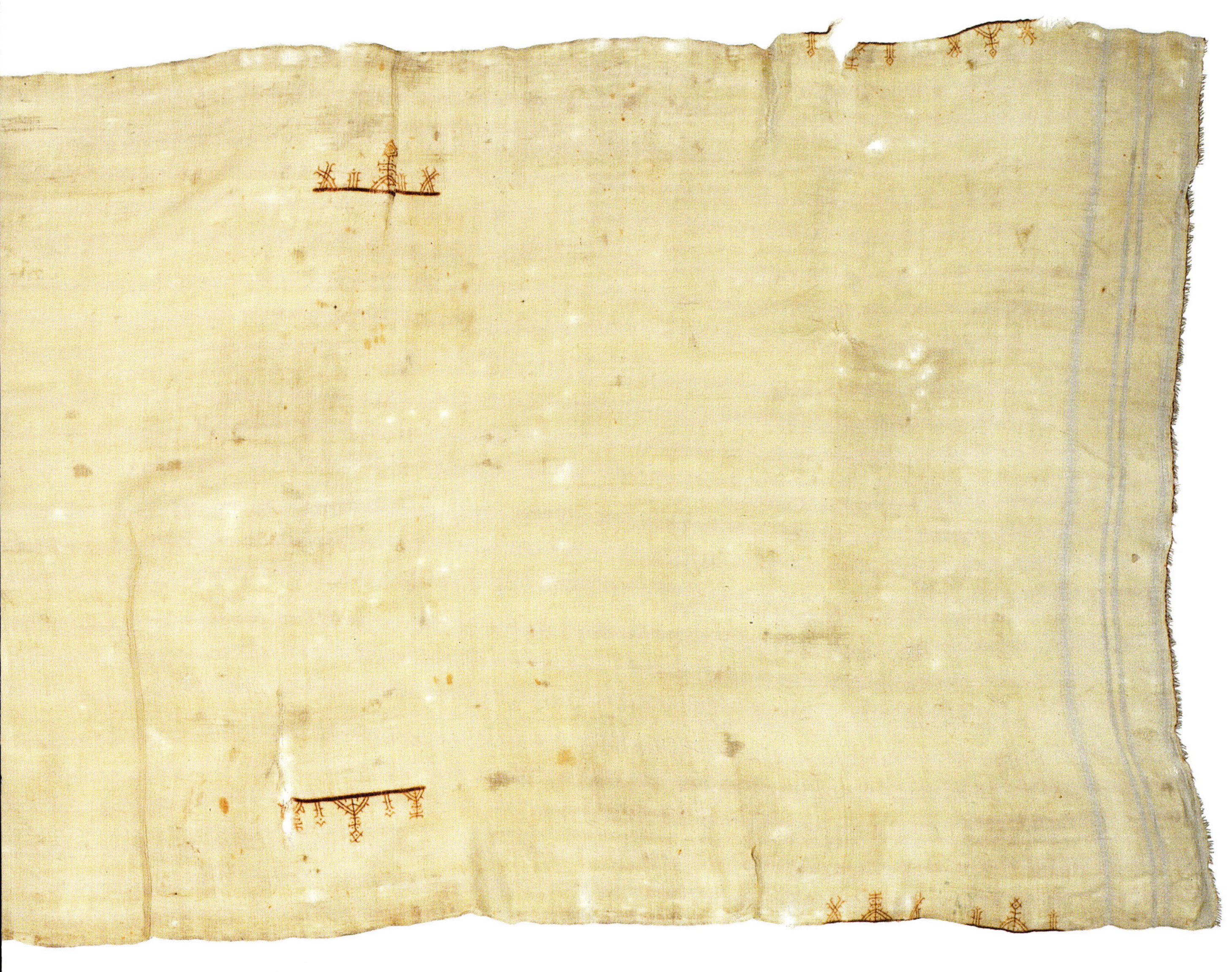

This piece may have been made as a wedding blanket or as a bridal veil instead of a woman's wrapper. The delicacy and transparency of this weaving suggest that this may have been the case. The division of the field corresponds to that of Feija woman's wrappers. The four recessed motifs are on a baseline; together the symbols form the lucky number five *(chamsa)*. The individual signs each have a meaning. Some of them may be Arabized *tifinagh* characters.

Es ist möglich, dass dieses Stück nicht als Wickeltuch hergestellt wurde, sondern als Hochzeitsdecke, als Umschlagtuch oder Schleier für eine Braut. Feinheit und Transparenz des Gewebes sprechen dafür. Die Feldeinteilung entspricht jener der Feija-Wickeltücher. Die vier nach innen versetzten Motive stehen auf einer Grundlinie; die Symbole bilden zusammen die Glückszahl Fünf *(chamsa)*. Die einzelnen Zeichen haben eine Bedeutung. Möglicherweise sind einige davon arabisierte *tifinagh*-Zeichen.

25 Haik

Woman's wrapper / Wickeltuch, ca. 1890
Imi n'Tatelt
Chorfa family of el Yâacoubi (previous owners) / *chorfa*-Familie el Yâacoubi (Vorbesitzer)
400 x 143 cm, Inv. no. K 171

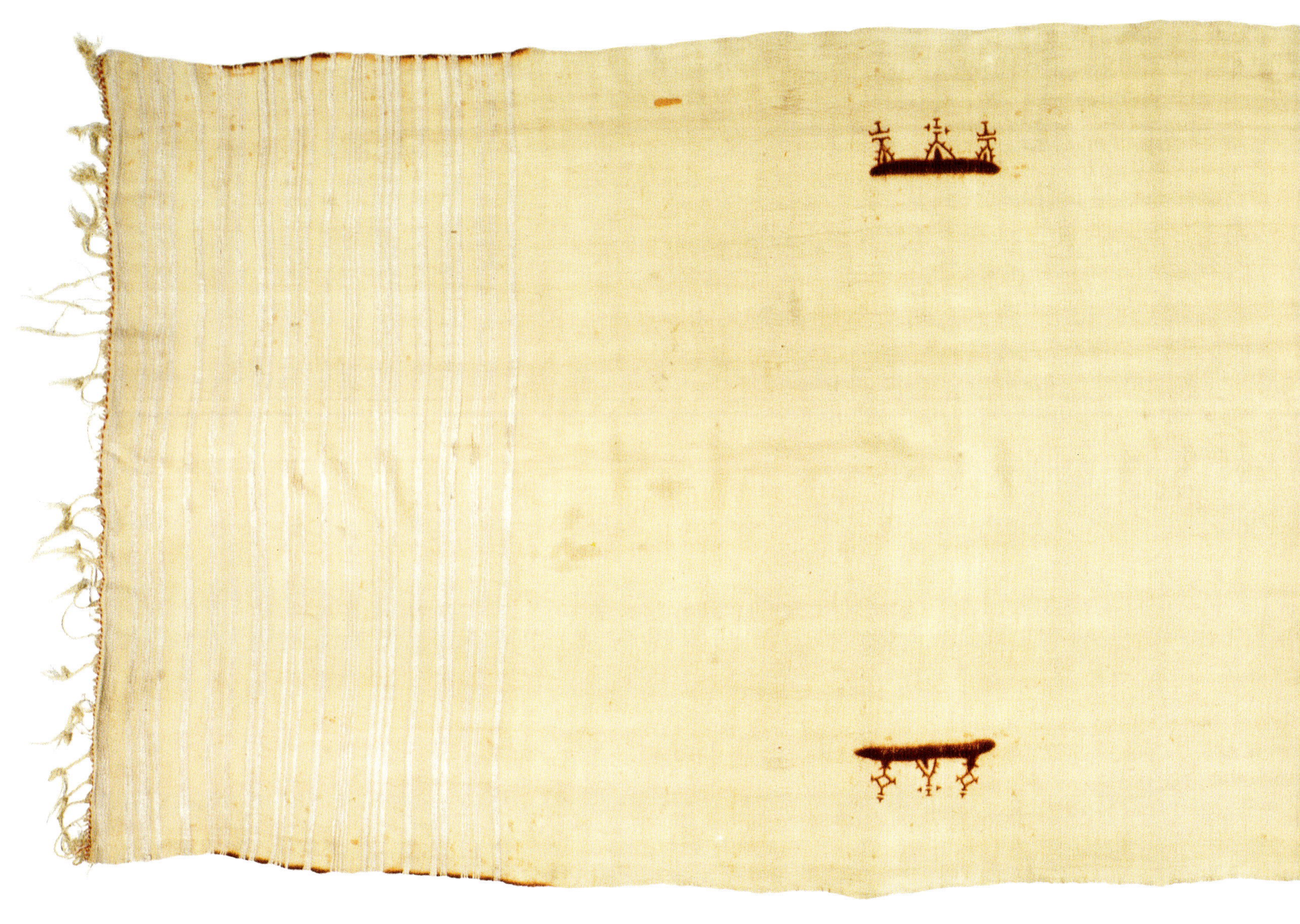

According to Saina Bellaz Ouaziz, who was born in 1950, this piece belonged to her aunt. She was married in Agadez (Niger). In addition to the indigenous signs, the recondite signs on Cat. no. 25 are here partly replaced by "Agadez crosses" (like those known from Tuareg jewelry). The symbolic five has given way to a triad combination.

Das Stück gehörte nach Auskunft von Saina Bellah Ouaziz, geb. 1950, ihrer Tante. Sie war in Agadez (Niger) verheiratet. Neben den gebietstypischen sind an die Stelle der geheimnisvollen Zeichen von Kat.-Nr. 25 teilweise "Kreuze von Agadez" (wie etwa beim Tuareg-Schmuck) getreten; aus der Fünfzahl der Symbole wurde eine Dreierkombination.

26 Haik

Woman's wrapper / Wickeltuch, ca. 1920

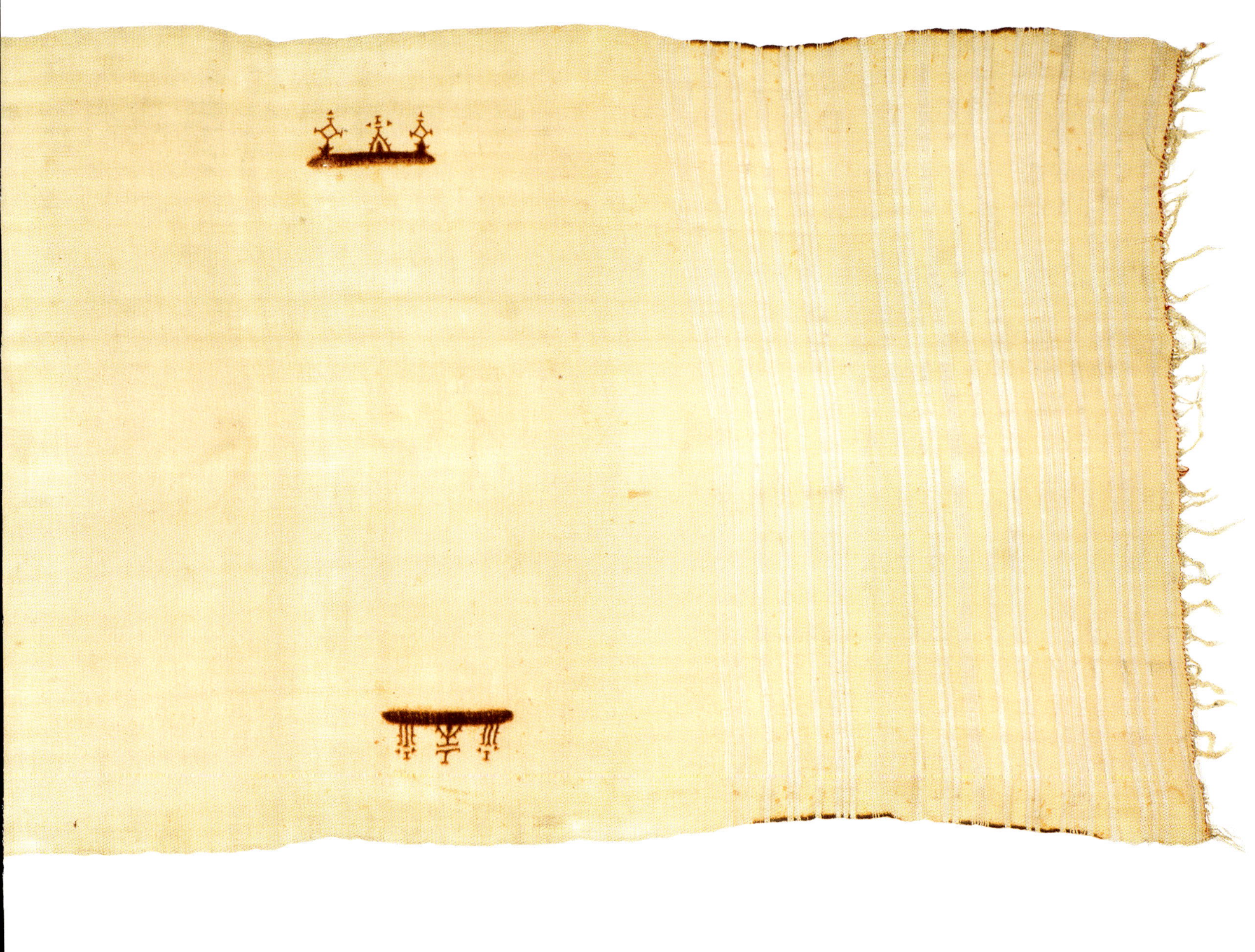

Textiles from the shrines at Imi n'Tatelt

The textiles that follow come from the shrines at Imi n'Tatelt (see also "The Feija and Islam", p. 38). They were kept for some time near the saint's tomb (fig. p. 39). The tomb of Beni Yâacoub was probably covered with them or they were laid on the floor of the *zaouia* so that pilgrims might lie on them or eat food set out on them.

The circumstance that an object, in this case a weaving, was kept for a certain length of time in a shrine means to believers that such weavings are "charged" with *baraka*. Some of the old, even very old, or at least worn, weavings used to be sold, and are still sold, by the *chorfa* and custodians of the Koran school *(zaouia)* to the pious so that they may attain *baraka*. Such pieces may not be resold by those who have thus acquired them but must remain in their families. Legends often cling to such pieces. Stirring but unprovable (see the descriptions of the individual pieces), these legends lend the pieces with which they are associated a highly mystical aura.

It was impossible to verify from which population groups or tribes the women who wove these pieces came since all resident tribal groups make identical wrappers and headscarves. What could, on the other hand, be ascertained was that most textiles were donated unpainted to the *zaouia*. The task of painting them with henna afterwards fell to *chorfa* women. The basic design of the henna painting on these pieces resembles that on Feija work yet the motifs are in a form encountered only in the *zaouia*: these are invariably "*baraka* symbols". The dates often found on these textiles may refer to the year they were consecrated or may be commemorative although they hardly indicate the date of weaving.

Textilien aus den Heiligtümern von Imi n'Tatelt

Die folgenden Textilien stammen aus den Heiligtümern von Imi n'Tatelt (siehe auch "Die Feija und der Islam", S. 38). Sie wurden einige Zeit in der Nähe des Heiligengrabes verwahrt (Abb. S. 39). Man bedeckte vermutlich das Grab von Beni Yâacoub damit, oder sie wurden in der *zaouia* auf den Boden gelegt, damit sich die Pilger darauf lagern oder ihr Essen einnehmen konnten.

Die Tatsache, dass sich ein Gegenstand, in diesem Falle ein Gewebe, eine gewisse Zeit im Heiligtum befand, bedeutet den Gläubigen, dass sich die Gewebe mit *baraka* "aufgeladen" haben. Die zum Teil alten, sehr alten oder jedenfalls abgenützten Gewebe wurden früher und werden heute noch vom jeweiligen *chorfa* und Wächter der Koranschule *(zaouia)* zur *baraka*-Erringung an zahlende Gläubige verkauft; sie dürfen dann vom Erwerber nicht weiterverkauft werden, sondern müssen in dessen Familie verbleiben. Die Stücke sind oft begleitet von abenteuerlichen, nicht überprüfbaren Legenden (siehe die Beschreibungen der einzelnen Stücke) und haben eine stark mystische Ausstrahlung.

Es konnte nicht einwandfrei geklärt werden, welchen Bevölkerungsgruppen bzw. Stämmen die Weberinnen dieser Textilien angehören, da alle ansässigen Stammesgruppen identische Wickel- und Kopftücher herstellen. Bekannt wurde dagegen, dass Textilien der *zaouia* gespendet werden, meist noch unbemalt. Die Henna-Bemalung wurde dann durch *chorfa*-Frauen ausgeführt. Die Henna-Bemalung orientiert sich im Aufbau zwar an den Feija-Arbeiten, die Motive sind in dieser Form jedoch nur in der *zaouia* anzutreffen: Es handelt sich durchweg um "*baraka*-Symbole". Die oftmals aufgebrachten Jahreszahlen könnten auf das Jahr der Widmung verweisen oder ein Erinnerungsdatum sein, kaum jedoch ein Herstellungsdatum.

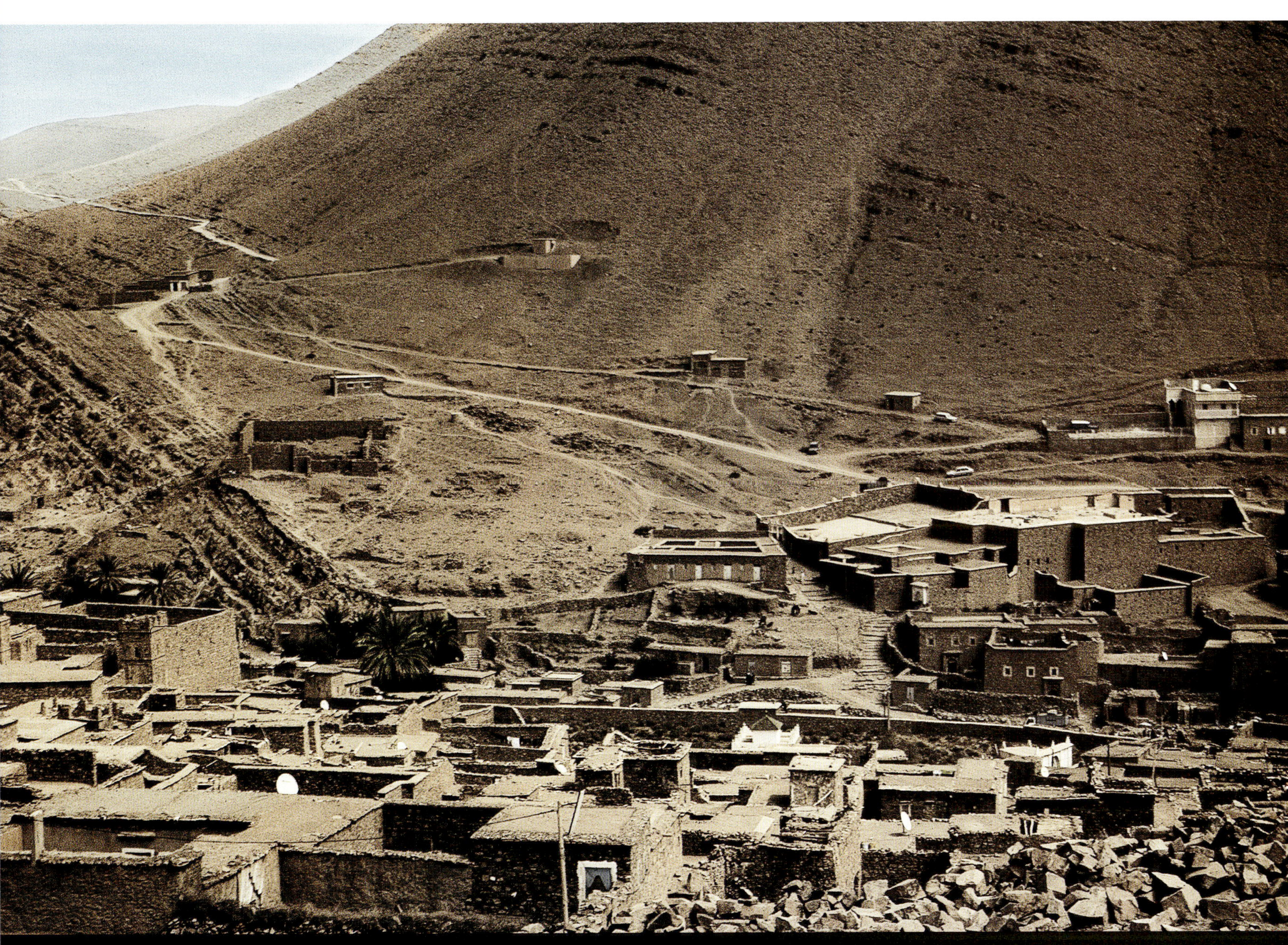

Imi n'Tatelt. The big 16th century building complex of the Beni Yâacoub *zaouia,* entirely sourrounded by a wall, is situated at the upper edge of the village (far right), 2000

Imi n'Tatelt. Der große, gänzlich ummauerte Gebäudekomplex der *zaouia* Beni Yâacoub aus dem 16. Jahrhundert liegt am oberen Dorfrand (rechts), 2000

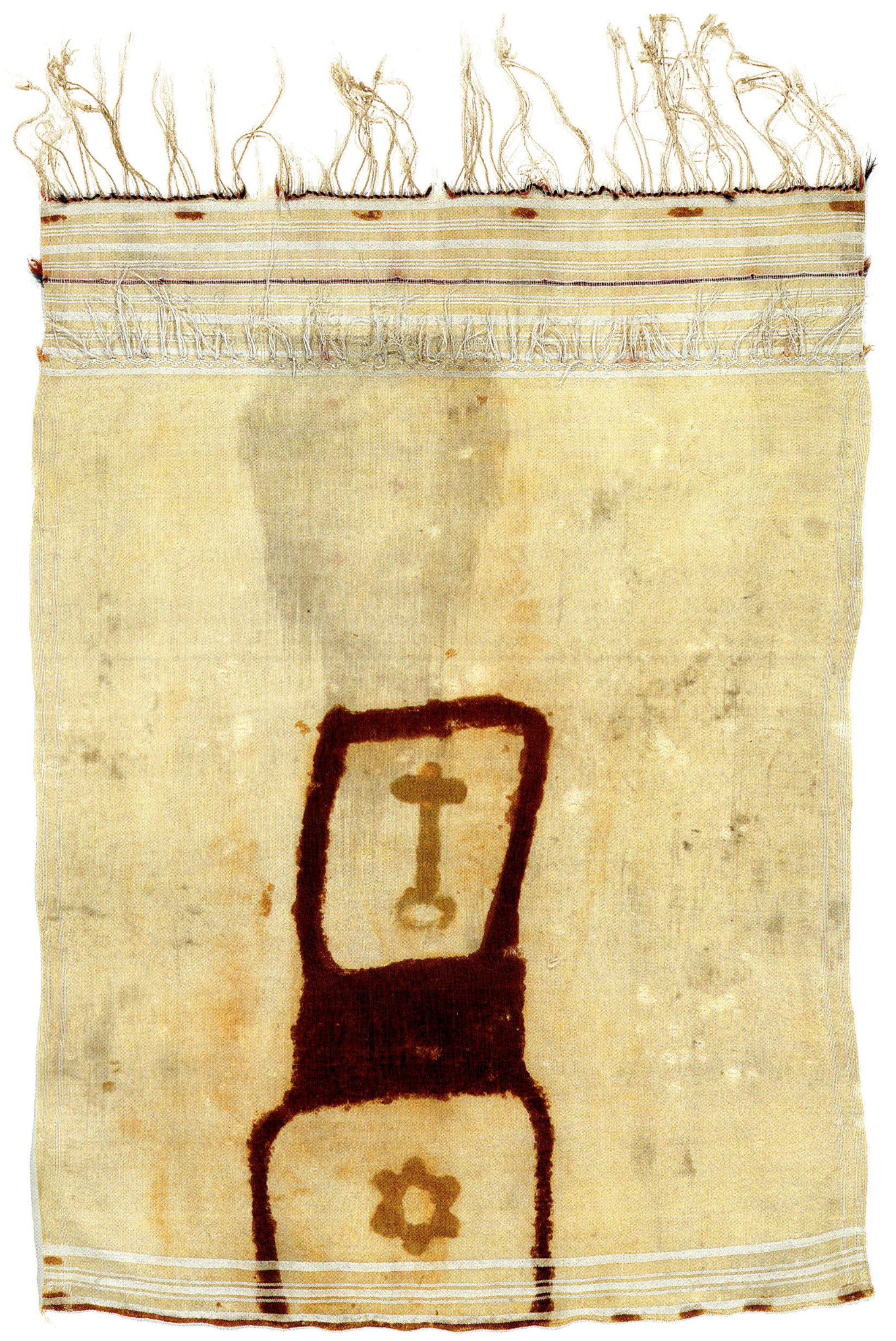

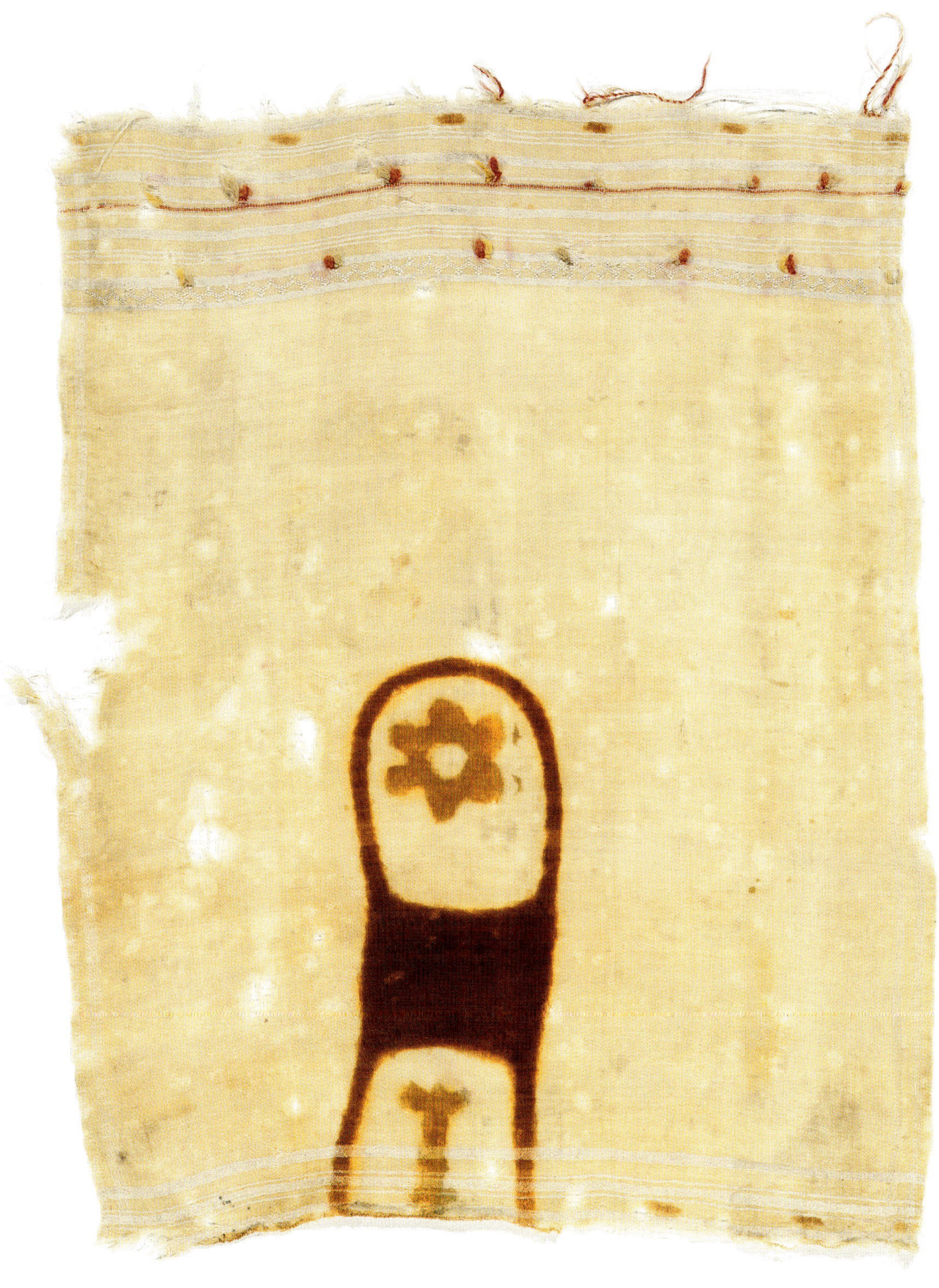

The basic design of both pieces is typically Feija (see "Iligh and Afouzar", p. 80). The motifs within the *bouitri* or gate symbols are different, however. These two headscarves may have been used at weddings; in any case the henna paintings were applied in two stages and at different times. The Solomon's Seal which has become a flower and the cruciform sign appear once in the upper zone and once in the lower of the main symbol. The legend associated with these headscarves is that they belonged to wives of the saint.

Die Grundgestaltung beider Stücke ist typisch für die Feija (siehe "Iligh und Afouzar", S. 80). Die Motive innerhalb der *bouitri-* oder Torsymbole sind jedoch verschieden. Möglich, dass beide Kopftücher für Hochzeiten verwendet wurden, jedenfalls sind die Hennabemalungen in mindestens zwei Etappen und zu verschiedenen Zeiten aufgetragen worden. Das blumengewordene Salomonsiegel sowie das kreuzartige Zeichen befinden sich einmal im oberen, einmal im unteren Teil des Hauptsymbols. Um diese Kopftücher rankt sich die Legende, dass sie Frauen des Heiligen gehört hätten.

28 Adrar

Headscarf/Kopftuch, ca. 1870-1890
Imi n'Tatelt, *zaouia*

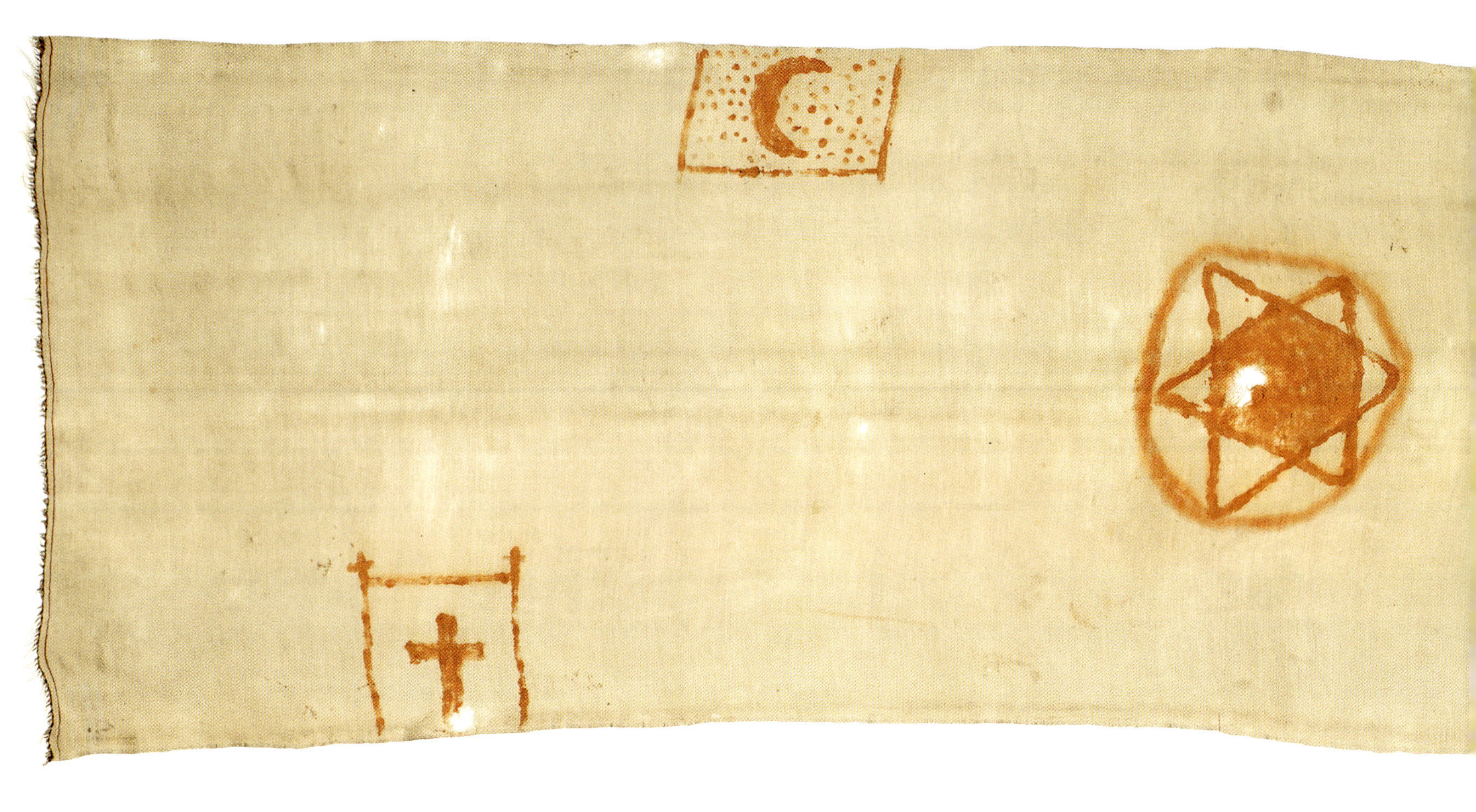

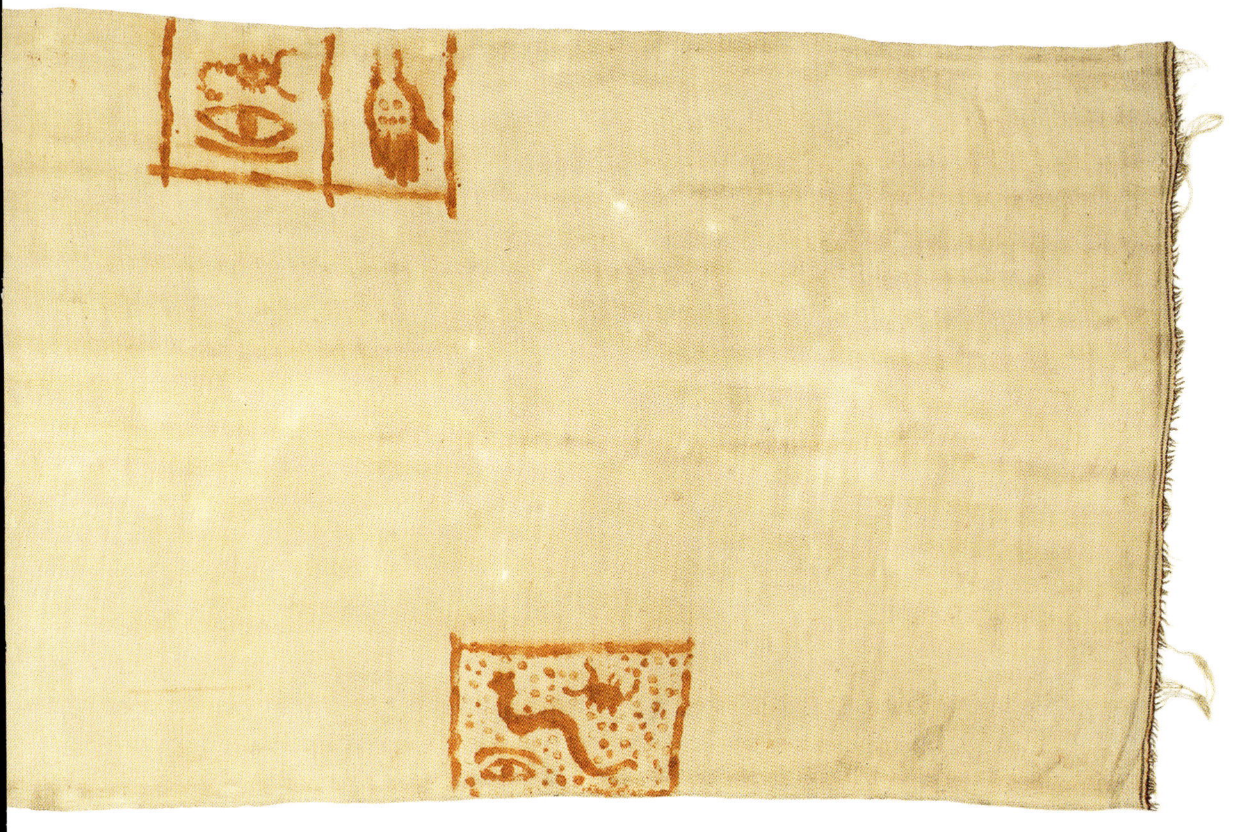

Except for the central motif, similar to Cat. no. 30. The six-pointed star (Solomon's Seal) is the symbol of Jewry - here used as a sign with special powers.

Mit Ausnahme des Zentralmotivs ähnlich wie das Stück Kat.-Nr. 30. Bei dem sechsstrahligen Stern (dem Salomonssiegel) handelt es sich um das Symbol für das Judentum – hier als Zeichen spezieller Kraft verwendet.

29 Haik

Woman's wrapper/Wickeltuch, 1912
Imi n'Tatelt, *zaouia*

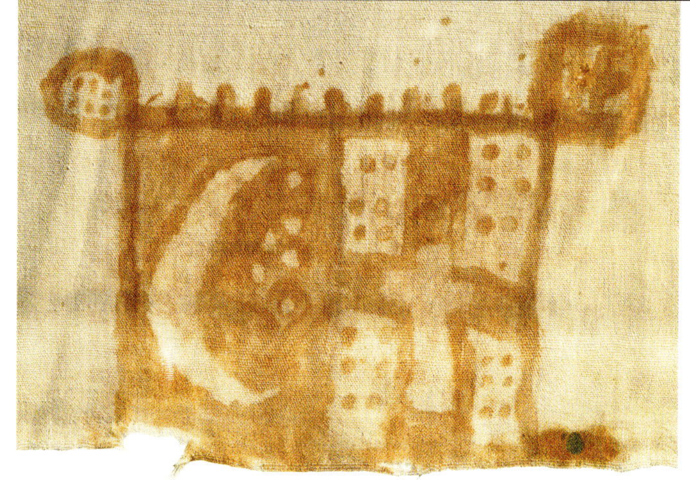

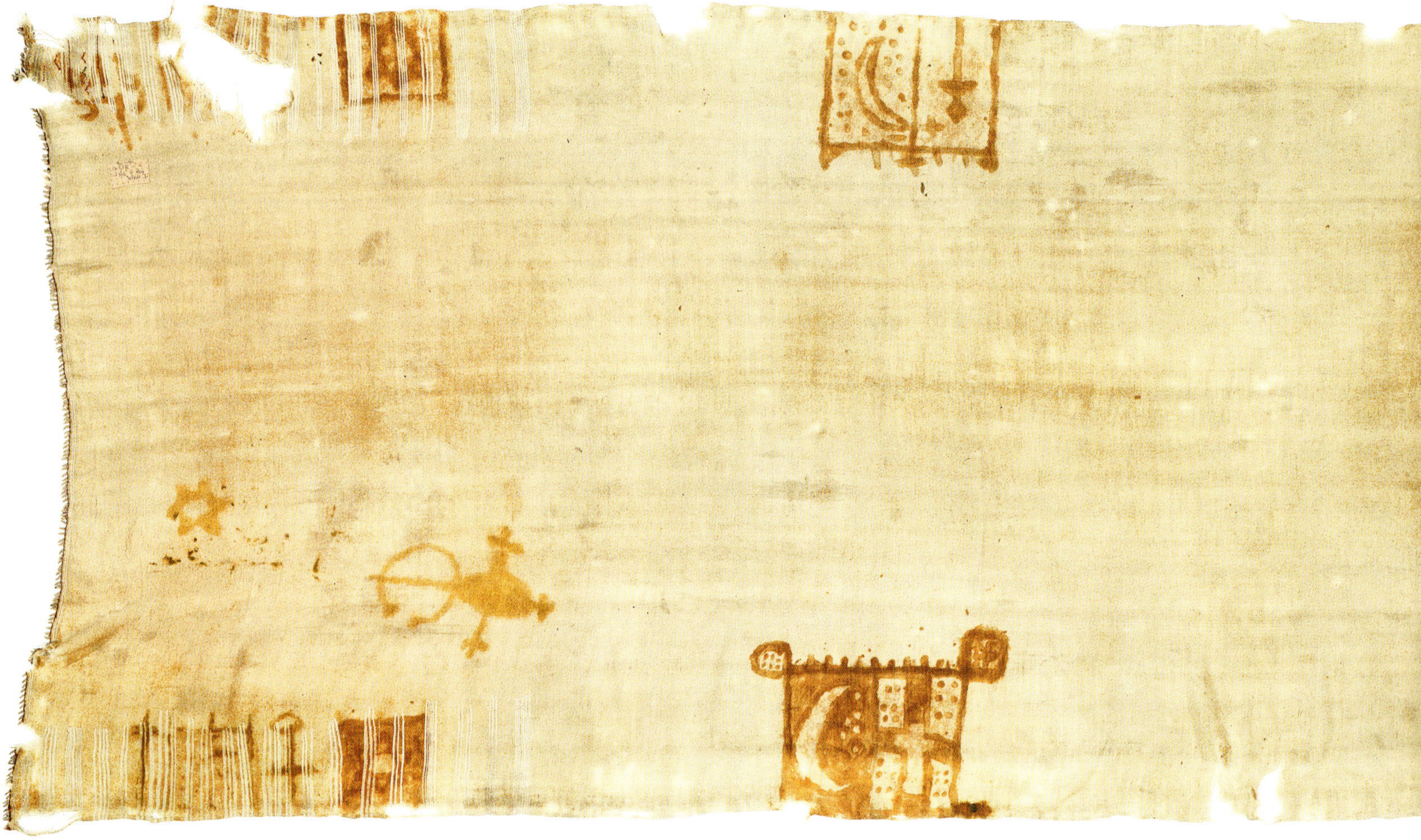

Arab dating: 919 (= 1513 AD). *Tismissine* motifs (see Cat. no. 15) along the sides, in them symbols such as the moon, stars, crosses and the Solomon's Seal turned into a flower. The corner motifs are a combination of short cotton shots and henna painting. The henna painting seems to have been applied in two work stages (the tortoise fibula and the "star flower" are probably earlier). The symbols in the cartouches as well as the date (possibly a commemorative date) belong to the context of the shrine. The piece has been dated to 1956 on the basis of ^{14}C dating carried out by the ETH Zurich on 15. Sept. 1999. Our own analysis of the fabric as well as our experience tend to make us prefer a date of ca. 1900.

Arabisch datiert: 919 (= 1513 n. Chr.). *Tismissine*-Motive (siehe Kat. Nr. 15) an den Seiten, darin Symbole wie Mond, Sterne, Kreuz, blumengewordenes Salomonsiegel. Die Eckmotive sind eine Kombination von kurzen Baumwollschüssen und Hennabemalungen. Die Henna-Bemalungen scheinen in zwei Arbeitsgängen aufgetragen zu sein (die Schildkröten-Fibel und der "Blumenstern" sind wohl älteren Datums). Die Symbole in den Kartuschen sowie die Datierung (eventuell ein Erinnerungsdatum) gehören in das Umfeld des Heiligtums. Eine ^{14}C-Datierung der ETH Zürich vom 15.9.1999 führte zu einer Datierung des Stücks auf das Jahr 1956. Nach unserer eigenen Gewebeanalyse und Erfahrung vermuten wir allerdings eine Herstellung um 1900.

30 Haik

Woman's wrapper / Wickeltuch, ca. 1900 or 1956 (^{14}C-AMS dating / ^{14}C-Datierung)
Imi n'Tatelt, *zaouia*
450 x 140 cm, Inv. no. K 175
Technical analysis / Strukturanalyse, p. 139

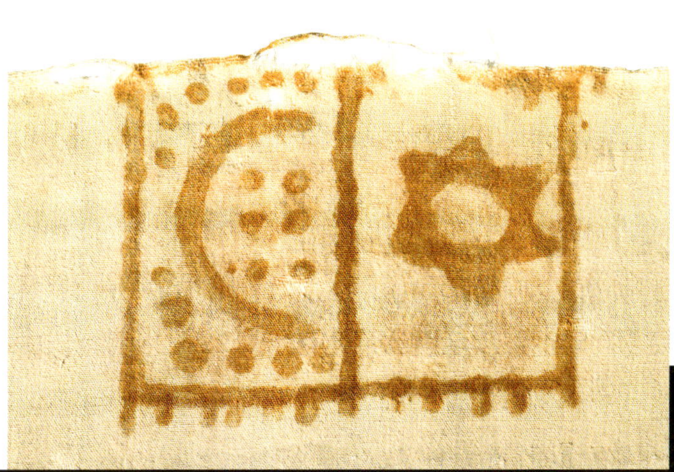

30 Details

Since this cloth is unusually wide, it is unlikely that it was made as an article of clothing. Its salient feature is the two eye symbols painted in henna with eyebrows and five dots: the eyes were also deliberately perforated; we do not know what this means. A date, 1074 (= 1664 AD) is painted on but does not stand for the year in which the piece was made.

Das Tuch ist ungewöhnlich breit; es ist daher wenig wahrscheinlich, dass es für Bekleidungszwecke hergestellt wurde. Hervorstechendstes Merkmal sind die beiden mit Henna gemalten Augensymbole mit den Brauen und den fünf Punkten: die Augen wurden zudem absichtlich perforiert; die Bedeutung entzieht sich unserer Kenntnis. Eine Datierung 1074 (= 1664 n. Chr.) ist zwar aufgemalt, bezeichnet aber nicht das Herstellungsjahr des Stückes.

31 Haik

Woman's wrapper/Wickeltuch, ca. 1920
Imi n'Tatelt, *zaouia*
475 x 153 cm, Inv. no. K 176

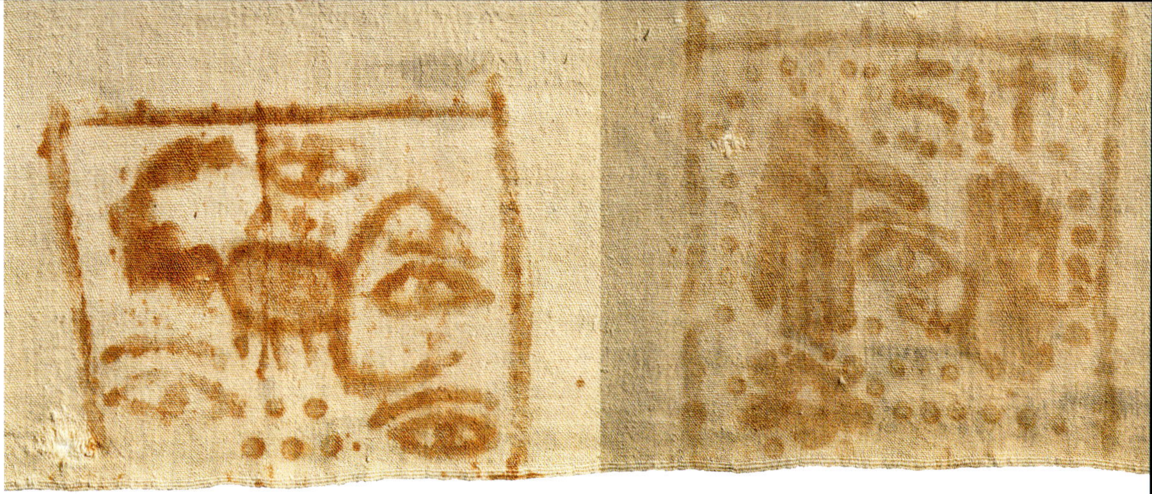

31 Details

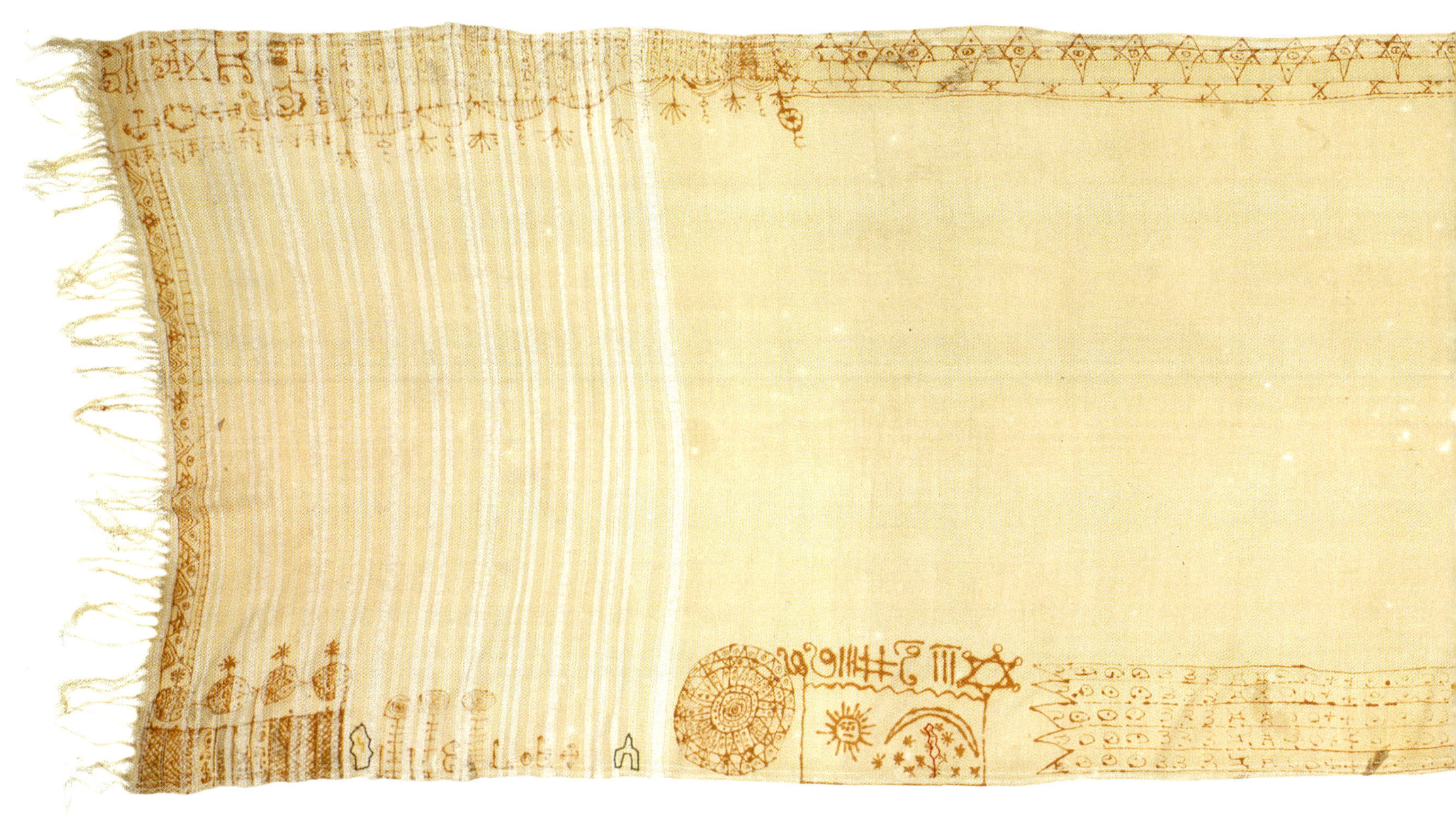

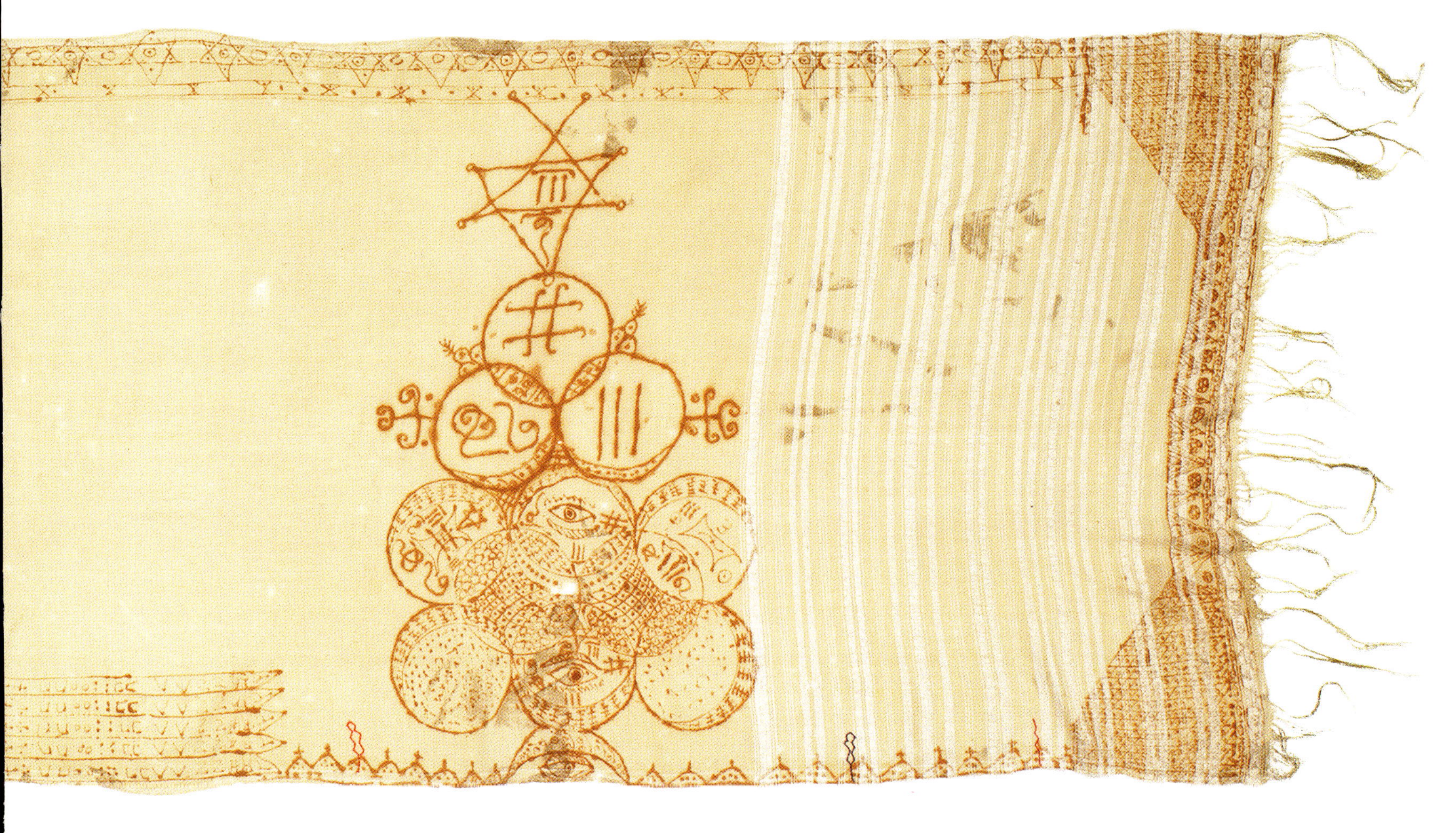

32 The *haik* of the *fqîh* / Der *haik* des *fqîh*

ca. 1850
Imi n'Tatelt, Feija weaving / Feija-Webarbeit
478 x 123 cm, Inv. no. K 201

The haik of the fqîh

This cloth has the same dimensions and facture as a cloth worn as drapery by women and was certainly woven by a Feija woman in Feija territory yet it was used by a *fqîh*[7]. This is why the henna paintings show special motifs. The *fqîh* probably used this cloth to wrap up sick persons or to cover them or he may have sat on it himself in order that he might be invested with the powers of the amulets painted on it.

The signs painted in henna with symbolism referring to Islam will be discussed in the following essay by Edward Badeen. However, the *haik* of the *fqîh* is also painted with *tifinagh* characters (cf. "The Imazighen and their Tifinagh", p. 22), a script which, as we have been told by the Feija, only one in one thousand can now read or write (this is probably the Moroccan *tifinagh*). Most of the words written in *tifinagh* characters in the Berber dialect spoken by the Feija on the *haik* of the *fqîh* designate the names of fruits and herbs of the kinds used in Berber medicine (see details).

The mid-19th-century date is based on statements made by the *fqîh's* family. The henna painting was evidently applied in several different onsets of work. No comparable piece is known.

Der Haik des Fqîh

Das Textil hat zwar die Abmessungen und die Machart eines Frauen-Wickeltuches und ist mit Bestimmtheit von einer Feija-Frau im Gebiet der Feija gewoben worden, doch wurde es von einem *fqîh*[7] verwendet. Daher zeigen die darauf befindlichen Henna-Malereien auch ganz besondere Motive. Vermutlich benutzte der *fqîh* das Tuch, um Kranke darin einzuwickeln oder zu bedecken. Oder er setzte sich selber darauf, damit sich die Wirkungen der aufgemalten Amulette auf ihn übertrugen.

Soweit sie sich auf den Bereich des Islam bezieht, wird auf die Symbolik der auf dem Tuch befindlichen Henna-Zeichen im nachfolgenden Beitrag von Edward Badeen eingegangen. Zusätzlich ist der *haik* des *fqîh* aber auch mit *tifinagh*-Zeichen versehen (vgl. "Die Imazighen und ihr Tifinagh", S. 22), eine Schrift, die laut unseren Informaten vor Ort, bei den Feija heute nur noch rund ein Promille der Bevölkerung lesen oder schreiben kann (es handelt sich dabei um das marokkanische *tifinagh*). Die mit *tifinagh*-Zeichen im Berberdialekt der Feija auf den *haik* des *fqîh* geschriebenen Worte bezeichnen mehrheitlich Namen von Früchten und Kräutern wie sie auch in der Berber-Apotheke verwendet werden (siehe Details).

Die Datierung auf die Mitte des 19. Jahrhunderts beruht auf Aussagen der Familie des *fqîh*. Die Henna-Bemalung ist offenbar in mehreren Schüben erfolgt. Ein vergleichbares Stück ist bisher nicht bekannt.

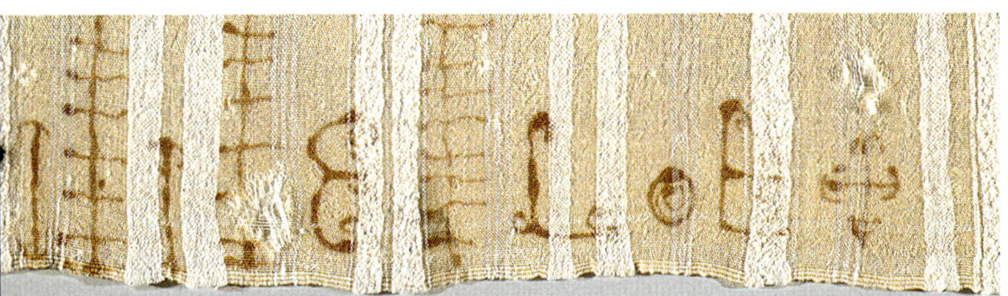

liqamt **= mint**

liqamt = Minze

Details from the ***haik*** of the ***fqîh***;
names of therapeutic herbs in ***tifinagh*** characters

Details aus dem *haik* des *fqîh*;
Namen von Heilpflanzen in *tifinagh*-Schrift

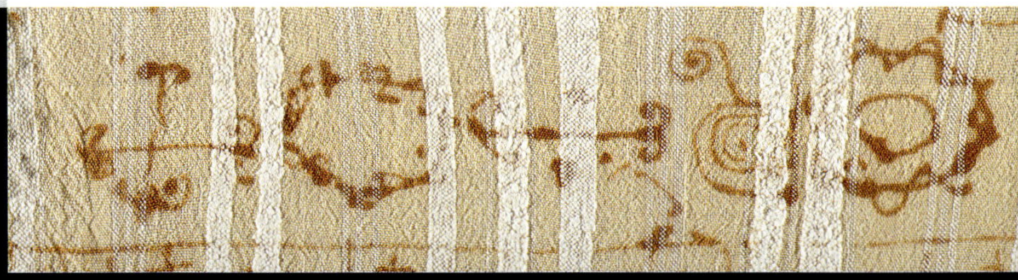

tiskert **= garlic**

tiskert = Knoblauch

The Symbols on the haik of the fqîh

Edward Badeen

With a relatively large rectangular surface, the *haik* of the *fqīh* is covered along all sides with magic signs and dashes. They represent a magic wall of protection to safeguard the *fqīh* against the hostile forces which beset his suffering patients with their evil magical powers. Magic symbols from several areas are represented, containing as much protective force as possible, tacit but highly eloquent all the same.

Some magical signs on the *haik* of the *fqīh* belong to the disfigured cuneiform writing represented in what is known as "spectacles script".[8] These are represented here by the reflection of a modified Arab letter "M" flanking the two impinging circles embedded in the pyramid of circles below the hexagram. We also encounter an echo of this in the circles of the two large hexagrams which are fitted out with small circles.

Apart from numerous dots and dashes, the following geometric figurations are present: triangles (parts of the plentiful hexagrams and the many X signs with surrounding parallels), quadrilateral forms (the rectangular cloth itself, the quadrilateral with sun, half moon and stars) and large circles which are recognizably such as well as countless small, often unrecognizable circles. We notice all sorts of arcs, both large and small, turned inwards or outwards in configurations. Some of these form half moons laden with small signs; others form the frame for eye signs. Still others are elements of eyelids and brows as well as the domes of churches, synagogues, mosques or *marabout* tombs. In the circles we find magical square cells, etc., drawn freehand and imprecisely.[9]

Die Symbole des Haiks des Fqîh

Edward Badeen

Der *haik* des *fqīh* ist eine relativ große rechteckige Fläche und von allen Seiten am Rande mit Zauberzeichen und Strichen versehen. Es handelt sich hierbei um eine magische Schutzmauer, die den *fqīh* gegen die feindseligen Kräfte, welche seine leidenden Patienten begleiten, samt ihren bösen Zauberenergien schützt. Es sind mehrere Bereiche der magisch wirkenden Symbole vertreten, die möglichst viel Schutzkraft in sich bergen, zwar wortlos, aber viel sagend.

Manche Zauberzeichen auf dem *haik* des *fqīh* gehören in den Bereich der entstellten Keilschrift, vertreten in der Form der sogenannten "Brillenschrift".[8] Diese sind hier durch die Wiederspiegelung eines abgewandelten arabischen Buchstabens "M" auf beiden Seiten der zwei sich berührenden Kreise vertreten, die in die Pyramide aus Kreisen unterhalb des Hexagramms eingebettet sind. Einen Widerhall davon finden wir auch in den mit kleinen Kreisen versehenen Ecken der beiden großen Hexagramme.

Neben vielen Punkten und Linien sind folgende geometrische Figuren vertreten: Dreiecke (Teile der zahlreichen Hexagramme und der vielen X-Zeichen mit den sie umfassenden Parallelen), Vierecke (das Tuch selbst, das Viereck mit Sonne, Halbmond und Sternen) und große erkennbare sowie zahlreiche kleine, manchmal unerkennbare Kreise. Wir bemerken allerlei Bögen, kleine wie große, in Figuren nach außen oder nach ihnen gerichtet. Manche bilden mit kleinen Zeichen beladene Halbmonde, andere formen den Rahmen für Augenzeichnungen, weitere sind Bestandteile von Augenlidern und -brauen, von Kuppeln von Kirchen, Synagogen, Moscheen oder *marabout*-Grabmälern. In den Kreisen finden wir unter anderem frei und ungenau gezeichnete magische Quadratzellen.[9]

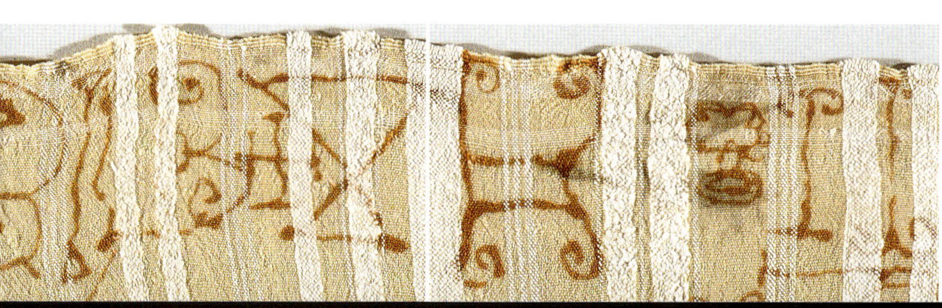

tiyni = dates (desert fruits) *louz* = almonds

tiyni = Datteln (Früchte der Wüste) *louz* = Mandeln

7 On the *fqîh* see "Traditional popular medicine and the fqîh", p. 45 f.
8 Winkler 1930, p. 37. Extensively on the spectacles letters, ibid. pp. 150-167.
9 Cf. the rock carvings at prehistoric cult sites in Spain: ibid. p. 43 f.

7 Zum *fqîh* siehe "Die traditionelle Volksmedizin und der Fqîh", S. 45 ff.
8 Winkler 1930, S. 37. Ausführlich über die Brillenbuchstaben, ebenda, S. 150-167.
9 Vgl. die Felszeichnungen vorgeschichtlicher Kultstätten Spaniens, ebenda, S. 43f.

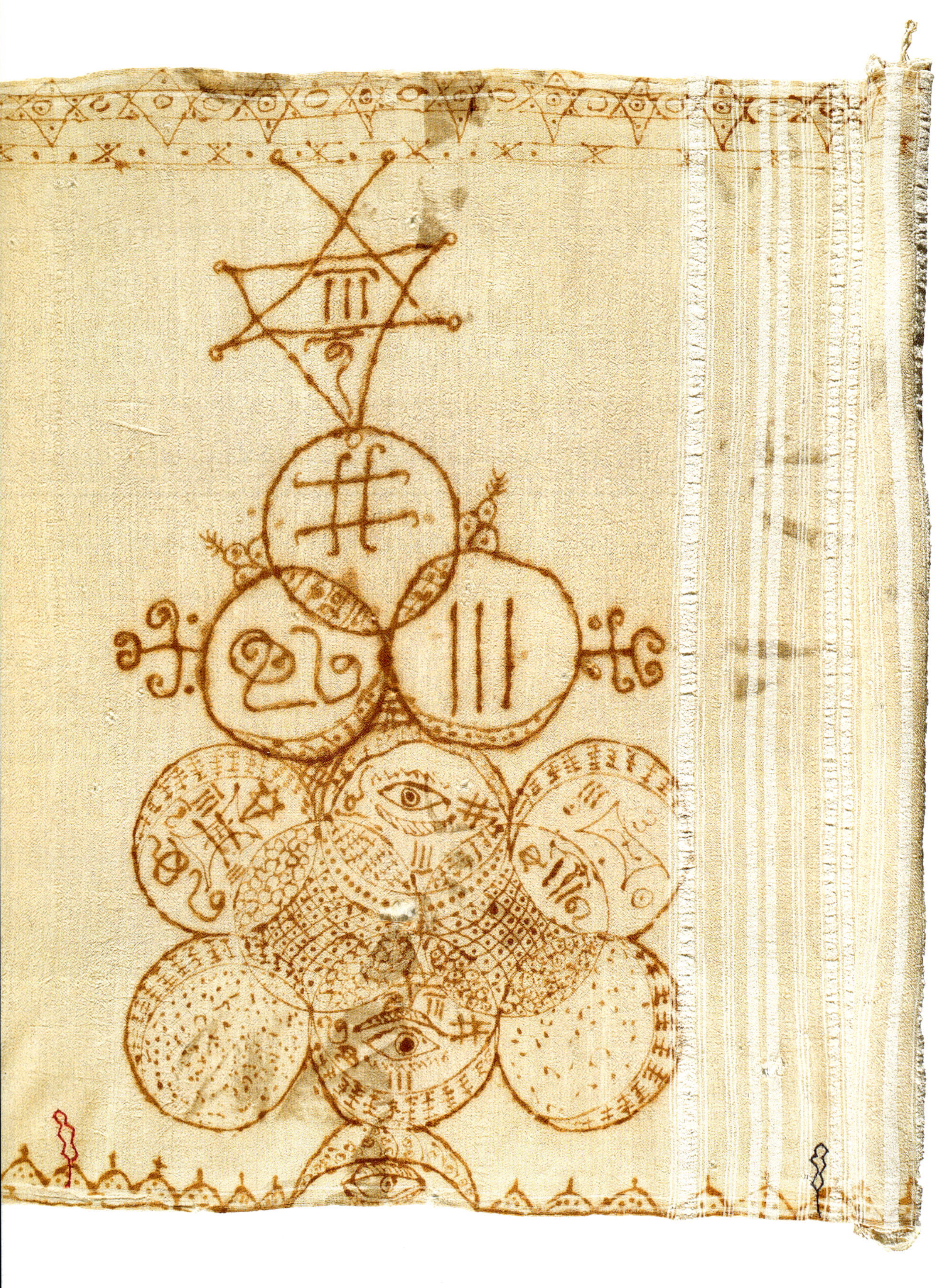

Main motif of the *haik* of the *fqîh*

Hauptmotiv auf dem *haik* des *fqîh*

It is obvious that the drawings of eyes with pupils with their penetrating stare and glazed look - sometimes with, at others without, eyelids or brows - are supposed to have an apotropaic effect, warding off the "evil eye" and the negative forces emanating from the envious. The concentrated healing and tutelary powers of the three monotheistic religions are clearly represented here symbolically by the various domes depicted. On the far left at the bottom we encounter signs which may represent Djinns which work their mischief on particular weekdays and cause specific diseases.[10]

In the midst of all these succinct symbols, the seven seals or "Solomon's Seal" or "Seals"[11] are particularly striking. They occur twice on the *haik* of the *fqīh*: above the box with the shining sun, the downwards pointing half moon and the stars (fig. p.134)[12] and again in the upper zone of the pyramid formed of circles (fig. p. 132).

This seal is basically encountered, with variants and also with different degrees of magical potency, not only in both old and new specialist handbooks on Islamic magic but also on printed or hand-written talismans, engraved on gems and the interiors of bronze magic dishes[13] or as the contents[14] or part of the contents[15] of magic quadrilaterals of various shapes and sizes.

Dass die Zeichnungen von Augen mit ihren eindringlich starr blickenden Pupillen – manchmal mit und manchmal ohne Augenlider oder -brauen – gegen den "bösen Blick" und die negativen Energiestrahlen der Neider wirken sollen, ist offenkundig. Auch die gesammelten Heil- und Schutzkräfte der drei monotheistischen Religionen sind klar durch die verschiedenen Kuppeln symbolisch vertreten. Ganz links unten treffen wir auf Zeichen, die möglicherweise Dschinnen repräsentieren, welche jeweils an gewissen Wochentagen ihr Unwesen treiben und gewisse Krankheiten verursachen.[10]

Aus der Menge der prägnanten Symbole stechen die sieben Siegel oder "das" bzw. "die Siegel Salomos"[11] ins Auge. Wir finden sie auf dem *haik* des *fqīh* zweimal vertreten: einmal über dem Kästchen mit der strahlenden Sonne, dem nach unten schauenden Halbmond und den Sternen (Abb. S. 134)[12] und ein zweites Mal im oberen Teil der Pyramide aus Kreisen (Abb. S. 132).

Dieses Siegel ist grundsätzlich in verschiedenen Varianten und auch mit anderen Zauberpotenzen zu finden, und zwar nicht nur in alten und neuen Fach- und Handbüchern zur islamischen Magie, sondern auch auf gedruckten oder von Hand geschriebenen Talismans, eingraviert auf Gemmen und Innenseiten von bronzenen Zauberschalen[13] oder als Inhalt[14] oder Teil eines Inhalts[15] von magischen Quadraten verschiedener Formen und Größen.

Normalerweise besteht die Reihe – von rechts nach links – aus einem Penta- oder Hexagramm. An zweiter Stelle folgen drei senkrechte Striche, die mit einer darüber schwebenden horizontalen Linie überdacht werden. An dritter Stelle folgt der unverbundene arabische Buchstabe "M" *(mīm)*. Dann kommt eine Art Leiter mit zwei, drei und mehr Sprossen. An fünfter Stelle folgen vier senkrechte Striche, gefolgt vom etwas veränderten arabischen Buchstabe "H" *(hā')*. Dieser Buchstabe wird manchmal durch einen achteckigen Stern ersetzt. An der siebten und letzten Stelle steht der arabische Buchstabe "W" *(wāw)*.[16]

Djin Merra:

Djin Berkane:

Djin Chemharouch:

Djin Mimoun:

Each of these signs stands for a *djin*. From: Akhmisse 1985

Jedes dieser Zeichen steht für einen *djin*. Aus: Akhmisse 1985

10 Cf. Akhmisse 1985, p. 50, where some Djinns are explicitly named, with characteristic signs allocated to them.

11 On this Winkler 1930, p. 55, 127f.

12 What is probably meant here is a propitious constellation and a position of the moon. Cf. Winkler 1930, p. 84.

13 For details on individual pieces see Winkler 1930, pp. 56-65.

14 E.g. Būnī, *Šams al-ma'ārif al-kubrā*, p. 93; Būnī, *Manba' uṣūl al-ḥikma*, pp. 98, 99, 175, 182, 197, 198; Dayrabī, *Muğarrabāt*, p. 60.

15 E.g. Būnī, *Šams al-ma'ārif al-kubrā*, p. 93; Būnī, *Manba'*, pp. 176, 179, 181, 182; Tilismānī, *Šumūs al-anwār*, p. 82; Suyūṭī, *ar-Raḥma fi aṭ-Ṭibb wa-l-ḥikma*, p. 240.

10 Vgl. Akhmisse 1985, S. 50, wo einige Dschinnen beim Namen genannt und deren charakteristische Zeichen angegeben werden.

11 Dazu Winkler 1930, S. 55, 127f.

12 Gemeint sind hier wahrscheinlich eine Glück bringende Konstellation und Mondstation. Vgl. Winkler 1930, S. 84.

13 Für Einzelheiten über Einzelstücke siehe Winkler 1930, S. 56-65.

14 Z.B. Būnī, *Šams al-ma'ārif al-kubrā*, S. 93; Būnī, *Manba' uṣūl al-ḥikma*, S. 98, 99, 175, 182, 197, 198; Dayrabī, *Muğarrabāt*, S. 60.

15 Z.B. Būnī, *Šams al-ma'ārif al-kubrā*, S. 93; Būnī, *Manba'*, S. 176, 179, 181, 182; Tilismānī, *Šumūs al-anwār*, S. 82; Suyūṭī, *ar-Raḥma fi aṭ-Ṭibb wa-l-ḥikma*, S. 240.

16 Winkler 1930, S. 56 und ausführlich S. 114-149.

The row - read from right to left - normally consists in a pentagram or a hexagram. Second, there follow three vertical lines which are roofed over with a horizontal line hovering above them. Third, there follows a free Arab letter "M" *(mīm)*. Then comes a sort of ladder with two, three or more rungs. In fifth place come four vertical lines, followed by a slightly modified Arab letter "H" *(hā')*. This letter is sometimes replaced by an eight-pointed star. In seventh and last place stands the Arab letter "W" *(wāw)*.[16]

The sequence is rather different on this cloth: the Arab letter "M" is on the lower left-hand selvedge, written with an extra downwards curve (see detail). It looks like a spectacles letter. A horizontal dash, curving downwards and to the left, is above this letter. Only three instead of four vertical lines follow the ladder with two rungs. Then come the Arab letters "W" and "H" instead of the usual sequence "H" and "W".

On the pyramid of circles we spot a hexagram which is linked with the writing on the frame of the cloth by the two extended legs of the upper triangle. In its central field it contains the three vertical lines with the horizontal roof line and in the bottom triangle the Arab letter "M" together with the horizontal dash which curves downwards. The ladder-like sign is in the circle placed below the hexagram. Below these two circles are juxtaposed. The right-hand circle contains the three vertical lines, of which there are four in other versions. The letters "W" and "H" are in the left-hand circle. The letter "M" is on both sides, outside the circles. It is so curvilinear that it is unrecognizable, hanging decoratively from the circles in the form of a spectacles letter. All or some of these signs recur in the three circles that follow in the sequence of circles below and in the central circle of the bottom row.

32 **Detail (cf. figs. pp. 132 and 133)**

Detail (vgl. Abb. S. 132 und 133)

Auf dem Tuch ist die Reihenfolge etwas anders: Am unteren linken Rand finden wir den arabischen Buchstaben "M", geschrieben mit einer weiteren Rundung von unten (siehe Detail). Er sieht aus wie ein Brillenbuchstabe. Über diesem Buchstaben steht ein horizontaler Strich, der nach unten links abgebogen ist. Nach der Leiter mit zwei Sprossen folgen dann anstatt vier nur drei senkrechte Striche. Dann folgen die arabischen Buchstaben "W" und "H", und nicht wie sonst "H" und "W".

Auf der Pyramide aus Kreisen entdecken wir das Hexagramm, das durch die zwei weiter gezogenen Linien des obersten Dreiecks mit der Beschriftung des Tuchrahmens Kontakt aufnimmt. Es beherbergt in seinem Mittelfeld die drei senkrechten Striche mit der horizontalen Überdachung und in seinem untersten Dreieck den arabischen Buchstaben "M", zusammen mit dem horizontalen Strich, der sich nach unten biegt. In dem Kreis, der unter dem Hexagramm liegt, finden wir das leiterähnliche Zeichen. Darunter stehen zwei Kreise nebeneinander. Der rechte Kreis beinhaltet die drei senkrechten Striche, die in anderen Fassungen vier sind. Im linken Kreis sind die Buchstaben "W" und "H" zu finden. Auf beiden Seiten, außerhalb der Kreise, ist der Buchstabe "M" zu entdecken, der bis zur Unkenntlichkeit verbogen ist und in Form eines Brillenbuchstabens wie ein Zierschmuck an den Kreisen hängt. In den drei folgenden Kreisen der darunter befindlichen Kreisreihe und in dem mittleren Kreis der untersten Reihe sind jeweils alle oder einige dieser Zeichen wieder zu entdecken.

16 **Winkler 1930, p. 56 and extensively pp. 114-149.**
17 **Būnī invariably uses a pentagram but never a hexagram.**
18 **Būnī, *Šams al-ma'ārif al-kubrā,* p. 93.**
19 **This is what he calls the four vertical lines.**
20 **Būnī, *Šams al-ma'ārif al-kubrā,* p. 89 f., Winkler 1930, p. 80.**
21 **Būnī, *Manba' uṣūl al-ḥikma,* p. 100.**
22 **Ibid., p. 171.**

17 Būnī verwendet immer ein Pentagramm niemals ein Hexagramm.
18 Būnī, *Šams al-ma'ārif al-kubrā,* S. 93.
19 So nennt er die vier senkrechten Striche.

The importance of a symbol depends on the significance lent to it by those who use it. Ahmad al-Bûnî (d. 1225), probably the best-known and most frequently quoted author in books of magic written in Arabic, mentions these signs several times.[17] In them he sees "the recondite arcana of God and his most highly prized name."[18] The "H", "W" and the four "little staves"[19] come from the Torah; the ladder and the "M" from the Gospels and the pentagram with the three vertical lines and a horizontal dash hovering over it from the Koran.[20] This means that all three monotheistic religions are represented in these signs.

In the *Manbaᶜ uṣūl al-ḥikma*, its author, the same Aḥmad al-Būnī, writes that these signs are among the "arcana" which may not be revealed until God has explained them to a magician's pupil either by divine inspiration or in a dream.[21] In the same book he calls them: "Solomon's Seal" and "The Greatest Name of God."[22]

Die Wichtigkeit eines Symbols wird von der Bedeutung bestimmt, welche seine Benutzer ihm verleihen. Aḥmad al-Būnī (gest. 1225), der wohl bekannteste und am meisten zitierte Autor in arabischer Sprache verfasster Magiebücher, kommt mehrfach auf diese Zeichen zu sprechen.[17] Er erkennt in ihnen "das verborgene Geheimnis Gottes und dessen hochgeschätzten Größten Namen".[18] Das "H", "W" und die vier "Stäbchen"[19] stammen aus der Tora, die Leiter und das "M" aus dem Evangelium und das Pentagramm mit den drei senkrechten Strichen und einem schwebenden horizontalen Strich darüber aus dem Koran.[20] Das heißt, alle drei monotheistischen Religionen sind in diesen Zeichen vertreten.

In seinem Buch *Manbaᶜ uṣūl al-ḥikma* aber erklärt uns derselbe Aḥmad al-Būnī, dass diese Zeichen zu den "mysteriösen Geheimnissen" gehören, die man nicht verraten darf, bis Gott sie dem Zauberlehrling durch Eingebung oder einen Traum erklärt.[21] Im selben Buch nennt er sie: "das Salomonische Siegel" und "der Größte Name Gottes."[22]

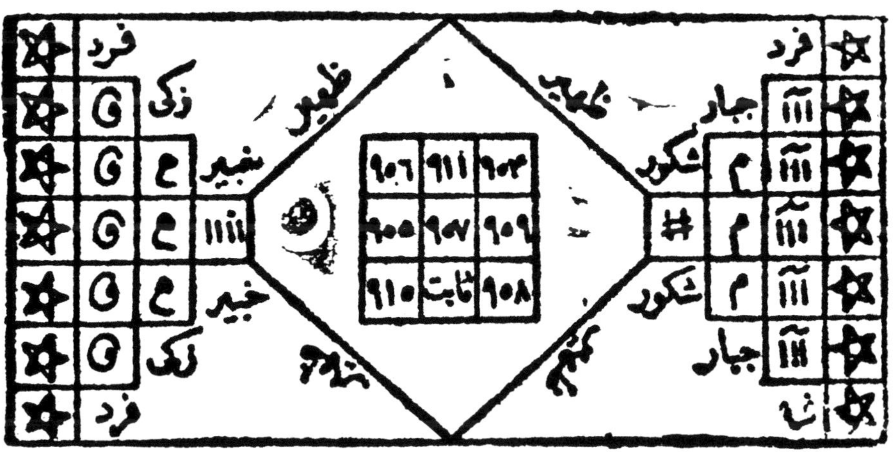

Amulet.
From: Būnī, *Manbaᶜ uṣūl al-ḥikma*, **S. 175.**

Amulett.
Aus: Būnī, *Manbaᶜ uṣūl al-ḥikma*, S. 175.

Talisman.
From: Būnī, *Manbaᶜ uṣūl al-ḥikma*, **S. 182.**

Wunschtalisman.
Aus: Būnī, *Manbaᶜ uṣūl al-ḥikma*, S. 182.

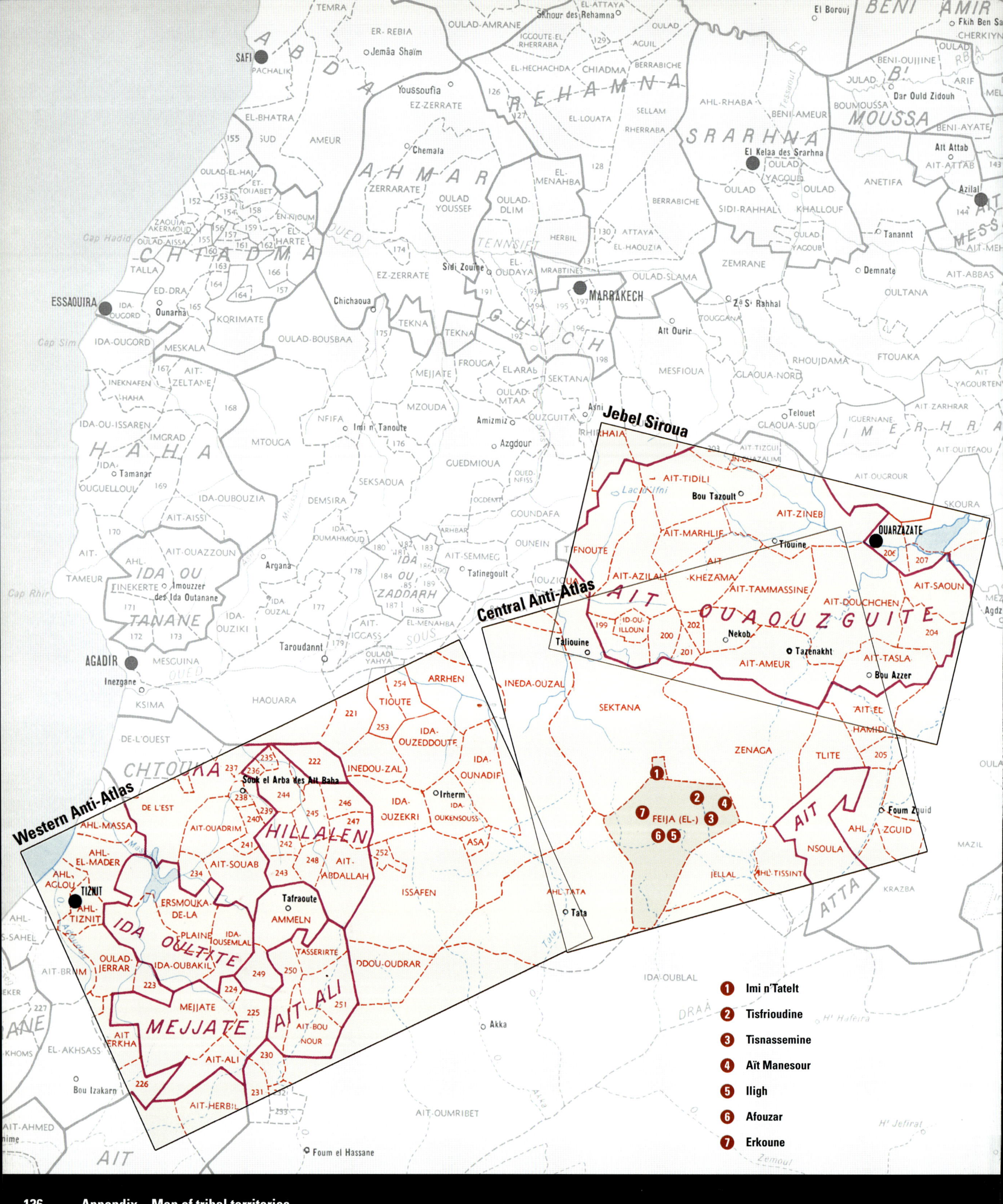

Jebel Siroua
Central Anti-Atlas
Western Anti-Atlas
SAFI
ESSAOUIRA
AGADIR
MARRAKECH
OUARZAZATE
TIZNIT
Taroudannt
Tafraoute
Tata
Akka
Taliouine
Nekob
Tazenakht
Bou Azzer
Foum Zguid
Souk el Arba des Aït Baha
Irherm
El Kelaa des Srarhna
Demnate
Azilal
Chichaoua
Imi n' Tanoute
Amizmiz
Asni
Aït Ourir
Inezgane
Bou Izakarn
Foum el Hassane
ABDA
REHAMNA
SRARHNA
AHMAR
CHIADMA
HAHA
GUICH
IDA OU TANANE
IDA OU ZADDARH
AIT OUAOUZGUITE
HILLALEN
IDA OULTITE
MEJJATE
AIT ALI
AIT NSOULA
ATTA
CHTOUKA
FEIJA (EL-)
SEKTANA
ZENAGA
TLITE
ISSAFEN
AMMELN
1 Imi n'Tatelt
2 Tisfrioudine
3 Tisnassemine
4 Aït Manesour
5 Iligh
6 Afouzar
7 Erkoune

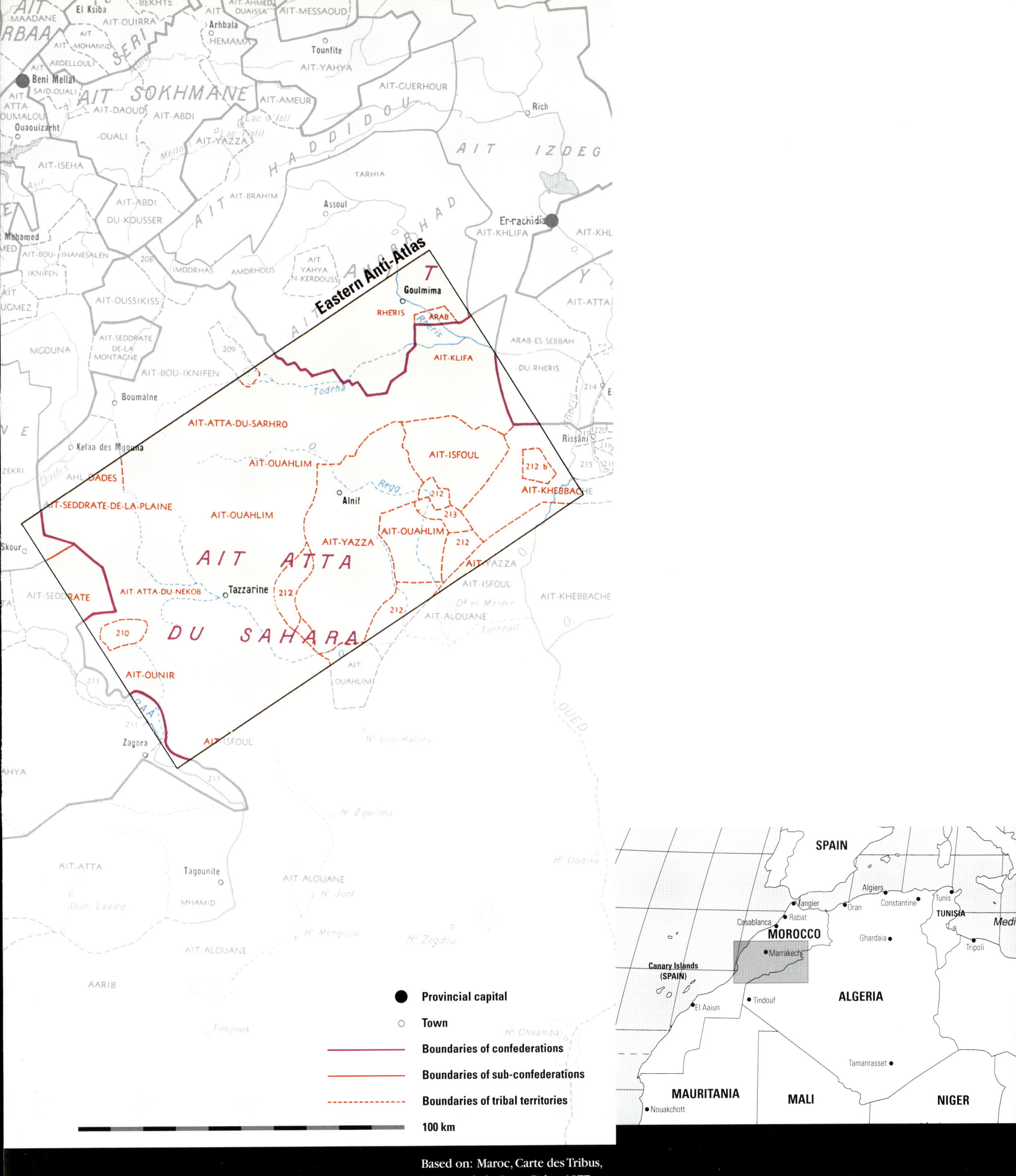

Based on: Maroc, Carte des Tribus, Division de la Carte, Rabat 1977

Technical Analyses

Ina von Woisky-Niedermann

Cat. no. 8: Adrar (Headscarf/Kopftuch), Inv. no. K 202

- Length of fabric including fringe 116 cm
- Length of woven fabric 97 cm, fringe 24 cm
- Width of fabric = loom width = 75 cm
- Weft patterned tabby, wool, natural colored
- Warp: natural colored wool, Z-spun, 11 warp ends per centimeter
- Selvedge: the ten outermost warp ends doubled and cotton warp, 2 stripes, material equal to weft I
- Main weft: natural colored wool, Z-spun, approx. 18 threads per centimeter
- Weft I: cotton, white, S-ply, double; always 2 picks per pick
- Weft II: cotton, white, irregularly Z-spun
- Weft III: wool, colored red and green, Z-spun
- Weft I-III: additional stripes inserted by hand (equal to weft I) Additional knotted tassels, wool and silk
- Warp fringes: S-plied, ends knotted
- In places painted with Henna without coloring the cotton threads

Cat. no.14: Adrar (Haedscarf/Kopftuch), Inv. no. K 181

- Length of fabric including fringes 118 cm
- Length of woven fabric 99 cm, fringes 18 cm
- Width of fabric = loom width = 66 cm
- Weft patterned tabby, wool, natural colored
- Warp: natural colored wool, Z-spun, approx. 11 warp ends per centimeter
- Selvedge: the two outermost warp ends doubled and warp cotton S-ply, 2 stripes
- Main weft: natural colored wool, Z-spun, approx. 19 picks per centimeter
- Weft I: cotton, white, S-ply
- Weft II: cotton, white, Z-spun
- Weft III: wool, colored, no noticeable spin, greenish and red, attached tassels green-red-natural colored
- Weft I-III: stripes inserted by hand
- Warp ends left as fringes on reverse side
- Warp fringe: a) several S-plied, b) then several Z-spun
- In places painted with Henna

Translation by/Übersetzung von:
Bettina Niekamp, Abegg-Stiftung, Riggisberg BE/Schweiz
Ina von Woyski-Niedermann, Textilkonservatorin SKR

Strukturanalysen

Ina von Woisky-Niedermann

Kat. Nr. 8: Adrar (Headscarf/Kopftuch), Inv. no. K 202

- Gesamtlänge 116 cm
- Gewebelänge 97 cm, Fransen 24 cm
- Gewebebreite = Webbreite = 75 cm
- Leinwandbindiges Grundgewebe Wolle naturfarbig mit Schussmusterung
- Kette: Naturfarbene Wolle, Z-Drehung, ca. 11 Fäden/cm
- Webkante: die äußersten 10 Kettfäden doppelt, beidseitig Baumwollkette in 2 Streifen, Material wie Musterschuss 1
- Grundschuss: Naturfarbene Wolle, Z-Drehung, ca. 18 Fäden/cm
- Musterschuss 1: S-Zwirn 2-fach, Baumwolle weiß; immer 2 Fäden pro Eintrag
- Musterschuss 2: unregelmäßig gesponnene Baumwollfäden weiß, Z-Drehung
- Musterschuss 3: Wolle, eingefärbt rot und grün, Z-Drehung
- Zusätzlich von Hand eingelegte Musterschüsse (wie Musterschuss 1) Zusätzlich eingeknüpfte Zotteln, Wolle und Seide
- Fransen: bestehen aus Kettfäden, welche zu S-Zwirn verdreht worden sind, am Ende geknotet
- Teilweise mit Henna bemalt, dabei keine Einfärbung der Baumwollfäden

Kat. Nr. 14: Adrar (Haedscarf/Kopftuch), Inv. no. K 181

- Gesamtlänge 118 cm
- Gewebelänge 99 cm, Fransenlänge ca. 18 cm
- Gewebebreite = Webbreite = 66 cm
- Leinwandbindiges Grundgewebe, Wolle, naturfarbig, mit Schussmusterung
- Kette: Naturfarbene Wolle, Z-Drehung, ca. 11 Fäden/cm
- Webkante: 2 Kettfäden, doppelt geführt und Baumwollkette, S-Zwirn, 2 Streifen
- Grundschuss: naturfarbene Wolle, Z-Drehung, ca. 19 Fäden/cm
- Musterschuss 1: Baumwolle weiß, S-Zwirn
- Musterschuss 2: Baumwolle, weiß, Z-Drehung
- Musterschuss 3: farbige Wolle, ohne erkennbare Drehung, grünlich und rot, eingeknüpfte Zotteln grün-rot-naturfarben
- Von Hand eingelegte Musterschüsse (Musterschuss 1)
- Rückseite des Gewebes: Die Enden der eingelegten Musterschüsse stehen gelassen
- Fransen aus Kettfäden: a) mehrere zu S-Zwirn verdreht, b) dann mehrere zu Z-verdreht
- Teilweise Henna-Bemalung

Cat. no. 16: Haik (Woman's wrapper/Wickeltuch), Inv. no. K 144

- Length of fabric including fringes 450 cm
- Width of fabric = loom width = 135 cm
- Weft patterned tabby, wool, natural colored
- Warp: natural colored wool, Z-spun, approx. 7 warp ends per centimeter
- Selvedge: the three outermost warp ends tripled
- Main weft: natural colored wool, Z-spun, approx. 12 picks per centimeter
- Weft I: cotton, white, S-ply
- Weft II: cotton, white, Z-spun
- Both pattern wefts woven in tabby as underlay for henna painted parts without coloring the cotton threads
- Fringes: approx. 4 warp ends tightly wrapped, approx. 1 cm, then separated into 2 x 2 threads, then again wrapped displaced over 4 threads. 2 rows of fringes
- Randomlike placed colored wool woven in tabby

Cat. no. 20: Veil/Umschlagtuch, Schleier, Inv. no. K 122

- Length of fabric, including fringes 190 cm
- Length of woven fabric 164 cm, fringe both ends length 1 x 19 cm, 1 x 9 cm
- Width of fabric = loom width = 143 cm
- Weft patterned tabby, wool, natural colored
- Warp: very fine, natural colored wool, Z-spun, approx. 16 warp ends per centimeter
- Selvedge: cotton, white, S-ply, 13 picks, 1 selvedge; other selvedge 16 picks, mixed with wool
- Main weft: fine, natural colored wool, Z-spun, approx. 14 picks per centimeter
- Weft I: cotton, white, Z-spun
- Weft II: wool, different colors, S- and Z-spun in red, blue and yellow
- Weft III: wool, colored; cotton, white, inserted by hand
- Wool patterns mixed with silk tassels, not knotted but drawn in by hand
- Fringes: consist of warp ends, S-plied, then several Z-spun
- Small area painted with Henna without coloring the cotton threads

Cat. no. 30: Haik (Woman's wrapper/Wickeltuch), Inv. no. K 175

- Length of fabric including fringe approx. 470 cm
- Length of woven fabric approx. 466 cm, fringe both ends length 1.5 or 2.5 cm
- Width of fabric = loom width = 144 cm
- Weft patterned tabby, wool, natural colored
- Warp: natural colored wool, Z-spun, approx. 12 picks per centimeter
- Selvedge: the three outermost warp ends doubled
- Main weft: natural colored wool, Z-spun, approx. 12 picks per centimeter
- Weft I: cotton, white, S-ply
- Weft II: cotton, white, Z-spun
- Weft III: wool, red and blue, Z-spun
- Weft I-III: randomly placed stripes on both sides woven by hand
- Fringe: approx. 4 warp ends tightly wrapped with natural colored wool
- In places painted with Henna without coloring the cotton threads

Kat. Nr. 16: Haik (Woman's wrapper/Wickeltuch), Inv. no. K 144

- Gewebelänge 450 cm
- Gewebebreite = Webbreite = 135 cm
- Leinwandbindiges Grundgewebe, Wolle, naturfarbig mit Schussmusterung
- Kette: naturfarbene Wolle, Z-Drehung, ca. 7 Fäden/cm
- Webkante: 3 x 3-fach geführte Kettfäden
- Grundschuss: naturfarbene Wolle, Z-Drehung, ca. 12 Fäden/cm
- Musterschuss 1: Baumwolle, weiß, S-Zwirn
- Musterschuss 2: Baumwolle, weiß, Z-Drehung
- Beide Musterschüsse als Eintrag in Leinwandbindung, nur als Unterlegung bei Hennabemalung, dabei keine Einfärbung der Baumwolle
- Fransen: Umwickelte Kettfäden über 4 Fäden, ca. 1 cm, dann Trennung in 2 x 2 Fäden, dann versetzt wieder über 4 Fäden gewickelt. 2 Reihen Fransen.
- Wie zufällig Schusseinträge in farbiger Wolle.

Kat. Nr. 20: Veil/Umschlagtuch, Schleier, Inv. no. K 122

- Gesamtlänge 190 cm
- Gewebelänge 164 cm, Fransen, beidseitig, Länge 1 x 19 cm, 1 x 9 cm
- Gewebebreite = Webbreite = 143 cm
- Leinwandbindiges Grundgewebe, Wolle naturfarbig mit Schussmusterung
- Kette: sehr fein, naturfarben, Wolle, Z-Drehung, ca. 16 Fäden/cm
- Webkante: Baumwolle, S-Zwirn, 13 Fäden, 1 Seite; andere Seite 16 Fäden gemischt mit Wollfäden
- Grundschuss: feine, naturfarbene Wolle, Z-Drehung, ca. 14 Fäden/cm
- Musterschuss 1: Baumwolle weiß, Z-Drehung
- Musterschuss 2: verschieden farbige Wolle, S- und Z-Drehung in Rot, Blau und Gelb
- Musterschuss 3: Von Hand eingetragene Musterschüsse in Wolle, farbig, und Baumwolle, weiß
- Wollmotive gemischt mit Seidenzotteln, nicht eingeknüpft, sondern eingezogen
- Fransen: bestehen aus Kettfäden, zu S-Zwirn verdreht, dann mehrere zu Z gedreht
- Kleine Hennabemalung, dabei keine Einfärbung der Baumwollfäden

Kat. Nr. 30: Haik (Woman's wrapper/Wickeltuch), Inv. no. K 175

- Gesamtlänge 470 cm
- Gewebelänge ca. 466 cm, Fransen, beidseitig, Länge 1,5 cm bzw. 2,5 cm
- Gewebebreite = Webbreite =144 cm
- Leinwandbindiges Grundgewebe, Wolle naturfarbig mit Schussmusterung
- Kette: naturfarben, Wolle, Z-Drehung, ca. 7 Fäden/cm
- Webkante: äußere 3 Kettfäden doppelt
- Grundschuss: naturfarbene Wolle, Z-Drehung, ca. 12 Fäden/cm
- Musterschuss 1: Baumwolle weiß, S-Zwirn
- Musterschuss 2: Baumwolle weiß, Z-Drehung
- Musterschuss 3: Wolle, rot und blau, Z-Drehung
- Musterschüsse nur vereinzelt streifenweise an den Seiten von Hand eingelegt
- Fransen: ca. 4 Kettfäden dicht mit naturfarbener Wolle umwickelt
- Stellenweise mit Henna bemalt, dabei keine Einfärbung der Baumwollfäden

Bibliography / Bibliographie Selection / Auswahl

Adam, André, "Le costume dans quelques tribus dans l'Anti Atlas", in: *Hespéris* 1952, pp. 465-480

Akhmisse, Mustapha, *Médecine, Magie et Sorcellerie au Maroc*, Casablanca 1985

Badeen, Edward, "Amulette im Islam", in: *Boubou – c'est chic, Gewänder aus Mali und anderen Ländern Westafrikas*, Bernhard Gardi (ed.), Basel 2000

Badeen, Edward, "Zwei mystische Schriften des ʿAmmār al-Bidlīsī", *Beiruter Texte und Studien*, vol. 68, Stuttgart 1999

Bartel, Günter/**Stock**, Kristina, *Lexikon der arabischen Welt*, Darmstadt 1994

Benabid, Abdelmalek, *Flore et écosystèmes du Maroc*, Paris 2000

Benchaâbane, Aabderrazzak/Abbad, Abdelaziz, *Les plantes medicinales commercialisées à Marrakech*, Marrakech 1997

Besonçenot, Jean, *Costumes du Maroc*, Aix-en-Provence 1988

Bertrand, Albert, *Tribus berbères du Haut Atlas*, Lausanne 1977

Brestowski, A., *Handwörterbuch der Pharmacie*, Vienna/Leipzig 1893

Brett, Michael/**Fentress**, Elizabeth, *The Berbers*, Oxford 1996

Būnī, Aḥmad b. ʿAlī, *Šams al-maʿārif al-kubrā wa-laṭāʾif al-ʿawārif.* In the appendix four treatises of the ʿAbdalqādir al-Ḥusaynī al-Adhamī follow: 1. *Mīzān al-ʿadl fī maqāṣid ar-raml* 2. *Fawātiḥ ar-raġāʾib fī ḫuṣūṣiyyāt al-kawākib* 3. *Zahr al-murūǧ fī dalāʾil al-burūǧ* 4. *Laṭāʾif al-išāra fī ḫaṣāʾiṣ al-kawākib as-sayyāra*, 4 vols., Beirut 1970

Būnī, Aḥmad b. ʿAlī, *Manbaʿ uṣūl al-ḥikma*, Beirut, no date

Camps, Gabriel, *Aux origines de la Berberie. Monuments et rites funéraires protohistoriques*, Paris 1961

Camps, G., *Les Berbères – Mémoire et identité*, Paris [2]1987

Census 1936, Protectorat de la France au Maroc – Direction des Communications – Service du Travail: *Répertoire alphabétique des Agglomérations de la zone française de l'empire chérifien classées par tribus et par fractions de tribu, d'après les résultats de recensement quinquennal du 8 mars 1936-1941*, Rabat

Chaker, Salem, *Textes en linguistique berbère. Introduction au domaine berbère*, Paris 1984

Dayrabī, Aḥmad, *Muǧarrabāt ad-Dayrabī al-Kabīr*, genannt: *Fatḥ al-malik al-maǧīd al-muʾallaf li-nafʿ al-ʿabīd wa-qamʿ kull ǧabbār ʿanīd*, Cairo 1924

De Candolle, A., *Der Ursprung der Kulturpflanzen*, Geneva 1884

Diamond, Jared, Arm und reich. *Die Schicksale menschlicher Gesellschaften*, Frankfurt/Main 1999

EI = The Encyclopaedia of Islam, New Edition, Leiden/London [2]1960 ff.

Ensel, Remco, *Saints and servants in Southern Morocco*, Leiden 1999

Fennane, Mohamed/**Ibn Tattou**, Mohamed/**Mathez**, Joel/**Ouyahya**, Aicha/**El Oualidi**, Jalal, *Flore pratique du Maroc*, vol. 1, Rabat 1999

Flamand, P., *Diaspora en terre d'Islam, "La carte des mellah"*, vol. 1, Casablanca 1959

Fournier, P., *Les quatre Flores de la France*, Paul Lechevalier (ed.), Paris 1961

Gabus, Jean, *Sahara*, Neuchâtel 1982

Galand, Lionel, *Langue et littérature berbère (25 ans d'études)*, Paris 1979

Garcia, Michèle Maurin, *Le henné, plante du paradis*, Georges Naef (ed.), Geneva 1992

Grammet, I./**De Meersman**, M. (eds.), *Splendeurs du Maroc*, exhibition catalog, Musée Royal de l'Afrique Centrale, Tervuren 1998

Grammet, I. Niloo Paydar, *Fabrics of Moroccan Life*, exhibition catalog, Indianapolis Museum of Art, Indianapolis 2002

Gsell, Stephane, *Histoire ancienne de l'Afrique du Nord*, vol. I., 1913, vol. VIII., Paris 1929

Hawkes, J.G., *The diversity of crop plants*, Boston 1983

Hawkes, J.G., *Genetic conservation of world crop plants*, London 1991

Hegi, Gustav, *Illustrierte Flora von Mitteleuropa*, vol. V/part 2 1926

Hmamouchi, Mohamed, *Les plantes medicinales et aromatiques Marocaines*, 1999

Hoffmann, Bernard G., *The structure of traditional Moroccan rural society*, The Hague 1967

Ibn Khaldûn, *Histoire des Berbères*, Paris 1890

Kerner von Marilaun, Anton/**Hansen**, Adolf, *Pflanzenleben*, 3 vols., Leipzig/Vienna [3]1913

Kessler, Michael et al., *Strömung, Kraft und Nebenwirkung*. Eine Geschichte der Basler Pharmazie, Basel 2002

Knapp, Rüdiger, *Die Vegetation von Afrika*, Stuttgart 1973

Laoust, Emile, *Noces berbères*, Aix-en-Provence 1993

Maçais, G., *La Berbèrie musulmane et l'Orient au Moyen-Age*, Paris 1946

Mann, Vivian B., *Morocco – Jews and art in a Muslim land*, New York 2000

Meier, Fritz, "Almoraviden und Maraboute", "Bausteine II", in: *Beiruter Texte*, vol. 53b, Glasen, Erika/Schubert, Gudrun (ed.), Istanbul 1992, in Kom. bei Franz Steiner Verlag, Stuttgart, pp. 712-796

Minges, Klaus (ed.) et al., *Berber. Teppiche und Keramik aus Marokko*, exhibition catalog, Museum Bellerive, Zurich 1996

Muller-Lancet, Aviva/**Champault**, Dominique (eds.), *La vie juive au Maroc*, Jerusalem 1986

Nehr, Rudolf, "Zur Prähistorie der Maghreb-Länder (Marokko – Algerien – Tunesien)", in: *Materialien zur Allgemeinen und Vergleichenden Archäologie* 49, Mainz 1992

Oliel, Jacob, *Les Juifs au Sahara, le Touat au Moyen Âge*, Paris 1994

Ortega, Carlos (ed.) et al., *Tejidos Marroquíes – Teresa Lanceta*, exhibition catalog, Museo Nacional Centro de Arte Reina Sofía, Madrid 2000

Pickering, Russel W./**Pickering**, Brooke/**Yohe**, Ralph, *Moroccan Carpets*, London/Washington 1994

Pomet, Peter, *Der aufrichtige Materialist und Spezereihändler*, Paris 1717

Rabaté, Marie-Rose, *Bijoux du Maroc*, Aix-en-Provence 1996

Rainer, Kurt, *Tasnacht. Teppichkunst und traditionelles Handwerk der Berber Südmarokkos*, Graz 1999

Rikli, Martin/**Schröter**, Carl, *Vom Mittelmeer zum Nordrand der Sahara*, Zurich 1912

Riser, J., *Encyclopédie Berbère V, Anti Atlas*, Aix-en-Provence 1984

Rübel, Eduard, *Pflanzengesellschaften der Erde*, Bern 1930

Schneider, Wolfgang, *Lexikon der Arzneimittelgeschichte*, Frankfurt/Main 1974

Schweppe, H., *Handbuch der Naturfarbstoffe*, Landsberg/Lech 1992

Segonzac, Marquis de, *Au coeur de l'Atlas*, Paris 1910

Soldini, Giovanna M. et al., *Tuareg*, Zurich 1983

Spillmann, G., *Villes et tribus du Maroc: tribus berbères*, vol. IX; *districts et tribus de la haute vallée du Dra*, vol. II, Paris 1931

Striedter, Karl-Heinz, *Felsbilder der Sahara*, Munich 1984

Suyūtī, Ǧalāladdīn ʿAbdarraḥmān, *Ar-Raḥma fī aṭ-ṭibb wa-l-ḥikma*. Diyārbakir: al-Maktaba l-Islāmiyya, no date

Tietzel et al., *Zarte Bande aus Marokko*, exhibition catalog, Deutsches Textilmuseum, Krefeld 2000

Topper, Uwe, *Sufis und Heilige im Maghreb*, Munich 1984/1991

Tschirch, A., *Handbuch der Pharmakognosie*, Leipzig 1925

Vavilov, N.I., "The origin, variation, immunity and breeding of cultivated plants", in: *Chrinica Botanica*, vol. 13, pp. 1-364

Volkszählung 1936, see **Census** 1936

Weberling, Focko/**Schwantes**, Hans Otto, *Pflanzensystematik*, Stuttgart 1972

Westermarck, Edward Alexander, *Marriage ceremonies in Morocco*, London 1914

Westermarck, Edward Alexander, *Ritual and belief in Morocco*, 2 vols., London 1926

Winkler, H. A., *Siegel und Charaktere in der muhammedanischen Zauberei*, Berlin/Leipzig 1930

Zavada, M., "The historical use of Henna in the Balkans", in: *Thaiszia* 1993, vol. 3, pp. 97-100

Journals/Zeitschriften:

Awal – Cahier d'Etudes Berbères 2, 1986

Etudes et Documents Berbères 2, 1987

Tifawt – Tasghunt tadelsant n tamazight 4, 1994

Tifinagh 9, 1996

Abbreviations / Abkürzungen

Abb.	—	Abbildung
Bd.	—	Band
Cat. no.	catalog number	—
cf.	confer	—
cm	centimeter	Zentimeter
comp.	comparison	—
e.g.	example given	—
f./ff.	following	folgende
fig.	figure	—
ibid.	ibidem	—
Inv. no.	inventory number	Inventar-Nummer
Kat.-Nr.	—	Katalog-Nummer
p.	page	Seite
pp.	pages	—
S.	—	Seite
vgl.	—	vergleiche
Vergl.	—	Vergleichsstück
vol.	volume	—
z.B.	—	zum Beispiel

Glossary / Glossar

adrar	The term used for headscarf in the Anti-Atlas / Im Anti-Atlas Bezeichnung für Kopftuch
agadir	Fortified communal granary / Befestigter Gemeinschaftsspeicher
agadir romanni	Granary, fort and caravanserai / Speicher, Wehrburg und Karawanserei
agoual (ahouach among the Sektana/bei den Sektana)	A Berber dance in southern Morocco / Berber-Tanz in Südmarokko
aït	Tribe, clan among the Berber / Stamm, Clan bei den Berbern
bab	Gate / Tor
baraka	Blessed virtues in popular religion / Segenskraft im Volksglauben
bournous	Hooded cloak worn by men / Kapuzenumhang für Männer
chamsa	Five, a magic number / Fünf, magische Zahl
chorfa, (pl.; sing.: cherif)	Members of religious aristocracy, descendants of the Prophet / Angehörige des religiösen Adels, Abkömmlinge des Propheten
darija	The Moroccan colloquial vernacular / Die marokkanische Umgangssprache
djin (pl.: djinnun)	A spirit or demon in popular religion / Geist im Volksglauben
fqîh	Koran teacher, scribe, healer, blessed with supernatural powers, practitioner of white magic / Koranlehrer, Schreiber, Heiler, Besitzer übernatürlicher Kräfte, betreibt weiße Magie
haik	Cloth worn as a wrapper by women / Wickeltuch als Frauenbekleidung
hamada	Stony desert / Steinwüste
harar	Free farm laborer from the old Sudanic lands / Freie Feldarbeiter aus dem alten Sudan
haratin (or/oder hartani)	Descendant from black slaves and Arabs or Berbers / Mischling aus schwarzen Sklaven und Arabern oder Berbern
imazighen	Term used by the Berber for themselves / Bezeichnung der Berber für sich selbst
issouqen	Derogatory term for slaves = those who were bought in the souq / Abschätzige Bezeichnung für Sklaven = die im souq Gekauften
itri	Star / Stern
jebel	Mountain / Berg
jellabah	Hooded garment / Hemdkleid mit Kapuze für Männer und Frauen
jemaa	Assembly / Versammlung
kasbah	Fortified village or Berber fort, usually built of mudbrick / Befestigtes Dorf oder Berberburg, meist Lehmarchitektur
ksar (pl./Mz. ksour)	Fortified tribal village in southern Morocco / Wehrdorf in Südmarokko
lef	Part of tribal territory / Teil des Stammesgebietes
Maghreb	Sunset / Sonnenuntergang, al-Maghreb-al-Aksa = Land in the sunset / Land im Sonnenuntergang, Morocco is the westernmost Islamic country / Marokko ist das westlichste Land der islamischen Welt
marabout	Saint's tomb / Heiligengrab
mellah	Settlement or quarter of a city inhabited by Jews / Siedlung oder Ortsteil für Angehörige des mosaischen Glaubens
moussem	Religious feast day / Kirmes, Jahrmarkt
oulad	Arab tribe, clan / Stamm, Clan bei den Arabern
ramadan	Month of fasting / Fastenmonat
schedwi	Special weaving technique for making patterns / Spezielle, musterbildende Webtechnik
souq	Market, also weekly market / Markt, auch Wochenmarkt
Sous	Fertile valley between the western High Atlas and the Anti-Atlas / Fruchtbares Tal zwischen dem westlichen Hohen Atlas und dem Anti-Atlas
Sudan	The old kingdom of Sudan included what is now the Sahel Zone with the countries of Mauretania, Mali and Niger / Das alte Königreich Sudan umfasst die heutige Sahelzone mit den Staaten Mauretainien, Mali und Niger
sufi	Member of an Islamic brotherhood of mystics / Anhänger einer mystischen islamischen Bruderschaft
tahdicht	Feija wedding blanket / Hochzeitsdecke bei den Feija
tamazight	A Berber language / Eine der Berbersprachen
taschelheit	A Berber language / Eine der Berbersprachen
tifinagh	Tuareg alphabet / Alphabet der Tuareg
tismissine	Name of a Feija textile pattern, allegedly without meaning / Name eines Musters bei den Feija-Textilien, angeblich ohne Bedeutung
zaouia	Islamic monastry which can have an educational institution and a hospice for pilgrims and the sick attached to it; also a religious center of supraregional importance / Islamisches Kloster, dem eine Koranschule und eine Herberge für Pilger und Kranke angeschlossen sein kann; auch religiöses Zentrum von überregionaler Bedeutung

In transcribing terms from Arabic or the Berber languages, we have retained the French spelling since it

Für die Wiedergabe von Begriffen in arabischer oder berberischer Sprache halten wir uns an die franzö-

Authors

Edward Badeen

Born in Nazareth, Palestine, in 1944. Studied Islamic studies, English and Arab letters and literature, psychology and Semitic philology in Jerusalem and Basel. Taught at the universities of Bern, Freiburg im Breisgau and Tübingen. Currently teaching at Basel and Zurich Universities in Switzerland. Has published extensively in the field of Islamic studies; numerous translations of modern Arab literature. Strong commitment under the auspices of the Israeli-Palestinian discussion group in Switzerland to promoting the peace process.

Annette Korolnik-Andersch

Born in Bonn, Germany, in 1950. Studied at Kunstgewerbeschulen (colleges for the applied arts) in Basel, Zurich and London. Trained as an academic draughtswoman, painter and textile designer. Since 1971 freelance artist. Exhibitions in Europe and recipient of awards and study grants. Lives and works near Zurich, Switzerland. Since the early 1990s has collected and conducted field studies in the field of Moroccan tribal rugs and textiles together with Marcel Korolnik. Has contributed essays to several exhibition catalogs and lectured at international conferences. Nominated for the McMullan Award in 2002.

Marcel Korolnik

Born in Zurich, Switzerland, in 1945. After taking a diploma at Handelsschule (commercial college), trained in stages leading to advertising director. Retrained as an author and director of films and audiovisual productions. Since 1980 has owned an advertising agency; has received several awards for creative achievement. Also works as a freelance photographer. Exhibitions at galleries and published photographic work. Lives and works near Zurich, Switzerland. Since the early 1990s has collected and conducted field studies in the field of Moroccan tribal rugs and textiles together with Annette Korolnik-Andersch. Has published articles on this subject in specialist journals and exhibition catalogs and lectured at international conferences. Nominated for the McMullan Award in 2002.

Mourad Kusserow

Born in Berlin in 1939, fled from the GDR at the age of 15. In 1954 contacts with the FLN (Algerian National Liberation Front), from late 1959 member of the FLN and the ALN (Algerian National Liberation Army in Morocco). Journalist since 1960. From 1965 until 1994 editor on the chief editorial staff for politics and economics at the Deutsche Welle radio channel in Cologne. Has published in newspapers and magazines in Germany and abroad. His many books include: *Marokko - Land zwischen Orient und Okzident, Der weise Sultan - Im Märchenland Marokko, Flaneur zwischen Orient und Okzident* and *Maghrebinische Träume*. Has lived in Agadir, Morocco, since 1994 and, since summer 2001 also in Adelsheim, Germany. Special areas of interest and study: Islam, Near Eastern and Sephardic Jewry, the Maghreb countries. Is North Africa correspondent for Afrika Post (Berlin) and a freelance journalist.

Markus Ritter

Born in Basel, Switzerland, in 1954 in Basel. Trained as an agricultural and biological laboratory assistant before enrolling at Basel University to study zoology, botany and history. Since 1980 freelance consultant in the fields of environmental protection and nature conservancy. Since 1996 a partner in the ecological agency Life Science AG in Basel, Switzerland. Special areas of interest and study: nature conservancy, ecological urban planning, public relations.

Autoren

Edward Badeen

Geboren 1944 in Nazareth (Palästina). Studium der Islamwissenschaft, Englischen und Arabischen Literaturwissenschaft, Psychologie und Semitischen Philologie in Jerusalem und Basel. Dozenturen an den Universitäten Bern, Freiburg im Breisgau und Tübingen. Zur Zeit Lehrtätigkeit an den Universitäten Basel und Zürich (Schweiz). Umfassende Publikationstätigkeit im Bereich Islamwissenschaft; zahlreiche Übersetzungen aus der modernen arabischen Literatur. Starkes Engagement innerhalb der jüdisch-palästinensischen Diskussionsgruppe in der Schweiz zur Förderung des Friedensprozesses.

Annette Korolnik-Andersch

Geboren 1950 in Bonn (Deutschland). Studium an den Kunstgewerbeschulen in Basel, Zürich und London. Ausbildungen als Wissenschaftliche Zeichnerin, Kunstmalerin und Textilentwerferin. Seit 1971 freischaffende Künstlerin. Ausstellungen in Europa und Gewinnerin verschiedener Auszeichnungen und Stipendien. Lebt und arbeitet in der Nähe von Zürich (Schweiz). Seit den frühen 1990er Jahren gemeinsam mit Marcel Korolnik Sammlerin und Feldforscherin im Bereich von Stammesteppichen und -textilien aus Marokko. Beiträge in mehreren Ausstellungskatalogen und Vortragstätigkeit bei verschiedenen internationalen Kongressen. 2002 nominiert für den McMullan Award.

Marcel Korolnik

Geboren 1945 in Zürich (Schweiz). Nach dem Diplom an der Handelsschule mehrstufige Ausbildung bis zum Werbeleiter. Zweitausbildung als Autor und Regisseur für Filme und audiovisuelle Produktionen. Seit 1980 Inhaber einer Werbeagentur; mehrfach für kreative Leistungen ausgezeichnet. Nebenberuflich tätig als freier Fotograf. Ausstellungen in Galerien und publizierte Arbeiten. Lebt und arbeitet in der Nähe von Zürich. Seit den frühen 1990er Jahren gemeinsam mit Annette Korolnik-Andersch Sammler und Feldforscher im Bereich von Stammesteppichen und -textilien aus Marokko. Publikationen zu diesem Thema in der Fachpresse und in Ausstellungskatalogen; Vortragstätigkeit bei internationalen Kongressen. 2002 nominiert für den McMullan Award.

Mourad Kusserow

Geboren 1939 in Berlin, mit 15 Jahren Flucht aus der DDR. 1954 Kontakt zum FLN (Algerische Nationale Befreiungsfront), ab Ende 1959 Mitglied der FLN und ALN (Algerische Nationale Befreiungsarmee in Marokko). Seit 1960 Journalist. 1965 bis 1994 Redakteur in der Zentralredaktion Politik/Wirtschaft bei der Deutschen Welle in Köln. Veröffentlichungen in in- und ausländischen Tageszeitungen und Magazinen. Zahlreiche Buchveröffentlichungen, darunter: *Marokko – Land zwischen Orient und Okzident, Der weise Sultan – Im Märchenland Marokko, Flaneur zwischen Orient und Okzident* und *Maghrebinische Träume*. Seit 1994 Wohnsitz in Agadir (Marokko), seit Sommer 2001 zeitweise auch in Adelsheim (Deutschland). Spezialgebiete: Islam, orientalisches und sephardisches Judentum, Maghreb-Länder. Heute Nordafrika-Korrespondent der Afrika Post (Berlin) und freier Publizist.

Markus Ritter

Geboren 1954 in Basel (Schweiz). Ausbildung zum Agro-Biologielaborant, anschließend Belegung von Universitätsvorlesungen in Basel in den Fächern Zoologie, Botanik und Geschichte. Seit 1980 Freiberufliche Beratertätigkeit im Bereich Umwelt- und Naturschutz. Seit 1996 Teilhaber des Ökobüros Life Science AG in Basel. Spezialgebiete: Naturschutz, ökologische Stadtplanung, Öffentlichkeitsarbeit.

Copyright 2002 by ARNOLDSCHE Verlagsanstalt GmbH sowie Autorinnen und Autoren

All rights reserved. No part of this work may be reproduced or used in any forms or by any means (graphic, electronic or mechanical, including photocopying or information storage and retrieval systems) without written permission from the copyright holder.

Alle Rechte vorbehalten. Vervielfältigung und Wiedergabe auf jegliche Weise (grafisch, elektronisch und fotomechanisch sowie der Gebrauch von Systemen zur Datenrückgewinnung) – auch in Auszügen – nur mit schriftlicher Genehmigung der ARNOLDSCHEN Verlagsanstalt GmbH, Liststraße 9, D-70180 Stuttgart.

This book has been printed on paper that is 100% free of chlorine bleach in conformity with TCF standards.

Dieses Buch wurde gedruckt auf 100% chlorfrei gebleichtem Papier und entspricht damit dem TCF-Standard.

Die Deutsche Bibliothek –
CIP-Einheitsaufnahme

Die Farbe Henna : bemalte Textilien aus Süd-Marokko / Autoren: Annette Korolnik-Andersch ; Marcel Korolnik. Mit Beitr. von: Edward Badeen ... Hrsg.: Annette Korolnik-Andersch ; Marcel Korolnik. Engl. Übers.: Joan Clough. – Stuttgart : ARNOLDSCHE, 2002

ISBN 3-89790-178-1

Made in Europe, 2002

Editors/Herausgeber
Annette Korolnik-Andersch
Marcel Korolnik

Editorial work/Lektorat
Winfried Stürzl

English translation/Englische Übersetzung
Joan Clough, München

Layout/Grafische Gestaltung
projektpartner, Laurenz Theinert, Stuttgart

Offset reproductions/Offset-Reproduktionen
mb Satz und Repro, Stuttgart

Printing/Druck
Rung-Druck, Göppingen

Photo credits/Bildnachweis

Alf Dietrich, Zürich: pp. 26, 72/73, 76/77, 78, 79, 82, 83, 84, 85, 86/87, 88/89, 90/91, 94, 95, 96/97 above, 96/97 below, 98/99, 100/101, 102/103, 108, 109, 112, 114/115, 116/117, 120, 121, 122/123, 124/125, 126/127, 128/129, 130, 131, 132, 134, cover

Annette Korolnik-Andersch, Zürich: pp. 16, 17, 19, 22, 54, 56, 57, 58, 59, 61

Marcel Korolnik, Zürich: pp. 4, 9, 12, 13, 14, 15, 18, 20, 21, 28, 30, 31, 32, 34, 35, 36, 37, 38, 39, 42 left, 44, 70, 72 below, 74, 75, 80, 92, 93, 106, 119

Simone Korolnik Jablonka, Tübingen: pp. 10, 42 right, 48, 49, 50, 51, 52, 53, 62, 63, 64, 65, 66, 67, 81, 107, 111

Museum Bellerive, Zürich (Marlen Perez): pp. 6, 27, 69, 71, 73 detail, 77 detail, 100 detail, 104, 105, 113 left, 114 detail, 124 detail, 125 detail, 127 details

The Minneapolis Institute of Arts: p. 113 right

Exhibitions/Ausstellungen

Museum Bellerive, Zürich
3.10.2002 – 5.1.2003

Städtisches Museum Schloss Rheydt,
Mönchengladbach
9.2. – 29.3.2003

Museo civico e archeologico,
Castello Visconteo, Locarno
Sept./Oct. 2003

Museum of International Folk Art,
Santa Fe, New Mexico, U.S.A.
13.6. – 12.9.2004

and further exhibition venues
und weitere Ausstellungsstationen

We are indebted to:

**Hamou Oukira and his family, Iligh,
without his generous help and the valuable information he gave us (all of it accurate and to the point), we could not have been able to conduct our study**

Brahim el-Medikki and his son Mustapha, Zagora, driver, translator, cook and tent constructor

Librairie La Source, Rabat, and staff

**Dr. Peter Jablonka, Tübingen,
for re-reading and checking in the chapter "Early traces of man", p. 16**

**Frieda Sorber,
Curator for Textiles and Costumes, Antwerp Fashion Museum, Wynegem, Belgium, for clarifying technical points in the chapter "Wool and weaving among the Feija", p. 48**

**Bettina Niekamp,
Abegg-Stiftung, Riggisberg BE/Schweiz, for her collaboration in translating the "Technical Analyses", p. 138**

Dank an:

Hamou Oukira und Familie, Iligh,
ohne seine uneigennützige Mithilfe und seine wertvollen Informationen (welche sich alle als stichhaltig erwiesen), wäre unsere Studie nicht durchführbar gewesen

Brahim el-Medikki
und seinen Sohn Mustapha, Zagora,
Fahrer, Übersetzer, Koch, Zeltbauer

Librairie La Source, Rabat, und ihre Mitarbeiter

Dr. Peter Jablonka, Tübingen,
für die Durchsicht von "Frühe menschliche Spuren", S. 16

Frieda Sorber,
Kuratorin für Textilien und Kostüme, Mode Museum Antwerpen, Wynegem, Belgien, für webtechnische Hinweise in dem Kapitel "Wolle und Weben bei den Feija", S. 48

Bettina Niekamp,
Abegg-Stiftung, Riggisberg BE/Schweiz, für ihre Mitarbeit bei der Übersetzung der "Strukturanalysen", S. 138

Supported by/Mit freundlicher Unterstützung der Familien-Vontobel-Stiftung